Textbook of
# Animal Breeding

# Textbook of Animal Breeding

**Dr. S.S. TOMAR**
*M.Sc. (Ag.), Ph.D. (Animal Gen. & Breeding)*
Principal Scientist, National Dairy Research Institute,
(Deemed University)
Karnal-132 001 (Haryana) **INDIA**

**KALYANI PUBLISHERS**
LUDHIANA * NEW DELHI * NOIDA (U.P.)
HYDERABAD * CHENNAI * KOLKATA * CUTTACK

# KALYANI PUBLISHERS

***Head Office***

B-I/1292, Rajinder Nagar,
**Ludhiana**-141 008

***Administration Offices :***

4779, Ansari Road,
23, Daryaganj, **New Delhi**-110 002

***Works***

B-16, Sector 8, **Noida** (U.P.)

***Branches***

1, Mahalakshmi Street,
T. Nagar, **Chennai**-600 017

110/111, Bharatia Towers, Badambadi
**Cuttack**–753 009 (Orissa)

3-5-1108, Narayanaguda,
**Hyderabad**-500 029

10/2B, Ramanath Mazumdar Street,
**Kolkata**-700 009

**T-395 70 05**

**V-43073 05**





***Reprinted, 2025***

***TYPESETTING & DIAGRAMS***

(File name—TBAB)

*At* Gautam Graphic Printers,

**ISBN 81-272-1290-3**

***PRINTED IN INDIA***

*At* Kalyani Printings, B-15, Sector 8, NOIDA
and Published by Mrs. Usha Raj Kumar for
Kalyani Publishers, New Delhi-110 002

# FOREWORD

I am extremely delighted to write a foreword for the book entitled, "Text Book of Animal Breeding" written by Dr. S.S. Tomar of this Institute. There are some books on animal breeding published in developing countries as well as some sporadic efforts have been made by Indian authors which do not meet the requirement of post-graduate students completely as they have not been written as per syllabus of the course of Animal Breeding taught in SAU's and ICAR Institutes and meant for various competitive examinations. Therefore, there was a great need of having this type of book.

The author has made very appreciable effort and commendable contribution to bring out this book as per syllabus of post-graduate programme covering all aspects of genetic improvement of farm animals and that too in a simple and illustrative language, with solved numerical examples, understandable to every reader. The present publication being brought out by very experienced author is thus very beneficial and is most welcome.

The author is highly qualified and experienced in the subject of Animal Breeding having about 38 years experience of research and teaching and has many published research papers & books to his credit, besides having practical knowledge of Agriculture & Animal Husbandry.

I am confident that this text book will go a long way in helping the students in qualifying the examinations and the teachers in teaching and planning of research in the subject. I hope this book will serve as a model text book and with this I wish the author all the best.

**(Nagendra Sharma)**
**Director**

# PREFACE

The domestication, being an evolutionary process, together with artificial selection by man, had changed the genetic structure of animal population, the environmental conditions and the changes in morphological, production and reproduction traits as well as behaviour of the domestic animals. The changes in genetic structure have caused the genetic variability in animal populations. Man had been making continuous efforts to exploit this genetic variability by use of selective breeding since long.

With the advancement of the science of genetics during 20$^{th}$ century, the knowledge of population genetics had been of great use for the genetic improvement of animal populations. The Animal Breeding stems on the principles of population genetics to exploit genetic variability using biometrical techniques for improvement of animal population and development of new strains/breeds of different species to meet the demand of different geographical areas. Thus the application of the principles of population genetics using the biometrical techniques for genetic improvement of livestock is known as the Animal Breeding.

In India, the Animal Breeding as a separate subject at Post Graduate level was started almost with the establishment of SAU's in 1960. Sporadic efforts have been made by some Indian authors to publish certain information on animal breeding, which do not meet the requirements of the Post Graduate students and teachers. Therefore, it was essentially required to bring out a text book on animal breeding to meet the requirement as per syllabus prescribed for various SAU's and Institutes. The present book entitled "Text Book of Animal Breeding is an attempt in this direction, to cover the syllabus taught in SAU's, ICAR and other institutes as well as the syllabus meant for All India Competitive Examinations conducted by UPSC and ASRB (ICAR), in continuity of earlier two text books on population Genetics by the author. The main features of this book are the use of simple language, numerical solved examples, listing of questions asked in ARS exam upto date and the coverage of complete syllabus of Animal Breeding covering domestication, AnGR and their conservation, livestock contribution, data collection and adjustment, prediction and measurement of response to selection, different selection criteria, selection experiments, mating systems, breed improvement programmes and the breeding strategies for different species of livestock and poultry. Hope this book will be of great use and help to the Post Graduate students and teachers as well as those involved in livestock development programmes.

I am highly thankful to Dr. Nagendra Sharma, Director, NDRI, Karnal for appreciating my efforts and for writing foreword for this publication. Thanks are also to the Post Graduate students and teachers who read my two Text Books on Population Genetics and encouraged me to write a book on Animal Breeding. I am also highly thankful to my family members – my wife Smt. Shakuntla, my sons Dr. Arun, Dr. Ajay, Dr. Amit, my daughter Archana, my daughters in laws Mrs. Poonam and Mrs. Nidhi and my grand sons Mr. Vijay, Vinay and Vaibhav.

I welcome the readers to give their suggestions for further improvement.

**2004** **S.S. Tomar**

# CONTENTS

| Chapters | Pages |
|---|---|

| Chapters | Pages |
|---|---|

| Chapters | Pages |
|---|---|

| Chapters | Pages |
|---|---|

| Chapters | Pages |
|---|---|

# 1
# DOMESTICATION OF ANIMALS

## 1.1. GENERAL

The exact period of domestication is not known, perhaps started very late in the Old Stone Age, or early in new Stone Age. Man used to hunt and eat the animals in Old Stone Age, **Paleolic period** (1000-8000 BC). This period was marked by the use of stone and bone implements without agriculture. The new Stone Age, **Neolithic period** (8000-6000 BC) was marked by the use of ground and polished bone and stone weapons and tools. The domestication of animals of nearly all the species started and the agriculture was also started in a crude way when man used to live in huts or wooden houses. The first animal to be domesticated probably was the dog and goat 8500-9000 years ago from today whereas the cattle and sheep 6000-6500 years ago from today. The period of new Stone Age extended upto about BC 3000.

The use of cow ghee in religious ceremonies had been mentioned in Vedas (Rig Veda) and there are mentions of the cow **"Kam Dhenu"** in ancient writings. In Shiva Temples are found the references of sculptures of **"Nandi Bull"**. The cow has been said to be the mother of **Rudras**, the daughter of **Vasus** and the sister of **Aditayas** in Vedas. In Hindu mythology, the male buffalo has been referred to as the vehicle of the God of death, **"Yama"** and also regarded as the physical form of the demon **Mahishasur** a symbol of inertia - **"Tamas"**.

## 1.2. DEFINITION OF DOMESTICATION

According to Lush (1945) the domestication of animals includes several aspects viz., tameness, raising them at farm which implies to keep the domestic animals in or near man's own residential places, to bring their growth and reproduction under man's control, to make use of animal's products or services to man's own advantages and dependency of animals on man's care for their existence.

The domestication can be defined as the man's activity of taming the wild animals and to control the breeding, feeding and care (management and health control) of animals.

It involves some biological changes (morphological, physiological or behavioural) in the animal. Thus domestication differs from taming which is defined as the elimination of tendencies to flee from the man. The wild animals (species occupying natural habitats) may be tame, whereas individuals of most domestic species require taming only if their association with man is limited during early age. The untamed domestic animals should be differentiated from feral animals or domestic animals which have reverted to the wild state.

## 1.3. BASIC CHARACTERISTICS OF DOMESTIC ANIMALS

The domestic animals have certain basic characteristics related to their adaptation, behaviour and reproduction favouring domestication. These are :

1. **Social group:** The domestic animals and birds are highly social and their wild relatives form elaborately (with great care or labour) organized groups under natural conditions.
2. **Adaptability:** They have the ability to adapt to a wide range of environmental conditions other than those in which they normally used to live. Thus they do not have any specialized habitat requirement.
3. **Sexual behaviour:** They live in large numbers together in the form of herds or flocks including both the sexes. This helps the animals to have little social stress under confinement as they have minimum fighting attitude and they can mate. They do not have any pair-bonds between two sexes but any female can mate to any male. The males dominate over the females. This reduces the conflict between animals and facilitates the mating. They provide sexual signals by movements or posture rather than colour patterns or morphological structures which commonly change under domestication and would result in failure to breed in the absence of essential stimuli.
4. They adapt the sexual pattern in a limited space and have the ability to reproduce in confinement.
5. They can live on the by-products of agriculture (herbivovous) and hence do not have specialized dietary habit.
6. The parent young interaction is such that the female accept the other young soon after parturition or hatching. Removal of young one from their parents during early life and cared for by man, establishes a bond to man. The rearing of young ones in groups away from their parents under intensive human care make them to bond to their own species and adapted to successful reproduction under confinement.
7. They are little disturbed by man or sudden change in environment. The wild animals have the tendency to flee by seeing man from a specific distance which may differ for different species. This flight distance can be reduced, by careful handling and approach, to zero by taming. Thus they respond to man.
8. They provide service or useful products with economic value.
9. They are tame and have evolved by selection from wild type.

## 1.4. METHODS OF DOMESTICATION

The starting of domestication had certainly been need based. Man thought the need of certain animals and attempted to domesticate them. The needs of man could have been for religious rites (as sacrifice to the God) and for meeting his requirements like meat for food and skin for clothing. Thus animals of economic value to man were started to be domesticated viz., sheep, goat, cattle, pig and fowl. These could have been another reason of domestication of animals by man like attraction of some animals (dogs) by waste of food available around man's dwellings. Such animals acted as scavengers of man's surroundings and they slowly became pet.

There can be two methods of domestication The first is the **imprinting method** and second is **hunger sympathy method**

**(i) Imprinting method:** This involves to bring home a few young as pets or to capture the cripples (those which are unable to run away). Such animals are well fed and cared.

The rearing of pets was started for the tendency of women and children to keep pets. This suggests the most probable stimuli to domestication. The wild animals are easily caught, tamed in young age and well cared and fed. The hand rearing become attached to human being and respond to them as they might do to their own species and prefer their human foster parents. This forms the social bond. This is called as imprinting. The evidence to support this view is that primitive (ancient) people in all parts of the world used to tame and rear the wild animals. However, there was a problem to provide milk to rear the infant mammals. But there are reports indicating that there are still women of tribes in tropical America and South West Asia who nurse pups, kids and piglets. The human nurses were gradually replaced by lactating animals of one domesticated mammalian species. This helped to domesticate another species. Once the goat and sheep were domesticated the milk became available for orphaned calves and colts. This helped to domestication of large species.

**(ii) Hunger sympathy method:** In this method a pit is dig out in the jungle and then covered with grasses. The wild animals are either carefully derived in a planned way to that pit or they themselves came across that pit and fall down in the pit while crossing it. After few days a man visits that site and provides some feed and fodder to that animal in the pit. This process goes on for few days till the animal starts recognizing and loving that man. The man then brought home the animal probably in a cage and takes care. The wild elephants are captured by this planned drives method. This is the effective method of taming the most unruly among the wild ones. The tame elephant is then used to bring more number of wild ones and to teach them to work. However, one point in domestication play very important role in taming the wild animals and the same is the temperamental aptitude of wild animals. This makes the success or failure of attempts of domestication.

The domestication had been completed in multi stages viz., loose contact of animals with man in the beginning, confinement of the animals within human environment where they bred at random in captivity, selective breeding by man, and finally the development of breeds with desired characteristics. The development of breeds started as early as BC 3000.

## 1.5. EVOLUTIONARY SEQUENCES UNDER DOMESTICATIONS

The evolutionary changes have occurred in different species of animals due to the major forces (mutation, migration, genetic draught and selection) responsible to alter the gene frequencies. The basic requisite of these forces is the mutation. The species have migrated in small numbers from their centres of domestications to other countries having different cultures and environmental conditions. Thus migration and genetic drift had played their role. The geographical isolation by distance determined by dense forests, mountains, hilly rivers, deserts etc., the physical environment, ecological constraints, social preferences, disease prevalence and the natural selection have resulted in the origin and development of different regional breeds/types because these had been intermating within the geographical region. The artificial selection had played its role in changing the gene frequencies, in order to meet the needs of different geographical areas.

The evolutionary progress is favoured by the availability of unoccupied environmental niche. A range of physical environment in which a species is found or multidimensional space within which the environment permits an individual or species to survive is called the ecological or environmental niche. In ancient time there was human culture of food collection by hunting the animals and this culture was followed by culture of plant cultivation. This has created an unoccupied niche which favoured rapid domestication of a number of animal species. There had been then the selection between species to serve human culture and needs viz. milk producers, draught animals, scavengers etc.

**Divergent selection:** The domesticated species diverged for different functions. The dogs have diverged into types selected for herding, bird hunting, trail hunting, guarding and draught purposes; horses selected for speed and riding; chickens selected for fighting, meat and egg production. The divergent selection divides a well established breed into different types. Short horn cattle had diverged into beef and milk production to the extent that they converged with other breed selected for the same function. The dairy Short horn now resembles the Friesian breed more than it resembles the beef Short horn which now resembles the Angus breed.

Improvement was started for a specialized function viz., increased milk/egg/wool production, speed etc. This developed the breeds and varieties by morphological diversification and imposed reproductive isolation.

## 1.6. CHANGES BROUGHT BY DOMESTICATION IN EVOLUTIONARY PROCESS

The domestication is an evolutionary process. It had changed the genetic structure of populations by differential reproduction of genotypes. The domestication has shifted the emphasis from natural selection to artificial selection, from random mating to the mating systems, migration of animals in small numbers and hence genetic drift. Moreover, the domestication has also made the changes in the environment. It is known that neither selection nor the change in environment from wild to domesticated conditions create any new gene, but the change in environment allows the genetic differences to express themselves. The changes in environment exploits the hereditary differences and this makes the selection more easy and accurate.

## (1) Change in selection and mating systems

The domestication had intensified forces of evolution which bring change in genetic structure of population. Before domestication, the wild animals used to move widely in groups and bred at random. After domestication, animals were confined in captivity within human environment and the man chose the breeding pattern as to which animal should be saved for breeding. Thus this resulted a change in population size (which became small) and in the mating system together with artificial selection.

Man had the idea of resemblance among relatives since very beginning. Keeping this idea in mind, man started breeding the most desirable animals and castrating others. The practice of castration is an ancient practice. No doubt that man had practiced the artificial selection for thousands of years. The process of artificial selection by man had resulted the genes of favoured animals to become more abundant in the population compared to the genes of less favoured animals. Thus scientifically speaking, the artificial selection has changed the gene frequencies and hence the genetic structure of population. Now, the selection is known to be the main force of changing the genetic structure of population. Under domestication, the animals were more narrowly restricted by herding or fencing to grow, remain and reproduce in the same area where they were born, this together with small population size resulted in increase in inbreeding and relatedness among domestic animals. The inbreeding resulted from restricted movement and from limiting the number of breeding males had been an important force to produce diverse races of domestic animals. The concentration on a few good animals for breeding inevitably led to some inbreeding and thus a particular type, colour and conformation tended to become fixed. This had thus resulted into differed breeds of today.

Man had transported the breeding animals far beyond the area in which they were born and could have wondered before their domestication. A number of examples on this aspect may be cited to support that how this process went on during historic times. The cattle were brought from Holland to England across water, Merino sheep from Spain to many lands, Angora goat from Turkey to USA and South Africa, Zebu cattle from India to Brazil and USA, Short horn cattle from England to Argentina and Australia etc. The invading armies and the migrating people brought with them the animals from their native lands. Alexander, the Great, brought large number of livestock with his armies form Greece to India. Genghis Khan during 1300th century with his armies traveled with enormous reserves of cavalry horses all the way from China to Central Europe. Such cases of migration of animals are known since the beginnings of domestication. Thus domestication had resulted in an increased amount of out breeding by transporting of animals by men with him. Therefore this process had changed the genetic structure of domestic animals.

## (2) Change in environment

The environment play its role in changing the expression of a character. The change in environment after domestication allowed the differences in heredity to express more clearly than could have been in the environment of wild animals. The genetic differences are not clearly expressed in poor environment as expressed in better environment. The example of feeding regime on fattening ability is well fitted in this case. The genetic differences in the feed conversion efficiency are more clearly expressed in a well managed feed lot experiment than under the condition of malnutrition/under feeding/feed scarcity. After domestication, the environment has improved in terms of nutritional changes (quantity and quality of feed, feeding times etc.), way of life, protection from extreme climate, better management practices etc. This permitted the hereditary differences to express themselves and this has been exploited by man to develop better animals.

A new phenotypic expression of the genotype can be developed under drastically different than normal environment. There may occur morphological changes in muscle and fat, skin and bone proportions during growth under nutritional changes and the changes related to way of life like more sedentary life (habit of too much sitting) e.g. body conformation of local **lalas** (shop keepers) is different than a farmer or labourer. The body conformation of modern pigs fed on a low plane of nutrition is similar to the wild boars.

The high quality feed and better management practices like protection from adverse climate influence the growth rate and sexual behaviour. The growth rate is high and the sexual maturity is earlier and continue longer (prolonged breeding season).

In mammals, more thorough milking may prolongs the lactation. The maternal care may also be prolonged if provided to new young at appropriate interval. There is interference in milk let-down in case of disturbance in the activation of the secretion of adrenaline due to mishandling of animal.

The removal of eggs from the nest immediately to laying prolongs the egg laying in many species of birds. Under modern management conditions, the unselected jungle fowl hatched and reared more eggs than in natural habitat.

# 1.7 CHANGES IN ANIMAL CHARACTERISTICS UNDER DOMESTICATION

The domestication has brought changes in economically useful animals with respect to morphological characters, production and reproduction traits, and psychology/behavioural attributes. The changes resulted from the domestication can be observed by comparing the wild ancestors with domestic animals. The degree and trend of change have been under control of man to a great extent. The traits of interest to man have been subject to greater change due to directional selection and breeding. Secondly, the trend of changes had been depended on the objectives set by man viz. the change in size of domestic animals of different species. The size of cattle has decreased but of the horses has increased. Man has influenced the evolutionary process of domestic animals (population size, selection, migration and mating systems) These evolutionary changes have caused differentiation in anatomy, morphology, physiology and behaviour of animals which are inherited with slow change from generation to generation.

## (I) MORPHOLOGICAL CHARACTERS

The changes have occurred under domestication in size and shape of body, colour and type of colour etc. The **size** of domesticated cattle has decreased whereas the size of horses has increased as compared to wild ancestors as a result of selection and breeding of cattle for smaller body size as the milk production is not related to body size but the draught power is related to body weight. The birds have also increased in size.

The **proportions of different body parts** have also been subjected to change along with changes in body size. The changes have occurred in skeleton and limbs depending upon the purpose for which the animals had been domesticated. The draught animals tended to have larger limbs and compact skeleton whereas the animals developed for meat had deep body and shorter legs. The parts in which the most valuable meat is to be found (loins and buttocks) have become more developed in domestic swine. There has been shortening of facial part in skull under domestication.

There had been changes in **body colour** from wild colour which was typically one which blended well with the environmental background so as to act as protective colouring favourable to survival from predators. The deviations from protective colouring are unfavourable to the survival of animals under wild conditions whereas, domestic animals need no protective colouring. As a result, various coat colours were developed.

The **hair coat** of ancestral forms has also changed form mixed hair type with medullary and fluffy (soft) hairs to increased amount of fluffy hairs e.g., in case of sheep fine wool breeds have been developed.

The **bones** of animals after domestication have been changed in their shape and compositions. The bones of domestic animals have become smoothed from nodosity and sharp edged crest for muscle attachment in wild ancestors. The proportion of hard matrix has been reduced with increasing spongy matrix. The internal **organs** have also been modified in domestic animals. The intestines of domestic rabbit have become shorter while in case of domestic pigs are longer than wild boar. The **weight of heart** in domestic sheep has reduced to half of their wild ancestors.

## (II) REPRODUCTIVE CHARACTERS

The reproductive processes of domestic animals have undergone significant changes. The wild animals are **seasonal breeders** so as their young ones are born in a favourable season of the year whereas most of the domestic animals do not have the seasonality. The **puberty** in domestic animals is earlier. The **litter size** has also increased in litter bearing domestic animals e.g., the domestic swine has twice as many young per litter as the wild boar and has **two breeding seasons**. Thus the breeding season has prolonged under domestication.

## (III) PRODUCTION CHARACTERS

The **egg laying capacity** of domestic chicken has increased significantly. A domestic hen may lay an egg daily against laying and brooding of about 10 eggs by a wild hen.

After domestication, man has developed many breeds of livestock through selection and breeding for their **high productivity**. The nature has provided the udder and teats to the mammals for nursing their young ones. Thus a wild cow (urus) produced as much milk as required to her calf in first or two months of life and can not produce more than 500-700 kg milk whereas the milk production of a cow at present has increased to 10,000 kg in a lactation.

The **wool yield and quality** in case of sheep has increased tremendously.

## (IV) BEHAVIOUR CHARACTERISTICS

### Relative stability of behavioural components

There are specific aspects of behaviour viz., patterns of behaviour, effective stimuli which bring (elicit) behaviour, and the level of response indicated by the intensity or frequency at which appropriate stimuli release specific response pattern. The behaviour patterns are less subject to change (conservative) than the stimuli which release them whereas the levels of response are least conservative and most readily modified. There is no evidence that the behaviour patterns of domestic ungulates, carnivores and gallinaceous birds differs from those of their wild progenitors. The wolves do bark but less frequently than some breeds of dogs. The domestic rabbits under semi-natural conditions having no prior experience of digging, also burrow and construct nest like that of wild forms. Likewise, there is no basic difference in social organization of red jungle fowl and domestic hens.

### Behavioural changes

The domestication may bring change in behaviour through learning or physiological adjustments. The animals get signals for some events through **hearing under confinement**. e.g., animals learn to expect feeding time by moving to the area where fed, preparation of milking like rattling of milk pails and concentrate feeding may elicit the release of milk before the udder is actually manipulated. Likewise, the stimus for milk let-down has shifted form the calf to man. The animals rapidly learn to locate feed, water and their mates, under confinement.

The **physiological adjustments** under domestication may also bring change in behaviour. For example, the **physiological needs for energy and water** are changed under changed environmental conditions which follow the changes in feeding behaviour. The level of feed intake and selection of specific nutrients are changed for increase in growth rate and egg production. There is an increase in water and feed consumption during milk production.

There are certain unique stimulus conditions which may produce changes under domestication e.g., suitable conditions for optimal **nesting behaviour** are absent under confinement and man provides artificial nests for birds or nesting materials for pigs. Even some birds do not use these nests and require man's efforts to train them to use nests. Placing of eggs in nests attract the hens to the nest.

Some **husbandry practices** are also important to bring change in behaviour e.g. separation of two sexes, castration etc. A number of males with marginal levels of sexual response, if kept separate, behaved like those which have higher sexual potential. The castration of non-breeders reduces aggressiveness and can be kept in large groups.

The selective breeding has played its role in shaping behaviour. The selective pressure under domestication has resulted in presumed **reduction of flight, swimming** and **tree roosting** (taking rest on tree) in muscovy ducks. The **territorial patterns of behaviour** tend to break down under domestication and the selection pressures favour the animals with more flexible territorial and social behaviour. The feral (wild, brutal) horses started living in groups with one stallion and his harem. Likewise, fighting cocks in pen areas show some territorial behaviour and each territory has a single cock and a harem of females. Another examples is of wild mallards (ducks) which are monogamous in the natural habitat but become polygamous **failing** to develop pair-bonds with specific females under confinement.

Lorenz(1940, 43) studied the consequences of domestication among ducks and found that in contrast to wild mallard (duck), the male domestic ducks forced copulation with females which try to escape.

The selection changes the behavioural thresholds. The examples of successful selection for increased sexual and fighting behaviour as well as the decreased broody, sexual, fighting and emotional behaviour can be cited. The non broody strain of turkeys under selective breeding became broody and stopped laying if eggs were left on the nest continuously.

Selection of bulls for refined characteristics has often nearly eliminated masculine secondary sexual characteristics, having feminine appearance and they are very docile and often show reduced sexual behaviour.

It is well known that castration eliminates or atleast greatly decreases sexual activity for the reason of reduced supply of androgenic hormones. The castration also reduces the aggressiveness and makes possible to live in large groups.

Some domestic animals contain many females who fail to provide adequate maternal care to their offspring, due to the unnatural living condition which do not provide the stimuli necessary for the expression of full-fledged parental behaviour. The domestication had a deleterious effect upon the biological requirements for parental behaviour, for the reason of selection for economic characters. For example, the selection in domestic fowl has been deliberately done against broodiness (a form of parental or care taking behaviour).

The domestic breeds are more tractable (docile) than a related wild species. There are evidences for inheritance of differences in behaviour viz. variation in sexual behaviour, parental behaviour, agonistic behaviour, learning ability etc. Any quantitative behavioural character can be changed by changing the genotype and similarly that any change in the genotype probably will have some effect on behaviour.

Environmental forces can drastically modify the future behavioural and physiological capabilities of the organism. The ability to learn, to copulate or to survive under severe stress depends on the characteristics of the environment prevailed during early life. The environment actively interacts with the psychobiological processes of the being organism and this interaction changes these processes. The environment forces have broader and longer lasting effects when acts early in life.

## 1.8. CLASSIFICATION OF DOMESTIC ANIMALS

All living organisms vary considerably in their form (size and shape), structure and mode of life. It is not possible to arrange and study the heterogenous collection of all the organisms without proper classifications and without keeping them in systematic order. It was felt necessary to arrange and classify the animals and plants into certain groups and subgroups to have a broad idea and minute details of life in the world.

Man may have started giving names to animals and plants as soon as the power of speech was acquired. Upnishads and Vedas (1500-600 BC) have references of classification of organisms. However, Aristotle (384-322 BC) started the work of biological taxonomy writing 9 volumes discussing history of plants and laid foundation for the study of floral morphology.

The arrangement or classification of different kinds of organisms and their relationship amongst them is known as systematic, which is as old as human civilization, and covers taxonomy (law of arrangement) which is the study of classification and identification. The classification is a system of arrangement of organisms into groups showing relationship while the identification is to know the correct place (position) of an organism in the plan of classification. After an organism is identified (find a place in classification) it is then given a name by which it is referred to. This is called as nomenclature which is a process of giving scientific names to animals and plants. The scientific/botanical/zoological name of an organism consists of two words viz., generic name (first word) and the species name (second word). This is the binomial system of nomenclature proposed by Linnacus (1958) a Swedish Botanist who is often referred to as the **father of taxonomy**. The importance of binomial system of nomenclature lies in the fact that same animal or plant is known by different local names in different countries, states and localities. This makes the same and only one name of a particular plant or animal scientifically all over the world. For example, the scientific name of zebu cattle in Bos indicus which means that the animal belongs to the genus Bos and to the species indicus.

### Hierarchy of taxonomy

All the plants and animals are ranked/arranged in a hierarchy of categories (groups, sub groups) such as kingdom, phylum (for animals) and division (for plants), class, order, family, genus and species. The hierarchy means a series or succession of different ranks and it is a system of arrangement or framework for classification in which the different categories are placed in order to logical sequence.

The kingdom is the highest taxonomic category. All animals are included in animal kingdom while all the plants in the plant kingdom. The lowest base category in both the kingdom is the species. The **species** is a basic unit in taxonomy as well as in evolution. A species is a group of individuals (animals or plants) which are similar in morphological characteristics, reproductively isolated and genetically distinct from other group of individuals.

A **genus** comprised the related species having more features in common than in other closely related group of species. All the species of a genus have been evolved from a common ancestor.

A **family** includes related genera and in separated from other related families by important characteristic differences.

The next higher taxonomic category is the **order** which includes related families. The organisms of related orders are kept under the next higher category named as **class**. The classes of animals having some features in common are included in a **phylum**.

## Place of domestic animals in the animal kingdom

The animal kingdom is detailed into 10 phyla. The domestic animals are kept under the phylum ***chordate*** (which has 4 sub phylum) and in its sub phylum ***vertebrate*** or ***craniata*** (with backbone). The vertebrate have the characteristic features of body with bony or cartilagiuous endoskeleton, presence of vertebral column, caranium or brain box distinct, head well developed provided with sense organ, paired lateral appendages being usually present.

The sub phylum vertebrate has two super classes, Agnata having animals with no jaws and no lateral appendages (includes 50 species) and the second is ***Gnathostomata*** having animals in which jaws and lateral appendages are present.

The super class gnathostomata has 6 classes viz, **mamalia** (3700 speceis), Aves (8600 species), amplibia (2500 species), reptila (6300 species), Osteichthyes (30000 species – marine or fresh water), and chondrichthyes or pisces (550 species – all are morive). All the farm animals except poultry are kept under the class mammalian which have the following features.

(i) Body is covered with hair
(ii) Presence of mammary glands, sweat and sebaceous glands
(iii) Body is divided into head, neck, trunk and tail except in man
(iv) Presence of external ears in pair
(v) Digits usually evading in claws, nails and hoofs
(vi) Foetus is nourished by the mother through placenta
(vii) Heart is four chambered
(viii) Presence of teeth in jaw bones
(ix) Animals are warm blooded
(x) Higher animals are viviparous

**Class** Mammalia
**Sub-class I** Eutheria
**Order I** Ungulata (hoofed mammals)
**Sub order :** (i) Artiodactyles (Even toed hoofed)

A. **Suina** : Families – 1. Hippopotamidae
2. Suidae: Genus : Sus (non ruminat)
S. scrofa (wild boar)
S. domestica (domestic swine)

B. **Tylopoda** : Family = Camenelidae (ruminants)
Genus : Camelus
C. bactrianus (Asian two humped)
C. dramedrius (Arabian one humped)

C. **Pecora** : Families 1. Cervidae (Deer)
2. Giraffidae (giraffes)
3. Bovidae (hollow horned)
**Sub family : bovinae**

Genus : (1) Ovis (sheep)
Species : O. aries (domestic sheep)
O. Canadensis
O. vignei etc.

(2) Bovis (Bos)
(i) Taurinal (Bos)
B. Taurus
B. indicus
(ii) Bibovinal (Bibos)
B. gaurus (gaur)
B. frontalis (gayal-Mithun)
B. sondaicus (Banteng)
(iii)Bisontinal (Bison)
B. grannies (yak)
B. bonasus (European Bison)
B. bison (American Bison)
(iv) syncerinal or bubalus
S. caffer caffer (African cape and congo buffaloes)
(v) Bubalinal (Bubalus)
B. bubalis (Indian Water buffaloes)
B. depressicornis (Celebes of Indonesia)
B. mindorensis (tamaraw or mindora)

(3) Capra (goat)
C. hircus (bezoar)
C. falconeri
C. caucasia
C. pyrenaica
C. ibex

Sub order (2) : Perissodactyles (Even toed)
Families : 1. Rhinocerotidae
2. Equidae (non ruminant)
Genus : Equus
E. caballus (Horse)
E. asinus (Ass)
E. kiang (half asses)
E. zebra (Zebra)

Order 2 : Rodentia Rabbits
Mice

Order 3: Carnivora
Suborder : Fissipedes

| Families : | 1. | Felidae | Cat |
|---|---|---|---|
| | 2. | Ursidae | Bears |
| | 3. | Camidae | Dogs, Wolves, Jackals, Foxes |

Order 4 : Primates
Suborder 1: Anthropoidea
Monkeys
Man

Sub class 2: Metatheria
Order 5: Marsupialia - Kangaroo

There are 6 more orders in class mammalia

## Species and breeds

The morphological and physiological characters formed the basis of dividing the animal kingdom into species and breeds within a species. The first division is into species. The most important feature of division is the reproductive discontinuity which means that two species do not interbred or the progeny of two species do not produce fertile progeny when they are further mated together. For example, horses and asses are two species and on mating produce viable but sterile progeny, except few rare cases. The interspecies crosses have variable fertility e.g., the female progeny produced by mating yak and cattle are fertile but their male ones are sterile. However, fertile male progeny of yak and cattle can be produced by two back crossing to cattle. Therefore, the reproductive discontinuity as a dividing criterion between species in some cases is liquidated.

A species is further divided into breeds or sub species. Different breeds have both qualitative and quantitative characters which differ for one breed to the other. These qualitative characters are morphological such as colour and type of hairs, shape and size of horns, presence or absence of some body parts like zebu breeds of cattle are humped whereas European breeds are hump less for which they are regarded as subspecies of the same genus, Bos. The quantitative characters can be considered as differences in type and size of the body, milk production and fat per cent in milk etc. However, there is no clear dividing line between breeds for quantitative characters for the reason that these traits show continuous variation under the control of polygenes.

Each species of farm animals contains a number of breeds. A group of animals of the same species having same origin (related by descent) and having common characteristics like general appearance, body colour, feature, size, configuration etc. is said to be a breed. The mating of animals within a breed maintains the purity of breed. A breed is a genetic entity developed over a long period of time as a result of planned mating and selection. Therefore a breed has certain well defined physical conformation different from other breeds in the vicinity and has distinct local names.

The breeds are not included in the Linnean Taxonomic classification and hence the binomial nomenclature of different breeds of a species is same.

There is further division of a breed into strains based on isolation from each other due geographical conditions or due to different aims of breeding the animals.

This is called as strain breeding. The individuals of a breed or strain are more closely related to each other than others due to interbreeding. This group is called a line. A line is called an inbred line when the inbreeding coefficient is reached at lest 0.375 as a result of two generations of full sib mating. The full sib or half sib group of animals in cattle is the sire dam or sire family and all the individuals of a family are equally closely related to each other.

## Breed formation

The different breeds and strains of domestic animals and birds have developed over thousands of years during the process of evolution in wild and domesticated stages as well as through intensive systems of production to meet the marketing demands. They must have gone through stress conditions for developing different genes and gene combinations in them regarding their adaptability to different geoclimatic conditions, resistance to diseases and parasites, heat tolerance and utilization of locally available roughages. The natural selection and genetic drift caused the breed differences. Secondly, man's attempt to influence the evolutionary process of domestic animals by selecting the animals with desirable characteristics, migrating and crossing to produce desired animals over a period of time also caused breed differences. All these caused the evolution of new types of animals with distinct appearance within a species. The natural selection increases an individual's fitness over others and this develops a stable population in a given environment. Thus the geographically isolated groups eventually form the breeds. The migration plays its role to develop new type of animals with differential survival and reproduction. Highly specialized breeds and strains have been produced and developed in developed world by recent advances in animal breeding techniques of genetic manipulation (A.I. with frozen semen and E.T.T.). These techniques have made easy, fast and inexpensive to introduce new genetic resources all over the globe.

The local agroclimatic conditions and socio-cultural preferences have played significant role in evolving the Indian breeds. Indian people prefer milk with high fat content and this has caused the buffalo breeding for milk. The type of cattle breeds evolved in the country had been the utility based viz., draught, milk and dual purpose breeds have been evolved. The major factors in development of breeds of different livestock breeds had been the farmer's preference, geographic isolation, natural selection and the intended utilities.

# 1.9 THEORIES ABOUT ORIGIN OF PRESENT DAY SPECIES

There are two schools of thought about the origin of the present day domesticated animal viz. monophyletic and polyphyletic origin. The monophyletic theory states that the animals have descended from a single wild species whereas the polyphyletic theory states that they have been descended from two or more wild species. However, there is dispute in this regard for the reason of scantiness of the evidence. It is not certain to say that which contemporary wild species was the ancestor for the reason that the original wild ancestor has become either extinct or the domesticated animals have been changed too much.

The polyphyletic origin stands on the fact of tremendous diversity of domesticated animals e.g. there are too many contrasts between different breeds of dogs or species. On the contrary, it is said that the variations among races of domesticated animals are largely man-made as enough of variability in wild populations is hereditary. The selection having diverse goals together with other breeding practices like inbreeding can produce distinctly contrasting races from a single wild population in few generation. Therefore, the observed diversity does not seem to be an explanation in favour of the polyphyletic origin of species.

## 1.10. ORIGIN AND DOMESTICATION OF DIFFERENT SPECIES

The domestication of animals and plants had laid the foundation of civilization and modern agriculture on which had rested the social and scientific progress. There are about 100000 species of animals listed in literature but man has domesticated 40 species of domestic animals including poultry to serve various purposes. The exact time of domestication is not known but it has been certain long before the time of recording historical data. It is generally believed that domestication must have started at the end of the Old Stone Age or in the beginning of New Stone Age.

The Llama, alpaca, guinea pig and turkey are native to the Americas. The domestication of other species took place in the Old World, largely in central or Western Asia with some domestication in Egypt and Europe. The chickens and elephants were domesticated in India and one center of domestication of swine was in China. It is also likely that domestication may have been in several regions for some species like sheep and swine. Upper Egypt or Ethiopia was one of the centres of domestication for the ass.

An attempt has been made here to give the information on the origin of different species of domestic animals in terms of their wild ancestors (progenitors) form which the present day species have descended, the probable time and place of their domestication.

### 1.10.1 Cattle

The term cattle is much broader than thought in general. It is rather a sub family (bovinae) or a genus (Bos or Bovis) of the family bovidae (hallow horned animals). The genus Bos (Bovis) includes 5 sub genera or sub groups viz.

(1) Bos or Taurine (humpless and humped cattle))

(2) Bibos or Bibovine (gaur, gayal-mithun, bantang, Kouprey)

(3) Bison or bisontine (American bison, European bison, yak);

(4) Syncernia (African Cape and Congo buffalo); and

(5) Bubalina (Bubalus arnee, the arni and its domestic descendant, the water buffalo, **Bubalus bubalis**; the anoa, **Bubalus depressicornis**, the Celebes buffalo of Indonesia; and the tamaraw, **Bubalus mindorensis** found in island of Mindoro in the Philippines for which called as Mindoro buffalo).

The above classification of genus Bovis can be simplified as true cattle, bison and buffaloes. The true cattle have 6 species viz. aurochs (humpless and humped cattle), gaur, gayal (mithun), yak, banteng and kouprey, and all these are interbreedable with male offspring as infertile.

The domestic cattle are of two types living now: Bos Taurus (humpless cattle of temperate zones) and Bos indicus (humped cattle of tropical countries). The cattle of United States are purely of European origin. The cattle were domesticated during New Stone Age (Neolithic period, 8000-6000 BC) both in Europe and Asia.

Mason (1985) and others had mentioned that all the domestic cattle descended from aurochs or urus (*Bos primigenius*). It was a very large animal of the elephant size but of a bull shape and was a wild ox of Europe.

Another progenitor (ancestor) of present day breeds of European origin has been reported by Rice (1962) and Lush (1945) as the *Bos longifrons* (brachyceros) which was in Europe as a domesticated animal early in Neolithic. This was small type. The present day European or American breeds of cattle may have been developed as a result of various degrees of crossing between the ancestors.

The cattle of India and Africa (B. indicus) were domesticated as early as 2100 BC and thought to the descended from the wild Malayan Banteng (Rice, 1962). The humped cattle or zebu were produced by manipulating the morphology of domestic cattle for adoption to a hot, dry environment with two new features – a large hump and a long hanging dewlap. The zebu cattle's voice is more of a grunt than a low. They have dropping ears, upright horn, long face and slender (long and thins) legs, have variation in body colour from white to grey and black. They have comparatively low basal metabolic rate, better capacity for heat dissipation through cutaneous evaporation and resistance to some diseases like tick born diseases. The jaws are large and hind limbs are sloping.

Lush (1945) have further mentioned some more names of the ancestors of domestic cattle. These are primarily the *B. namadicus* which was contemporary with man in India in the early Pleistocene (about 30,000 years ago).

According to Herre (1958), the wild cattle (B. primigenius) which are generally considered the progenitors of all domestic cattle including the Zebus, originated in India and then spread over most of Asia and Europe and across northern Africa. Domestication of wild cattle (Aurochs) probably first occurred in India (Baluchistan, Sindh and Afghanistan), the Near East (Iran, Iraq, Jordan, Syria, Turkey, and USSR) and Egypt from 6000 to 4000 BC. The seals of Sivikotaka in Gujarat and Kalibhangan in Rajasthan bear images of animals' favourite of Harappans (2200 – 1600 BC). In Siwaliks occur fossils of Bos acutifrons, regarded as the possible ancestor of the Pleistocene wild cattle, that is Bos namandicus of India and Europe. It is assumed that domestic cattle were brought by immigrants for Southern Europe from the New East during Neolithic time (8000-6000 BC) and these were probably descended from Asiatic wild cattle or from interbreeding between European and Asiatic races.

A schematic development of modern breeds of cattle from wild cattle by domestication is given here:

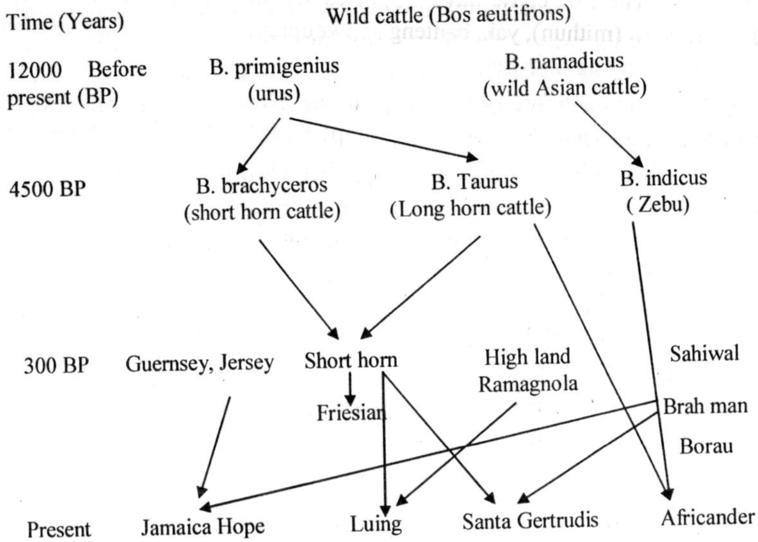


## 1.10.2 Other tribes of cattle

The **banteng, gaur** and **gayal** are all restricted to south-eastern Asia and nearby islands. The banteng is the common work ox of Java, Bali and Borneo.

The **gayal (Mithun)** may be only the domesticated form of the gaur or say that the gaur of Assam, Bangladesh and Burma has been domesticated as Mithun or gayal exclusively for sacrificial purposes. There are conflicting hypotheses about the origin of mithun. Some considered it as the hybrid of gaur and cattle while others regarded it as the domestic form of gaur. Mithun is quite similar to gaur in appearance, colour etc..

The **yak** is long haired and bushy tailed cattle, domesticated from its wild progenitor, Bos mutus. The **European bison** (wisent) and the American bison have never been really domesticated.

## 1.10.3. Buffalo

The buffaloes have close zoological relationship with the cattle, both belong to the same sub family Bovini of the family Bovidae. The buffaloes belong to two sub genera/groups viz. Bubalina or Bubalus (Asian buffaloes) and syncernia or syncerus (African buffaloes). The sub genus bubalus has the following 3 species.

**(i) Bos (Bubalus) Bubaline :** It is known as Indian water buffalo. The arni is the ancestor of domestic water buffalo of India, Pakistan and elsewhere. It was domesticated in India during pre-historic times between 2500-3000 BC. The water buffaloes are of two types viz. River buffaloes and Swamp buffaloes. Cockrill (1982) mentioned that all buffaloes of river group, including Egyptian and Mediterranean breeds have their origin in the Indian subcontinents. 5000 years ago or even earlier whereas the swamp buffaloes were probably first domesticated in China some 5000 years ago.

The river buffaloes are found through out India where clean water of rivers, irrigation canals and ponds is available to wallow. It is very much docil. The river buffaloes have been developed by selection in India and Pakistan into many dairy breeds. The important breeds are Murrah, Nili-Ravi, Kundi, Mehsana, Surti, Jaffarabad and Bhadawari.

The Swamp buffaloes prefer mostly lands to wallow in mud. It is found in Assam and T.N. in India. This type comprises Nagpuri/Pandarpuri, Toda and Marathwada. The Swamp buffalo had a diploid number of 48 chromosomes against 50 of the river type but the amount of chromosomal material is similar in two types because swamp buffalo lacks one of the small chromosome pair but had longer first chromosome pair. The crosses between two types are fertile.

**(ii) Bos (bubalus) mindorensis - the tamaraw :** It is a dwarf buffalo (3-3½ feet height), native to the island of mindoro in the Philippine. It is nocturnal, wild and fierce animal. It lives in mountain forests.

**(iii) Bos (Bubalus) depressicornis – the Anoa or Celebes buffalo :** It is the smallest member of the bubaline group in the world. There is no evidence of its existence elsewhere other than the island of Celebes, Indonesia. The size of anoa varies from 2 feet to 3 feet depending on its three races. It is widely hunted by the local people.

The subgenus syncerus has only one species, known as *Bos (syncerus) caffer* or sometimes Bos (Bubalus) Caffer. It is also called as the African cape and congo buffalo for its natural habitat extending from the cape to the south bank of the Congo river. The cape buffaloes are still wild and have not been domesticated. They live in bushy country and graze during the first half of night and hide in shady places during the day.

## 1.10.4 Sheep and goats

The two genera (ovis and capra) of sub family bovinae of the family Bovidae are closely related. However, a sheep is different from goats (i) by glands in both forefeet and hind feet (ii) by the absence of strong goaty odors in males, a gland beneath the tail known as subecious gland and (iii) absence of beard. They also differ in horns which are generally spiral in opposite directions in two genera – the right horn of the sheep to the right like a corkscrew and the goats to the left. The tails of the two are different in the way that tails of goats are erect upwards but of sheep droop downwards. Sheep have tear gland.

The domestic sheep (ovis aries) have descended form Mouflon (ovis musimon) of Europe and urial (ovis vignei) of Asia. Some other ancestors of domestic sheep have also been mentioned viz., *ovis ovientalis* which was domesticated in Indian sub-continent and argalis group (ovis poli) of central Asia etc.

Rice (1962) mentioned that sheep probably originated in Europe and cooler regions of Asia in Pleistocene era.

The domestic goat (Capra hircus) have descended from wild goat or bezoar (Capra aegagrus) of south west Asia. The wild goat is divided into 3 groups' viz., the bezoar of Pasang (*C. aegagrus), the ibex* (*C. ibex)* and the morkhor (*C. falconeri*). Lush (1945) mentioned that domestic goats descended from *C.aegagrus* or *E. prisca* which is known from Pleistocene fossils from Greece.

### 1.10.5 Pigs

The present day breeds of domestic pig (sus domesticus) have originated form two wild ancestors viz.

(i) *Sus scrofa* (European wild boar), the progenitor of the Northern European breeds. Its crossbred progeny with domestic swine are fertile. It was domesticated in Neolithic times around Baltic sea.

(ii) Sus vittatus (collared Malayan pig) which is native to Middle Eastern Asia, domesticated in China and the progenitor of the breeds of Southern Europe, Asia and Africa.

### 1.10.6 Poultry

The red jungle fowl of India (Gallus gallus) is considered as the progenitor of domestic fowl. The chickens were domesticated in India (Indus valley) about 2000 B.C. from where they spread to the east and west.

### 1.10.7 Camel

The camels are of two types viz. singe humped camel (Camelus dromedarius) and two humped camel (c. bactriansus). The first was domesticated probably in Arabia or north eastern Africa during Egyptian civilization whereas the later was domesticated in Asia somewhere between Iran and the Gobi desert.

### 1.10.8 Horse

The origin (ancestry) and date of domestication of horse is not clear. However, it is mentioned that the domestic horse is the result of probably two or three wild types viz., steppe horse, desert horse and forest horse. The domesticated horses of Europe and Western Asia have probably descended from the Tarpan or Mongolian horse. It has been also mentioned in literature that horses were present in Europe in Paleolithic times about 25,000 years ago. The Greece and Egyptian records of the domestication of the horse date from about 2000 BC and 1600 BC, respectively. Probably the last animal to be domesticated by man was the horse whereas the dog was the first animal domesticated.

## Order of domestication

(i) Pre-agricultural period – mammals like dog, reindeer, goat and sheep were domesticated.

(ii) Early agricultural period – mammals which were crop destroyer and used for human food like cattle, buffalo, gaur, banteng, yak and pig.

(iii) Mammals were domesticated for transport and labour like elephant, horses, camels and ass.

## 1.11. HISTORY OF ANIMAL BREEDING

Pure breeding in human is an ancient idea for a number of reasons particularly the caste system of society. Emphasis on ancestry in human genealogies is older than history. Man's attempts to breed livestock to serve his purpose go far back into man's own history.

More than a thousand years ago, the Arabs in their horse breeding were memorizing the genealogies of their horses but the way they used these genealogies to breed their horses is not known. Lush (1945) presumed that like modern Arabs, the pedigrees could have been kept only in female line as an aid to selection and taking some care to avoid close inbreeding.

The Romans of the time of Varro and Cato (20000 years ago) made many comments about kinds and types of animals to be selected for breeding purposes, although they made no attempt to record long pedigrees for their livestock. The Roman, Varro advocated the idea of progeny testing 2000 years ago.

**Pure breeding :** The use of pedigrees was started in rural England late in the eighteenth century. Robert Bakewell (1726-1795) is remembered for setting the pattern of modern animal breeding and called the founder of animal breeding. The pedigree breeding was established in his time and he made it popular. He was born in England in 1725 and died in 1795. He was an experimenter. He made efforts to produce farm animals (cattle, sheep, and horses) with increased efficiency. He developed theories, tested them with experiments and laid down the following principles

(i) like begets (produces) like

(ii) Breed the best to the best regardless of relationship, this lead to extremely close mating and he thereby introduced inbreeding as a tool in livestock improvement.

(iii) Inbreeding produces prepotency and refinement, and development of relatively true breeding strains.

(iv) He initiated sire testing by leasing the sire to other breeders. He started the practice of ram-letting instead of selling his best males. He rented best males for use for a year at a time and the best sires were used to come back to him each year, and those whose progeny had proved them much better than the others, could be kept for use in his own flocks or herds. Thus he used the progeny testing idea of the Roman, Varro.

Robert Bakewell laid the foundation for the Shire horse, Longhorn cattle, and Leicester sheep. His success attracted many imitators (who follow examples) and many ambitious stockmen from many parts of England went to work with him so as to know his methods. The greatest contribution of Bakewell to breeding methods was that he appreciated the inbreeding as the most effective tool to produce refinement and fixing type.

Collings, who was one of those who visited and learned from R. Bakewell, laid the foundations of the Short horn breed in 1775.

Thomas Bates (1975-1849) studied the methods of collings. He started to keep records of feed consumption in relation to both beef and milk production. He selected with great care and inbred very closely, and developed one of the great herds of cattle.

In the seventeenth century, the Arab horse came to Britain. About this time, the imported horses were crossed with those locally available and a belief in purity of pedigree was adapted.

Buffon (1708-88) a French naturalist advocated systematic crossbreeding. As a result of the efforts of the Bakewell followers, these soon began groups of animals closely related to each other and similar in type all over England. These were the groups from which came the modern breeds most of which were not formally organized as such until later.

When the people of other lands came to know about the improvement in breeding stock of Bakewell and his followers, the export of breeding stock to those lands was started and this become a considerable source of income to the British stockmen. This encouraged them for further improvement to attract foreign customers for breeding stock.

## Breed association and pedigree recording

With time there was an increase in the number of animal breeders and the number of generations in the pedigrees. No one could remember all of the animals far back in the pedigree and also no one can believe in the statements or records of others. Therefore, the herd books were formed in order to supply correct information..

The first herd book was "An introduction to the General Stud Book" for the thorough bred horse and it was started in 1791. This contained the records of the pedigrees of the horses winning important races.

The next herd book "Short horn herd book" was published by Coates in 1822. An English Hereford herd book was published in 1846 and a Polled herd book for Aberdeen Angus cattle in 1862.

The first swine herd book in the world was that of the American Berkshire Association which appeared in 1876.

Stud herd books for horses were founded in France in 1826, in Germany in 1827 and in Australia in 1847.

The first cattle herd book in France was established in 1855, the first German one in 1864, the first Dutch one is 1874 and the first Danish one in 1881.

In the continental countries of Europe pure breeding and registration were generally organized at a later date than in Britain. In Germany and adjoining lands, extensive efforts for improvement were developed first in sheep breeding, then in horse breeding and in cattle breeding. Dauben ton used to measure wool fineness with a micrometer as long ago as 1779 and Abilgaard in 1802 started marking sheep individually so that their production could be recorded and used as a basis of selection.

After the turn of the eighteenth century, there was no intellectual background to the efforts of animals breeders in Europe and there was resurgence (revival) of the theory of pure breeding (pedigree breeding). In the period about 1800 it was common practice to cross extensively in accordance with the idea expressed by Buffon (1780) that perfection could be attained only through widespread crossing and mixing all individuals with desirable points. Then for a half century the trend changed to follow pure breeding for improving a breed from within itself. Krunitz (1845) wrote that the English improve a race from within the same race and mating them together, and to keep the stock unmixed to produce a race of desired qualities. This lead to the theory of "**racial constancy**" which held that each animal transmitted according to its race rather than to its other characteristics.

In 1860, attention was devoted to the individual than to the "racial constancy". During the nineteenth century a "doctrine of the indigenous breed" was popular in Norway, which held that locally adapted types of the animal were the best to use.

In 1859, Darwin published "the origin of species" and in 1865 Mendel published the results of his studies on the inheritance of garden pea which had no immediate impact on animal breeding.

The production of all cows has been recorded continuously since 1871 in Strickhof Agr. School at Zurich, Switzerland. The first cow testing association in the world was established in 1892 in Denmark.

Allen, R.L. (1847) stated in his book "Domestic Animals" that every country and almost every district has its peculiar breeds of cattle".

Galton (1822, 1911) introduced the quantitative approach to variation among relatives and it could have been made valuable but it was ignored and had to wait for Fisher, Wright, Haldane, and Lush in the period 1918 to 1939.

## WORK DONE IN INDIA

Sukhatme (1944) statistically analysed the breeding data of goat breeding scheme of ICAR being in operation at Etah (UP). The ICAR then initiated to scrutinise all the research schemes, programmes and reports from statistical point of view. This followed several investigations.

A series of studies were followed by Amble and his colleagues to analyse the breeding data of cattle viz., Red Sindhi, Tharparkar and Kangayam maintained at GLF, on crossbred cows and buffaloes maintained at MDF and on sheep and goats kept at different research stations. They worked out the vital statistics like mortality and fertility rates and the estimates of genetic parameters.

The analysis of breeding data accumulated in the past at different farms has become a routine of animal breeders. This helped the animal breeders to know the genetic structure of the herd/flock which aided in selection for genetic improvement. This emphasized the need to record and maintain the records in a herd and to analyze the data for drawing plans for P.T. of bulls.

Side by side, the statistical techniques were also improved. The application of discriminant function for selection of genetically superior animals was demonstrated by Panse (1946). The new sire indices were also developed by Krishnan (1956) which was the corrected daughter average index, by Sundersan and Collegues (1965) known as dairy search index accounting the period variations.

Kampthorne and Tandon (1953) developed the method of estimating $h^2$ from data with different number of daughters per dam. Tomar et al. (1991) and Tomar (1998) worked out the method of estimating $h^2$ of threshold data withou' transformation. Tomar and Verma (1981) gave the formula to estimate the standard error of $h^2$ of threshold characters.

Prediction equations were given by Sunderason et al. (1954/1960) to predict life time milk production and to predict lactation yield from partial yield, by Tomar et al. (1971) to predict the body weight of cows from body measurements.

Tomar and his collegues in a series of studies (1985-2001) opened a new area of research and gave the formula to work out the replacement rate, replacement index, and the selective value of cows, buffaloes and goats.

Basic researches on quantitative genetics were also carried out by Mathur (1953) and Puri (1954) to estimate the effective number of factors responsible for inheritance of quantitative characters. Gopalan (1962) studied the effect of linkage on quantitative characters. Narain and his collegues studied the gene action and interaction with multiple alleles (1963), variation in presence of epistasis and G-E interaction (1965) and the genetic and assortative mating (1967)

Amble and Jacob (1974) reviewed the work on development of statistics in animal science research in India.

## QUESTIONS

**1.1.** Enumerate the basic characteristics of domestic animals. Describe in detail the changes caused by long term domestication in animals. (*ARS 1992*)

***Or***

What changes did domestication bring about the economically useful animals with respected to psychology, reproductive characters, anatomical conformation, production traits? (*ARS 1990*)

**1.2.** (*a*) Give the zoological classification of genus bovis. (*ARS 1993, 1996*)

(*b*) What are the various methods of animal domestication? (*ARS 1993 1996*)

**1.3.** Describe origin and domestication of cattle and buffalo leading to eventual evolution of their present day modern breeds. (*ARS 1994*)

**1.4.** (*a*) Discuss origin and domestication of sheep and goat. (*ARS 1996*)

(*b*) Discuss origin and domestication of buffalo

**1.5.** What do you mean by domestication of animals? What are the theories of origin of present day species?

**1.6.** (*a*) Give in brief the history of animal breeding.

(*b*) When and for which breed the herd book was first started? (*ARS 1978*)

**1.7.** (*a*) Define the terms: domestication, breed, environmental niche, taming, imprinting.

(*b*) Write the evolutionary sequences under domestication.

(*c*) What domestication had brought changes in evolutionary processes?

***

# 2

# ANIMAL GENETIC RESOURCES (AnGR)

## 2.1. BIODIVERSITY

The life is greatly diversified into various forms to the extent that no two organisms are alike how closely genetically related they are except clones and identical twins. This is called the biodiversity. The biodiversity exist in domestic and pet animals as well as among wild life. The biodiversity in domestic animals is taken as the genetic diversity in the form of different breeds and forms within species. The genetic diversity has resulted due to the process of evolution over thousands of years during wild and domesticated stages and for the efforts made by man to meet the market demand, in present day context. Since beginning man has tried to exploit many species of plants and animals. This leads to domestication of some species of animals having desirable characteristics for mankind. However, man has domesticated a mere handful (about 40 species) for his own use like milk, meat, eggs, fibre, hides/ skin, fuel, manure and draught power etc. The various breeds and distinct animals types developed through selection and breeding practices and quest for development of need based animal types in different agroclimatic conditions have acquired specific morphological and physiological characteristics grouped as adaptation. The farm animals of India have the unique features of adaptation to adverse climatic factors, diseases and parasites of tropics, survival on inadequate quantities of feeds, fodder and water.

## 2.2 ANIMAL GENETIC RESOURCES (AnGR) OF WORLD AND INDIA

The AnGR includes all types of species and breeds that exist. Mason, I.L. (1988) had published a book "A World Dictionary of Livestock Breeds, Types and Varieties". It is the most comprehensive book on domestic AnGR.

According to world watch list, FAO, 1995, the numbers of breeds of livestock species are as under.

**TABLE 2.1: NUMBER OF BREEDS**

| Species | World | Asia and Pacific | Europe | America | Africa | India | |
|---|---|---|---|---|---|---|---|
| | | | | | | FAO | ICAR |
| Cattle | 787 | 190 | 305 | 110 | 120 | 61 | 30 |
| Buffalo | 72 | 57 | 2 | 3 | 2 | 19 | 15 |
| Sheep | 920 | 226 | 42 | 70 | 73 | 59 | 42 |
| Goat | 351 | 126 | 113 | 23 | 34 | 29 | 20 |
| Pigs | 358 | 157 | 129 | 52 | 13 | 3 | 3 |
| Ass | 77 | 17 | 16 | 10 | 6 | 3 | 3 |
| Horse | 384 | 72 | 185 | 65 | 31 | 9 | 6 |
| Camel | 56 | 14 | | | | | 6 |
| Chicken | 606 | 72 | 406 | 45 | 57 | | 18 |
| **Total** | **3606** | **931** | | | | **183** | **145** |

The India's share to the world and Asian total population (in million) of livestock species according to FAO Data bank (1998) is as under:

**TABLE 2.2 TOTAL POPULATION (MILLION)**

| Species | World | Asia | India | Indian share to | |
|---|---|---|---|---|---|
| | | | | World | Asia |
| Cattle | 1315 | 453 | 209 | 15.9 | 46.1 |
| Buffalo | 164 | 159 | 92 | 56.1 | 57.9 |
| Sheep | 1061 | 402 | 56 | 5.3 | 14.0 |
| Goat | 693 | 437 | 121 | 17.4 | 27.6 |
| Pig | 957 | 577 | 16 | 1.7 | 2.8 |
| Horse | 61 | 17 | 1 | 1.6 | 5.8 |
| Camel | 19 | 5 | 1.5 | 7.7 | 30.5 |
| Chicken | 13683 | 6828 | 343 | 2.5 | 5.0 |

## 2.3. LIVESTOCK POPULATION TREND IN INDIA

The population of various species of farm livestock and poultry in India is exceedingly high but their overall productivity is markedly lower than that of the European and American counter parts. Not only this, but there had also been marked increase in population of various animal species which is indicated by the following figures.

**TABLE 2.3: POPULATION (MILLIONS) OVER THE PERIODS (INDIA)**

| Species | 1951 | 1961 | 1972 | 1982 | 1992 |
|---|---|---|---|---|---|
| Cattle | 155.3 | 175.6 | 178.3 | 192.45 | 204.58 (64.36) |
| Buffalo | 43.4 | 51.2 | 57.4 | 69.78 | 81.21 (43.81) |
| Sheep | 39.1 | 40.2 | 40.0 | 48.76 | 50.78 |
| Goat | 47.2 | 60.9 | 67.5 | 95.25 | 115.28 |
| Camel | 0.6 | 0.9 | 1.1 | 1.08 | 1.03 |
| Pig | 4.4 | 5.2 | 6.9 | 10.07 | 12.79 |
| Yaks | - | 0.02 | 0.04 | 0.13 | 0.06 |
| Mithuns | - | - | - | - | 0.15 |
| Mules | 0.06 | 0.05 | 0.08 | 0.13 | 0.19 |
| Donkeys | 1.3 | 1.1 | 1.0 | 1.02 | 0.97 |
| Horses and ponies | 1.5 | 1.3 | 0.9 | 0.9 | 0.82 |
| Total livestock | 292.8 | 335.4 | 353.4 | 419.59 | 470.86 |
| Poultry | 73.5 | 114.2 | 138.5 | 207.74 | 307.07 |

Figures in parenthesis are the breedable females

**Stocking rate :** India has 328.8 million hectares of total land area and only 193 m hectares is under cultivation of which about 60 m hectares is irrigated. According to 1982 census, the stocking rate per sq. km had been 58.5 cattle, 21.2 buffalo, 14.8 sheep, 28.9 goat, 0.27 equines, 0.3 camel, 3.0 pigs, 63.2 poultry and the overall livestock density was estimated as 127.64 animals per sq. km in 1982.

## 2.4 STATEWISE POPULATION OF DIFFERENT SPECIES

**TABLE 2.4: STATE/UT WISE ANIMAL POPULATION (THOUSANDS) IN 1992**

| State/UT | Cattle | Buffalo | Sheep | Goat | Pigs | Camels |
|---|---|---|---|---|---|---|
| J & K | 3055+ | 729+ | 2945+ | 1767+ | 12+ | 2 |
| HP | 2165$ | 701+ | 1076$ | 1118+ | 5- | - |
| Punjab | 2906 | 6008+ | 527- | 544- | 101- | 42 |
| Haryana | 2136 | 4372+ | 1043+ | 800+ | 516+ | 128 |
| UP | 25635- | 20084+ | 2403+ | 13110+ | 2905+ | 35 |
| Rajasthan | 11699- | 7708+ | 12496- | 15309$ | 253+ | 749 |
| Gujarat | 6804- | 5268+ | 2028- | 4241+ | 102- | 63 |
| Maharashtra | 17646+ | 5448+ | 3037+ | 9943+ | 376+ | - |
| Goa | 98 | 42 | - | 14 | 89 | - |
| MP | 28588+ | 7970+ | 836- | 8370+ | 729+ | 12 |
| Orissa | 13841+ | 1536+ | 1838- | 4943$ | 584+ | - |
| Bihar | 22154+ | 5352+ | 1689+ | 17459+ | 1127+ | - |
| West Bengal | 17453+ | 1012+ | 1488+ | 14170+ | 955+ | - |
| Tripura | 949+ | 20+ | 5$ | 429+ | 188+ | - |
| AP | 10946- | 9150+ | 7788+ | 4328- | 650- | - |
| Tamil Nadu | 9278- | 2814- | 5848+ | 6343+ | 672- | - |
| Karnataka | 13173+ | 4252+ | 5430+ | 6287+ | 380+ | - |
| Kerala | 3524+ | 296- | 30+ | 1848- | 136+ | - |
| Assam | 10118+ | 959+ | 149+ | 3454+ | 1364+ | - |
| Arunachal Pradesh | 324+ | 5- | 32+ | 125+ | 237+ | - |
| Manipur | 719$ | 114- | 14$ | 38- | 383+ | - |
| Meghalaya | 535$ | 33- | 22- | 195+ | 295+ | - |
| Mizoram | 59+ | 7+ | - | 21- | 112+ | - |
| Nagaland | 332+ | 32+ | 1 | 151+ | 526+ | - |

| | | | | | | |
|---|---|---|---|---|---|---|
| Sikkim | 198+ | 2- | 15- | 114- | 44+ | - |
| UT's : Chandigarh | 5- | 23+ | - | - | 3$ | - |
| Delhi | 41- | 247+ | - | 17- | 10- | - |
| Pondicherry | 90- | 5- | 3- | 44- | - | - |
| Lakshdweep | 2- | - | - | 17+ | - | - |
| Daman and Diu | 8 | - | - | 5 | - | - |
| D.N. Haveli | 49+ | 3$ | - | 19+ | - | - |
| A, N. Islands | 50+ | 14+ | - | 56+ | 34- | - |
| Total | 204583+ | 84206+ | 50783+ | 115279+ | 12788+ | 1031 |

| State/UT | Horses & Ponies | Mules | Doneys | Yaks | Mithun | Total livestock | Poultry |
|---|---|---|---|---|---|---|---|
| J & K | 122+ | 19 | 19 | 33 | - | 8703+ | 4627+ |
| HP | 13- | 16 | 7 | 5 | - | 5106+ | 725+ |
| Punjab | 39- | 16 | 36 | - | - | 10222+ | 18331+ |
| Haryana | 50 | 25 | 73 | - | - | 9143 | 8578 |
| UP | 249 | 102 | 276 | - | - | 64799 | 10790 |
| Rajasthan | 24 | 3 | 200 | - | - | 48441 | 3053 |
| Gujarat | 13 | - | 79 | - | - | 18598 | 5657 |
| Maharashtra | 41 | - | 73 | - | - | 36564 | 33118 |
| Goa | - | - | - | - | - | 243 | 731 |
| MP | 73 | 8 | 58 | - | - | 46744 | 11800 |
| Orissa | - | - | - | - | - | 35090 | 37407 |
| Bihar | 16 | 4 | 29 | - | - | 47930 | 17655 |
| West Bengal | 12 | - | - | - | - | 35090 | 37407 |

| State/UT | Horses & Ponies | Mules | Doneys | Yaks | Mithun | Total livestock | Poultry |
|---|---|---|---|---|---|---|---|
| Tripura | - | - | - | - | - | 1591 | 1597 |
| AP | 8 | - | 41 | - | - | 32911 | 49884 |
| Tamil Nadu | 9 | - | 43 | - | - | 25007 | 24553 |
| Karnataka | 13 | - | 33 | - | - | 29568 | 16164 |
| Kerala | - | - | - | - | - | 5834 | 21907 |
| Assam | 18 | - | - | - | - | 16062 | 16394 |
| Arunachal Pradesh | 5 | - | - | 9 | 105 | 842 | 1187 |
| Manipur | - | - | - | - | 22 | 1290 | 3259 |
| Meghalaya | 2 | - | - | - | - | 1182 | 1824 |
| Mizoram | 2 | - | - | 1 | 1 | 203 | 1086 |
| Nagaland | 6 | - | - | - | 26 | 1074 | 2164 |
| Sikkim. | 2 | - | - | 10 | - | 385 | 302 |
| UT's : Chandigarh | - | - | - | - | - | 31 | 180 |
| Delhi | - | - | - | - | - | 315 | 28 |
| Pondicherry | - | - | - | - | - | 142 | 120 |
| Lakshdweep | - | - | - | - | - | 19 | 61 |
| Daman and Diu | - | - | - | - | - | 13 | 27 |
| D.N. Haveli | - | - | - | - | - | 71 | 117 |
| A, N. Islands | - | - | - | - | - | 154 | 611 |
| Total | 817- | 193 | 967 | 58 | 154 | 47085 | 307069+ |

The signs '+' and '-' indicate the increase and decrease in population during 1992 over 1982 whereas the sign $ indicate the almost static population

The population distribution in different states clearly indicate the significant differences among states and regions for the importance of the type of genetic resources and the animal husbandry practices

The AnGR of India has the following special features

1. The India is a gold mine and vast reservoir of the germplasm of domestic animals and poultry. This includes the various species viz. cattle, buffalo, sheep, goat, pig, yak, mithun, camels, equines (horses and Ponies, mules, donkeys), poultry and ducks. Further there is a large biodiversity within each of these species having well recognized breeds viz. 26 breeds of cattle, 8 of buffalo, 42 of sheep, 22 of goats, 8 of camels, 6 of horses, 17 of poultry in addition to other useful animals like mithun, yak, donkeys, pigs etc.
2. About 80% of the total indigenous animals are non-descript and hence remained undocumented.
3. All the breeds have not been properly documented and evaluated for their utility.
4. The Indian breeds have better adaptability to cope with harsh climatic conditions and to certain diseases, have better efficiency to utilize coarse feed and fodder.
5. The population density is high but production potential is low compared to exotic breeds.
6. The crossbreeding programme for genetic improvement had resulted in marked decline in availability of pure breeds.
7. The bulls of superior genetic merit (progeny tested bulls) are not available to the extent required.
8. The better female germplasm particularly the buffaloes are sold and taken to metropolitan cities for milk production but after completion of lactation they are slaughtered.
9. The farm livestock and poultry provide milk, meat, skin, wool, dung, eggs and draught power, employment to rural poor, landless and marginal farmers as well through animal based industry besides that some animal species provide companionship and entertainment.

## 2.5. CATTLE GENETIC RESOURCES

The cattle is a sub-family, known as bovinae, of the family bovidae of horned animals, having 9 sub-species of cattle under genus Bos. These are Zebu cattle, hump less cattle, buffaloes, bison, mithun (gayal), yak, banteng, gaur and kouprey. The domestic cattle, descended from the aurochs and divided into two sub groups viz. zebu cattle of Asia and Africa and the exotic cattle or hump less cattle predominantly of Europe. The humpless cattle also occur in Africa and East-Asia. The six species of cattle (Aurochs, mithun, yak, banteng, gaur and Kouprey) can interbred but the male crossbreds are almost infertile and hence the breeding can be made with crossbred females.

### 2.5.1. Main features of cattle population in India

About 80% of the total cattle population in India is non-descript. Further the large majority of descript cattle belong to draught and dual purpose breeds. The distribution of different classes of cattle (millions) during 1992 in India was as under:

| | Total | Crossbreds | Indigenous | | |
|---|---|---|---|---|---|
| | | | Total | Descript | Non descript |
| All cattle | 204.58 | 15.21 | 189.37 | 28.41 | 160.96 |
| Adult female | 64.36 | 6.49 | 57.87 | 8.68 | 49.19 |

There were 18032 indigenous cattle bulls and 431 crossbred cattle bulls in the country in 1992.

India has excellent quality of draught cattle which significantly contributed as draught animal power. Besides it, there are some milch type and dual purpose breeds which also provide milk and good quality bullocks.

The FAO had estimated 61 breeds of cattle in India but there are about 26-30 well defined breeds according to Indian literature.

The population density of cattle is very high (58.5 cattle per sq. km) which is increasing constantly. Due to increase in population number, the overall milk production has increased in the country but the milk production per animal is decreasing.

The indigenous cattle are, able to perform under harsh climate and stressful environment, less susceptible to certain diseases, able to consume and convert coarse and dry fodder into animal products and thereby can be raised on zero input system.

The crossbreeding for breed improvement programme has resulted into the reduction of high producing animals of indigenous breeds. Moreover, the indigenous cattle are also being replaced by milch breeds of buffaloes.

The cattle of India vary in size and body conformation perhaps due to their origin, adaptation to different agro-climatic conditions and the use which they have been put to. The cattle breeds of India have been divided into milch breeds which produce good quantity of milk but do not produce good quality bullocks, dual purpose breeds which are fairly good milkers and produce bullocks of good draught powers, and the draught breeds providing only a little amount of milk.

### 2.5.2. Cattle breeds of India

Olivery (1938) was perhaps the first to survey the important breeds of cattle in India. The names of breeds under different categories of utility alongwith their home tract, body colour, adult body weight (males and females) and the milk yield (kg) in a lactation have been given in the tabular form below:

| Sr. No. | Breed | Home tract | Body colour | Adult weight (kg) | | Milk (kg)/ lact. |
|---|---|---|---|---|---|---|
| **Milch Breeds** | | | | **M** | **F** | |
| 1. | Sahiwal | Organized farms in Pb., Haryana, UP, Bihar, MP, WB | Red | 540 | 400 | 1800 |
| 2. | Red Sindhi | Organized farms in Haryana, TN and other parts of India | Red | 460 | 320 | 1600 |
| 3. | Gir | Junagarh, Kathiawar and Baroda | Red or red and white | 550 | 400 | 1500 |
| 4. | Tharparkar | Ajmer, Jodhpur | White or light grey | 540 | 350 | 1700 |
| **Dual – purpose Breeds** | | | | | | |
| 5. | Rathi | Rajasthan (mixture of Sah, RS and TP) | White or grey or brown patches | 380 | 325 | 1800 |
| 6. | Hariana | Rohtak, Hisar, Karnal, Gurgaon, Western UP, Rajasthan | White or light grey | 500 | 350 | 900 |
| 7. | Mewati | Mathura (UP), Alwer and Bharatpur | White with grey patches | 400 | 350 | - |
| 8. | Kankrej | Kutch and Ahmedabad (Gujarat) | Silver or iron grey | 550 | 430 | 1600 |
| 9. | Deoni | AP, Karnataka, MS | Black and white , Red and white | 590 | 340 | 900 |
| 10. | Ongole | Ongole, Nellore and Guntur (AP) | White or greyish | 550 | 440 | 700 |
| 11. | Gaolao | Chhindwada (MP), Wardha and Nagpur, AP | White | 430 | 330 | 500 |
| 12. | Krishna Valley | MS, AP, Karnataka | Grey white | 500 | 340 | - |
| 13. | Dangi | MS, Valsad (Gujarat) | Red and white, black and white | 365 | 295 | 600 |

| Sr. No. | Breed | Home tract | Body colour | Adult weight (kg) | | Milk (kg)/ lact. |
|---|---|---|---|---|---|---|
| **Draught Breeds** | | | | **M** | **F** | |
| 14. | Nagori | Rajasthan | White or grey | 400 | 340 | 500 |
| 15. | Malvi | MP | Grey | 430 | 340 | 500 |
| 16. | Kharigarh | Lakhimpur Khari (UP) | White | 475 | 320 | 400 |
| 17. | Kankatha | Bundelkhand and Banda (UP), MP | Grey | 340 | 295 | - |
| 18. | Nimari | Nimar and Indore (MP) | Red with white spots | 390 | 320 | 300 |
| 19. | Panwar | Pilibhit and Lakhimpur (UP) | Black with white | 320 | 295 | - |
| 20. | Bachur | Darbhanga, Bhagalpur, Sitamarhi, Muzaffarpur, Champaran (Bihar) | Grey | 385 | 320 | 500 |
| 21. | Khillari | MS | White to grey | 500 | 345 | 300 |
| 22. | Amritmahal | Karnataka | White or grey | 500 | 320 | - |
| 23. | Hallikar | Tumkor, Hassan, Mysore (Karnataka) | Dark or light | 450 | 300 | - |
| 24. | Bargur | Coimbatore | Red and white | 340 | 295 | 350 |
| 25. | Kangayam | Coimbatore | White or gray | 500 | 330 | 600 |
| 26. | Siri | Sikkim, Darjling | Black and white | 450 | 350 | 900 |
| The following 4 breeds of cattle (draught type) have also been documented in Indian literature making a total of 30 breeds of Indian cattle | | | | | | |
| 27. | Red Kandhari | Maharashtra | Dark red | - | - | - |
| 28. | Punganur | Andhra Pradesh | White or light grey | 130 to 200 | | 500 |

| Sr. No. | Breed | Home tract | Body colour | Adult weight (kg) | | Milk (kg)/ lact. |
|---|---|---|---|---|---|---|
| | | | | M | F | |
| 29. | Umblechery | Tamil Nadu | Grey with white makings on face and legs | - | - | - |
| 30. | Vachur | Kerala | Red, black and white | 95 to 150 | | 500 |

The crossbred strains/breeds evolved at different places are as under:

Cattle breeds evolved in India:

1. Taylor — Shorthorn and Jersey with local cows around Patna.
2. Jersind — Jersey x Red Sindhi at Allahabad
3. Sunandini — Brown Swiss x non descript at Munar (Kerala)
4. Frieswal — 3/8 to 5/8 level of exotic inheritance of Friesian and rest Sahiwal at M.D.F.
5. Karan Fries — Friesian x Tharparkar at NDRI, Karnal.
6. Karan Swiss — Brown Swiss x (Sahiwal & Red Sindhi) at NDRI, Karnal.
7. Jerthar — Jersey bull x Tharparkar cows at Bangalore

Cattle breeds developed in other countries:

8. Australian Milking Zebu — 20 to 40 % Zebu blood (Sahiwal, Red Sindhi) and rest from Jersey at CSIRO
9. Australian Frisian Sahiwal — Sahiwal bulls x H.F. cows of Queensland Deptt. of Primary Industry
10. Jamaica Hope — 80% Jersey, 15% Sahiwal and 5 % Holstein blood, developed in Jamaica
11. Mambi — ¾ HF and ¼ Zebu in Cuba
12. Siboney — 5/8 HF and 3/8 Zebu in Cuba
13. Pitanquieras — 5/8 Red Poll and 3/8 Zebu in Brazil
14. Santa Gertrudis — Brahman x Shorthorn at Texas
15. Brangus — Brahman x Angus
16. Beefmaster — Brahman x Shorthorn x Hereford
17. Charbray — Brahman x Charolais
18. Guernsey — Brown and White cattle of Brittany x Brindle cattle of Normandy

## 2.5.3. Important Exotic Breeds of Cattle

### Dairy Breeds

**1. Holstein Friesian:** originated in two provinces of Netherlands (North Holland and West Fries land). Immigrated to Netherlands from Europe. Imported into USA by Dutch settlers in 1621. Large size body with black and white colour. Adult body weight 800 kg of males and 550 kg of females. Best milk producer of the world with world record of about 19000 kg in a lactation and an average production of 6000-7000 kg with low fat % (3-3.5%). AFC about 30 months and CI 13-14 months.

**2. Brown Swiss:** Native of Switzerland. Introduced into United States in 1869. Fairly large size body with light brown to grey colour. Adult body weight 700 kg males and 500 kg females. Medium milker with average 5000 kg milk per lactation. AFC and CI equal to HF cattle.

**3. Jersey:** Originated on the island of Jersey (English Channel). Imported into England in 1811 and United States in 1850. Smaller size cattle with reddish grey to brown colour. Adult weight about 600 kg males and 400 kg females. AFC and CI almost equal to HF cattle. Average herd average of 4500 kg per lactation with 4.5% fat.

**4. Ayrshire:** Developed in Ayrshire country of Scotland during 18th century by crossing many strains of cattle. Medium size body with cherry red to brown colour. Adult males weight about 700 kg and females 500 kg. Outward and upward horn. Imported into United States in 1822. AFC and CI almost equal to HF cattle.

**5. Guernsey:** Home tract in Guernsey in the Channel Island. Developed by Brown and White cattle of Brittany and large brindle cattle of Normandy. Smaller body with yellowish brown colour weighing about 600 kg males and 400 kg females. Herd average 4000 kg milk per lactation with 4.5-5% fat.

### Beef Breeds

**1. Hereford**: Developed in Hereford (England) during 1800 and imported into USA in 1817. Red in colour with white face and compact body weighing 600 kg males.

**2. Short horn**: Developed during 18th century in Durham Country in England. Solid red in colour or red with white markings or white or roan.

**3. Angus**: Originated in Aberdeen country of Scotland. Completely black body with polled head. Compact body. Introduced in USA in 1873.

**4. Santa Gertrudis**: Developed in Texas (USA) by crossing Short horn with Brahmin crossbred bull (any Indian breed is Known as Brahmin in USA). This breed has 5/8 Short horn and 3/8 Brahmin. Deep cherry-red colour body.

**5. Brangus**: Developed in USA by crossing Angus with Brahmin.

**6. Beef Master**: Developed in USA by crossing Hereford with Brahmin bulls and Shorthorn bulls. The Brahmin inheritance is about 15%.

## 2.6. BUFFALO GENETIC RESOURCES

The total population of buffalo in India as per livestock census of 1992 was 84 million out of which the breedable buffaloes were 43 million. The annual growth rate during 1987-92 registered an increase of 2.08%. There were 2864 buffalo bulls in the country. Asia has 96% and India 50% of the world buffalo population followed by China, Pakistan, Thailand, Philippines, Indonesia, Nepal, Vietnam, Burma, Bangladesh and Sri Lanka.

About 60% of the total buffaloes in India are non-descript and rest 40% population is descript classified into 19 breeds according to FAO but into 15 breeds according to ICAR.

| S. No. | Breed | Home tract | Body colour | Weight M | Weight F | Milk/lact. (kg) |
|---|---|---|---|---|---|---|
| 1. | Murrah | Rohtak, Hisar, Jind, Nabha, Patiala, Ludhiana, | Black | 570 | 450 | 1800 |
| 2. | Nili Ravi | Ferozpur (Pb.) | Black with white markings on forehead, muzzle, legs and tail | 600 | 450 | 1700 |
| 3. | Surti | Surat, Kaira, Baroda (Guj), | Brown | | | 1600 |
| 4. | Mehsana (Murrah x Surti) | Mehsana, Sabarkanta, Baroda (Guj) | Black to grey with white markings on face, legs, tail tips | 600 | 450 | 1600 |
| 5. | Jafrabadi | Junagarh, Jamnagar, Kutch (Guj.) | Black with white patches on face and legs | 600 | 450 | 1800 |
| 6. | Bhadawari | Agra, Etawah (UP), Gwalior (MP) | Copper coloured with short hair of black or brown colour | 475 | 385 | 900 |
| 7. | Nagpuri or Berari or Ellichpuri | Nagpur, Akola, Amravati (MS), MP and AP | Black with white patches on face, legs and tail | | | 1000 |
| 8. | Toda | Nilgiri (TN) | Grey skin | | | 800 |

The other breeds of buffaloes are localized in their small tracts: These are as under:

9. Pandarpuri or Marathwadi of Maharashtra state
10. Sambalpuri of Orissa and MP with black or brown skin
11. Manda or Ganjam of Orissa and A.P. with grey but yellowish tufts of hair may present on knee and fetlock.
12. Jerangi of A.P. and Orissa
13. Kalahandi or Paddakiwadi of Orissa and A.P.
14. Tarai of U.P. (Bareilly, Rampur, Sahajanpur)
15. South Kanara of Karnataka

## 2.7. SHEEP GENETIC RESOURCES

The total population of sheep in India (50.8 million) ranked fourth in the world in 1992 accounting for about 4.57% of the world sheep population whereas in 1997 sheep population in India was 56.47 million and ranked 3rd in the world with 5.3% of the world and 14.0% of the Asian sheep population. The sheep population in India registered an annual growth rate of 2.2% during 1987 to 1992 and 0.74% during 1951 to 1992 with an annual increase of 0.288 millions.

Sheep population and wool production in different regions of India

| Traits | North Temperate | North Western | Southern Penisular | Eastern |
|---|---|---|---|---|
| Sheep population (m) | 3.63 (7.2%) | 21.45 (42.2%) | 0.86 (41.1%) | 4.85 (9.5%) |
| Wool Prod. (m kg) | 4.8 (10.5%) | 29.8 (65.4%) | 9.1 (20.0%) | 1.9 (4.1%) |

There are 6 types of sheep breeds according to types of wool fibres viz.,

Fine wool – fine quality fleece

Medium wool – The fleece is medium in fineness and length

Long wool – wool fibres are long approaching 30 cms. The wool is coarse.

Carpet wool – It is coarse, wiry and tough

Fur – Pelts are used for fur purposes

Crossbred wool – produced from long wool and fine wool breeds crossing

### Sheep breeds of India

| Sr. No. | Breed | Home tract | Adult body M | Adult body F | Utility |
|---|---|---|---|---|---|
| **North Temperate Region Breeds** | | | | | |
| 1. | Bhakarwal | J&K, migratory flock | | | Carpet wool |
| 2. | Changthangi | Changthangi region of Laddakh | 38 | 34 | -do- |
| 3. | Gurej | Gurej (Kashmir) | | | -do- |

| Sr. No. | Breed | Home tract | Adult body Wedight | | Utility |
|---|---|---|---|---|---|
| | | | M | F | |
| 4. | Karnah | Karnah (North Kashmir) | 40 | 30 | Apparel wool |
| 5. | Poonchi | Poonch & Rajori (J&K) | | | Carpet wool |
| 6. | Kashmir | Kashmir valley | | | Apparel wool Merino |
| 7. | Gaddi | Kulu, Kangra & Chamba (HP) | 25 | 24 | Carpet wool |
| 8. | Rampur Bushari | Rampur, Bushair, Shimla, Kinnour, Nahan, Bilaspur & Lahaul Spiti (HP) | 29 | 25 | -do- |
| **North Western Arid and Semi Arid Breeds** | | | | | |
| 9. | Muzaffarnagri | Western UP | 50 | 40 | Meat and Carpet wool |
| 10. | Jalauni | Jalaun, Jhansi, Lalitpur (UP) | 40 | 30 | -do- |
| 11. | Munjal | Punjab, Haryana | | | Carpet wool, meat |
| 12. | Hisardale (Merino x Magra) | Hisar | 54 | 34 | Apparel wool |
| 13. | Chokla or Shekhawati | Nagaur, Siker, Churu, Jhunjhunu (Raj.) | 34 | 23 | Carpet wool |
| 14. | Jaisalmeri | Jaisalmer, Barmer, Jodhpur (Raj.) | 28 | 28 | Meat and carpet wool |
| 15. | Magra (Bikaneri) | Bikaner, Jaisalmer (Raj.) | 27 | 24 | Carpet wool |
| 16. | Malpura | Jaipur, Tonk, Ajmer, Bhilwara, Bundi (Raj.) | 40 | 24 | Meat and carpet wool |
| 17. | Marwari | Marwar region (Raj.) | 30 | 26 | -do- |
| 18. | Nali | Ganganagar, Churu, Jhunjhunu (Raj.) | 34 | 24 | Carpet wool |
| 19. | Pugal | Bikaner, Jodhpur (Raj.) | 31 | 27 | -do- |
| 20. | Sonadi | Udaipur, Dungarpur & Chittorgarh (Raj.) | 38 | 21 | Meat and carpet wool |
| 21. | Patanwadi or Kutchi or Kathiawari | Patan distt. Of Gujarat | 33 | 26 | Carpet wool |

| Sr. No. | Breed | Home tract | Adult body Weight | | Utility |
|---|---|---|---|---|---|
| **Southern Peninsular Region** | | | **M** | **F** | |
| 22. | Deccani | Pune, Satara, Sangli, Ahmedanagar, Kolhapur (MS) | 34 | 34 | Meat |
| 23. | Bellari | Bellari distt. (Karnataka) | 35 | 27 | Meat, carpet wool |
| 24. | Hasan | Hasan distt (Karnataka) | 25 | 23 | Meat |
| 25. | Kenguri | Raichur distt. (Karnataka) | 32 | 27 | -do- |
| 26. | Mandaya or Bannur | Mandya and Banglore (Karnataka) | 34 | 24 | -do- |
| 27. | Nellore | Nellore (AP) | 36 | 30 | -do- |
| 28. | Coimbatore | Coimbatore, Dindigul (TN) | 25 | 20 | Meat & carpet wool |
| 29. | Kilakarsar | Virudunagar, Ramnathpuram (TN) | 30 | 21 | -do- |
| 30. | Madras Red | Chingalpet, Madras (TN) | 36 | 23 | -do- |
| 31. | Mechari | Salem, Erode, Namakkal (TN) | 35 | 22 | -do- |
| 32. | Nilgiri | Nilgir hills (TN) | 30 | 25 | Apparel wool |
| 33. | Ramnad white | Ramnathpuram, Virdunagar (TN) | 30 | 22 | Meat |
| 34. | Trichi black | Trichy, Pramblur, Salem, Tiruvannamali, Dharampur (TN) | 25 | 18 | -do- |
| 35. | Vempur | Tuticorin, Virudnagar (TN) | 34 | 28 | -do- |
| **Eastern Region Breeds** | | | | | |
| 36. | Chotta Nagpuri | Chottanagpur, Ranchi, Palamodh, Hazaribagh, Singhbhum, Dhanbad (Bihar) | 20 | 20 | Meat, Carpet wool |
| 37. | Shahbadi | Shahabad, Patna, Gaya (Bihar) | 37 | 21 | Meat |
| 38. | Ganjam | Ganjam (Orissa) | | | Meat, carpet |
| 39. | Garole | Sunderban (WB) | | | Meat |
| 40. | Balangir | Balangir, Sambalpur, Sundargarh (Orissa) | 24 | 18 | Meat, carpet wool |
| 41. | Bonpala | Sikkim | | | Meat, carpet |
| 42. | Tibetan | Sikkim, Kamag distt. of Arunachal | | | Carpet wool |

The following crossbred strains of sheep have been evolved in India:

| Sr. No. | Name | Exotic inheritance | Crosses made with place |
|---|---|---|---|
| 1 | Bharat Merino | 75% | Chokla and Nali withRambouillet and Merino at Avikanagar |
| 2 | Avivastra | 50% | Chokla and Nali with Ramborilet and Merino at Avikanagar |
| 3 | Avikalin | 50% | Malpura with Rambouillet at Avikanagar |
| 4 | Avimans | 50% | Malpura and Sonadi with Dorset and Suffolk at Avikanagar |
| 5 | Indian Karakul | 75% | Marwari, Malpura and Sonadi with Karakul at CSWRI, Bikaner |
| 6 | Kashmir Merino | 50-75% | Gaddi, Bhakarwal and Poonchi with Merino & Rambouillet |
| 7 | Nilgiri synthetic | 62.5-75% | Nilgiri with Merino and Rambouillet at Sandynallah (TN) |
| 8 | Patanwadi synthetic | 50% | Patanwadi with Rambouillet & Merino at GAU, Dantiwara |
| 9 | Hissardale | 75% | Bikaneri with Australian Merino at GLF, Hisar. |

Some breeds of exotic sheep developed by crossbreeding are as under:

| | | |
|---|---|---|
| 1 | Columbia | Rambouillet x Lincoln rams |
| 2 | Panama | Lincoln x Rambouillet rams |
| 3 | Targhee | Rambouillet x Long wool breed |
| 4 | Romnelet | Romney Marsh rams x Rambouillet ewes |
| 5 | Suffolk | Dark face South down rams x Norfolk strain |
| 6 | Corriedale | Merino ewes x Lincoln rams |
| 7 | Karakul | It was also developed by crossbreeding of two local breeds |

## Exotic breeds of sheep

### I. Fine wool breeds

**1. Merino:** Developed in Spain, imported into America in 1801 and used to develop American Merino from which Delaine Merino were developed. Rams weigh about 60kg and ewes about 45 kg. Rams shear 10kg wool and ewes 7 kg wool in a year. Medium size breed with short head. Ewes polled and Rams spiral horns. Imported to India from USSR.

**2. Rambouillet:** Originated at Rambouillet in France by importing Merino from Spain and hence descended from Spanish Merino. Imported into America in 1840. Rams weigh about 100 kg and ewes 70 kg and produces about 5 kg long fleece annually. Large breed with wide head and well balanced horns curving backward and upward. Ewes polled, Rams have large spiral horns or polled. Imported to India from USA.

## II. Medium wool breeds

**3. Corriedale:** Developed in New Zealand by crossing Merino ewes and Lincoln Rams and also Licester Rams subsequently. It has 50% Merino inheritance and rest Lincoln and Licester. Introduced in America in 1914. It is hardy breed producing wool and mutton. Rams weigh 80 kg and ewes 60 kg. Rams and ewes produce 7 kg and 5 kg wool per year. Dual purpose breed (meat and wool). Imported in India from Australia.

**4. Hampshire:** Originated in England by crossing two strains of sheep. Imported in USA in 1840. Large breed good for mutton as well. Rams weigh more than 100 kg and ewes about 80 kg producing 4 kg fleece annually.

**5. Cheviot:** Developed in Scotland by infusion of black face high land, Licester, South Down and Merino. Rams weigh 80 kg and ewes 60 kg producing 4-5 kg wool per year.

## III. Long coarse wool breeds

**6. Lincoln:** Developed in Lincoln (England) in 1749 with Licester inheritance. Largest breed in the world. Rams weigh about 150 kg and ewes about 100 kg. Fleece is 25-38 cm long often twisted into spiral.

**7. Licester:** Originated in Licester (England) in 1960 by Robert Bakewell from local sheep by close inbreeding. Rams weigh 120 kg and ewes 80 kg. Fleece coarse, 15-25 cm long with annual yield of 5 kg.

**8. Romney Marsh:** Originated in the Marshy district of Kent (England). Resistant to parasites, medium size breed weighing about 100 kg rams and 70 kg ewes.

## IV. Fur breeds

**9. Karakul :** Native to Bokhara (Central Asia), derives it name after the area Karakul (black lake). Originated by crossing two breeds of this area. Medium size breed, rams weighing 80 kg and ewes 60 kg, producing light white fleece of low grade of about 3 kg annually. Poor in mutton quality. Produces fur pelt from prematurely born lambs or killed soon after birth. Imported in India in 1975.

## V. Mutton breeds

**10. Dorset:** Medium size, origin exactly not known but developed through selection, native of England (Dorset region). These are horned and polled strains, wool is short and 2.75 to 3.2 kg, rams weighs 80 kg and ewes 60kg. Imported in India in 1973 at CSWRI, Avikanagar.

**11. Suffolk:** Native of England (Suffolk region). Developed from dark faced south down rams used in Norfolk strain. It is black faced free from wool. Both rams and ewes polled, though rams have scars, short, dense and fine fleece of 2.75 to 3.75 kg annually. Ewes are prolific, mature rams weigh 100 kg and ewes 80 kg. Imported in India in 1973 at Avikanagar (Rajasthan)

**12. South Down:** Originated in South down hills of England and developed by selection and inbreeding of local sheep. It is hornless and mutton breed Rams weigh 80kg and ewes 60 kg producing 3-4 kg wool per year.

## 2.8. GOAT GENETIC RESOURCES

The goat population in India was estimated to be about 120.6 million in 1997 and 128 million in 1999-2000. India stands 2$^{nd}$ in goat population. The goat population had increased by 3.6% (1.66 million) annually during 1951 to 1992 which is higher than cattle, buffalo and sheep. This is inspite of the fact that the current mean rate of slaughter of goats is about 40% and mean mortality rate of about 15%.

There is a history of migration of goats from western Asia to India from 7500 -7000 BC onwards. The geographical isolations due to hilly rivers, high mountains, dense jungles and deserts etc; physical environment, ecological constraints, social preferences, diseases resistance and the natural selection had resulted into the origin of present day Indian breeds over thousands of generations.

There are nearly 20 well recognized breeds of goats in India constituting 20-25% of the total goat populations and the remaining populations are considered as mixed and non descript. Different breeds have been developed in India to produce milk, meat and fibre through natural selection and have been adapted to diversified agro-climatic conditions based on their utility. The good quality fibres are produced by the goats of temperate Himalayan region and they possess the finest quality under coat called pashmina. Primarily milch type breeds which are large in size are found in North and North-Western region of the country. The goat breeds found in southern and peninsular region of India are of dual purpose for milk and meat. The different goat breeds of different regions have been listed as under:

| S. No. | Breeds | Home tract | Utility |
|---|---|---|---|
| **North temperate region** | | | |
| 1. | Changthangi | Changthang (Ladakh), Hills of Leh | Meat, fibre, pashmina |
| 2. | Chegu | Lahaul & Spiti, hill region of UP | -do- |
| 3. | Gaddi | Kangra, Kulu, Simla, Chamba (HP) | Meat, fibre (long hair) |
| **Northern arid and semi arid region** | | | |
| 4. | Barbari | Etawah, Agra, Aligarh (UP | Milk, meat |

| S. No. | Breeds | Home tract | Utility |
|---|---|---|---|
| 5. | Jamnapari | Etawah, Agra, Mathura (UP) | -do- |
| 6. | Beetal | Gurdaspur, Ferozpur, Amritsar (Pb.) | -do- |
| 7. | Jhakrana | Alwer, Nagaur (Rajasthan) | -do- |
| 8. | Marwari | Jodhpur, Pali, Nagaur, Bikaner, Jalore, Jaisalmer, Badmer (Rajasthan) | -do- |
| 9. | Sirohi | Sirohi (Rajasthan) | -do- |
| 10. | Zalawadi | Sundranagar, Rajkot, Zalawad (Guj.) | -do-, long hair |
| 11. | Gohlwadi | Bhavnagar, Junagarh, Amreli (Guj.) | -do- |
| 12. | Kutchi | Kutch, Kathiawar (Guj.) | Milk, Meat |
| 13. | Mehsana | Mehsana, Banaskantha, Baroda, Gandhinagar (Guj.) | -do- |
| 14. | Surti | Surat, Baroda (Guj.) | -do- |
| **Southern peninsular region** | | | |
| 15. | Osmanabadi | Osmanabad, Ahmednagar, and Solapur (MS) | -do- |
| 16. | Sangamneri | Pune, Ahmednagar (MS) | -do- |
| 17. | Malabari | Calicut, Kottayam, Malabar hills (Kerala) | -do- |
| 18. | Kanniadu | Ramnathpuram, Trinelochi, Tuticorin (TN) | Meat |
| 19. | Ganjam | Ganjam, Kovput, Phoolbani (Orisa) | Meat |
| 20. | Black Bengal | Nadia (WB) | Meat |

## Exotic goat breeds

The important exotic breeds of goats are as under:-

**1. Saanen :** Originated in Saane and Simmental valleys of Switzerland. White or light cream colour body, have pendulous udder, produces about 100 kg milk per lactation. Legs short in comparison to body, ears erect pointing forward, bucks weigh about 80 kg and Does about 60kg.

**2. Alpine:** Originated in Nubia (Africa), large animals, long lagged and hardy, small ears and Roman nose, Bucks weigh 80 kg and Does 60kg.

**3. Anglo Nubian:** The development of this breed is exactly not known. This is one of the largest and heaviest breeds among all European breeds of goats, produces 3 kg milk daily.

**4. Toggenburg:** Originated in Toggenburg valley of Switzerland, very hardy and high milk producing breed, light brown to dark chocolate body colour. Small white ears pointing forward, white strips on both sides of face. Bucks weigh ab0ut 70 kg and Does about 60 kg.

**5. Boer:** It is from Southern Africa and exported to many countries. Mean adult body weight is about 30 kg with birth weight of 4.0 kg and produces about 1.4 kg milk per day.

**6. Angora Goat :** Originated in Angora region in Asia Minor (Turkey). It is most important goat breed for fibre (Mohair or Pashmina) production. The fibre produced by these goats is called Mohair. Bucks weigh 60 kg and Does 40 kg. Average yield of mohair is 3 kg annually.

**7. Orenberg :** Originated from local goats of kaazakhstan and later on improved by selection for quality of pashmina. The adult body weight is about 40 kg for does and 70 kg bucks. They produce pashmina fibres of 16 microns diameter and 5.5 cm in length of about 300 gm per year.

## 2.9. CAMEL GENETIC RESOURCES

The north-western African countries have about 73% (14.6 million) of the total world camel population (19.2m). About 28% (5m) are present in Asia and rest 1.36% (0.225) population is in rest of the world. In India Rajasthan contributes about 70% of the country's camel population with more number of camels in 10 districts viz. Barmer, Churu, Bikaner, Hanumangarh, Jodhpur, Jaisalmer, Junjhunu, Nagaur, Sikar and Ganganagar. India stands third possessing 1.5 million camel after Somalia (6.2 m) and Sudan (2.9m). The camel is known as ship of desert capable of travelling long distances on sand carrying men and material. It provides energy to agricultural operations. It utilizes various adaptive mechanisms particularly the water retention and ability to thrive on water deprivation.

There are four well defined breeds of camel. These are Bikaneri, jaisalmeri, Mewari and Kuchchhi. The other breeds are the crosses of different breeds viz. Marwari, Mewati, Shekhawati and Sindhi are such breeds of camel.

1. **Bikaneri Breed:** This breed was evolved by selective crossbreeidng of different breeds like Sindhi, Baluchi, Afgan and Thari. Its home tract is Bikaner and adjoining districts. It is used for draught, meat, milk, hair, hides and dungs. The birth weight is 42 and 39 kg, gestation length 382 days, AFC 1885 days, adult body weight 650 -580 kg, milk yield in 300 days in 1650 kg with an average of 5.5 kg per day. Annual hair production 0.8 kg.
2. **Jaisalmeri camel:** Its home tract is Jaisalmer district. It is riding camel. It has been descended from Tharparkar camel of Sind regions. The birth weight is 37 and 34 kg and adult weight is 590-500 kg. Milk yield 2 to 4 kg per day. Annual hair production 0.758 kg.

3. **Mewari camel:** Originated from hill camel of Punjab. The hilly region of Udaipur is the home tract.
4. **Kuchhi camel:** The habitat is Kutch region of Gujarat. They are heavy, well built. The birth weight is 35 kg and 32 kg, adult body weight 630 and 500 kg. Females are good milkers producing 4-6 kg per day.

## 2.10. EQUINE GENETIC RESOURCES

The equine comprising horses, donkeys (ass) and their inter-species hybrids – the mules have made significant contribution to mankind. They are used for draught/ cart and riding animals. The riding horses were being used to carry the urgent messages before mechanized transport in old days. They had important role to win battles in the warfare. The ponies, donkeys and mules had significant contribution in agriculture as a means of transport, draught and pack purposes.

There has been a sharp decline in horse and donkeys population in India for the reasons of mechanization, small land holdings and abolition of Jagirdaris. The horse breeding in India remained in the hands of Rathore's of Marwar and Maharawals of Kathiawar whereas donkeys were kept by rural poor for their livelihood. There are six horse breeds of India. These are kathiawari, marwari, Spiti, Zanskari, Manipuri and Bhutia. Besides these, the FAO has also recognized 3 more breeds of horses viz. Chummarti, Deccani and Sikang.

### 2.10.1. Horse (Equus caballus ) breeds

| S.No. | Breeds | Origin and home tract | Utility |
|---|---|---|---|
| 1 | Marwari | It has Arab blood. Marwar and Mewar region of Rajasthan. | Riding, sports and safari |
| 2 | Kathiawari | Evolved from wild horses of Kathiawar and Arabian horses. Saurashtra Province of Gujrat (Rajkot, Junagarh, Bhavnagar, Surendranagar and Amreli) is the home tract | Riding, sports and safari |
| 3 | Spiti | Spiti ponies originated in Tibet and found in spiti division of lahaul, Kullu and Kinnaur district of HP | Riding and pack animal |
| 4 | Zanskari | Leh and Ladakh area of J & K. | Draught, Transport and riding |
| 5 | Manipuri | These ponies are found in Manipur and Assam. Originated from Asiatic wild horse and Arabian horses | Beauty, fastness and hardiness |
| 6 | Bhutia | Sikkim and Darjeeling. Resemble to Tibetian pony | Riding and pack animal |

There had been the dilution of horse breeds for indiscriminate breeding. The crossbreeding between Kathiawari and Marwari horses has considerably reduced the number of purebreds. There are only about 13% (3000) purebred Marwari horses out of total population of horses (23300) in its home tract. Likewsie, the purebred population of Kathiawari horses in its home tract (Gujarat) is about 56% (8000) of the total horse population of 12900.

## 2.10.2. Ass or donkeys (Equus asinus) breeds

The donkey is low input requirement animal and available everywhere. The modern domestic asses have mainly originated from Nubian race of Africa. Three distinct types of Indian asses are Indian donkeys, Indian wild asses and Kiang. The Indian wild asses are found in the Rann of Kutchh of Gujrat known as Kulau. The Kiang is found in Sikkim and Ladakh.

## 2.10.3. Mules

The mules are the species hybrid producing by crossing of horse mare (female) with Jack as a stallion (male ass). The mules are used as draught, pack and transport animals particularly in hills. Adult bodyweight of draught mules vary from 450 to 650 kg with 155 to 172 cm height. The size, speed, strength and sprit are of horse type whereas sure footedness, lack of excitability, endurance (patience) and ability to survive on poor feed came from ass side.

## 2.11. MITHUN

The Mithun or gayal (Bos or Bibos frontalis) is a bovine species and also called as 'Mountain cattle' or 'ceremonial ox' of north eastern hill region. Mithun originated in Himalayan region about 45oo years ago. It resembles domestic cattle in most of the physical, production and reproduction traits, but it has no hump, its dewlap is small, tail is short and horns are short stumpy. It has an oily sweat gland which acts as insect repellent. There are different views about its origin. These are that it is the domesticated gaur, or a hybrid of crossing of gaur bull and zebu cow, or descendent from of wild Indian bovine. The mithun resemble with gaur in appearance, colour, body features and some habits and produce fertile crossbred progeny when crossed with gaur whereas it differs from zebu cattle in hemoglobin, transferrin and blood group genotypes. It is thus considered more to have originated from the gaur. It has 58 (2n) chromosomes.

Mithun cows produced 1.4 to 3.5 kg milk per day with 4 to 5% fat, 3.5 to 4% protein, 4-5% lactose and 0.8% ash.

The birth weight of mithun varies from 20 to 30 kg, adult body weight from 450-500kg, body height 1.2 to 1.4 m. Sexual maturity attained at 2.5 to 3 years, G.P 272 days, S.P. 60-180 days, productive life 12 years and total life span is 20 years.

In India, there are two different types of mithun. These are known as Arunachalees and Nagamees

**Arunachalees :** They are found in Arunachal Pradesh. These are small in size than Nagamees. They have been developed for milk and meat.

**Nagamees :** They are found in Nagaland and Manipur. They are heavier in size and weight (400-500kg). They are good for beaf (meat) purpose having long and massive body.

## Hybrids

In order to increase the milk production, the mithun males have been mated with cows. The hybrids are given names according to the species involved and sex of ancestor. The $F_1$ males produced by crossing cows with mithun bull are called as **Jatsa** which are good for draught purpose while the $F_1$ female are called as **Jatsamin** which produce milk higher than mithun cows. The backcross is also made by crossing Jatsamin with mithun male and the two sexes are called as **Nupsa** (male progeny) and **Nupsamin** (female progeny).

Siri cows were crossed with mithun bulls in Bhutan. The male and female $F_1$ are called **Jechha** and **Jessam**.

A farm of mithun has been setup by Govt. of Arunachal Pradesh at Kambi in West Siang Distt. whereas the National Research Centre on Mithun of ICAR has been working in Phek distt. of Nagaland.

## 2.12. YAK

Yak (Bos grunniens) is locally known as **banchour** for wild and **chour-gau** for domestic variety. It was originated in China which still has 90% of the total world yak population of 14 million.

No breed of yak has been described so far. But Indian yaks have been described of four types' viz. **Ladakh yaks, Himachal yaks** of Spiti valley, **Arunachal yaks** of Twang and Dirang region, and **Sikkim yaks** which are of two types depending upon rearing community viz. Bho and Aho yaks.

The yaks interbred with bison, banteng, gayal, zebu and European cattle. The chromosome number of yak is 60 (2n).

## 2.13 PIG GENETIC RESOURCES

The age at fist conception in pigs is 300 days, gestation length of 112 days, farrowing interval 227 days, litter size at birth and weaning 6-8 and 4 to 6, average litter weight at birth and weaning 4.5 to 4.8 and 21 to 42 kg, the average birth weight is 0,52 kg and average weaning weight (8 weeks) ranged from 6 to 12 kg. No attempt has been made to catalogue the pigs breeds in India and hence there is no definite breed. However, the following types/breeds of domestic pigs are known

| S. No. | Breeds | Distribution | Adult body weight (kg) |
|---|---|---|---|
| 1 | Desi | UP, Bihar, MP, Punjab | 168 |
| 2 | Ghori | North eastern India Kerala, | |
| 3 | Ankamali | Karnataka, T.N., Maharashtra- | 40-70 |

## EXOTIC BREEDS OF PIGS

1. **Yorkshire:** originated in Yorkshire (England), developed from Leicester pigs by Robert Bakewell, migrated into USA in 1893, good bacon breed, white in colour with small ears tilting to the front, broad face.
2. **Berkshire:** Developed in Berkshire (England) by crossing of English hog with sows of Chinese and Siamese origin. Large and long body with arched narrow back, adult weight 500 kg, black coat with white feet.
3. **Duroc :** Originated in USA, developed by crossing pigs from Africa, Spain and Portugal. Light golden to dark red in colour, body medium length with tall legs, adult weight 450 kg, for boars and 350 kg for sows.
4. **Tamworth:** Developed in Ireland, colour varies from golden to dark red, large, long and tall breed known for lean meat.
5. **Landrace:** Developed in Denmark by crossing English pigs on native pigs, also having some Chinese pig inheritance, white in colour, long narrow body.
6. **Poland China:** Originated in USA, developed by crossing Berkshire, Hampshire, Tamworth and some inheritance of Russian pigs, large, long body with long legs, black colour with white extremities, prolific but poor mothering ability.

Some breeds of exotic pigs have been developed by crossbreeding. These are as under:

| | |
|---|---|
| Minnosota No. 1 | Tamworth x Landrace |
| Minnosota No. 2 | Poland China x Yorkshire |
| Beltsville No.1 | Poland x Landrace |
| Beltsville No.2 | Yorkshire x Duroc x Landrace x Hampshire |
| San Pierre | Berkshire x Chester white |
| Palouse | Landrace x Chester white |
| Maryland No. 1 | Berkshire x Landrace |

## 2.14 POULTRY GENETIC RESOURCES

The term poultry implies a wide variety of birds of many species viz. chickens, pigeons, guinea fowl, pea fowl, turkeys, ducks, geese, swans, pheasants, quail, ostriches, Emu and others. The alternate term to the poultry science is the *ormithology* which is the study of birds other than poultry. The distinguish feature of poultry is the presence of comb. Fowls have relatively high breathing and pulse rate as well as high body temperature (105°F to 109°F) than other domestic animals.

The fowl are classified into different types viz. egg type, meat type, dual purpose, game birds, ornamental and bantam (dwarf) on the basis of economic value and fancy purpose. The further grouping is into-

* **Classes** depending upon the region of their development viz. Asiatic, English, American, Polish, French, Mediterranean etc.
* **Breeds** within class having some common characters

**Classification of the class Aves**

| | |
|---|---|
| Phylum | Chordata |
| Sub phylum | Vertebra |
| Class | Aves (Feathered, warm blooded verteba with 4 chambered heart) |
| Sub class | Neornithes (without teath) |

| **Order** | **Galli form** | | | | | **Ansariform (Aquatic birds)** | | |
|---|---|---|---|---|---|---|---|---|
| Family | Meleagridiae | | | Phasianidae | | Antidae | | |
| Genus | Maleagris | Coturnix | Phasians | Gallus | Pavo | Aser | Cairina | Anas |
| Species | M. galloopavo | C. japonica | P. colchicus | G. domesticus | P. cristatus | A. anser | C. maschata | A. platyrhynchos |
| Common name | Turkey | Japanese quail | Pheasant | Fowl | Pea fowl | Gosse | Muscovy | Duck |
| 2n Chrom. | 80 | 78 | 82 | 78 | 80 | 80 | 80 | 80 |

* **Varieties** within breed which are different in colour pattern, comb type, feather pattern, shape etc.

* **Strains** within variety developed by a particular breeder.

The native birds (chickens) show great variability in their morphological traits viz. body weight (dwarf, normal and heavy weight), plumage pigmentation (blackish, brownish), flumage distribution (nacked neck, frizzle, crest, philopody), comb (single, rose, pea, and walnut), shank and skin (green and blue pigmentation) and melanin deposition in skin, meat, internal organs and bones in some birds like Khadakanath. The major morphological marker genes creating these variations increase the adaptability to tropical environment. Some of the examples of the effects of major genes are as under:

1. Frizzle gene (f) is incomplete dominant causes curling of feathers and reduced feathering with side effect of improving the convection ability.
2. Dwarf gene (dw) which is sex linked recessive reduces the body size by 10-30% and has its effect on metabolism (reduction), fitness (increase) and disease tolerance.
3. Slow feathering gene (k) is sex linked dominant causes delay of feathering with side effect on reduction in fat deposition and protein requirement, increases heat loss and delay the immune response mechanism.
4. Naked neck gene (Na) is incomplete dominant with direct effect on loss of neck feathers and secondary feathers and its side effect to increase convection ability and fitness but reducing the hatchability.
5. Pea comb gene (P) is dominant and causes the compact comb size with side effect to improve the convection ability.

In literature, 20 breeds of desi fowl (chickens) have been documented. These are as under:

| S.No. | Breed | Habitat | Important character |
|---|---|---|---|
| 1. | Faverolla | Kashmir | Feathered comb |
| 2. | Punjab Brown | Pb and Hariana | Meat type with brown plumage |
| 3. | Brown Desi | UP | Layer type single comb |
| 4. | Ankaleshwar | Gujarat | Single comb, hardy with poor production |
| 5. | Bursa | Gujrat and MS | No particular character |
| 6. | Frizzle fowl | Hot & humid costal region and N.E. region | Curved feather, better heat dissipation and adaptability in arid region |
| 7. | Naked neck | -do- | Neck naked which make them well adopted to high temperature due to heat dissipation |

| S.No. | Breed | Habitat | Important character |
|---|---|---|---|
| 8. | Kadaknath or kalamasi | MP | Black pigmentation on external and internal surface |
| 9. | Aseel | AP | Game bird with fighting quality and biggest in size among native breeds |
| 10. | Denki | AP | Males (cocks) good fighter with long neck and legs |
| 11. | Kalasthi | AP | Resemble to Denki but small in size |
| 12. | Ghagus | AP and Karnataka | Small size with small comb and wattles, thick neck and feathered shank |
| 13. | Tellichery | Kerala | Small bird with black skin |
| 14. | Haringhata black | W.B. | Good layer, small size black bird |
| 15. | Daothigir | Assam | Fairly heavy breed |
| 16. | Miri | Assam | Small size black bird |
| 17. | Chittong or Malay | N.E. Regions | Large heavy bird with fighting nature |
| 18. | Nicobari | Nicobar islands | Short legs, small size, good layer |
| 19. | Teni | All parts of country | Small all purpose bird, tolerates high temperature |
| 20. | Titri | | Small bird, yellow beak and neck, black and white feathers, poor layer |

A number of crossbred genotypes have been evolved at different centres by the ICAR institutes and SAU's. There are:

| Name | Breeds involved | | Purpose | Institute |
|---|---|---|---|---|
| | Male | Female | | |
| Vanraja | Cornish | Synthetic population | Dual | ICAR, Hyderabad |
| Grama priya | Synthetic | White leg horn | Dual | ICAR, Hyderabad |
| Cari gold | Selective breeding of RIR | | Egg | CARI, Izatnagar |

| Name | Breeds involved Male | Female | Purpose | Institute |
|---|---|---|---|---|
| Giriraj | | | Dual | UAS Bangalore |
| Krishna-J | Synthetic | | Egg | JNKVV, Jabalpur |
| Yamuna | Kadaknath | New Hampshire | - | |
| Kalinga Brown | Selective breeding of RIR | | Egg | CPBF, Bhubneswar |
| Gramalakshmi | Australorp | white leghorn | Dual | KAU, Kerala |
| Nandanam | RIR population - | | TNVASU, Chennai | |
| Cari-Nirblik | Assel cross | | 190 eggs | CARI |
| Cari-Shyam | Kadaknath cross | | 210 eggs | CARI |
| Upcari | Frizzle cross | | 220 eggs | CARI |
| Hitcari | Naked neck cross | | 220 eggs | CARI |

## Exotic breeds of poultry

There are 5 classes of poultry breeds based on their origin viz. Asiatic, American, English, Mediterranean and continental European. The important breeds are:

1. **Leg horn :** Mediterranean breed of number one egg producer, Developed in Spain, white in colour with yellow skin and single combed, heavy egg layers (250-300 eggs annually)
2. **Minorca :** Also called as Red Faced Black Spanish, largest and heaviest Mediterranean breed, produces large white eggs; long wattles and large white ear lobes with black beak, shanks and toes.
3. **Australorp :** Developed in Australia, single combed with black plumage and white skin, good egg producer
4. **Sussex:** Developed in England, single comb, white skin, good layers, small size bred.
5. **Orphington** : English breed, single comb, colours are black, white, blue or buff, moderate egg producers
6. **Cornish :** Developed in England, white in colour, heavy breed, excellent meat breed
7. **Phode Island Red :** Developed in Rhode Island (USA), heavy breed, single combed, dark red colour, good strains for both egg and broilers
8. **Plymouth rock :** American breed heavy breed with strains for both eggs and broilers, single combed with yellowish skin.

9. **New Hampshire:** American breed, chestnut red plumage, single comb, good producer of large brown shelled eggs.
10. **Brahaman** : Asiatic breed developed in India, pea comb, have three varieties viz., light, dark and buff.

## 2.15. OTHER POULTRY SPECIES

The other poultry species are Guinea fowl (Titri). Japanese quail (Bater), Ducks, Turkeys, Pigeons, Ostrich and Emu. They constitute only a small segment of the total poultry population. These species except pigeons were introduced in the country (India).

### 1. Guinea Fowl (Numeda meleagris galeata) : Titari or Tatiri

It is native of France. Its population rank third after chickens and ducks. It is known by different local names viz. **titri** in Northern plains, **chittra** in western parts and **chinha** (Cheena) **murgi** in south and eastern parts. They are raised in Punjab, UP, Bihar, Rajasthan, MP, Maharastra, Orissa, AP, TN and Karnataka.

The **breeds of guinea fowl** are based on the plunge colour variations. The main varieties recognized world over are: **Pearl, Lavender and White**

In India, Pearl guinea fowl are most common. They have dark-grey feathers with white spots having pearl like appearance. The lavender birds have light gray spotted feathers. The feathers of these two varieties are often used for ornamental purpose. The white variety has completely white plumge.

CARI Izatnagar (Bareilley) maintains all the 3 varieties while pearl is maintained at PAU Ludhiana. UAS Bangalore, Central Poultry Breeding Farm, Bhubneshwar and AVM hatcheries, Coimbatore.

A new variety of guinea fowl has been developed at CARI, Izatnagar and named as **Guncari**. It produces about 100-120 eggs per year from March to October and hence seasonal layer. The egg weight is about 40 gm and hatchability is about 70%, the body weight at 12 weeks is about 1.0 kg.

The CARI Izatnagar has also developed 3 crossbred genotypes for meat viz. **Swetambari, kadambari, Chitambari**

The Guinea fowl has a low input requirement with excellent foraging scavenging potentials. They have flocking instinct hence offer no management problems. They are raised for egg and meat.

### 2. Ducks (Anas platyrhynchos)

They are popular in Assam, W.B., Orissa, AP, TN, Kerala and Tripura. They are reared for egg and meat. There is Central Ducks Breeding Farm at Hessarghata (Banglore) and few farms of State Govts and SAU's. The ICAR has undertaken a scheme for comparing pure and crossbred duck's egg and meat. Ducks constitute about 9% of the total poultry populations. They are resistant to chicken diseases, exterminators of snails, harmful weeds and beetles. Asia is considered as a homeland of Mellard ducks but most of the modern breeds have been developed in Europe and America. The age at first egg is about 150 days.

The important Indian breeds are:

**Nageswari**, **Sythetemete** and **Indian Runner** which produce about 200, 80-120 and 80-150 eggs per annum, respectively.

## 3. Turkeys (Meleagris gallopavo)

The turkeys are raised almost exclusively for meat production. Turkey meat is low in fat with higher percentage of edible meat. The males weigh between 5-8 kg and females between 3-4 kg. The egg weight is about 60gm and lay about 30 eggs before going broody. It takes about 12-14 weeks to produce Turkey broilers.

The turkeys were first domesticated in West Central Mexico. The birds are flightless. The important breeds are:

- Bronze
- White Holland Bourbon Red
- Narragansett
- Beltsville Small white (BSW)
- Broad Breasted Large white (BBLW)
- Broad Breasted Bronze (BBB)

The breeds of turkey raised in India are:

- B.S.W. at CARI Izatnagar, HAU Hissar, College of Agriculture, Udaipur (Rajasthan)
- BBLW at College of Agriculture Udaipur (Rajasthan)
- BBB at UAS Bangalore, Central Poultry Breeding Farm, Hessarghata

The CARI has developed a new breed known as **CARI-Virat** which has white plumage and meat type.

## 4. Japanes Quail (Coturnix coturnix japonica) – Bater

The common wild quail (coturnix coturmix) distributed widely in Asia and Europe gave rise to the Japanese quail during 11th century from Japanese sub species of coturnix or may be introduced there from China or Korea. It is raised for both eggs and meat. It is a small bird with rapid growth and early maturity, has high rate of lay (more than 250 eggs annually) and require less feed and space. It has also short generation interval for which it is also used as laboratory animal.

In India, the quail is known as **'Bater'**. The Indian native quail (C.C. indica) has 3 sub species viz. **Rain quail**, **Grey quail** and **Button quail**. It has small size of 40 gm adult weight and is a wild avian species but C.C. japonica has been commercialized. The domestication of Bater could not be successful.

India imported the domesticated Japanese quail in 1974 from USA, Germany and Korea to Central Avian Research Institute, Izatnagar (UP) and at other centres also. The Japanese quail weigh between 100-300 gm depending upon the breed. The different lines maintained at CARI are Broiler quail, white breasted, white feathered, brown feathered and white shell egg line. The other centres which maintain quails are PAU, Ludhiana, Central Poultry Breeding Farm Chandigarh, CPBF

Bombay, Deptt. of Farms and Gardens Steel Plant Bokaro, B.C. K.V. Mohanpur (WB), UAS Bangalore, APAU, Hyderabad, AVM hatcheries Coimbatore etc.

Quails attain about 90% of their mature body weight by the market age of 6-7 weeks and starts laying at this age. Quails are maintained for one year only because the egg production, fertility and hatchability are reduced in second year. Quail eggs may be stored for nearly one month at 13°C with 70% RH. The quail meat is tender and tasty and each quail may yield 100-150 gm meat at market age of 5 weeks.

The CARI Izatnagar has evolved some crossbred genotypes of quail viz.

Meat Production – **Cari Sheweta, Cari Uttam, Cari Ujjawal**

Egg type – **Cari pearl**

## 5. Domestic Pigeons (Columba livia domestica):

It is the first bird tamed by man 45oo B.C. The pigeons are most commonly present at the places of worship and memorial estates. The domestic pigeons have been descended from wild rock pigeons (Columbia livia) of Asia and Europe. The pigeon rearing is for recreation, pleasure and meat production. The Mughal kings introduced the pigeon farming in Indian sub continent.

The pigeon breeds are of two types viz. flight and show purpose breeds, and meat breeds. The first category has the breeds as Kabli, Patiala, Lotan, Saharanpuri, Hyderabadi, Kherni, Nisvari, Aseel, Lakka, Girbaz, Zeera, Maina Jog, Chandan Chuha etc. The heavy weight or **meat breeds** are Naqab poosh, Gola, Umer, Lahores etc. The meat breeds are less active but good feeders, less prolific, quite in temperament.

The mature pigeons may weigh about 0.5 to 1.0 kg and some large breeds upto 1.4 kg. They are mainly reared for meat production by producing squabs (pigeon young before appearing feathers) that grow quicker having larger breasts. They start flying usually at 21-30 days of age. A pair of pigeons may raise 15 young ones per year. The body weight of male and female squals at 28-30 days is about 270 and 240 gm while that of adults at about 5 months of age is 320 and 290 gm. The sexual maturity is attained at about 6-7 months of age. They may bred round the year producing two eggs in a clutch and 8 clutches per year. They produce for about 4-5 years. The squab meat is delicate, tender, fine textured, attractive flavour and hence always fetches more prices but once the flying begins, the meat turned tough. Therefore, the squabs are harvested at 21-30 days of age.

## 6. The big birds – Ostrich and Emu

The ostrich (Struthio camelus) and the Emu (Dramaius novehollandiae) are the two species of birds of giant size. The ostrich is reared in the country for about 100 years but the Emu which is an Australian bird only about 15 years. However, the farming of these two species is now gaining global popularity. In India, recent attempts have been initiated at two places viz.

**Ostrich :** Maruti Ostrich Research & Training Farm, Bangalore

**Emu :** Kainaka Retite Farm, Gorantla, Guntur (AP)

Both these species can comfortably adapt to a varied climatic conditions between 5 to 56°C. But they can not be raised in confinement and prefer free ranging with short grasses and few shady trees.

The adult body weight of ostrich and Emu are about 11.5 kg and 55 kg with average height of 2.5 m and 1.6 m respectively. The egg weight is about 1.6 kg and 0.6 kg and the average number of eggs produced for breeding season is about 40-100 and 45-50 for two species of Ostrich and Emu. They live longer for about 70 years and 50-60 years, respectively. The age at sexual maturity is 2-3 years and 3-4 years for female and male Ostrich and the corresponding figures are 2-2.5 years and 3.0 years for Emu female and male. Both these species are farmed for feathers, nutritive lean meat, leather and oil.

## 2.16. RABBIT FARMING IN INDIA

The rabbits and hares are different from each other belonging to different genera of the family Leporidae of the order Legomorpha, super order Glires of the class Mammalia. The rabbits belong to the genus *Oryctologus* whereas hares belong to the genus *Lepus.* The rabbits belongs to the species *Cuniculus.* Thus the zoological name of rabbit is *Oryctologus cuniculus*. The rabbits are small running animals with relatively short ears and legs, giving birth to blind and naked young whereas the hares are larger hopping animals with longer ears and legs giving birth to open eyed furred young. The rabbit are mostly nocturnal, live in holes dugged by them but the hares do not burrow and hidden in vegetation.

The rabbits and rodents (rats, mice, squirrels and guinea pigs which belong to the order Rodentia of super order Glires) have the similar habit of passing food twice through G.I. tract. This double passage of the food is necessary for their life. This practice is known as *Coprography.*

The origin of all domestic rabbits is the European wild rabbit. The Europe (USSR, France, Italey, Spain) has about 85% rabbit population of the world followed by China. The rabbits are herbivovus, prolific and efficient convertor of fodder to food.

The rabbit farming in India is only in its infancy. The Kerala state had 77187 rabbits according to 1987 census whereas the numbers of Angora rabbits in H.P. during 1991-92 were 29982. The CSWRI supplied the breeding stock to different development agencies, universities and private entrepreneurs. The CSWRI regional station at Garsa (Kulu, HP) was the first in India to import meat type rabbits from U.K. (New Zealand White rabbit) and USSR (White Giant, Grey Giant and Soviet Chinchilla). There are about 30-36 rabbitries in Kulu Distt. (HP), with an average population of 150-200. About 500 farmers of HP, some from Punjab and UP are engaged in Angora wool production. The annual Angora wool production is about 15000 kg in HP.

The rabbit fur is not considered to be a true fur and fetches much lower price than those of mink and foxes. The rabbit fur is a byproduct from the animals reared mainly for meat production. However rabbit fur is very important. The rabbit fur skins constitute more than 50% of fur trade in international market. India imports about half a million rabbit fur skins annually from France and other countries to meet the demand of fur industry.

The males and female rabbits mature at about the same age of about 5 months whereas the breeding age in larger meat producing breeds is little delayed. The gestation period is about 31 days. The female rabbit does not have oestrus cycle and can stay in heat for several days. There is no regular period of heat and the ovulation occurs only after mating. The acceptance or refusal of service indicates whether she is in heat or not. A doe accept mating and ovulate when its vulva become red in colour and this happens in 90% cases. The ovulation, occurs 10-12 hours after mating, and induced by coitus stimuli. A doe can become pregnant after 7 days of kindling (giving birth of young rabbit i.e. the act of parturition). Average kindling per year is about 4 producing 25 kits per doe per year. Daily milk production is about 200 gms.

A young rabbit whose eyes are not yet opened is called **Kit** and below 20 weeks of age is called **Bunney**. The culled rabbit is called **Roaster** whereas a newly weaned rabbit is called **Weaner** and the rabbits grown for meat are called **Broiler**. The rabbit wool is called **Fur** and its skin as **Pelt**. The mature male and female are called **Buck** and **Doe**, respectively.

There are two types of rabbits viz. **Fur type** and **Meat type**. The fur type is the Angora breed which has 3 strains viz. German Angora (GA), Russian Angora (RA) and British Angora (BA). The German strain is best fur producer for yield, fineness etc. All these 3 strains were introduced at Garsa initially in 1980's and were crossed with German Angora. Half breeds and three breed crosses were maintained. The performance of various Angora breeds and their crosses at Garsa (H.P.) were as under.

| Characters | GA | RA | BA | GRA | GBA | GBR |
|---|---|---|---|---|---|---|
| Litter size at birth | 5.5 | 6.2 | 5.4 | 6.1 | 5.5 | 5.0 |
| Litter size at weaning | 4.8 | 5.8 | 5.2 | 5.6 | 4.0 | 4.4 |
| Litter weight at birth (kg) | 0.24 | 0.30 | 0.27 | 0.28 | 0.25 | 0.24 |
| Individual weight at weaning (kg) | 0.52 | 0.56 | 0.60 | 0.62 | 0.62 | 0.68 |
| Kit survival (%) | 87.5 | 94.2 | 95.0 | 92.5 | 71.2 | 87.1 |
| Annual wool yield (gm) | 612 | 307 | 378 | 436 | 392 | 426 |
| Staple length (cm) | 5.5 | 6.6 | 6.1 | 6.0 | 6.2 | 6.2 |
| Medullation (%) | 2.6 | 2.9 | 3.1 | 2.9 | 2.6 | 2.7 |
| Fibre diameter (m) | 12.6 | 12.7 | 13.2 | 12.7 | 12.6 | 12.7 |

The broiler rabbit breeds are as under:

| Breed | Fur colour | Origin | Mature weight (kg) | Av. Litter1 at (birth) | Av. Litter wieth t | | |
|---|---|---|---|---|---|---|---|
| | | | | | at weaning | Birth | Weaning |
| New Zealand White | White | UK | 3.0 | 7.5 | 6.2 | 0.32 | 0.65 |
| Gray Giant | Gray | Russia | 3.5 | 6.5 | 5.8 | 0.31 | 0.62 |
| White Giant | White | Russia | 4.0 | 7.1 | 6.5 | 0.31 | 0.63 |
| Soviet Chinchilla | Chinchilla | Russia | 3.5 | 6.6 | 6.0 | 0.30 | 0.68 |

These four strains of broiler rabbits were introduced in 1979 at Garsa (HP). A **black brown strain** was developed by crossing SC and GG. Another colour strain '**Duch**' was also developed.

## QUESTIONS

**2.1.** Explain genetically what do you mean of a breed with emphasis on why the individuals of a breed resemble closely in colour and markings but not in production traits. (*ARS 1976*)

**2.2.** Name home tract and one important characteristic of five important breeds of buffaloes. (*ARS 1978*)

**2.3.** What is a breed? When would you recognize a particular group of animals as a breed? Describe recently claimed breeds of sheep and cattle in India with particular reference to their place of origin, genetic architecture and production performance (*ARS 1981*)

**2.4.** What new categories (type) of animals and birds show economic promise for introduction to India? Describe the possible genetic resources of these species and consideration which must be made in their import. (*ARS 1984*)

**2.5.** (*a*) Describe the genetic resources of Indian dairy buffaloes. (*ARS 1984*)

(*b*) What is an animal breed? (*ARS 1992*)

(*c*) How do we differentiate breeds/types from each other? (*ARS 1993*)

**2.6.** (*a*) Briefly explain farm animal diversity in India.

(*b*) What kind of genetic information should be used?

(*c*) What is the basic theory behind genetic diversity?

(*d*) How are genetic distances interrupted?

(*e*) What are the practical considerations? (*ARS 2001*)

# 3

# CONSERVATION OF ANIMAL CENETIC RESOURCES (AnGR)

The technical aspects of conservation of animal breeds which are at the verge of extinction were considered jointly in 1980 by FAO and UNDP and laid down definite procedures after analysing the problems for establishing gene and data bank. The efforts in this direction in India were started with the establishment of National Bureau of Animal Genetic Resources Karnal in 1984 under the control of ICAR.

## 3.1. CONSERVATION VS PRESERVATION

The word conservation is closely related to the preservation. The preservation covers the continued maintenance of genetic variability. The preservation of a breed is required when it reaches an endangered level of population or near to extinct. The preservation and multiplication may also be required in case of individuals having unique traits or exceptional genetic merit.

The conservation includes the preservation along with upgradation (improvement) of the genetic potential and management of a breed for use in future. Thus the conservation covers both continued maintenance of genetic variability, improvement and sustainable utilization by exploiting the genetic variability. The conservation can also be defined as the management of the biosphere of human use for benefits in present time together with maintaining its potential to meet the future needs.

## 3.2. THREAT TO GENETIC DIVERSITY AND ITS REASONS

The different indigenous (Indian) breeds of different species of farm animals and poultry are essentially the result of evolutionary processes, they have adapted to harsh climatic conditions with low management inputs interms of feeds/fodder and health care, capable to convert low quality feeds and fodder more efficiently into animal products (milk, meat, eggs, wool etc.) and better adapted to withstand tropical diseases. They are integral part of agriculture. However, they are now getting diluted and facing degeneration. The **dilution of a breed** is in terms of purity of breed. There is a decline in the availability of pure bred animals conforming to the model attributes of the breed. Some of the breeds of farm animals of India are under constant risk of their extinction. The endangered breeds or the breeds which need attention for their conservation are as under:

| Species | Breeds at risk |
|---|---|
| Cattle | Red Sindhi, Sahiwal, Tharparkar, Vachur, Punganur, Mewati, Kankatha, Kharigarh, Bargur, Panwar, Siri, Krishna valley |
| Buffaloes | Nili-Ravi, Toda, Bhadawari |
| Sheep | Bhakarwal, Gurez, Karnah, Kashmir Valley, Poonchi, Munjal, Hissar dale, Muzaffarnagri, Malpura, Chokla, jaisalmeri, Magra, Lohi, Pugal, Nilgiri, Bonpola, Changthangi, |
| Goats | Beetal, Barbari, Jamnapari,Surti, Jhakrana, Chegu, Changthangi |
| Camel | Double humped, Jaisalmeri, Sindhi |
| Horse | Bhutia, Manipuri, Spiti, Zanskari |
| Poultry | All the breeds. |

The following reasons/facts can be assigned to affect the domestic animal diversity and the dilution and declining trend of population of the breeds.

## 1. Breeding systems and breed dilution

(i) **Upgrading:** There had been unrestricted interbreeding among different breeds particularly in rural areas. The native animals/breeds are crossed with superior (improver) breed for better economic returns. This has resulted into the mixture of various breeds. Bhadawari buffaloes have been upgraded with Murrah. The sheep breeds like Malpura and Chokla showed declining trend possibly because of introduction of Marwari inheritance through migratory flocks. There is also inter mixing of Jaisalmeri and Chokla sheep. The reason is that recommended breeding strategies are neither mandatory to follow nor these are backed by the support service.

(ii) **Crossbreeding:** The efforts have been made to improve the productivity of indigenous breeds of livestock and poultry by introducing exotic germplasm of superior genetic merit through crossbreeding the native breeds with exotic ones. The crossbreeding has been widely used as a major force for achieving rapid genetic change to increase animal productivity than selection within breed. The use of A.I. with frozen semen and ETT have further made easy and fast to introduce elite germplasm all over the globe. However, the crossbreeding has adverse effects viz. overall reduction of genetic variability in a species and also to put at risk to the low producing breeds. Thus crossbreeding has resulted the dilution of breed and declining the number of purebred animals. Thus there is threatening to the virtual replacement and elimination of many native breeds viz Sahiwal and Red Sindhi cattle, almost all native breeds of sheep of J & K and Beetal goats have been crossed with exotic breeds. This resulted these breeds to come under vulnerable/endangered category.

In view of the above, there had been absence of planned strategies for conservations of indigenous breeds.

**2. Geographical reorganization:** The breeding tracts and organized farms of some breeds of cattle (Sahiwal, Red Sindhi), Buffalo (Kundi, Nili-Ravi), Sheep and goats have gone to Pakistan

**3. Purpose based farming system (use of few breeds):** The different breeds of farm animals served different purposes of the owner viz. milk and draught in case of dairy animals; milk, meat, wool/fibre in case of sheep and goats; eggs and meat for poultry etc. Therefore, specific breeds are raised for specific purpose. The breeds that do not serve the purpose are neglected. They are either not kept or put in crossbreeding programme. The Nilgiri, a fine wool breed of sheep of T.N. is at risk because wool is not required in south India, also there is no market of wool whereas the mutton is in great demand in the area. Toda buffaloes of T.N. are getting endangered due to neglect. Some breeds like Vachur and Punganur cattle have lost for the reason that they did not get recognition at proper time.

**4. Economic viability:** The economically useful breed is automatically conserved. There are certain breeds which have lost their utility due to poor performance and declining economic returns to farmers. These are Mewati, Kankatha, Kherigarh, Bachur cattle.

**5. Modern Agricultural practices:** There has been change in agricultural productive system after 1970 viz. mechanization, growing of cash crops etc. The large scale of mechanization has reduced the requirement of draught power. These animals have lost their utility and became economically unviable because of their low milk production ability and intensification of mechanized agriculture.

The agricultural production system has been completely changed due to increase in human population pressure, high density and availability of low inputs. As a result more land has come under irrigation for crop production. Thus there has been reduction in land holding and the common grazing area. This has caused the reduction in herd size also. To keep a bull for breed improvement by small farmer with poor resources is not possible and hence he is forced to depend on the bull, available in or around the village, which may not be of the same breed or good genetic merit. This caused the genetic dilution and reduced performance of progeny.

The Muzaffarnagri sheep in UP and Munjal sheep in Punjab are decreasing in numbers due to non-availability of grazing area. The wasteland and grass land are being converted into irrigated cropping area. Likewise, mass degradation of forests has shown continuous decrease of Mithun population which is a browser of broad leaved trees/shrubs.

**6. Other factors:** Increase in livestock population is also causing deterioration due to inadequate inputs of feeding, healthcare etc.

Some sheep breeds like Changthangi, Tibetan and Bonpala are at risk due to smaller flocks scattered in large area of fragile ecology. The flood and avalanches (snow storms) have also caused endangerment of some breeds.

## 3.3. ENDANGERED LEVEL (RISK) OF A BREED

The number of breeding females of a breed is the main detrimental factor to decide the endanagered status. The estimates of minimum population size for different species to declare the endangered status have been given by different workers. However, it depends on species, local circumstances like breed management system, rate of crossbreeding, rate of decline and utility of breed. The mortality rate, growth rate, sexual maturity, fertility rate in different species are different and hence the endangered status differ for different species.

According to FAO, the survival risk of the breed should be studied when breed population size reaches 5000 breedable females and total population of 10,000.

The population size in thousands for consideration of endangered status of a breed under Indian conditions for different species have been suggested as under by NBAGR.

| Species/ Status | >10000 Normal (intermediate) | 5000-10000 Insecure | 1000-5000 Vulnerable | 100-1000 Endagered | <100 Critical (Rate) |
|---|---|---|---|---|---|
| Cattle | 25 | 15-20 | 5-15 | 2-5 | < 2 |
| Buffalo & goats | 30 | 20-30 | 10-20 | 5-10 | < 5 |
| Sheep | 50 | 30-50 | 15-30 | 8-18 | < 8 |
| Camels & Horses | 20 | 15-20 | 5-15 | 2-5 | < 2 |
| Pigs | 10 | 5-10 | 1-5 | 0.5-1.0 | < 0.5 |

## 3.4. OBJECTIVES (NEEDS) OF CONSERVATION

The native breeds need to be conserved to meet the following objectives

**1. Genetic insurance:** There is growing awareness to conserve the endangered breeds for future use. The native breeds have been developed over thousands of years, have better adaptability to harsh climate, diseases, heat tolerance and utilization of locally available poor quality roughages. They have unique genes or gene combinations which are associated with adaptability and producing capacity under adverse climate and inadequate feed resources. Thus loss of such breeds means the loss of DNA sequences responsible for specific adaptive traits which may be required to introduce in highly productive germplasm evolved through new techniques of biotechnology. It is not known that what might be needed in future. Thus as a genetic security the conservation of native breeds for their use in future is required.

**2. Scientific study:** The conservation of native breeds provides useful research material in genetics, biochemistry, physiology, morphology and anatomy. It is also useful to understand the process of evolution, domestication and the effects of natural and artificial selection etc.

**3. Economic potential in a particular environment:** The crossbred animals fail to exploit their genetic potential under Indian conditions of low input and harsh climate, are more susceptible to tropical diseases, and their production level goes down beyond $F_1$'s. Moreover to produce $F_1$s also requires the conservation of indigenous breeds for future use.

**4. Environmental considerations:** Every organism has its own role to play within an ecosystem and the loss of germplasm has adverse effect on the ecosystem which is hazardous to the existence of mankind. The domesticated breeds are integral part of our eco-system.

**5. Cultural and ethical requirements:** If a breed is not economical viable, it should be preserved for cultural and public interest of historical importance (monuments) since the animal genetic resources are the part of the natural heritage, culture and ecosystem. Moreover, to take care of the existence of all forms of life is required on ethical and moral grounds.

**6. Energy source:** India has a number of good draught breeds of cattle used to perform a number of agricultural operations before intensification of mechanized agriculture. However, the non-renewable source of energy may be exhausted sooner or later. In such situation, the animal draught power will be required and hence these breeds should not be allowed to extinct.

## Unique features in indigenous breeds

| **1. Cattle breeds** | **Unique features/traits** |
|---|---|
| Sahiwal, Red Sindhi Gir, Rathi | Milch type, heat and drought tolerant |
| Hariana, Ongole | Dual purpose, Milch type, heat and drought tolerant |
| Nagori | Excellent drought animal for hot climate |
| Vechur | Miniature cattle |
| Punganur | Dwarf cattle |
| Umblicherry | Excellent for wet ploughing |
| Siri | Dual purpose, high altitude breed |
| **2. Buffalo breeds** | |
| Bhadawari | High fat content (10-12%) |
| Jerangi | Small size (deer buffalo) |
| **3. Sheep breeds** | |
| Changthangi | Alpine sheep of high altitude for fine wool |
| Garole | High fecundity, survive under salincondition |
| Magra | Lustrous carpet wool |
| Marwari, Jaisalmeri, Deccani and Chokla | Hardy and capable of traveling long distances |
| Mecheri | High quality skin |
| Chokla, Patanwadi | Best carpet quality wool |

| | |
|---|---|
| Mandya | High quality and palatable meat |
| **4. Goat breeds** | |
| Barbari | Short oestrus cycle, high yielder |
| Jamnapari | High yielder |
| Black Bengal | High ovulation rate and kidding percent |
| Black Bengal, Surti | Tender low fat meat and delicate skin |
| Chegu, Chagthangi | Low fibre diameter (8-10 m), |
| Andman | High tolerance of salt and capable to survive on sea water. |
| **5. Poultry breeds**<br>Kadaknath, Tellicherry | Meat of medicinal value |
| Naked Neck | Ability for convection, improved adult fitness |
| Frizszle fowl | Ability for convection |

## 3.5. MANAGEMENT OF AnGR

The approach for managing effectively the AnGR over time to better understand, use, develop and maintain them in order to meet the challenge should include the following aspects:

(i) Identification, characterization, evaluation, documentation and conservation

(ii) Training of manpower for successful completion of the above activities

(iii) To develop breed improvement programmes on national level for proper management of AnGR (utilization)

The breed identification and characterization based on phenotypic characteristics was done in early thirties on the basis of limited and cursory observations. This resulted that many breeds having distinct attributes were not recognized. On the other hand, a number of varieties of a breed in different species have been reported over time e.g. Deccani, Patanwadi, and Nellore breeds of sheep. The varieties of Deccani are Lonad, Sangamneri, Solhapuri (Sangla), and Kolhapuri; of Patanwadi are the fine fleeced Patanwadi, Coarse fleeced (Kathiawadi) and meat type coarse fleeced (Charotari). Therefore, there is a need to identify, characterize, evaluate and document the AnGR for monitoring the status of breeds. To accomplish these tasks require the livestock survey.

**Livestock Survey:** The livestock census is conducted species wise in most of the countries including India. This does not serve the purpose of conservation of AnGR. The breed wise livestock census data is essentially required to know the population and production trends so as to enlist the endangered breeds. This requires a well planned survey of AnGR for their identification, characterization, evaluation, documentation and conservation. The survey programme helps to provide information on breed descriptors, the status of a breed required for its conservation and use by the planners, scientists and development agencies. It also helps to provide information on unique characteristics and to enlist the elite animals of a breed.

The survey of a breed should ensure the recording of the following information:

- Geographical distribution and native environment.
- Demographic information (age and sex wise)
- Qualitative and quantitative characteristics of morphological, productive and reproductive traits of the breed as a whole and of unique animals, elite producers.
- Collection of blood samples for genetic evaluation (characterization) from 50 unrelated animals of a breed.

**Breed Descriptors:** This means the information on habitat, physical and morphological characteristics, performance and genetic architecture of breed. The habitat of a breed should include the history of breed and geographical distribution (home tract), soil, topography, climate, feeds and fodder availability. These may be recorded from district headquarters of the breeding tract of the breed. The morphological and physical characteristics include the body size, the size and shape of different physical traits like horns, ears, tails, body colour etc. The data to be recorded on performance include the information on growth in terms of body weight at different ages, production (milk, fleece, eggs, meat etc.) and reproduction traits. These can be collected either from the farmers or by field recording. The genetic architecture of a breed may be known from blood groups, biochemical polymorphism and DNA markers. To develop breed descriptors of a breed requires the survey in the breeding tract. The purpose of descriptor is to facilitate valid comparison and classification of breeds within a species.

**Identification:** The term identification with respect to conservation of AnGR consists of:

- Country and source of data viz. published scientific papers, case studies, annual reports of different agencies involved in AnGR, thesis, store of unpublished data etc.
- Species, breed or population and location within country where breed is found.
- Animals of a breed with unique characteristics or unique genetic potential.
- Breeds and animals that may be at risk and declining in number.

**Characterization:** It is the description of a breed in terms of breed descriptors. This includes the distillation of all available knowledge (published and unpublished) which contributes to the reliable prediction of genetic performance in a defined environment.

**Evaluation:** It is contemporary comparison of performance records of two or more breeds under the same environment. Therefore, evaluation should provide characterization information for two or more breeds.

**Documentation:** It is simply the collection (to compare in detail) of existing data.

**Methodology of characterization:** Depending on the level of knowledge, the time and means available, the different methods of breed characterization can be used.

A net work project with NBAGR, Karnal, India as the nodal agency for genetic characterization and conservation of indigenous breeds of livestock and poultry came into operation in later half of VIII five years plan. This project aimed to develop breed descriptors, to characterize the breeds for phenotypic traits (qualitative and quantitative) and molecular genetic characterization, and finally to conserve the germplasm of elite/unique animals and birds. The technical programme for survey and characterization of AnGR under Network Project is as under:

To conduct survey in 3 districts by one supervisor and 4 enumerators in each district to determine the demographical and geographical distributions of breeds and to record information on morphological and physical characteristics, performance and utility traits together with feeding and management practices for animals of different age groups viz. 1-3 months, 3-12 months, yearlings, milking and dry animals, and the breeding males.

Three different levels of description varying from general to the specific can be used. These are as given below:

**Macro:** Phenotypic characterization, conservation

**Meta:** Phenotypic characterization

**Micro:** Phenotypic and genetic characterization

The details are as under

(i) **Macro level:** This consists of on-farm surveys based on stratified sampling procedure to collect information about herds and animals. The basic information are collected about the location, village identification of the herd and the animal details like type or breed, sex, age and some simple measurements (body height etc.). The information may also be collected by direct questioning the farmer about the farming system and herd production

(ii) **Meta level:** It is based on a monitoring of on-farm husbandry practices. This is an individual recording system for performance of identified animals so as to allow comparing breeds with respect to the mean and the phenotypic variance of performance traits. To accomplish the task, a stratified random sampling procedure is most appropriate for sampling of farms and animals within the farm. The number of farms and individuals within farm to be sampled (selected) depends on the variability among farms, among animals within farm and the breeding structure within farm particularly the number of sires used per year. The number of farms should not be less than 40 and that too using two or more sires whereas the number of animals per breed should not be below 400. The information should be recorded on the sampled animals on all the performance traits viz. physical traits (linear measurements, body score), performance traits (milk yield, fleece yield, body weight, fertility, viability), health records (abortion, blood and faecal sample, tick infestation), and environmental conditions like location, climate, feed resources (feed type and availability), management (shelter/housing, watering frequency, herding practices), herd structure (animal movement), breeding structure (number of males and females, castration, use of A.I. and age distribution of animals).

(iii) **Micro level:** It is complementary to macro and meta studies for comparing and testing animal populations. The micro level is based on selected methods that can be used to gain knowledge of the genome of individual animals within a population. It is considered a detailed study measuring the performance of animals of selected population under controlled and standardized conditions for a precise phenotypic and genetic evaluation of a population. The sampling should follow a stratified random sampling procedure assuring as broad a genetic sample from as many different farms as possible and not more than one sire per farm. A total of 200 breedable females and 10 males per breed are required for estimating breed differences whereas for estimating genetic parameters require at least 20 sires each mated to 20 dams. However these numbers can be built up over time.

## 3.6. ANIMAL DATA BANK

The data base or data bank is collection of data on any aspect of life in well organized, meaningful and easily accessible way. A database file is for storage and maintaining the records.

The data bank for animal genetic resources has a key role to play in listing and describing the breeds, in documenting the erosion of these resources and in highlighting the breeds that are likely to disappear in near future unless specific action is taken.

The first data bank was initiated by European Association of Animal production (EAAP) in 1980's organizing the survey of EAAP member countries and established a data bank at the Institute of AB&G in Hannover, Germany to store information on European breeds. The EAAP also tried later on in 1990 to recover data from non – EAAP countries but could not success due to poor response. In 1991 the FAO was assigned the work to establish a data bank in Rome to cover all the non-European countries and that EAAP in Hannover would keep data bank solely on Europe. The data bank in Rome is called the **FAO Global Data Bank** for domestic livestock. The types of information stored in data bank are as under:-

**General information:** Species, geographical location of breed, local name, synonyms and international name of the breed after Mason (1988), name of organization provided the information.

**Origin and development of breed:** Origin of breed, wild or primitive, population size, risk status, use of A.I. and storage of semen.

**Breed description:** Coat colour, horn description, hair or wool type, adult weight and size, genetic characters (marker genes, ch. aberrations)

**Use and qualities of breed:** Main use, special quality like disease resistance, adaptability to harsh climate

**Management condition:** Type of management, housing period, feeding.

**Performance trait information:** Various types

**Additional information:** Estimates of genetic distance to other breeds, analysis of genetic material of the breed, conservation programme in operation for the breed

The sources of information for data bank are the Dictionary of Mason (1988), scientific literature, and FAO/UNDP Global Breed Survey.

The Global Data Bank first dealt with only seven species viz., cattle, buffalo, sheep, goat, pig, horses, and ass. The documentation on camel and poultry breeds started later on.

The FAO Global Data Bank had 2047 entries of which 86 (5%) are wild or feral, 502(25%) are descended as a variety, sub variety or strain of a breed., and 164 (8%) are found in more than one country. Out of 2047, there are 564 cattle, 68 buffaloes, 600 sheep, 259 goat, 245 pigs, 247 horses and 64 asses.

The FAO had developed **Domestic Animal Diversity Information System** (DAD-IS) for management of animal genetic resources. It is a multi language, multi faceted, computerized information and communication system. This provides support for teaching, research, formulating policies, early warning for conservation of DAD. It now contains information on about 5300 breeds of 35 species of domestic animals of 180 countries. It is used to monitor breeds, their population and status, contains performance and production attributes of breeds.

## 3.7. PRINCIPLES OF CONSERVATION

The conservation of AnGR should be based on the following basic principles

1. **Population size:** The stock should be maintained with optimum population size above the level of risk.
2. **Characteristics of the stock:** The stock for preservation/conservation should be of the following types
   - pure form
   - Having special traits
   - Select diverse stock
3. **Environmental conditions:**
   - Maintain and conserve the locally adapted breeds and that too in the same location.
   - Maintain live animals providing the similar feeding, management and environmental conditions under which they had been traditionally kept
4. **Breeding methods:** The genetic merit and diversity should be maintained using appropriate breeding programme.

## 3.8. METHODS OF CONSERVATION OF AnGR

The conservation of AnGR can be done *in situ* as well as *ex situ,* for which two methods of conservation are called as the *in situ* conservation and *ex situ* conservation.

### *1. In situ* conservation

This involves the maintenance of live population of animals in their adaptive environment (original and natural conditions) and animal population continues to evolve and be developed for more sustainable use. There are two aspects of *in situ* conservation viz., active and passive. The active *in situ* conservation is equivalent to breed development through animal breeding programme whereas the passive *in situ* conservation is the maintenance of live animal populations within their environments for the breeds which are at risk of loss.

This method is best for conserving a breed. The sufficient genetic variability in the breed population can be maintained if the sample size is fairly large. The proper breeding plan for genetic improvement can effectively work to make the breed economically viable. Moreover, the breed can gradually adapt to the changing environment over time. However, the limiting factor for its implementation is the high cost involved in maintaining large herds/flocks.

The *in situ* conservation can be done in a better and scientific way at the organized farms under the control of Govt. to ensure purity of breed. This method is also feasible in field conditions i.e. in herds maintained by farmers and NGO like BAIF, AFPRO, Goshalas. The conservation can be done in field conditions by forming breed societies.

**Institutional herds:** Some important indigenous breeds are kept by ICAR institutes, SAU's animal breeding farms, central and state Govt. livestock farms. However, the population size is too small for improvement through selection. The conservation of breeds on organized farms together with improvement in their productivity can be done by the followings:

- Effective population size
- MOET
- Nuclear herd both ONBS and CNBS
- Improving the management and environment

The organized farms have small number of breedable populations. It is, therefore, very important to know the minimum population size of a breed for *in situ* conservation so as to avoid the risk of inbreeding and genetic drift which are increased with the decrease in population size. The organized farms having a nucleus herd of 100 breedable females' atleast can run the selective breeding programme for improvement and *in situ* conservation.

The details of MOET, ONBS etc. have been given elsewhere in this book (Chapter 16)

**Farmers herds:** The individual farmer maintains small herds/flocks. Therefore, they can not keep the male germplasm of good quality. This forces them to mate their females with the unselected bulls of low genetic merit available in and around the village. This result in production of non-descript population. Secondly, no data recording system is followed in farmer's herds/flocks. These problems of maintaining the purebred population of indigenous breeds and data recording can be solved;

- by forming **breed societies** for development, improvement and conservation of indigenous livestock breeds. The breed society may be constituted having the Distt. Collector, Deputy Director AH/Distt. Livestock Officer/VAS, Block Pramukh/ Pradhan, Farmers, Animal Breeders etc.

- by covering the area of breed under **Herd Registration Scheme** for data recording and
- by giving **incentives to the farmers** in different ways viz. an amount for keeping purebred animal, provision of semen and A.I. facilities and support price of products from purebreds etc.

  The following strategies to increase fodder resources may be helpful for *in situ* conservation of indigenous breeds:

- To maintain the common grassland and other feed/fodder resources for grazing of animals.
- To reduce the grazing pressure on depleted vegetation and feeding resources by improving migrating grazing system during lean period (summer) in a way to move the animals to the forests, riverside wasteland and harvested agricultural fields and return to native place in rainy season.
- Re-seeding of wastelands/grasslands and controlled grazing
- Controlled grazing in forests because livestock and grassland ecology are complimentary to each other for the overall maintenance of sustainable ecological balance.
- Planting the high yielding species of plants which provide optimal lopping in common grasslands and pastures, so as the livestock can be supplemented with tree lopping when grazing resources are depleted in lean period. This is known as silvipasture and multi tier vegetation.

Besides above strategies to increase the fodder resources, the following programmes will be helpful for *in situ* conservation:

- Improving economic efficiency of indigenous breeds through use of superior germplasm by selective breeding, better health coverage and providing balanced ration
- To create public awareness about the local breeds for their suitability and special attributes under nature conditions.

## 2. *Ex situ* conservation

The *in situ* conservation may not be feasible for the breeds which are economically not viable and hence they may be lost due to economic pressure. The *ex situ* conservation can be done to handle this situation. The *ex situ* conservation can be in *in vivo* and *in vitro.*

### *In vivo* method

It is *ex situ* conservation of live animals in small numbers at a place away from the main breeding tract of the breed viz. organized herd of research station, central/ state government animal farms, bull mother farms, zoo and breeding park. This type of conservation has the limitation in terms of population size to avoid the adverse effect of inbreeding. It is not possible to keep the large herds/flocks of breeds which are economically not viable. Inbreeding in small population is unavoidable and hence the genetic defects appear. Therefore, the breeding population should be maintained in such a manner that the inbreeding is minimum and the performance of the population showed improvement over the years so as the breed becomes self sustaining. The effective population size can be maintained on organized farms or with farmers in the native breeding tract or under livestock breed safari/parks on the pattern of wild life.

The live animal reservoir/breed safari/park may help to preserve the natural habitat keeping all species of plants, animals and other organisms. It will be a good system to conserve the precious germplasm of breeds of domestic animals as a self-sustaining unit. This may also attract the tourist industry as in developed countries. These may serve as the amusement parks if managed properly keeping diverse population of distinct breeds and may thus provide opportunity for urban people to know about the animals.

## *In vitro* method

It is the storage of living cells for long period of time. It is done by (i) deep freezing of sperms (semen) and oocytes, (ii) deep freezing of embryos, and (iii) storage of DNA. The *in vitro* conservation has the following basic objectives

- Regeneration of endangered breed
- New breed development
- Supporting the *in vivo* populations
- Research for determining the effect of single major gene
- DNA studies and genome mapping

(i) **Cryopreservation of sperms and oocytes:** The semen (sperms) of all the species is suitable for deep freezing. The technique of freezing, storing and thawing of semen is simple and a routine one. Likewise, the cryogenic storage of oocytes as a portion of ovaries from slaughtered animals can be done for most of the species of farm animals, except cattle. The conservation of haploid genome as semen, but not the oocytes, has great limitation of the requirement, for IVF of the animals of opposite sex or both types of cells (sperms and oocytes) of the same breed.

(ii) **Cryopreservation of embryos:** It has been found successful with varying degree in case of cows, buffaloes, sheep, goats and horses. The embryo being a diploid zygote contains all the genetic information and hence it is an excellent tool of conservation. But it is relatively expensive to obtain embryos. Secondly, the cryo preservation techniques need further refinement for economical use. It requires 8 to 12 embryos to be frozen to get one live animal. This can be used for conservation of atleast endangered breeds. About 300 frozen embryos are required for conservation of a breed assuming the pregnancy rate of 40% and survival rate of 50%.

(iii) **Storage of DNA:** The genetic material can be preserved as the cryogenic storage of NDA. This method avoids the spreading of disease during its transportation. The storage of uncatalogued DNA is already possible but the genome maps of different species are not yet available for want of which, the storage of DNA could not become the normal method of preservation.

## Recent/New approaches

**Embryonic stem cells:** These are obtained from culture of inner cell mass of a young blastocyst. These are known as totipotent (undifferentiated) cells which are cultured *in vitro* for a very long period. These cells can be multiplied indefinitely and can be obtained relatively easily from cultured young embryos or cultured cells (primordial germ cells) and are routinely kept frozen before use. The cells have potential to develop into several embryos i.e. the single fertilized zygote gives rise to many embryos capable to frozen for a very long time.

**Somatic cells cloning:** The live animal can be produced from stored somatic cells. The cloning produces series of exact replica/copy of the concerned animals from which the somatic cells have been used. Two techniques (Roslin and Honolulu) which are in use at present enucleate the egg cell to eliminate majority of the genetic information. The Honolulu method is quicker than Roslin as well as it does not require the *in vitro* culture of donor cells. In Roslin technique, the donor cell is forced to remain in dormant cell stage and cultured *in vitro* to produce multiple copies of same nucleus. The enucleated recipient cells and the nucleated donor cell are fused by electric pulse to develop an embryo. The survived embryo is incubated in sheep's oviduct and finally placed in the uterus of surrogate mother ewe. In Honolulu method, the unfertilized mouse egg cells are used as the recipient of donor nucleus. The egg cell, after acceptance in new nucleus, is grown in a chemical culture. The developing embryo is transplanted in surrogate mother.

## 3.9. UTILIZATION OF INDIGENOUS AnGR: See section 17.1.

## 3.10. STRATEGIES FOR CONSERVATION

The conservation of livestock genetic resources in the country should have the broad based objectives with following lines of action:

### *1. National survey programme*

- To determine the demographical and geographical distribution of breeds in their home tracts
- To characterize the different breeds of livestock species with respect to their morphological, productive and reproductive characteristics, management practices
- To identify superior germplasm and rare variants within the specific breed.
- A national data bank should be established to keep complete information on all AnGR of the country
- To identify the breeds/types which are declining and heading toward endangerment or extinction
- Planning improvement and conservation programme

### *2. In situ* conservation programme

- Herd registration programme should be started for all the breeds with active participation of the farmers for which they need incentive and technical support

- Farmers will not come forward to conserve such breeds which are not economical to them. Such breeds should be kept at Govt. farms
- The breed societies should be formulated. The breed societies and voluntary agencies should be given financial and scientific support by the Central and State Govts. for conservation of native breeds.
- The capacity of Govt. animal farms should be increased with all types of infrastructural facilities to keep the indigenous breeds of livestock for their *in situ* conservation
- Different breeds should be adopted by different organization viz. Central and State Govts Farms, SAU's, ICAR institutes, A.H. Deptt. etc. located in home tract of the breed. They should be responsible for the characterization and further improvement and conservation of the breed. One farm for each breed in the breeding tract should be established.
- Inter-institutional associated herd programme should be developed for genetic evaluation and conservation.
- Goshalas having purebred animals should be supported by providing semen from bull mother station free of cost.
- The crossbreeding should be restricted to non-descript population and low productive animals of the breed.

### 3. *Ex situ* conservation programme

- India has good infrastructure for semen collection, storage and deep freezing. Wherever such facilities are available, it should be made mandatory for them to keep reserve the semen doses in addition to their requirement. The semen and embryo banks should be established.
- Training programmes should be organized.

## 3.11. AGENCIES FOR IMPROVEMENT AND CONSERVATION PROGRAMMES

There are a number of departments, institutions and agencies involved in different aspects of AnGR improvement programmes like research, education/training/manpower development, animal health services, counseling and guidance to farmers etc. These are as under:

1. **Department of A.H. and Dairying, Govt. of India.**
2. **I.C.A.R.**
3. **SAU's and Veterinary colleges**
4. **State Animal Husbandry Department**
5. **Non-Govt. Organizations (NGO) which are mainly on dairy animals**

(i) **Gaushalas:** There are about 1000 gausalas engaged in cattle development in India. Some are as under :

- Shree Gaushala Trust, Bhiwani (Haryana) maintains about 1000 crossbred animals of Jersey and Friesian crosses.
- Shree Gaushala Society, Panipat (Haryana) maintains over 200 cattle of HF, Jersey, Hariana and Sahiwal
- Amritsar Pinjrapol Gaushala maintains a large herd of Sahiwal breed (600 animals)
- Kasturbagram Krishi Gaushala, MP has about 150 purebred Gir cattle.
- Lok Bharti Gaushala, Gujarat has Gir and its crosses with HF and Jersey
- Gorakshan Pinjarapol Sanstha, Ahmednagar (MS) maintain Gir and its crosses of HF and Jersey
- Bombay Pinjarapol has about 1300 purebred Gir cattle.
- Sabarmati Ashram Gaushala, Gujarat, produces bulls and supply the liquid and frozen semen as well as provide training in A.I.
- Nasik Panchvati Pinjarapol has also the facilities of A.I. work.
- Bombay Gow Rakshak Mandli has devoted to research and development of dairy cattle

(ii) **Dairy cooperatives:** The cooperative has played significant role in dairy development programmes by providing to their members the inputs viz., A.I. and Veterinary aids etc. The cooperative sector in the year 1987 had 8 bull mother farms and 11 frozen semen bull stations. Village cooperatives have the involvement of lay inseminators

(iii) **Voluntary organizations:** These are as under:-

- Bhartiya Agro-Industries Foundation (BAIF), Urlikanchan (MS) is involved in crossbreeding of cattle in rural areas under the sponsorship of State Govt., Sugar Cooperatives, Milk Unions, industries and other funding agencies. It has covered about 8000 villages through 400 cattle breeding centres of 6 states in the country. The BAIF has the infrastructural facilities of Bull Mother Farm, Frozen Semen Lab, Research Lab, Demonstration Farms and Training Institute.
- Action for Food Production (AF PRO), Aligarh (UP) is involved in development of good breed of draught animal with improved milk production. It has its crossbreeding work at farm and in the nearby villages.
- Raymond's Embryo Research Centre (MP) is involved in MOET technology
- Janaki Devi Bajaj Trust, Maharastra, has also started cattle crossbreeding work in tribal belts of Pune district.

(iv) **Private companies:** These are the commercial breeding companies and the produce processing companies which are dealing with poultry, sheep and goat keeping.

**6. Other Departments**

- National Dairy Development Board – Operation Flood

- Department of Biotechnology – involved in genetic Engineering, Veterinary diagnostics, E.T.T. etc.
- Department of Environment

## QUESTIONS

**3.1.** What are the needs of germplasm conservation? Discuss the various methods of conservation, their feasibility and importance to Indian breeds ? (*ARS 1993*)

***Or***

(*a*) Differentiate between conservation and preservation

(*b*) What are the needs of germ plasm conservation?

(*c*) Discuss in brief the various methods of conservation, their feasibility to Indian breeds of livestock. (*ARS 1996*)

**3.2.** (*a*) What is meant by conservation?

(*b*) Enlist objectives of conservation

(*c*) Discuss on methods of conservation

(*d*) What are the steps involved in wild life conservation?

(*e*) Briefly mention practical utility of conservation in farm animals including poultry. (*ARS 2001*)

**3.3.** (*a*) Discuss on reasons of threatening to genetic diversity

(*b*) Enlist the agencies involved for conservation programme

(*c*) What are the levels or risk of an animal breed?

(*d*) What do you mean by management of AnGR?

**3.4.** Write short notes on

(*a*) Animal Data Bank

(*b*) Methodology of breed characterization

(*c*) Principles of conservation

(*d*) Utilization of indigenous AnGR

(*e*) Strategies for conservation

(*f*) FAO Global Data Bank

(*g*) Domestic Animal Diversity Information System

***

# 4

# LIVESTOCK CONTRIBUTION

The livestock and poultry have important position in economic development and prosperity of a country like India being primarily an agricultural country. India lives in villages and the main occupation is agriculture which mainly depends on livestock. Crop cultivation and animal husbandry are dependent on each other and traditionally practiced in rural areas of India. This integrated farming system of mixed crop animal farming is sustainable and efficient. The sustainable means the successful management of resources to meet the requirement without adverse effect on the environment and resources.

M.L. Darling said "Without cattle, fields remain unploughed, store and bins stand empty, and food and drink lose half their savour for in a vegetarian country what can be worse than to have no milk and ghee".

## 4.1. LIVESTOCK CONTRIBUTION

The contribution of livestock to the rural economy is enormous and can not be fully realized by counting only the income from sale of milk, meat, hides etc. The contribution in the form of draught power and manure etc. needs to be accounted besides the value related to social and cultural aspects. A brief account of livestock and poultry importance and contribution is given here.

### 4.1.1 Livestock in agriculture

The livestock particularly the cattle and buffaloes have important contribution in different agricultural operations, to maintain soil fertility and to provide cash for purchase of various inputs used in crop production.

**(i) Agricultural operation:** Livestock is basic to all operations related to agriculture like ploughing, sowing of seeds, irrigation, threshing, cane crushing, transportation of fodder and all kinds of agricultural produce from filed to home and then to market. They provide motive/tractive power to the agriculture

**(ii) Maintenance of soil fertility:** The manure is the sole source to maintain soil fertility. All classes of livestock and poultry produce organic manure in the form of faeces (dung) and urine. The animal bones are used to manufacture the bone meal.

The dung is a complete manure having all the major elements required by crop plants. The cost of dung as manure was estimated Rs. 2156 crores in 1990-91. About 50% of the total dung produced is used as farm yard manure and rest as fuel.

**(iii) Help in purchase of inputs (Income from livestock products):** The sale of various livestock products like milk and milk products, meat, egg and wool is a good source of income for livestock owner. The cash received is used for purchase of various inputs like quality seeds, fertilizers, pesticides and agricultural implements etc.

## 4.1.2. Livestock products

The various products produced by different classes of animals are the sources of human diet, clothing and raw material for a number of industries

**(i) Source of food-milk, meat and eggs:** In ancient days before domestication man used to hunt and eat animals. Even today, the animals provide essential foods of animal origin like milk from cattle, buffalo and goat and meat from pig (pork), sheep and goat (mutton, chevon) and poultry, and eggs from poultry. The milk and eggs are the main source of animal protein in human diet today. The milk production data of different species, per capita availability and milk utilization pattern over the periods is as under:

**TABLE 4.1: MILK PRODUCTION (MILLION TONES) IN INDIA.**

| Species/year | 1951 | 1961 | 1972 | 1982 | 1990 | 1995 |
|---|---|---|---|---|---|---|
| Cow | 7.75 | 8.75 | 7.5 | 14.0 | 24.0 | 29.8 (52.5%) |
| Buffalo | 9.25 | 11.0 | 14.75 | 20.75 | 29.0 | 34.8 (45.0%) |
| Goat etc. | 0.4 | 0.65 | 0.75 | 1.05 | 1.9 | 1.7 (2.5%) |
| Total | 17.40 | 20.40 | 23.00 | 35.8 | 54.9 | 66.3 |

About 90% of the milk is produced in rural sector and rest 2% in urban areas. There are about 70 million milk producers in rural areas. In 1995, there were 57 million milch cows and 39 million milch buffaloes out of which 31 and 25 millions were in milk, respectively. About one-third of the total milk produced is retained by producers for home consumption and two-third is sold.

The per capita availability of milk has increased from 132 gm/day in 1950-51 to 195 gm/day in 1994-95.

**TABLE 4.2: THE MILK UTILIZATION PATTERN (%) OVER THE YEARS**

| Product/years | 1951 | 1961 | 1989-90 | 1990 | Value in 1995 (Rs. crores) |
|---|---|---|---|---|---|
| Liquid milk | 39.3 | 45.1 | 46.0 | 45.7 | 36364 |
| Ghee | 39.3 | 31.8 | 28.0 | 27.5 | 9060 |
| Curd | 8.8 | 8.1 | 7.0 | 6.9 | 6863 |

| Makhan/Butter | 6.0 | 6.4 | 6.5 | 6.5 | 3000 |
|---|---|---|---|---|---|
| Khoa | 4.0 | 4.7 | 5.5 | 6.5 | 4500 |
| Milk Powder | | | 3.8 | 3.7 | 1338 |
| Cheese/Paneer | | | 2.0 | 1.9 | 1050 |
| Others | | | 1.2 | 1.3 | 1016 |
| **Total** | | | | | **80781** |

**Meat Production:** Presently, India produces about 4.5 million tones of meat which is about 27% of 221 MT (million tones) produced in the world. The meat production by different species is as under:

**TABLE 4.3: MEAT PRODUCTION**

| **Species** | **Meat Production (MT)** | **Av. carcass weight (kg)** | **Slaughter percent** |
|---|---|---|---|
| Cattle | 1.30 | 103.0 | 6.5 |
| Buffalo | 1.20 | 138.0 | 11.05 |
| Sheep | 0.17 | 12.0 | 31.78 |
| Goat | 0.47 | 10.0 | 39.83 |
| Pig | 0.41 | 35.0 | 97.08 |
| Poultry | 0.44 | - | - |

In India about 30% of sheep and 40% of goats are slaughtered every year

The distribution of 221 million tones of meat produced in the world is

| | |
|---|---|
| Beef and buffalo meat | 64.0 mt, |
| Sheep and goat | 13.0 mt, |
| Pigs | 92.6 mt, |
| Poultry | 51.5 mt. |

**(ii) Source of wool** : There were 50.79 million sheep in India during 1992 to produce wool which is used to manufacture of woolen cloths to protect the human from cold. The wool production statistics in India in 1995 was as under:

| **Traits/ Zones** | **North Westerns** | **North Temperatre** | **Southern Peninsular** | **Eastern** | **Total (India)** |
|---|---|---|---|---|---|
| Sheep Population (million) | 21.45 (42.2%) | 3.63 (7.2%) | 20.86 (41.1%) | 4.85 (9.5%) | 50.79 |
| Greasy wool Proudction (m kg) | 29.82 (65.4%) | 4.79 (10.5%) | 9.12 (20.2%) | 1.87 (4.1%) | 45.6 |
| Per sheep wool Production (kg) | 1.39 | 1.32 | 0.44 | 0.39 | 0.9 (world av 2.4 kg) |

Sheep population in India is 4.5% of world sheep population but the wool production is only 1.4%. However, in India the wool production has increased from 27.0 million kg in 951 to 45.6 million kg in 1995. About 30 metric tones of Pashmina is produced

**(iii) Source of bones, hides and skin:** Large quantities of animal by products like bones, hides and blood are produced. These are important from industry and business point of view. About 30 million pieces of skins weighing 45.5 x 1000 tonnes are reported to be available from sheep costing about Rs. 375 crores whereas, the skin of goat amounted to 101 million kg.

**(iv) Source of fuel and gobar gas :** The livestock are indirect source of fuel. The dung from cattle and buffalo is used as fuel in place of coal and wood to cook food etc. The gobar gas plant is run using gobar (fresh dung) and is used to cook food, to enlighten bulbs and to run chaff cutter etc.

**(v) Source of livestock feed:** The slaughter house by products and carcass wastes are being processed for manufacturing of meat meal, blood meal, bone meal, feather meal for farm animals and poultry. Poultry droppings, cow dung and other wastes of farm yard are used in the rations of pigs and poultry.

**(vi) Converter of agricultural byproducts into valuable food:** The animals convert the roughages viz., cereal straw, bhusa, grasses, fodder tree leaves, rice and wheat bran into milk, meat, eggs for human consumption.

### 4.1.3 National economy

The contribution of livestock and poultry sector to the gross domestic product (GDP) in Rs. crores is as under:

**Contribution of livestock sector to the gross domestic product (Rs. crores)**

| | 1950-51 | 1980-81 | 1990-91 | |
|---|---|---|---|---|
| **Milk** | **692** | **6884** | **29269** | **67%** |
| **Meat group** | **131** | **1570** | **6982** | **16%** |
| Meat | 87 | 1227 | 6047 | |
| Beef | 12 | 178 | 730 | |
| Mutton | 48 | 537 | 2424 | |
| Pork | 3 | 68 | 487 | |
| Poultry | 24 | 444 | 2406 | |
| Meat product | 9 | 93 | 238 | 0.5% |
| **By products** | **35** | **250** | **697** | **1.6%** |
| Hides | 21 | 125 | 271 | |
| Skin | 10 | 85 | 312 | |
| Others | 4 | 40 | 114 | |
| Eggs | 45 | 351 | 1343 | 3.1% |

| | | | | |
|---|---|---|---|---|
| **Wool and Hair** | **14** | **49** | **145** | **0.3%** |
| Wool | 11 | 39 | 117 | |
| Hair & bristles | 3 | 10 | 28 | |
| **Dung** | **180** | **1352** | **4347** | **10%** |
| Dung fuel | 80 | 673 | 2191 | |
| Dung manure | 100 | 679 | 2156 | |
| Silk work cocoons & harey | 8 | 136 | 860 | |
| Increment in livestock | 19 | 255 | 713 | 1.6% |
| Total | 1089 | 10597 | 43659 | 100% |

The value of output from livestock stood at about Rs. 123076 crores and from fisheries Rs. 25078 crores during 1998-99. This accounted about 27% of the value of the output of Rs. 553,175 crores from total agriculture and allied fields as per report of Planning Commission, 2001. India has become largest producer of milk in the world reaching 86 million tones during 2001-2002.

**Buffalo** is the backbone of India's dairy industry and considered as India's milking machine contributing about 52% of the total milk produced in the country despite the fact that buffalo number is less than half of the country's total cattle population. Buffalo in India contribute about 30% of total meat production, producing about 1.42 million tones meat during 2000. The buffalo is a unique species for its feed conversion efficiency using low grade fibrous feeds. It sustains under harsh climatic conditions, has resistance to diseases and produces high quality milk rich in fat (7%) and various minerals like calcium, iron and phosphorus but low cholesterol value compared to cow milk. The cattle contribute about 30% of the total meat production in India.

According to an estimate (FAO, 1998), the **sheep** in India produce annually about 46.5 millions kg wool, 51 million of skins, 222 million kg mutton and 2977 million kg manure. The estimated value is about 2220 crores rupees. The productivity of indigenous sheep is low for want of proper selection of germplasm, limited feed resources and nutritional deficiency, heat stress, poor health monitoring and the husbandry practices adopted.

There is wide gap in the availability and requirement of wool in our country. Out of the wool produced in India (46.5 million kg) 29% was of apparel quality and rest 71% was of carpet quality. About half quantity of carpet wool is of $36^s$ to $46^s$ quality which can be used for carpet making and rest half quantity falls below $36^s$ quality which can be used for making of low quality carpets, barrack blankets and kamblies (rugs) etc. The total fine wool which is combs worthy and suitable for worsted manufacture was about 7.2 million kg against the requirement of about 34 million kg as per installed capacity of industry. Therefore, this gap has to be filled up either by importing fine wool or by mixing synthetic material or by increase in production.

Meat production in India is estimated at 4.9 million tones, standing eighth in rank in the world's meet production. During 1998-99, the meat group contributed

Rs. 21900 crores and meat products Rs. 828 crores while by products comprising mainly of hides and skins contributed Rs. 2232 crores. There is wide gap between the availability and requirement of meat in our country. The total mutton production in India was estimated to be 171 million kg in 1994 on the assumption of 25 kg average body weight, dressing percentage of 40 and the percentage of sheep being slaughtered every year as 32%. The requirement of mutton, for 60% non vegetarian people of the country on the assumption of 1.57 kg per capita consumption of meat per year, workout to be 1343 million kg. The average mutton production of Indian sheep is low because of low body weight, poor efficiency of feed conversion and dressing percentage, non-adoption of improved method of sheep production by shepherds and lack of adequate inputs etc.

The sheep also produce pelts. The most popular breed for producing lamb pelts is the Karakul in countries like USSR, Afghanistan, Iran and South Africa. It is coarse carpet wool breed with fat tailed thriving on poor vegetation and extreme climatic conditions. The pelts are produced from lambs which are either killed within 24-28 hours of birth or before birth at around 130-140 days of pregnancy. The pelts produced by killing of lambs before birth are more valuable. About 80% lambs are slaughtered for pelt production and rest are used as replacement stock. The USSR, South Africa, Afghanistan and Iran contribute 95% of the estimated 18 million pelts of world Karakul total pelt production. The ornaments (type of curls, their size and tightness), lusture and its weight determine the quality of pelt. The various types of pelts are classed as jacket, ribbed, flat and Caucasian. The lamb pelt production has certain advantages viz. high market value of pelts compared to other sheep products, killing of lambs for pelt production eliminates the risk of infant mortality, the adult females can be rebred to produce lambs more often or they can be used as foster mothers, results in reduced pressure of inputs (feed/fodder) required for larger period for meat and wool production.

The earliest discovery of man in prehistoric times was the **goat**, primarily as easy source of meat in the beginning but later on for its value for milk, hair and skin. The goats have survived to diversified agro-climatic conditions and sustained the poor people. The goat can sustain themselves on sparse (scattered) forage and extreme climatic conditions and specially useful to the people in semi arid and arid zones where droughts are common and the other species of animals may perish (to an end). The number of goats can be reduced during drought years but equally quickly recovered during better rainfall years for the reason of their better prolificacy (litter size).

**Goats** produce a variety of products. It is mainly meat animal in India. The demand of **goat meat** in India is high for its acceptability over other type of meat. Its meat is costliest of all meat because it is most preferred. However, it also provides skin and to some extent milk, fleece and manure. There are good **milk producing breeds** (Jhakrana and Jamnapari), **fibre producing goats** (Chegu and Changthangi) that produce elite quality pashmina fibres with imported breed (Angora) which produce mohair fibres. Goat hair fetches good price produced by Marwari breed.

The pashmina and shawls from goats is very lucrative (profitable) and export oriented industry. Pashmina produced by Indian goats is of high quality. India is on the top to export processed **goat skins**. The raw goat skins after proper processing are converted to quality leather for a variety of uses like clothing, shoes, ladies gloves, various kind of containers and water storage bags. The processed goat skins are of light weight with fine texture. The Indian breeds have superiority over other foreign breeds for skin quality. According to FAO (1998), goats produce 458 million kg meat (chevon) in India, about 3100 million kg milk representing about 3% of total milk produced in the country, 126 million kg skins, 30 metric tonnes pashmina and 8500 metric tonnes manure. The estimated cost is Rs. 6100 crores.

The Price of sheep and goat products, according to an estimate are as under:-

| Product | Milk | Meat | Skin | Wool | Pashmina | Offals |
|---|---|---|---|---|---|---|
| Price (Rs/kg) | 5.0 | 80.0 | 30.0 | 40.0 | 800.00 | 75/individual |

Manure Rs, 10/q @ 600 gm/adult/day and 200 gm/young/day

More than 0.16 million sheep and goats are slaughtered daily and produce 0.62 million tonnes of meat (0.17 mt mutton and 0.45 mt chevon) and constituted about 18% (5% of sheep and 13% of goats) of the total meat production in the country. About 1% of the total sheep and goat meat produced in the country is exported which is 3.87% of the total meat exported and it valued Rs. 62.66 crores.

**Mithun's meat** is very popular in its hometract but it is sacrificed only on religious and social functions i.e. marriage, feast of merit, celebration of victory over rival group. Mithun is a **status symbol** and **a measure of wealth**. They are called as currency being used in exchange of land, for payment of ransom, tax, fine or bride price. Among some tribes the irrigated land can be purchased only in mithuns and likewise the house and the orchards are purchased in mithuns.

Mithun **horns** have decorative value to display on house wall and used for various craft work. They are also used as drinking cups, flask for keeping powder and valuables and making of some value added products. The **bones** of mithun particularly the shoulder blades are used as implements like as a hoe for tilling or shovels for scrapping of garbage from house. The **hides** of mithun after removing hair is eaten, used as shields for chest covering as war dress, also used as sleeping mats and to make belts and purses as well as for making strings to tie the animals.

The **yak** provides milk, meat, fibre and used as pack animal in high altitude. The yak is known as **'ship of the high hills'** as it can carry 55-70 kg load for 13-16 km daily. The milk production of yak is 1.1 to 1.6 kg per day with variable fat% from 4.2 to 13.0%. The yak produces two types of wool viz. outer coarse wool and inner dense fine wool which are about 0.4 to -0.6 and 03 to 3.0 kg, respectively. The outer hairs are used for ropes and tents making.

The **pigs** are important meat producing animal. They are most prolific with fast growth rate, short generation interval and make up animal protein deficiency at a cheaper rate. They contribute about 10% (420 million ton meat) of the total meat produced in India. Pigs are most efficient to convert feed stuff and domestic and agricultural waste into the edible meat.

The pigs had been treated as dirty animals and hence the pig rearing in India remained in the hands of a particular class of people belonging to the lower socio-economic status having no means of pig farming on large scale and to use improved methods of pig raising viz. breeding, feeding and meat processing. During last two decades, the pork consumption and the proportion of pork consumers has been increased as a result of improvement in pig rearing on scientific lines. A number of private pig rearing farms have been started in the country using improved management systems for commercial purpose.

In India, the **poultry** is traditionally reared in the backyard of the houses with zero input system for eggs, meat and game purpose. India ranks fourth for egg production (35000 million eggs) in the world and it produces 5 million tones of poultry meat annually. The poultry production has now become industrialized by way of using superior germplasm and rearing the stock on scientific feeding, improved management practices and sound health coverage. It has been estimated that 75% of the eggs and broilers are supplied by those rearing the stock on modern intensive system. There are about one lakh poultry farms in the country.

Local or deshi fowl are preferred for their eggs and meat, because of their taste, leanness and special dishes. They are capable to adapt to unfavourable environment, and resist to certain diseases. They are good foragers, good mothers, require zero input and contribute the economic benefits in home tract.

## 4.1.4. Employment generation

Significant employment and income opportunities have been provided to different classes of people as a result of animal raising.

(i) Rearing of animals: Small and marginal farmers and landless labourers get opportunity to work in keeping/ raising of animals as it involves intensive use of labour usually on the part of family members.

(ii) Health care: Animal husbandry Deptt. of states and Central Govt. provide jobs to a number of Veterinary Graduates, Stockman, and other technical, ministerial and supporting staff.

(iii) Research activities: A number of scientists and extension workers get jobs/employment to conduct research on different aspects for animal improvement.

(iv) Fodder production, its supply, feeding of animals and manufacture of livestock and poultry feeds have generated employment to a number of people in the country.

(v) Manufacture of medicines, their distribution and marketing have also generated employment.

(vi) Livestock based industries: A number of small and large scale industries are livestock based viz., dairy industry, woolen industry, poultry farming, leather industry, bone industry to manufacture buttons and bone meal. A number of sports material are also prepared from hides and skins of the animals like football, volleyball, criket ball, hand gloves.

### 4.1.5. Transportation

The livestock, besides the transportation of agricultural products, is the main power of rural transport in the lack of means of other source of transport to carry load and passengers viz, camel, horse and asses

### 4.1.6. Source of entertainment and cultural activities

Man also keeps animals as a hobby (horse, poultry etc.) and also to use them for riding like horse and elephant. The animals are main part of circus to play a number of games for recreation. The animals kept in zoo also attract the man. Cultural life particularly in villages is intimately connected with cattle in many ways. The buffalo serves as a sacrificial animal in India, as a racing animal in some south east Asian countries, marriage and funeral procession in Indonesia and buffalo festival in Thailand.

## 4.2. SCOPE OF ANIMAL HUSBANDRY

The rearing of different classes of livestock species is essential part of human life for a number of reasons mentioned under section 4.1. These are in brief as under:

- To carry out various agricultural operations.
- To solve the problems of food, hunger and rural employment.
- To get other livestock products viz., wool, bone, hides and skin, manure/dung
- To generate employment
- As a source of transport to carry load and passengers in hilly areas and in some rural areas.
- As a source of income, entertainment and cultural activities.

## 4.3. LIMITATIONS OF LIVESTOCK REARING

The livestock rearing has the following limitations

(i) It is an expensive enterprise for poor people as it requires large capital investment to purchase the animals, to construct house (sheds) etc.

(ii) It requires hard labour

(iii) It requires good knowledge regarding better breeding, feeding, health care and managemental practices.

(iv) It requires the availability of green fodder through out the year for better productivity.

(v) Climatic factors also limit the rearing of all the species of livestock everywhere.

## 4.4. CAUSES OF BACKWARD STATE OF LIVESTOCK IN INDIA

There are certain reasons for backward state of livestock in India

**(i) Plenty and Poverty:** There is a paradox about the Indian livestock species "Plenty and Poverty". This means that the population of different species is excessive compared to land and other resources and their production potential is lower than their counterparts of American and European species. Further it has been estimated that 60 to 80% of native farm animals are non-descript i.e., they do not conform to the recognized breed characteristics. Secondly, among the descript breed majority is of the draught and dual purpose breeds of cattle. The genetic potential of native breeds of different species of animals is low for milk, meat, egg and wool production.

**(ii) Breeding policy:** There is no national breeding policy of animals. There is lack of progeny tested bulls and the A.I. services are not available to the entire population.

**(iii) Poverty:** Indian farmers who keep the animals are economically poor with small land holdings. This compelled them not to keep high producing animals and also not to provide proper sheds to protect their animals from environmental stress.

**(iv) Illiteracy:** The Indian farmers are mostly uneducated having no knowledge of scientific breeding, feeding etc. Thus the cows are bred with stray bulls of poor breeding value available in or around village. The cattle/buffalo owner remains interested to get his female stock conceived irrespective of breeding value of sire.

**(v) Malnutrition:** The area of grazing and to grow fodder crops has decreased. The scarcity of feed and fodder has also resulted due to more number of useless animals in the country. Consequently the growth, production and reproduction efficiency of female cattle/buffalo and working efficiency of bullocks has been adversely affected.

**(vi) Health and disease problems:** The Indian cattle and buffaloes are weak due to malnutrition and dirty sheds with no provision of ventilation, clean drinking water and protection from cold and hot winds. This makes the animals susceptible to certain diseases. Moreover, there is lack of veterinary facilities for proper and timely treatment of sick animals.

**(vii) Management problems:** The livestock rearing in India is a side business and hence proper attention is not paid for their proper management. This results weakness in animals which adversely affects their overall efficiency.

All the above factors are responsible for high mortality rate among young, late maturity, longer service period and dry period, and a number of reproductive problems.

## 4.5. SUGGESTED MEASURES FOR LIVESTOCK IMPROVEMENT

The quality of Indian livestock can be improved by removing the factors responsible for their poor quality. Therefore, the following remedial measures can be adopted to improve the quality of animals.

1. Proper utilization of native AnGR : See section 17.1
2. To keep the surplus, useless and old animals in Pinjarapoles and Gosadans
3. Provision of better feed and fodders
   - To develop natural pasture land and grass lands by reclaiming useless fallow land.
   - To grow good quality fodder of improved varieties
   - To establish feed and fodder storage for lean periods
   - To improve the quality of feeds and fodder by supplementation with leguminous forages, urea treated straw, urea molasses block etc.
4. Control of diseases by timely vaccination and treatment of sick animals
5. Improvement in housing system
6. To strengthen the extension education programmes
7. To develop processing and marketing facilities.

## QUESTIONS

**4.1.** Discuss on the livestock contribution.

***or***

Discuss on the scope of animal husbandry in India.

**4.2.** (*a*) What are the limitation of livestock rearing in India?

(*b*) What are the causes of backward state of livestock in India?

(*c*) What you would suggest the measures for livestock improvement?

**4.3** Write short notes

(*a*) Livestock in agriculture

(*b*) Livestock products from different species

(*c*) Livestock and national economy

(*d*) Employment generation of livestock industry.

***

# 5

# DATA RECORDING AND CORRECTION

An animal farm is a dynamic and complicated enterprise having the objective of increasing the productivity and profit. It is dynamic for the changes that occur every moment which include change in number of animals in milk and dry, number of animals open and pregnant, age structure of animals, daily production and requirement of inputs (feed, fodder, medicine, labour etc.) It is complicated as it requires sound planning for synchronization of all the inputs and activities related to each other. In order to achieve the objective of increasing the productivity and profit, it is essentially required for an efficient manager to keep track on all the changes, activities and requirements for which he has to keep the records and get useful information for taking right decisions about selection of genetically superior animals on the basis of their breeding values.

## 5.1. RECORD KEEPING

The animal farm data is being maintained for the past many decades on sheets and registers. More recently, the use of PC has come on the scene for maintaining the data. This enables faster analysis and quick results for monitoring the various farm activities etc. However, in spite of excellent potential of maintaining data on PC, there is still importance and existence of recording the data on registers. The data maintenance in either way has many reasons as the records are useful to the farm manager.

### 5.1.1. Purposes of record keeping

The records are kept for the following purposes.

- To know the pedigree and history of each animal pertaining to the production, reproduction and health performance
  - This helps to compare the between herd performance within breed as well as to make breed comparison

- The breeding value for different economic traits can be estimated which help in culling and selection of animals for breeding purposes which in turn bring the genetic improvement of future generations
- On the basis of production level, close management and appropriate feeding levels can be provided
- This also helps in fixing the price of the animal.
- Animals with optimum level of performance for the breed can be registered in central herd book and thus the herd and breed registration programmes can be implemented effectively.
- Based on the production performance the feeding requirement can be estimated.
- This also helps in research and development planning.

- To know the proper growth of young stock by weighing the animals at proper interval and recording the body weight. This will help in culling the animals with poor growth and late maturity.
- To avoid duplication in allotment of numbers to the young animals.
- To calculate the input/output relationship by keeping record on expenditure on feed and fodder.
- To know the financial status of the farm by keeping the sale register, death register, stock books, cash books etc.
- To know the health status by keeping records of the daily treatment of animals

## 5.1.2. Types of records

The important records kept at animal farm are listed below

1. Pedigree and history sheets – This contains the information of each animal regarding its brand number, its breed/genetic group, its dam and sire number, grand dam and grand sire number, date of birth/purchase, production and reproduction information of each lactation viz. lactation number, date of service, service sire number, number of services for conception, date of calving, types and sex of calf born, birth weight of calf, calf number, milk yield in 305 days, total lactation milk yield, peak yield, date of drying etc.
2. Birth register – This contains the information about date of birth, sire and dam number, birth weight, calf number and sex, date of death/disposal etc.
3. Growth register – The body weight recorded at different ages from calf hood age.
4. Daily treatment register – This contains the animal number of sick animal, name of the disease/disorder, treatment given.
5. Livestock register – This has the information about the number of animals present.

6. Daily milking register – This contains the information about the amount of milk produced by each cow in the morning and evening.
7. Milk feeding register – About the amount of milk fed to the calves in case of weaning and also to orphan calves
8. Feed and fodder register – to work out the expenditure on feed and fodder
9. Sale/mortality register
10. Cash book.

## 5.2. DATA CORRECTION

The phenotypic value for milk, meat, egg, wool and reproducing ability is the joint product of genotype of the animal and the environment received by it during the course of development and expression of any character. The environmental factors can be grouped as under:

(i) Random environment which includes sampling error and the error in data recording etc.

(ii) Environmental factors which may be year and season when production starts, feeding level and standards, health status, heat/cold stress, management level etc.

(iii) Physiological status viz. service period, dry period, lactation length, age and body condition etc.

### 5.2.1. Purpose of data correction

The above environmental factors influence greatly the ability to produce and reproduce and therefore mask the true breeding value of the animal. It is thus proper and logical to remove the effect of any environmental sources of variation and after eliminating or minimizing the effect of environmental factors, the data should be subjected to genetic analysis so as to obtain the accurate estimate of the genetic parameters. This is called as the correction or adjustment of data for environmental factors. Therefore, the purpose of adjustment of data is to minimize the environmental variation. The reduction in environmental variance increases the heritability and thereby the accuracy and response to selection is increased. Therefore, the adjusting records for environmental factors make the selection more effective. These adjusted records are the sum of the genetic and random effects. Therefore, the test of validity of correction is that the error variance ($\sigma_e^2$) should be less on adjusted data.

### 5.2.2. Methods of data correction

The different methods which can be used to adjust the data are:

1. Least squares constants
2. Ratio method
3. Difference method
4. Regression method

**1. Least squares method:** The most important and commonly used method to adjust/correct the data is the Least Squares constant method given by Gacula (1968).

This method adjust the data for several factors at the same time by the additive process viz. herd, year, season, age etc. The least squares constants of different levels of each effect are estimated by the method of Least squares technique of ANOVA (Harvey, 1966). To remove the environmental effects from the data, the correction factor for each source of variation irrespective of their significance are used. The correction factors (L.S. constants) are added to the original record of each individual with sign changed and the resultant quantity is the adjusted record as:

$$y = y_i - CF$$

Where, $y$ = adjusted record

$y_i$ = unadjusted or original record

CF = sum of all the corrector factors (L.S. constants)

**2. The ratio method:** It is **also** known as **gross comparison method** which uses the simple average of all animals of each level taken as a ratio of the base level. The resulting factor is used for adjusting the record of animal in that level. Mathematically, the corrected record ($y_i$) is:

$$y_i = x_i / R_i$$

Where, $X_i$ is the unadjusted record

$R_i$ is the conversion ratio taken as $\bar{x}_b / \bar{x}_i$

i is the level of record to be adjusted

b is the basal record

$\bar{x}_b$ is the average of base record

$\bar{x}_i$ is the average of record in i[th] level

Therefore, the ratio factors for adjusting the records to a common base are obtained by dividing the mean of a base record by the means of other lactation records to be adjusted. Taking the milk production of cows which calved in two seasons with different age at first calving considering the base record of winter calving at 4 years of age will take the following farm:

following farm:

| | Summer calvings | | | Winter calvings | | |
|---|---|---|---|---|---|---|
| | 3 yrs | 4 yrs | 5 yrs | 3 yrs | 4 yrs | 5 yrs |
| | $X_{S31}$ | $X_{S41}$ | $X_{S51}$ | $X_{W31}$ | $X_{W41}$ | $X_{W51}$ |
| | . | . | . | . | . | . |
| | . | . | . | . | . | . |
| | . | . | . | . | . | . |
| | $X_{S3n}$ | $X_{S4n}$ | $X_{S5n}$ | $X_{W3n}$ | $X_{W4n}$ | $X_{W5n}$ |
| Mean | $\bar{x}_{S3}$ | $\bar{x}_{S4}$ | $\bar{x}_{S5}$ | $\bar{x}_{W3}$ | $\bar{x}_{W4}$ | $\bar{x}_{W5}$ |

The different ratio factors will be:

$$\frac{\overline{X}_{w4}}{\overline{X}_{S3}}, \frac{\overline{X}_{w4}}{\overline{X}_{S3}}, \frac{\overline{X}_{w4}}{\overline{X}_{S5}}, \frac{\overline{X}_{w4}}{\overline{X}_{w3}}, 1, \frac{\overline{X}_{w4}}{\overline{X}_{w5}}$$

for the respective 6 groups of cows:

**3. Difference method:** It is used when the level of any effect is only two like sex effect. The mean value of either sex is adjusted to that of the other sex by adding the average of the difference between two sexes.

**4.** The **regression method**: It is used in two ways viz. **Simple regression** and **Partial regression**

**(a)** The **simple regression** is fitted when there is only one factor for which the adjustment is made viz. milk yield is to be adjusted for 300 days lactation length as:

$$\hat{y} = \bar{y} \pm b(x_i - \bar{x})$$

$\hat{y}$ is the adjusted milk yield

$\bar{y}$ is the average milk yield

$x_i$ is days in lactation

$\bar{x}$ is the average lactation length

$$b=by\ x = \frac{\Sigma xy}{\Sigma x^2}$$

x = days in milk, y = milk yield

**(b)** The **partial regression** coefficients are estimated and used when data is to be adjusted for two or more factors like, age, season, year etc. A partial regression coefficient describes the effect of one independent variable on the dependent variable keeping constant the effects of all other independent variables. The prediction equation is an under:

$$y - y = by_{1.2}(x_1 - \bar{x}_1) + by_{2.1}(x_2 - \bar{x}_2)$$

Where y = milk yield

$x_1$ = age

$x_2$ = lactation length

## 5.3. STANDARDIZATION OF RECORDS

The records on some animals are excluded before statistical analysis of data to study the effects of various environmental factors like year/period, season and parity of lactation etc. as well as before subjecting the data to genetic analysis for estimating genetic parameters. Such records are on the following animals.

- The incomplete records due to the death or culling of the cows/buffaloes during lactation.
- The records on animals which dried up before 100 days of lactation, depending on the nature of the traits under study viz. such records are excluded for 305 days/lactation milk yield, lifetime milk production,

lactation length and dry period whereas included for birth weight, gestation period, service period.

- The milk records following abnormal calvings. The effects of abnormal calvings on various production and reproduction traits are studied separately.

## 5.4. DATA GENERATION

There are two categories of traits. The first category includes those which are observed or measured directly and the second category includes those which are generated from the information recorded/available in history cum pedigree sheets of the animal.

### 5.4.1. Directly observed traits: These are as under-

Birth weight, body weight at different ages, type of calf born (normal and abnormal), sex of calf, mortality, body colour, body measurements (length, height etc.), measurements of various body parts, physiological traits (body temperature, pulse rate, respiration rate), greasy fleece weight, litter size, carcass weight, egg weight, incidence of diseases presence or absence of any part on the body, physical defect, etc.

The traits which are measured by some tests are chemical test (milk composition), biochemical/molecular polymorphic traits viz. blood groups, protein polymorphism, haemoglobin and potassium types in blood, transferrin types, molecular markers, etc.

### 5.4.2. Traits which are generated:

Most of the important economic traits in farm animals are generated from the information available in history cum pedigree sheets or other registers. Some of the traits are generated for each individual while others are for the whole population. The procedures to generate of the important traits are given as under:-

- **Age at sexual maturity** – date of birth to date of first heat
- **Age at first calving** – date of birth to date of first calving
- **Post portum breeding interval** – date of calving to date of first heat
- **Service period** – date of calving to date of conception
- **Gestation period** – date of conception to date of calving
- **Calving interval** – interval between two calvings
- **Fertility Index (bulls)** $\dfrac{\text{No. of conceptions}}{\text{No. of inseminations}} \times 100$

This is the fertility index for $i^{th}$ bull but if estimated for the entire herd, it is then called as the conception rate or pregnancy rate or fertility rate.

- **Breeding efficiency :** This is estimated for the lifetime of a cow/buffalo based on the number of calvings in lifetime as under:

(1) Tomar's formula (1965)

$$\text{Zebu cows} = \frac{n\ 365\ +\ 1020}{\text{AFC}+\text{CI}} \times 100$$

$$\text{Buffaloes} = \frac{n\ 365\ +\ 1040}{\text{AFC}+\text{CI}} \times 100$$

Where, n = no. of calving intervals

CI = sum of all calving intervals in days

AFC = Age at first calving in days

(II) Wilcox formula (1957)

$$\text{B.E.} = \frac{365\ (n\text{-}1)}{D} \times 100$$

Where, n = no. of total calvings

D = No. of days from first to last calving

- **Lactation length** – date of calving tu date of dry
- **Dry period** – date of dry to date of next calving
- **Sex ratio** – percentage of male births to the total birth
- **Abnormal calving** – percentage of abnormal calves to the total calves born
- **Mortality rate** =

$$\frac{\textbf{No. of animals died in particular age group}}{\textbf{Total no. of animals present in the begining of that age group}} \times \mathbf{100}$$

- **Incidence of disease** = $\frac{\text{No. of animals affected}}{\text{Total no. of animals}} \times 100$
- **Replacement rate**: Percentage of female calves reached to AFC out of total female calves born or total calves born (pregnancies) after Tomar and Varma (1988)
- **Replacement index**: Ratio of heifer calvings to the total adult females left the herd in a year or a period of many years after Ram and Tomar ('1993)
- **Selective value:** It is estimated as the number of female adults born reaching milking herd from each cow/buffalo after Ram and Tomar (1995).
- **Lactation milk yield** : Total milk yield produced by a cow/buffalo in complete lactation
- **305 days milk yield**: Milk yield produced upto 305 days of lactation
- **Milk yield per day of time**: It may be calculated for per day of lactation length or per day of calving interval or per day of total days in milk during life time or per day of herd life.
- **Total days in milk**: This is the sum of lactation length for all the lactations.
- **Days open (%)** : It is the percentage of total service period (days) in all lactations to the herd life.

- **Days dry (%):** It is the percentage of total days dry in all lactations to the herd life.
- **Life time milk production** : It is estimated as the sum of milk produced in all the lactations
- **Herd life**: Difference in days between date of first calving to the date of disposal (death or culling)
- **Longevity or life span** : date of birth to the date of disposal
- **Peak yield:** maximum amount of milk produced on any day in a lactation.
- **Days to attain peak yield**: date of calving to date of attaining peak yield.
- **Persistency of lactation:** This is as under

The rate of milk secretion throughout the lactation period follows certain patterns which are called as the **lactation curves**. These are the graphical representations of the daily or weekly milk production. The rate of milk secretion is maintained by some cows for longer period in a lactation and known as persistent producers while others go dry or drop the yield within a few weeks and hence called as non persistent. The persistent cows are more economical as it influences the lactation milk production. The degree with which the rate of milk secretion is maintained during decline phase of the lactation with the advancement of lactation is called the **persistency of lactation**. Mathematically, it is expressed as the average percentage or degree of decrease in milk production each month to that of the previous month.

It is more convenient to study the lactation curves from weekly milk yields. Different mathematical models describing the shape of lactation curve have been given by different workers. The different functions employed are exponential function, parabolic exponential, gamma type and inverse polynomial. The last two functions gave higher $R^2$ values.

The lactations milk yield is the function of **initial milk yield** (first week milk yield), **ascending phase milk yield** which includes initial milk yield plus the yield to the day of attaining peak yield and it is about 25% of the 305 day yield, and the **descending phase milk yield** starting from the day of peak yield to the date of drying or 305 days of lactation which accounts nearly 75% of 305 days milk yield. The descending phase milk yield decides the persistency of lactation. Different methods are available for estimating the persistency of lactation viz. lactation curves, regression coefficients of ascending phase milk yield on the descending phase milk yield, the ratios of production of different months of lactation and the analysis of variance method by estimating the intraclass correlation. The last two methods are mostly used for calculating the persistency of lactation (P).

Johansson and Hansson (1940) estimated the persistency as a ratio of production during 101 to 200 days to the production during first 100 days (P2:1) and the ratio of production during 201-300 days to the production of first 100 days (P 3:1)

Ludwick and Peterson (1943) defined the persistency of the consecutive ratios obtained by comparing production of each individual sub division of lactation period with the preceeding one as:

$$P = W_1 \frac{P_2}{P_1} + W_2 \frac{P_3}{P_2} + W_3 \frac{P_4}{P_3}$$

Where, $P_1$ = milk yield during $2^{nd}$ + $3^{rd}$ month

$P_2$ = milk yield during $4^{th}$ + $5^{th}$ month

$P_3$ = milk yield during $6^{th}$ + $7^{th}$ month

$P_4$ = milk yield during $8^{th}$ + $9^{th}$ month

$W_1 = R_1 / R_1 + R_2 + R_3$

$W_2 = R_2 / R_1 + R_2 + R_3$

$W_3 = R_3 / R_1 + R_2 + R_3$

$$R_1 = \frac{\overline{P_2}}{\overline{P_1}}, R_2 = \frac{\overline{P_3}}{\overline{P_2}}, R_3 = \frac{\overline{P_4}}{\overline{P_3}}$$

Mahadeven (1951) used the initial milk yield of ascending phase (upto peak yield) and 180 days milk yield to estimate persistency as:

$$P = \frac{A - B}{A}$$

Where, A = first 180 days milk yield

B = first 10 weeks or ascending phase (60 days) milk yield upto peak yield

## 5.5. EXTENDING AND PREDICTING MILK YIELD

It is sometime of interest to know 305 days milk yield of a dairy cow/buffalo before she has completed. This is possible to know the ratio factors which are developed on large number of data for different herds/breeds. The ratio factors are developed for each 10 days intervals of lactation period and for different lactations. The factors are obtained as:

$$\text{Factor} = \frac{\text{Av. 305 day milk yield}}{\text{Milk yield in y days}}$$

The worked example is the example No. 5.3 at the end of this chapter.

It is not possible to record the daily milk yield particularly in field conditions. However, one day milk yield in each month of lactation (known as test day milk yield) can be recorded easily.

Test day milk yield is multiplied by the number of days in that month (cow days in a month). The first test day should be after one week of calving atleast. The product of test day yield and number of days the cow being milked in that month yields the total yield for that month. See worked example No. 5.4.

## 5.6. NUMERICAL SOLVED EXAMPLES

**Example 5.1** From the information estimate the breeding efficiency and fertility index

| Sr. No. | Sahiwal cows | | | | Murrah buffaloes | | | |
|---|---|---|---|---|---|---|---|---|
| | AFC | Calving interval | | | AFC | Calving interval | | |
| 1 | 1120 | 400 | 390 | | 1080 | 430 | 435 | 460 |
| 2 | 1210 | 385 | 390 | 365 | 1050 | 370 | | |
| 3 | 1230 | 400 | 420 | | | | | |

| Bull No. | No of inseminations | No of Calvings |
|---|---|---|
| 1 | 90 | 70 |
| 2 | 135 | 100 |

## Solution:

1: B.E. of Cows : Tomar's method

Cow No. 1 $\frac{2\times365+1020}{1120+790}\times100=\frac{1750}{1910}\times100=91.6\%$

Cow No. 2 $\frac{2\times365+1020}{1210+1140}\times100=\frac{2115}{2350}\times100=90.0\%$

Cow No. 3 $\frac{2\times365+1020}{1230+820}\times100=\frac{1750}{2050}\times100=85.3\%$

By Wilcox formula

Cow No. 1 $\frac{365x2}{790}\times100=92.4\%$

Cow No. 2 $\frac{365x3}{1140}\times100=96.0\%$

Cow No. 3 $\frac{365\times3}{820}\times100=89.0\%$

II B.E. of buffaloes: Tomar's method

Buffalo No. 1 $\frac{3\times365+1040}{1080+1325}\times100=88.7\%$

Buffalo No. 2 $\frac{1\times365+1040}{1050+370}\times100=98.9\%$

Fertility index of bulls:

$$I=\frac{\text{No. of calvings}}{\text{No. of conceptions}}\times100$$

Bull No. 1 $\frac{70}{90}\times100=77.7\%$

Bull No. 2 $\frac{100}{135}\times 100 = 74.1\%$

**Example 5.2:** Calculate the persistency of milk yield from the following data of monthly milk production:

| Cow No. | Months M.Y. | | | | | | | | | |
|---|---|---|---|---|---|---|---|---|---|---|
| | 1 | 2 | 3 | 4 | 5 | 6 | 7 | 8 | 9 | Total |
| 1 | 250 | 260 | 270 | 280 | 300 | 305 | 300 | 290 | 260 | 2515 |
| 2 | 310 | 300 | 330 | 350 | 390 | 380 | 370 | 320 | 320 | |
| 3 | 260 | 290 | 330 | 340 | 330 | 330 | 330 | 320 | 290 | |
| 4 | 330 | 330 | 360 | 370 | 330 | 320 | 320 | 290 | 280 | |
| 5 | 290 | 280 | 300 | 320 | 310 | 300 | 280 | 290 | 280 | |
| 6 | 310 | 290 | 290 | 310 | 300 | 280 | 260 | 240 | 210 | |
| Total | 1750 | 1750 | 1880 | 1970 | 1960 | 1915 | 1860 | 1750 | 1640 | |

## Solution

### I. Ludwick & Peterson method:

$$\overline{P_1} = \frac{1750+1880}{6} = \frac{3630}{6} = 605 \qquad \overline{P_2} = \frac{1970+1960}{6} = \frac{3930}{6} = 655$$

$$\overline{P_3} = \frac{1915+1860}{6} = \frac{3775}{6} = 629.1 \qquad \overline{P_4} = \frac{1750+1640}{6} = \frac{3390}{6} = 565$$

$$R_1 = \frac{\overline{P_2}}{\overline{P_1}} = \frac{655}{605} = 1.082, \qquad R_2 = \frac{\overline{P_3}}{\overline{P_2}} = \frac{629.1}{655} = 0.96,$$

$$R_3 = \frac{\overline{P_4}}{\overline{P_3}} = \frac{565}{629.1} = 0.898, \qquad \sum R_i = 2.94$$

$$W_1 = \frac{R_1}{\sum Ri} = \frac{1.082}{2.94} = 0.368, \qquad W_2 = \frac{R_2}{\sum Ri} = \frac{0.96}{2.94} = 0.328,$$

$$W_3 = \frac{R_3}{\sum Ri} = \frac{0.898}{2.94} = 0.305,$$

| Cow No. | $P_1$ | $P_2$ | $P_3$ | $P_4$ | $\frac{P_2}{P_1}$ | $\frac{P_3}{P_2}$ | $\frac{P_4}{P_3}$ | P | Rank |
|---|---|---|---|---|---|---|---|---|---|
| 1 | 530 | 580 | 605 | 550 | 1.09 | 1.04 | 0.91 | 0.021 | 2 |
| 2 | 630 | 740 | 750 | 640 | 1.17 | 1.01 | 0.85 | 1.024 | 1 |
| 3 | 620 | 670 | 660 | 610 | 1.08 | 0.90 | 0.90 | 0.944 | 4 |
| 4 | 690 | 700 | 640 | 570 | 1.04 | 0.90 | 0.89 | 0.943 | 5 |
| 5 | 580 | 630 | 580 | 570 | 1.08 | 0.92 | 0.98 | 1.000 | 3 |
| 6 | 580 | 610 | 540 | 450 | 1.05 | 0.88 | 0.83 | 0.931 | 6 |

## II Mahdevan's Method:

| Cow No. | A | B | $\frac{A-B}{A}$ | Rank |
|---|---|---|---|---|
| 1 | 1665 | 570 | 0.69 | 3 |
| 2 | 2060 | 610 | 0.70 | 2 |
| 3 | 1880 | 550 | 0.71 | 1 |
| 4 | 2040 | 660 | 0.67 | 5 |
| 5 | 1800 | 570 | 0.68 | 4 |
| 6 | 1780 | 600 | 0.66 | 6 |

A = 180 days (6 months) milk yield

B = 60 days milk yield

## III Intraclass correlation method

$\Sigma X = 16475$, N = 54

C.F. $(16475)^2/54 = 5026400.46$

T.S.S. = 5091775-C.F=65324.54

Cow S.S. = 5506669.44 – C.F. = 30268.98

Error SS = TSS-Cow SS = 35055.56

ANOVA Table

| S.V. | d.f. | SS | MS | E.M.S. |
|---|---|---|---|---|
| Cows | 5 | 30268.98 | 6053.796 | $d_w^2 + d_B^2$ |
| Error | 48 | 35055.56 | 730.324 | $d_w^2$ |

$$\sigma_w^2 = \frac{6053.796 - 730.324}{9} = 591.4968$$

$$t = \frac{\sigma_B^2}{\sigma_B^2 + \sigma_w^2} = \frac{591.4968}{1321.8208} = 0.447 = P$$

**Example 5.3:** Consider the milk yield at 10 days interval and 305 days milk yield as under

| Days | 30 | 40 | 50 | .......... | 290 | 300 | 305 |
|---|---|---|---|---|---|---|---|
| Milk yield | 320 | 465 | 630 | .......... | 2260 | 2290 | 2325 |
| Ratio factors | 7.26 | - | - | .......... | 1.02 | - | - |

Find out the ratio factors and fill in the Table

## Solution

$$\text{Factor} = \frac{\text{Av. 305 day milk yield}}{\text{Milk yield y days}}$$

e.g. the factor for 30 days milk yield = 2325/320 = 7.26
the factor for 290 days milk yield = 2325/2260 = 1.02
and so on.

**Example 5.4:** Estimate 305 days milk yield of a cow which calved on 14th January and whose milk yield was recorded on 22nd of each month and these test day milk yield are as under

| Month | 1 | 2 | 3 | 4 | 5 | 6 | 7 | 8 | 9 | 10 | 11 |
|---|---|---|---|---|---|---|---|---|---|---|---|
| (a) Days | 17 | 28 | 31 | 30 | 31 | 30 | 31 | 31 | 30 | 31 | 15 |
| (b) Test day milk yield (kg) | 10 | 11 | 15 | 13 | 11 | 12 | 10 | 8 | 8 | 6 | 4 |
| (c) a.b | 170 | 308 | 465 | 390 | 341 | 360 | 310 | 248 | 140 | 186 | 60 |

## Solution

305 days milk yield = 170+308+465+.......+60=3078 kg

**Example 5.5:** The average lactation milk yields in first through eight lactations for Tharparkar herd are given below. Find out the ratio factors for each lactation considering the basal record of third lactation which is the highest among all lactations.

| Lactation No. | 1 | 2 | 3 | 4 | 5 | 6 | 7 | 8 |
|---|---|---|---|---|---|---|---|---|
| Milk yield | 1910 | 2080 | 2150 | 2080 | 1960 | 1955 | 1900 | 1840 |
| Ratio factors | 1.12 | 1.03 | - | - | - | - | - | |

## Solution:

$$\text{The ratio factor} = \frac{\text{Mean of basal record}}{\text{Mean of i}^{\text{th}}\text{ lactation}}$$

Thus the ratio factor for first lactation is 2150/1910 = 1.12

Similarly for second lactation = 2150/2080 = 1.03 and so on

**Example: 5.6:** The following hypothetical data pertain to the milk yield in kg averaged for 1000 cows each in the first through 5th lactation milked either twice or thrice. Find out the corrected milk yield of a cow yielding 900 kg in the first lactation for mature equivalent twice milked daily, taking 4th as the mature equivalent and the cow being milked thrice a day.

| Lactation No. | Twice | Thrice |
|---|---|---|
| 1 | 1000 | 1100 |
| 2 | 1160 | 1210 |
| 3 | 1360 | 1370 |
| 4 | 1370 | 1400 |
| 5 | 1400 | 1410 |
| Total | 6290 | 6490 |

The ratio to convert twice into thrice = 6490/6290 = 1.03

The ratio to convert first lactation milk yield into fourth lactation yield = 1400/1100 = 14/11 = 1.27

Now, had the cow been milked thrice in first lactation it would have yielded 900 x 1.03 = 927 kg. Similarly had the cow been in forth lactation, then its milk production would have been 927 x 1.27 = 1177.3 kg. Therefore, the corrected milk yield of cow

yielding 900 kg in first lactation with twice milking would be 1177.3 kg had it been milked thrice in fourth lactation.

**Example 5.7:** Find out the adjusted milk yield of a cow for service period which yield 2837 kg milk (y) and conceived after 266 days of calving. Consider the regression of milk yield (y) on service period (x) as 5.56 kg/day and the average service period as 145 days

**Solution**

The adjusted milk yield $(\hat{y}) = y - b_{yx}(x_i - \bar{x})$

$= 2837 - 5.56(266-145) = 2164.2$ kg

## QUESTIONS

**5.1.** Assuming that you are maintaining a dairy herd for breeding research. Keeping in view economy, objectivity and efficiency suggest a suitable recording system to be maintained. Give appropriate reasons for suggesting different proformae. *(ARS 1981)*

**5.2.** Enumerate production records to be standardized for the selection of dairy cow and why? *(ARS 1982)*

**5.3.** (*a*) What are the different purposes of record keeping?

(*b*) Give the purposes of data correction.

***

# 6

# RESPONSE TO SELECTION

## 6.1. GENERAL

Since domestication man has tried to apply artificial selection to change the animal population for making genetic improvement in performance. The different breeds of domestic animals that exist today are the result of natural and artificial selection. However, the aim has not been achieved so far and more genetic improvement is needed for production of milk, meat, egg, wool and other characters viz. race in horses, better show jumping, and more intelligent guide dogs.

The selection is a process of giving preference to certain individuals in a population to reproduce than other individuals which are denied the opportunity to produce next generation. Therefore, selection is the choice of individuals to produce the next generation. In genetic terms, the selection is a process of differential reproduction and survival of genotypes which may be natural or artificial or both.

The selection, without creating any new gene, changes the genetic structure of the population by changing the frequency of genes and genotypes. The frequency of desired genes is increased in the population through selection at the expense of the frequency of undesirable or less desirable genes. This is the genetic effect of selection. The selection is more efficient for dominant genes at low frequency but it is relatively easy to select for a recessive gene.

The characters are controlled by genes. Therefore, with the increase or change in the frequency of desirable genes, the phenotypic mean of the character of progeny generation is also increased or changed. The change in performance of progeny generation due to artificial selection is known as **response to selection** or **genetic change** or **genetic gain**. Now the point of discussion here is that how the performance of the progeny generation of selected parent is changed.

## 6.2. SELECTION DIFFERENTIAL AND RESPONSE TO SELECTION

The selection divides the parental population in two parts viz. selected and culled animals. The culled animals are inferior whereas the selected are superior for a trait under selection. Thus the two groups differ in their genetic structure and hence in their mean phenotypic value. The superiority of the selected parents over the population mean (for selected plus culled animals) is the phenotypic superiority and called as the selection differential denoted by S.

$$S = \overline{P}_S - \overline{P}$$

Where, $\overline{P}_s$ is the mean of selected parents

$\overline{P}$ is the population mean before selection was made

Thus, the selection differential (S) is taken as the mean of selected parents ( $\overline{P}_S$ ) expressed as deviation from population mean ( $\overline{P}$ ).

The phenotypic superiority of the selected parents is due to the followings.

- The selected parents may have better genotypes or they might have received better environment.
- The selected parents may have better genotypes as well as better environment.

Therefore, the phenotypic superiority of selected parents (selection differential) has two component parts viz.

S = Genetic superiority + Environmental superiority

The genetic superiority is more important and of more concern because it is the genetic superiority which is transmitted. Therefore, the selection of superior animals will be effective to improve the progeny generation if their superiority is genetic rather than the environmental. Further it is only the additive genetic variability ($\sigma^2_A$) which is inherited and fixed but not the whole of the genetic variability ($\sigma^2_G$). This is because the genotypes are broken up in every generation and hence the progeny do not get the same gene combination (genotypes) as their parents. Thus the gene combination superiority or variability ($\sigma^2_D$+$\sigma^2_I$) is not inherited. In this way, the additive genetic variability ($V_A$) of the total phenotypic variability ($\sigma^2_P$) is only responsive to selection and this is expressed as heritability ($h^2 = V_A/V_P$). The $h^2$ expresses the extent to which the total phenotypic superiority of a trait shown by selected parents is transmitted to their progeny. Therefore, the whole amount of selection differential is not transmitted to the progeny but its portion equal to $h^2$ is transmitted and it is called as the predicted response to selection. In other words, the **predicted response to selection** (R) is equal to the expected inherited part of the selection differential

$$R = h^2(P_S - P)$$

The heritability ($h^2$) is thus an important concept in relation to response to selection (R) and it can also be explained by taking the extreme values of $h^2$ as zero and one as under:

The zero value of $h^2$ means that $V_A$ is one. This indicates that there is no variation in B.V. of individuals of a population. In this case, the selection will not be effective because of no difference in the B.V. of selected and culled animals. This means that there is no genetic superiority of the selected parents to pass on to their progeny and hence there will be no difference in the average B.V. of the offspring of the selected parents and the B.V. of any individual of the parental population before selection.

In the second situation, when $h^2$ is one. This indicates that whole of $V_P$ is due to variation in B.V. ($V_A$). This means that individuals of a population differ entirely due to the differences in B.V. and hence the ranking based on phenotypic value will be equivalent to the ranking based on B.V. The genetic superiority of selected parents being solely due to the superiority in B.V., their progeny mean is expected to be equal to their mean (parental mean) because all of the genetic superiority of the selected parents has been passed on to their offspring

In the above two situations, the R will be as:

$R = 0$ when $h^2 = 0$

$R = S$ when $h^2 = 1.0$

And the general prediction equation of R for any value of $h^2$ will be

$$R = h^2.S \qquad \text{.....................} \ (1)$$

$$= h^2(P_S - P)$$

**Response to selection in relation to intensity and accuracy of selection**

The selection differential can not be estimated without practicing the selection among parent generation. Thus, R can not be predicted by the above equation. To overcome this, the selection differential (S) is taken in another form as:

$$S = i\sigma_p$$

Where, $i$ = intensity of selection

$\sigma_P$ = phenotypic standard deviation of trait

The i is also called as the standardized selection differential which is the number of $\sigma_p$ by which the mean of the selected group is above the population mean before selection. The i is expressed as:

$$i = s/\sigma_p = \frac{(P_S - P)}{\sigma_P}$$

the $s/\sigma_p$ expresses the S in standard measure for which it is called the standardized S or intensity of selection. Thus standardized S is the S divided by $\sigma p$. The standardized S is used to compare the different methods of selection. Now taking the S in standardized form requires the reorientation of the prediction equation of R as :

$$R/\sigma_p = S/\sigma_p \, h^2$$

$$R = i\sigma_p h^2 \qquad \text{since } [(s/\sigma_p = i)] \qquad \text{.......} \ 2$$

$$= i\sigma_p \, b_{AP} \qquad \text{since } (h^2 = b_{AP})$$

This reoriented equation of R can also be taken in terms of accuracy of selection as:

$$R = i\sigma_p \, h^2$$

$$= i\sigma_p \, (\sigma_A/\sigma_p) \, h$$

$$= i\sigma_A \, h$$

$$= i\sigma_A \, r_{AP} \qquad \text{since } (h = r_{AP}) \qquad \text{.......} \ 3$$

Where, $\sigma_A$ = Standard deviation of breeding values of trait,

$r_{AP}$ = correlation between B.V. and phenotypic value and equal h (square root of heritability). This is also called as the accuracy of selection

The response to selection (R) or the genetic gain ($\Delta G$) can be predicted from the above formula when the selection criteria are the individual's own record. But it can be made generalized for other criteria of selection viz. when the selection is based on the performance record of relatives of the individual under selection. The genetic gain can be predicted based on any criteria of selection (I) by using the following formula:

$$\Delta G = i\sigma_A r_{AI}$$

Where, $r_{AI}$ = correlation between the selection criteria (I) and the B.V. of individual (A)

## 6.3. ACCURACY OF SELECTION

The additive genetic relationship (**a**) between two individuals is taken to the extent to which they have breeding values (B.V.) or the genes in common. There are two situations to understand the concept. The **first** is that two animals are identical twins so as the **a** will be one and hence a record on other animal will be as accurate of the animal's true B.V. as a record on the animal's own record. In other words, the accuracy of selection on a record of other animal equals to the accuracy of selecting on individuals own record. The **second situation** is that the 'a' between two animals is zero and hence their B.V. will be independent of each other. Thus a record on other animal will not give any indication of the animals' true B.V. which means that the accuracy of selecting on a record of other animal will be zero. Therefore, the accuracy of selection based on a single record on a relative will be equal to the extent the individual and its relative have their B.V. in common (**a**) times the correlation between B.V. of individual and selection criteria ($r_{AP}$ which is the accuracy of relatives performance as a criteria to the relatives true B.V.). Therefore,

Accuracy of selection = Additive relationship between individual and relatives $\times$ $r_{AP}$ = a h.

In view of the above, the accuracy of selection based on single record on individual itself or on a relative's record will be as:

- Individual itself = h
- Based on pedigree performance

(i) One parent record = ½ h

Both parents = $\sqrt{^1/_2}$ h = 0.71 h

(ii) One grand parent's record = ¼ h

All four grand parentsh = $\sqrt{^1/_4}$ h = 0.5 h

(iii) One great grand parent's record = 0.125 h

All 8 great grand parents = $\sqrt{1/8}$ h = 0.35h

- Based on family records (i) F.S. = ½ h
  (ii) HS = ¼ h
- Based on progeny record = ½ h

It is thus clear that a single record on one relative is always less accurate than a single record on individual itself to predict its B.V.

Sometimes, the numbers of records used to predict the B.V. of an individual are more than one either of the individual itself or of its relatives. The $h^2$ based on n record is more than based on single record and hence the accuracy of selection will also be more as shown below:

| Selection Criteria | $b_{AP}$ or $h^2$ | | Accuracy of selection on n records |
|---|---|---|---|
| | Single record | N records | |
| Individual | $h^2$ | $\frac{\alpha\eta^2}{\alpha} + \frac{\delta\varsigma_\Delta}{\alpha\varsigma_\Pi} +$ | $\sqrt{\frac{nh^2}{1+(n-1)r}}$ |
| Pedigree | $h^2$ | $\frac{0.5nh^2}{1+(n-1)r}$ | $0.5\sqrt{\frac{nh^2}{1+(n-1)r}}$ |
| Family | | | |
| (i) HS | $0.25h^2$ | $\frac{0.25h^2}{1+(n-1)t}$ $= \frac{nh^2}{4+(n-1)h^2}$ | $0.25\sqrt{\frac{h^2}{1+(n-1)t}}$ |
| (ii) FS | $0.5\ h^2$ | $\frac{0.5nh^2}{1+(n-1)t}$ $\frac{nh^2}{2+(n-1)h^2}$ | $0.5\sqrt{\frac{nh^2}{1+(n-1)t}}$ |
| Progeny | $0.5\ h^2$ | $\frac{0.5nh^2}{1+(n-1)t}$ $= \frac{2nh^2}{4+(n-1)h^2}$ | $0.5\sqrt{\frac{nh^2}{1+(n-1)t}}$ |

Where, t = intra class correlation among HS/FS/Progeny

= 0.25 $h^2$ for HS

= 0.5 $h^2$ for FS and progeny

r = repreatability i.e. correlation among records

**Increasing the accuracy of selection:** The accuracy of selection can be increased by the following methods:

**1. To minimize the environmental variance:** It can be minimized by providing uniform environment, by use of multiple records to estimate $h^2$, by adjusting the data for environmental effects, by accurate measurement of data, and by analyzing the data based on contemporary group mean. The readers for the details may refer pages 320 to 322 of the "Text Book of Population Genetics. Vol. II. Quantitative Inheritance by S.S. Tomar (1998), Kalyani Publishers, Ludhiana.

**2. Combined selection:** When two or more criteria of selection are used to estimate an individuals' true breeding value (B.V.) it is called as the combined selection. This means to supplement the individuals' performance records with those of its relatives. This gives more accurate estimate of B.V. of the individual.

The family selection may be used to support individual selection when $h^2$ of a trait is low. It is better to select an individual with better record belonging to a superior family compared to an individual with similar performance belonging to a mediocre or inferior family. The half sib family selection is better than FS family selection. The reason being that family selection is more effective when the environmental variations common to all the members of a family are as small as possible. This means that environmental similarities among family members should be low. The common environmental variance is less among half sibs than among full sibs. Thus, the environmental correlation among F.S. is more than among H.S.

Secondly, the F.S. family selection reduces the genetic variability in the population and also results in a certain amount of inbreeding. The selected parents based on F.S. family averages are more closely related. Thirdly, the effective selection intensity is also reduced for a given testing facility for F.S. family selection.

**3. Selection based on future performance:** The selection should be based on the future performance (most probable producing ability or the expected producing ability) of the animal with more number of records.

The E.P.A. or M.P.P.A. is estimated as:

$$\overline{H} + \frac{nr}{1+(n-1)r}(\overline{C} - \overline{H})$$

Where, $\overline{H}$ = Herd average or contemporary average

$\overline{C}$ = Average of females based on all record

n = number of records

r = repeatability

$$\frac{nr}{1+(n-1)r}$$ = repeatability of n records which is based on more than single record.

The repeatability increases with number of repeated records. Thus the accuracy of evaluating an animal based on more records is increased when the temporary environmental effects are more

The accuracy of estimating MPPA or EPA of a cow is estimated as:

$$\text{Accuracy of EPA} = \sqrt{\frac{nr}{1+(n-1)r}}$$

**4. Large population:** In small size population the homozygosity is increased with consequent decrease in genetic variability and also the genetic drift occurs, which leads to the fixation of alleles. All these lowers the $h^2$, hence $r_{AP}$ and the genetic gain. Therefore, the population size should not be allowed to decrease. The population size also affects the S in a way that S is low in a population of small size.

## 6.4. INTENSITY OF SELECTION (i)

The intensity of selection denoted by i is the mean deviation of the selected animals in units of $\sigma_P$ of the trait i.e. it is the number of $\sigma_P$ of the trait by which the mean of the selected group is above the population mean before selection. The **i** is expressed as:

$i = s/\sigma_P$

The **i** expresses the **s** in standard deviation units and hence the intensity of selection is the standardized selection differential ($S/\sigma_P$). Thus, the **i** is the selection differential in units of standard deviation of the trait. The S in original units of measurement can be taken by multiplying **i** with standard deviation as:

$S = i\sigma_P$

The i is also taken as:

$i = Z/p$

Where, p is the proportion of animals selected

Z is the height of frequency distribution curve where the group of selected individuals is represented.

Thus Z is the height of normal curve at the point where the selected individuals with the lowest record fall. This point of separation is called the **point of truncation**. Thus, Z is the height of the ordinate at the point of truncation.

There are tables available showing the ordinate and area of normal frequency distribution curve to obtain the values of Z. This is known as the selection differential under truncation which indicates that all the animals are selected with records above a certain level of the trait. Therefore, the selection differential in standard deviation units may be taken from the mathematical properties of the normal distribution as:

$i = S/\sigma_P = Z/p$

Thus intensity of selection (i) is inversely related to the proportion selected (p). If the proportion selected (p) is given, the intensity of selection (i) can be estimated in terms of the number of standard deviation of the trait ($\sigma_p$) by which the mean of the selected individuals exceeds to the population mean.

The **i** can be known without actually measuring the superiority of parents. The approximate value of **i** can be obtained from **p** for any character based on their relationship after consulting a table of values given below:

**TABLE: THE i AS A FUNCTION OF P.**

| p | Intensity of selection (i) | | | | |
|---|---|---|---|---|---|
| | 10@ | 20 | 50 | 100 | ∝ |
| 1.0 | 0 | 0 | 0 | 00 | 0 |
| 0.9 | 0.17 | 0.18 | 0.16 | 0.19 | 0.20 |
| 0.8 | 0.32 | 0.33 | 0.34 | 0.35 | 0.35 |
| 0.7 | 0.46 | 0.48 | 0.49 | 0.49 | 0.50 |
| 0.6 | 0.60 | 0.62 | 0.63 | 0.64 | 0.64 |
| 0.5 | 0.74 | 0.77 | 0.79 | 0.79 | 0.80 |
| 0.4 | 0.89 | 0.93 | 0.95 | 0.96 | 0.97 |
| 0.3 | 1.07 | 1.11 | 1.14 | 1.15 | 1.16 |
| 0.2 | 1.27 | 1.33 | 1.37 | 1.39 | 1.40 |
| 0.1 | 1.54 | 1.64 | 1.71 | 1.73 | 1.76 |

@ No. of individuals from which the parents are to be selected

With standard rate of mortality, reproductive efficiency and perfect managemental conditions, the percentage of males and females required to maintain herd size are 4-5 and 50-60 in dairy animals, 2-4 and 40-50 in sheep and goats, and in swine 1-2 and 10-15.

## Determinants of i or S

The following factors determine the intensity of selection

(i) Proportion of population selected (p)

(ii) Phenotypic standard deviation of the trait ($\sigma_p$)

(iii) Sex of the animal under selection

(iv) No. of traits under selection

(v) Accurate measurement of the trait

The ways these factors affects the i have been discussed here:

**(i) Proportion selected (p):** This affects the selection differential in a way that if the proportion selected is high, the S will be low than when the p is low. The number or the proportion of animals selected depends on the breeding policy and the capacity of the farm. The proportion selected will be higher when increase in herd size is required. This will decrease the selection intensity and hence the S. In case to keep the herd size constant, fewer replacement animals will be required so as to select only the more desirable animals. This will increase the intensity of selection and hence the S. However, the population size put a restriction on p. In small size herd, the chances of inbreeding are more and this has three fold effects. The first is the inbreeding depression and the random drift, second is the reduction in genetic variability and thirdly the intensity of selection is reduced which also reduces the S. On the contrary, in large size herd, the chances of inbreeding are less and the i is increased. The size of the progeny generation though can be increased by increase in p but it will reduce i.

The p is affected by the number of replacement stock being available which is the function of the fertility (conception rate and number of offspring in a birth), prenatal losses, sex ratio, post natal mortality (health, survivability and longevity). The S is also larger in litter bearing species (pigs) than in species giving single birth (cattle, buffalo). The low breeding efficiency (late AFC and longer C.I.) and high calf mortality are great constraints in genetic improvement through selection. These constraints can be overcomed by adapting the following ways:-

**Large herd size:** To keep a large herd size requires increasing the capacity of the organized farms. The intensity of selection is increased in a large size herd and the level of inbreeding is reduced as mentioned above.

**Breeding efficiency:** Better nutrition and better management practices are required to increase the breeding efficiency and to reduce the calf losses.

The reproductive rate can be increased in males by use of A.I. and in females by use of MOET. These techniques should be used to increase the reproductive rate of the most superior animals.

**Longevity of elite dams:** The dams of elite herd should live longer and be retained in the herd for longer to get more calf crop. A large number of progeny per adult female reach the breeding age in a population of superior genotype with proper management and thus a smaller proportion of potential animals need to be selected. This will increase the selection differential and hence the response to selection.

Conclusively, the R increases with increase in S which in term increases with decrease in p. Therefore, R will be more when p is lower. However, more genetic variation in the population is preserved by higher p and results in a greater cumulative R. The lower value of p does not result in maximum long term R. The chance to get lost the favourable alleles with small effect linked with unfavourable alleles is reduced with larger p compared to smaller p each generation.

**(ii) Phenotypic standard deviation of the trait ($\sigma_p$) :** The second important factor to affect the S is the phenotypic standard deviation of the character which is a measure of phenotypic variability. If the character is less variable the S is consequently smaller and vice versa. The effect of the proportion selected and the $\sigma p$ on the magnitude of S is shown below.

| 50% selected | 20% selected | 20% selected |
|---|---|---|
| σp = 2 units | σp = 2 units | σp = 1 units |
| Sd = 1.6 units | Sd = 2.8 units | Sd = 1.4 units |

The above figures indicate that the S increases with the decrease in proportion selected and with the increase in σp of the character.

The σp will depend on the **breeding programmes of the herd.** If selection has been experienced for many years for a trait it will then affect the σp. Selection results in an increase of the production level of the herd and fewer animals will be available in the selected herd which exceeds the herd average. Consequently the variability in a trait and proportion selected will be reduced and therefore, the S will be small. On the other hand, if there has been no selection for years together in the herd, the S will be larger. This will result in low herd average and larger variability of the trait and it will also easy to find animals from other herds with high performance.

**(iii) Sex of the animal under selection:** The S is also affected by sex of the animal under selection. In case of males the S is large because fewer males are used for breeding. The use of AI and frozen semen technology has further increased the S for males. However, the effect of sex on S is further dependent on the species of livestock. For example, strong selection can be carried out in poultry breeding among both hens and cockerels.

**(iv) No. of traits under selection:** The number of traits selected for also influence the S. The S will be low with more number of characters under selection than for only one trait. It is because that an animal may not be outstanding in all the traits. It is, therefore, important to include only the most important economic traits in selection index.

**(v) Accurate measurement of the trait:** A mistake to decide which animal is actually superior for a trait results in small S. Likewise failure to use records in a proper way may also lower the S.

## 6.5. RELIABLE ESTIMATE OF HERITABILITY

The reliability of $h^2$ estimate depends on a number of factors listed below:

1. Data recording is correct or inaccurate.
2. Environmental conditions are similar or different to different animals.
3. Scale effect
4. Unadjustment of data
5. Violations of the assumptions in $h^2$ estimation viz. G x E interaction, G x E correlation, selection of parents, assortative mating and inbreeding

For details of the above factors, the readers may consult page 320 to 325 of "Text Book of Population Genetics. Vol. II. Quantitative Inheritance by S.S. Tomar (1998), Kalyani Publishers, Ludhiana (India).

6. Methods of estimation of $h^2$ : The methods of estimating $h^2$ are based on resemblance between relatives. The extent of resemblance between relatives depends on the extent to which the relatives have-

- genes in common
- genotypes in common and
- shared the common environment.

The factor of having genes in common by the relatives causes the additive genetic relationship between them denoted by '**a**' and this means that the relatives have the same breeding values because the additive genetic relationship is due to the additive effect of genes. The resemblance between relatives is also affected by the differences in B.V. of the individuals of a population. This can be understood by taking the similarity and differences in the B.V. of the members of a population:

**Similarity in B.V. ($V_A$=0):** When all members of a population, whether relatives or not, have exactly the same set of genes, it indicates that they all have the same B.V. and hence $V_A = 0$. In this case, there will be no contribution of having genes in common by the relatives to the resemblance between the relatives.

**Differences in B.V.:** This means that there exists the $V_A$ in the population for the reason of existing different genes in unrelated individuals within a population i.e. the variation exists in B.V. In this situation, the resemblance between relatives will increase along the extent to which the relatives have genes in common compared with unrelated individuals of the population. In this way, the importance of having genes in common depends on the extent of $V_A$ in the population. The maximum value of $V_A$ equals $V_P$ ($V_A$=$V_P$) and hence the relative importance of having genes in common equal $V_A/V_P$ which is the $h^2$. Therefore, the resemblance between relatives increases with the increase in additive genetic relationship (a) and $h^2$. The resemblance due to having genes in common equals **a h²** when the relatives are not inbred. This is the basis of estimating heritability. Thus,

$$h^2 = \frac{\text{resemblance}}{\text{additive relationship}}$$

In a similar manner, the contribution of having genotypes in common to the resemblance between relatives depends on the values of $V_D/V_P$ and $V_I/V_P$ whereas the contribution of having environment in common depends on $V_{EC}/V_P$

Now, taking the effect of all the 3 factors causing resemblance between relatives, the total resemblance will be as :

$$\text{Resemblance} = ah^2 + d\frac{V_D}{V_P} + \frac{V_{EC}}{V_P}$$

Where, d is the probability of relatives having same genotype (called as dominance relationship)

$V_i$ is ignored as it is not relatively important

The heritability is thus estimated as

$$h^2 = \frac{\text{resemblance}}{\text{additive relationship}} = \frac{ah^2}{a} + \frac{dV_D}{aV_P} + \frac{aV_{EC}}{aV_P} = h^2 + \frac{dV_D}{aV_P} + \frac{V_{EC}}{V_P}$$

It is thus clear that the $h^2$ estimate becomes biased upward if the relatives have genotypes or environments in common, though this biasness can be eliminated.

## 6.6. GENERATION INTERVAL

The generation interval is the time period between two successive generations with respect to the same stage of life cycle. It is defined and estimated as the average age of parents at the time of the birth of their offspring which became parents in next generation.

The selection response is also affected by the generation interval when the different schemes of selection are compared for their relative genetic progress. The conversation of genetic progress per generation into the progress per unit of time is also essential to compare the progress for the same trait in different species like milk yield in dairy animals (exotic, zebu, buffalo, goat, etc.).

### 6.6.1. Factors affecting generation interval (t)

**(i) Species:** The generation interval is different for different species.

**(ii) Selection schemes:** The selection schemes of varying number of offspring raised in any generation also affect the generation interval. The first selection scheme involving more number of offspring or more records per animal and the second selection scheme involves one offspring with one record. The first scheme will increase the intensity of selection as well as the accuracy of selection and thereby the response to selection will be greater. But this will also increase the generation interval and may result comparatively less progress per year than the progress per year obtained under the second selection scheme. Thus, the two schemes of selection can be compared on the basis of genetic gain expected per unit of time and the scheme resulting maximum progress per unit of time will be optimum.

The generation interval is affected by the number of progeny born before the selection is made. A breeder has to wait until more offspring have been reared so as to increase the intensity of selection which will increase the response to selection. The generation interval will be increased by including more offspring and thus response per unit of time will be reduced. The increase in number of offspring is beneficial to certain limit beyond which it reduces the relative speed of progress (measured as 1/t). The i will certainly be increased with additional number of offspring but the increase in t will be greater and faster than the increase in i. This will result in low relative speed of progress.

**(iii) Sex:** The generation interval (t) is also different for the two sexes depending upon their use to produce the offspring. For example, in a progeny testing programme in dairy cattle many sires are used even after their daughters are tested for milk production. This increases the t value for male side. Therefore, the t should be taken as an average from both male and female side in order to predict the response per year. This is also done because in dairy animals the generations overlap. In species like poultry the t is equal for both the sexes because the generations are distinct and do not overlap. This is because the selected progeny replace the entire population at the same time.

The generation interval is estimated species wise combined for the two sexes giving due weightage to the proportion of offspring raised. Both the sires and the dams produce the male as well as female progeny but at different ages. The generation interval is estimated as the weighted average of the following four averages:

$$t = n_1 t_{SS} + n_2 t_{SD} + n_3 t_{DS} + n_4 t_{DD}$$

Where,

$t_{SS}$ = average age of sire to produce male progeny (sons)

$t_{SD}$ = average age of sire to produce female progeny (daughters)

$t_{DS}$ = average age of dam to produce male progeny (sons)

$t_{DD}$ = average age of dam to produce female progeny (daughters)

$n_i$ are the weights being the proportion of offspring raised from four parts (of the formula) linking two successive generations.

**(iv) Breeding age:** The age at which the reproduction starts also influence the t. Breeding of animals at the earliest will reduce the t and increase the response per unit of time. The breeding age may be reduced by providing better feeding and care. This will increase the number of replacements available and the older animals are likely to be culled. It will have bidirectional effect on i. By increasing the number of replacements available will increase the i, whereas culling of older animals before their normal productive life will increase the requirement of replacements per year and thus the p will be increased. This in tern will increase i but S will be reduced. The gain attained by minimizing the t will be cancelled by reduction in selection differential. Therefore, more rapid population turn over (i.e. culling older animals) and reduction in t are the determining factors of relatives change in t and S which in turn will affect response per year.

The generation interval (years) in cattle is 4.5 in males and 3.0 in females, 5.0 and 3.5 in buffaloes, 4.0 and 2.0 in sheep and goats, 0.7 and 0.6 in poultry.

Thus, the generation interval is specific to species, sex within the species, and also influenced by the number of offspring raised in any generation, and by the age at which the reproduction starts.

## 6.6.2. Conflict of interest to influence generation interval

To maximize the genetic gain per year it is essential to minimize t. But on the contrary there is an important and interesting aspect of generation intervals which doesn't necessitate its minimization and raises a conflict of interest between generation interval and the genetic gain per generation. The magnitude and direction to which the t should be influenced is decided by the trait of interest with respect to its variability ($\sigma p$ and $h^2$) and its maximum production value (in terms of age of dam/ female at which the peak production is reached), goals and objective of the breeder viz. commercial production or seed stock, market price of the animals, and the cost of rearing the replacement stock, maintaining the animal during production. These are the factors which raise a conflict of interest to influence the generation interval.

To maximize genetic gain per unit of time is the main objective for those maintaining nucleus/breeding stocks. On the other hand, the main aim is not the maximum rate of genetic change for those interested in commercial farming viz. selling of milk and meat animals. But the main objective in commercial herds is to produce the animal products (milk, meat) in a more economically efficient way. For economically efficient production of animal product, it is not necessary to minimize generation interval particularly for females in order to maximize the genetic gain per unit of time. This is because the production in females increases upto a certain age, remains constant for some period and then declines. Thus by retaining older animals more production will be obtained. Therefore, culling the females at an early age to minimize the generation interval will affect adversely the productivity of the herd because the phenotypic potential of the new replacements will be less than older though the genetic potential of young progeny may be more. Moreover, the depreciation per year (taken as selling price at early age minus selling price at old age divided by generation interval) per female is decreased with the increase in generation interval because the selling price at old age after a certain age is constant. Finally, to retain the female stock for longer in the herd will require less number of new replacements per year and thus the new young progeny may be sold in more number. This will fetch more income because younger animals are more costly.

## 6.7. FACTORS AFFECTING RESPONSE TO SELECTION

The change in performance due to artificial selection known as response to selection depends on the following factors:

1. Additive genetic variability in the trait ($\sigma_A$)
2. Intensity of selection (i)
3. Accuracy of selection ($r_{AP}$)
4. Population size
5. Generation interval

### 1. Additive genetic variability in the trait ($s_A$)

The selection acts on additive genetic variability. The variation in breeding values (BV) of the individuals within the population is the raw material to act for artificial selection. The selection will not be effective to bring change if there are no genetic differences among animals. Therefore if $V_A = 0$, the $R = 0$. The magnitude of R increases with the increase in differences in B.V. between animals. However, the genetic variability of a trait (B.V.) within a population is determined by the population and the characters and hence it is beyond the control of breeder. It is therefore better to exploit other factors like intensity and accuracy of selection.

### 2. Intensity of selection (i)

The intensity of selection depends on the proportion (p). of the population selected. When p is small, the selection is said to be more intense or rigorous. But when p is large (increase in proportion selected) then there is decrease in intensity of selection. The R will be more when p will be small. This is a straight forward way to improve the rate of genetic progress. If all animals are selected, the S will be zero and no change in progeny mean will occur. The change occurs if some of the best animals are selected. Therefore, the proportion of animals selected should be less.

## 3. Accuracy of selection ($r_{AP}$)

The selection is effective only when the animals with highest B.V. are selected. The true B.V. of animals is not known. This requires one or more sources of information to know the estimate of B.V. of animal. The information to estimate the true B.V. of an animal may be collected on the performance of the animal itself and or of its any close relative. The estimate of true B.V. so estimated should be as much accurate as it can be to make the selection more accurate. The accuracy of selection is taken as the correlation between the true B.V. of an animal and the source of information (selection criteria) which is denoted as $r_{AP}$ where A is the true B.V. and P is the selection criteria. The selection criteria may be a single record or average of repeated records of the animals itself or on any relative viz. dam or average performance of a group of relatives like full sibs, half sibs or progeny groups.

The $r_{AP}$ is equal to square root of heritability ($r_{AP}$ = h). Thus if $h^2$ estimate is higher, the $r_{AP}$ will also be higher. The $h^2$ is an indication of the reliability of phenotypic value as a guide to the breeding value (B.V.) because the $h^2$ shows the correspondence between B.V. and phenotypic value. In other words, the $h^2$ shows the extent to which the B.V. constitutes the phenotypic value. Thus $r_{AP}$ is directly correlated to $h^2$ as $r_{AP}$ = h which is a measure of the accuracy of selection. It is, therefore, that for maximum accuracy of selection, the $r_{AP}$ must be as high as possible to make the selection accurate. Thus selection will be more accurate when the $h^2$ of the trait is high.

## 4. Population size

The effect of population size on response to selection can be viewed in terms of inbreeding and genetic drift.

**(i) Inbreeding:** The inbreeding is unavoidable in a population of small size. But inbreeding is less when the animals of both sexes are equal which is not possible in animal breeding for the reason that fewer males are required than females. This needs to estimate the effective population size (Ne). The Ne is the number of individuals that would give rise to the same rate of inbreeding, if they bred in the manner of an idealized population, in which the rate of inbreeding is $\Delta F = \frac{1}{2N}$. The Ne reflects the amount of inbreeding expected.

$$Ne = \frac{4SDt}{S+D} \text{ because } \frac{1}{Ne} = \frac{1}{4S} + \frac{1}{4D} \text{ or } Ne = \frac{4SD}{S+D}$$

$$\text{And } \frac{1}{2Ne} = \frac{1}{8S} + \frac{1}{8D}$$

Where, S and D are the number of sires and dams entering the population per year.

t is the average of males and females generation interval in years.

The increase in inbreeding per year is about $\Delta F = \frac{1}{2Net}$ which becomes in case of using few males as $\Delta F = \frac{1}{8St^2}$

The effect of inbreeding is to reduce the amount of genetic variability ($V_A$) and reduction in performance (inbreeding depression). This causes a decrease in response to selection. It is thus suggested that there should be sufficient Ne to reduce ΔF less than 1% per year.

**(ii) Genetic drift:** As a result of sampling of small number of genes in small size population, the genetic drift arises which means that the change is random in gene frequency. This may cause the loss of favourable alleles from the population. This will thus reduce the response to selection. Not only this but the ultimate limit to selection will be less and will be reached more quickly.

### 5. Generation interval

The response to selection or the genetic gain is obtained in next generation and the generation interval is different in different species. Therefore, in order to get the response per year, the response to selection is divided by the generation interval. The genetic gain per year is higher in the herd that breeds with younger animals (at younger age) than the herd that breeds comparatively at later age.

### Dependence of factors affecting response to selection

It has been discussed that $h^2$, S, and t are the three factors which affect the response per unit of time. All these three factors are related in such a way that the change in magnitude of one factor may affect the change in the magnitude of other factor in an adverse way.

The $h^2$ of a trait may be increased based on average of more number of records. This will increase the generation interval and decrease the selection differential because the average of more records is more close to the genotypic value of the animal. Secondly, if the generation interval is minimized by culling the animals after obtaining only one progeny, then the selection differential will be decreased. Therefore, in order to influence the overall genetic gain there should be a proper compromise between these factors affecting the response to selection.

## 6.8. COMPLICATIONS OF SELECTION

The selection had been effective in various species of animals by eliminating the undesirable genotypes and allowing the best to multiply. The animals best adapted to given environment survive and produce more number of progeny. Artificial selection had been effective to develop better breeds of livestock than ancestors. The natural and artificial selection have been operating even before the laws of heredity were known. After the discovery of the laws of inheritance, a number of new breeds of livestock have been developed. However, the selection is not so easy to imply and to give immediate results. The selection fails to give the desired results and thus dampen the enthusiasm of many breeders. There are some complications of selection which are responsible for not giving desired results. These can be grouped genetical or theoretical and operational/practical complications.

### 6.8.1. Genetical complications

The genetical complications which are responsible for the failure of selection effect are as:

**(i) Phenotypic value as joint effect of genotype and environment:** The environment has a great effect to mask the real genetic worth of an animal. Thus the environment may lead to mistake in selection when the different animals get different environment. It is therefore better to keep the animals under selection in suitable and uniform environment so as to recognize the real genetic differences to increase the accuracy of selection.

**(ii) Selection is based on phenotype:** Most of the economic characters are controlled by polygenes and hence it is not possible to identify the better genotypes accurately. The selection is thus made on the phenotype. Moreover, the G-E interaction affects the phenotypic value and hence the phenotypic value is changed over space and age of the animal.

**(iii) Heritability:** The heritability estimates of most of the traits are low and changes over space and time as well as by the mating system. The phenotypic value is a good indicator of the genotypic value only when the $h^2$ of a trait is high.

**(iv) Gene segregation:** The superiority of the individual is due to additive effect of favourable genes, better gene combinations, heterosis and better environment. The gene combinations are broken due to their segregation and independent assortment. Therefore, the progeny of better parents have a tendency to regress towards the population mean. The advantage of favourable combination of genes can be exploited by inbreeding to increase the homozygosity and by crossing the inbred lines to take the advantage of heterosis. However, the superior heterozygotes can not be used as breeding stock.

**(v) Gene action:** The genes act in different ways when combined viz. dominance, over dominance and epistasis. The selection favours the heterozygotes in this situation. This advocates the crossing of suitable inbred lines.

**Correlation among traits:** The selection is less effective when there is negative genetic correlation between desirable traits (milk yield and fat %) and when

**(vi)** there is positive correlation between desirable and undesirable traits (milk yield and susceptibility to mastitis).

**(vii) Inbreeding:** The selected lines are small in size and hence the inbreeding is unavoidable. Thus there is some effect of inbreeding depression. Therefore gain obtained by selection is offset by the effect of inbreeding. The depressing effect of inbreeding can be counteracted by selecting the superior foundation stock, followed by intense selection to offset the effect of inbreeding and to adopt the mating system of the 'mating best with the best' i.e. selective breeding or controlled breeding.

### 6.8.2. Operational complications

Some complications arise when the selection is exercised. These are as:

**(i) Foundation stock:** The parental population should be genetically superior with genetic variability so as to make the selection effective because the selection acts on additive genetic variability.

**(ii) Population size:** The population size is generally small and hence the intensity of selection and the selection differential is low. This makes the selection ineffective. Therefore, the herd size should be large.

**(iii) No. of traits:** The ranking of animals for single trait is easy but become difficult as the number of traits under selection is increased for the reason that an animal may be superior in one trait but inferior for the other trait. Therefore, only the traits of greatest economic value should be considered for selection. Moreover, the intensity of selection is decreased by selection for more than one trait and it is equal to $1\sqrt{n}$ for each trait.

**(iv) Change in goal of selection:** The goal of selection is changed without achieving the first goal and hence the primary objective of selection is forfeited.

**(v) Selection limit:** The genetic variability is reduced or completely vanished under long term selection and hence it makes the selection ineffective. This requires the introduction of new genes from outside.

## 6.9. CONSTRAINTS IN GENETIC IMPROVEMENT

In India, about 60-80% of the population of most of the species of farm animals are non descript with very low production performance and the animal rearing is mostly in the hands of farmers. However, in the past, some organized farms were established for maintaining purebred animals and to produce genetically superior bulls for distribution to various agencies engaged in animal rearing. The constraints in genetic improvement through selection are little different for farmer's herd and the organized herd.

At farmer's herd, the major constraints for improvement have been unscientific breeding, inadequate nutrition and poor management including the health care. The main reasons are that the farmers are not organized, keeping very few number of animals, their poor economic status and illiteracy. They are thus forced to mate the female animals with the sires, available in or around the village, irrespective of genetic merit. They are interested to get their female animals pregnant to initiate new lactation and to get the calf/lamb/kid crop.

The genetic improvement is possible by

(i) selection within improved breeds

(ii) upgrading of non descript and low producing females with sires of high genetic merit of improved breeds,

(iii) crossbreeding between two or more breeds

The genetic progress through selection depends mainly on heritability (genetic variability) of the trait and the selection differential. Besides, the genetic progress per unit of time is more important than the progress per generation and hence the generation interval is an important factor in reckoning the genetic progress. Lastly, the population size also influences the genetic progress of a herd. The effects of all these factors in influencing the response to selection have been discussed under section 6.7 of this chapter.

The constraints in genetic improvement and suggestion to overcome them are as under:

**1. Low heritability estimates of the economic traits:** The $h^2$ estimates of most of the traits are low to moderate which indicates small genetic variability in these traits. The magnitude of genetic improvement increases with the increase in differences in B.V. between individuals. The $h^2$ can be increased by reducing the environmental variance. Secondly, in view of low $h^2$ estimate, the progeny testing as criteria of selection is advocated.

**2. Low accuracy of selection:** The accuracy of selection is taken as the 'a h' as discussed under section 6.3. In view of low $h^2$ estimates, the $h = r_{AP}$ is low. Therefore, efforts should be made to increase the accuracy of selection, as discussed earlier in this chapter.

**3. Low intensity of selection (low scope of selection):** This primarily depends on the proportion of animals selected (p). The intensity of selection is very less particularly in case of female selection. There is no scope of selection of females on voluntary grounds (for the traits under selection like milk production in dairy animals). This reduces the selection differential and hence the genetic progress.

**4. Population size:** The herd/flock size is very small even on organized farms. This invites the inbreeding and the genetic drift as well as limits the intensity of selection. There is thus required to increase the capacity of the organized farms or to run the P.T. programme in associated herds.

## 6.10. NUMERICAL SOLVED EXAMPLES

**Example 6.1:** Clayton et al. (1957) worked out the expected and observed response to selection for abdominal bristle number in Drosophila. The $h^2$ from base population was 0.52 and the base population had an average of 35.3 bristle numbers whereas the selected parents had 40.6. The numbers of bristles in offspring generation were 37.9

### Solution

$S = 40.6 - 35.3 = 5.3$ bristles

$R = h^2S = 0.52 \times 5.3 = 2.8$ (expected response)

Realized $R = 37.9 - 35.3 = 2.6$

**Example 6.2:** In the example of 6.1, the standard deviation ($\sigma p$) was 3.35. The parents selected were 20 male and 20 females out of 100, giving the selection intensities as 1.40. The expected response can be estimated as:

## Solution

$R = i\sigma p\ h^2$

$= 1.4 \times 3.35 \times 0.52 = 2.44.$

**Example 6.3:** A herd of Sahiwal cows had the herd average of 2000 kg milk of first lactation and the average of the selected population was 2200 kg. The $h^2$ estimate of milk yield was 0.25 and the generation interval was 5 years. Estimate the time required to double the milk production.

## Solution

$S = 2200\text{-}2000 = 200$ kg

$R = h^2S = 0.25 \times 200 = 50$ kg

$\Delta G/\text{year} = 50/5 = 10$ kg

No. of generation required to double the milk production = 2000/40 = 50

And hence 40 generation = 40 x 5 = 200 years.

**Example 6.4:** The average annual greasy fleece weight of a flock of sheep was 2.0 kg and after culling the low producers the average increased to 2.5 kg. The EPA of 10 rams used in the flock was 3.0 kg and after culling the low producers the average increased to 4.0 kg. Assume the $h^2$ of fleece production as 0.4 and generation interval from dam to daughter as 4 years and that of sire to daughter as 3 years. Estimate the expected genetic gain per generation and per year

## Solution

$S = 2.5 - 2.0 = 0.5$ kg (females)

$S = 4.0 - 3.0 = 1.0$ kg (males)

$\Delta G(F) = 0.4 \times 0.5 = 0.2$ kg

$\Delta G(M) = 0.4 \times 1.0 = 0.4$ kg

$$\Delta G \text{ per generation} = \frac{0.2 + 0.4}{2} = 0.3\ kg$$

$\Delta G$ per year (F) = 0.2/4 = 0.05 kg

$\Delta G$ per year (M) = 0.4/3 = 0.13 kg

$$\text{Average } \Delta G \text{ per year} = \frac{0.5 + 0.13}{2} = 0.09\ kg$$

**Ans:** $\Delta G$ per generation = 0.3 kg = 300 gm

$\Delta G$ per generation = 0.09 kg = 90 gm

**Example 6.5:** Find out the observed selection differential, standardized and weighted (effective) selection differential from the data given below with = 1900 units and $\sigma p$ = 16 units.

| Sire No. | 1 | 2 | 3 | 4 | 5 | 6 | Total |
|---|---|---|---|---|---|---|---|
| Trait | 2000 | 1970 | 1920 | 1880 | 1850 | 1900 | 11520 |
| No. of progeny ($n_1$) | 10 | 15 | 12 | 14 | 11 | 8 | 70 |

**Solution**

(i) Observed $S = \overline{P}_S - \overline{P} = \frac{11520}{6} - 1900 = 1920 - 1900 = 20.0$

(ii) Standardized $S = S/\sigma P = 20/16 = 1.25$

(iii) Weighted $S = \frac{\sum x_i n_i}{\sum n_i} - \overline{P}_o = \frac{134460}{70} - 1900 = 1920.8 - 1900 = 20.8$

**Example 6.6:** The following are the date of birth in years for sires and dams of 10 calves born in the year 1975. Estimate the generation interval for sire and dam

| Calf No. | 1 | 2 | 3 | 4 | 5 | 6 | 7 | 8 | 9 | 10 |
|---|---|---|---|---|---|---|---|---|---|---|
| Sire | 1970 | 1968 | 1970 | 1968 | 1971 | 1970 | 1970 | 1972 | 1971 | 1970 |
| Dam | 1971 | 1967 | 1969 | 1970 | 1971 | 1968 | 1965 | 1970 | 1967 | 1967 |

**Solution**

G.I. = year calf born – year sire or dam born

$$\text{G.I. for sires} = \frac{(5+7+5+4+4+5+5+3+4+5)}{10} = 5.0 \text{ years}$$

$$\text{G.I. for dams} = \frac{(4+8+6+5+4+7+10+5+8+8)}{10} = 7.0 \text{ years}$$

**Example 6.7:** The AFK of 500 goats is given here. Find out the G.I. for AFK.

| Age at kidding (years) | 2 | 3 | 4 | 5 |
|---|---|---|---|---|
| No. of goats | 140 | 170 | 100 | 90 |

**Solution:**

$$\text{G.I.} = \frac{(140\times 2+170\times 3+100\times 4+90\times 5)}{500}$$

$$= \frac{1640}{500} = 3.28 \text{ years}$$

## QUESTIONS

**6.1.** What are the methods of increasing accuracy in selection of breeding females as well as males, separately? (*ARS 1976*)

***Or***

Discuss in detail the various methods of increasing the efficiency of selection in livestock (*ARS 1981*)

***Or***

How can you maximize the genetic progress for animal population undergoing continues selection for a heritable character (*ARS 1985*)

**6.2.** How selection brings about change in biological population? Discuss the obstacles for quick response through selection.

(*ARS 1993*)

**6.3.** Explain the following:

Improvement of an economic trait depends upon heritability as also on its selection differential. Illustrate your answer with specific examples for dairy cattle and poultry in India. (*ARS 1982*)

**6.4.** (*a*) In your opinion what are the major constraints experienced in the improvement of livestock production in the country.

(*b*) What strategy initiatives you like to take for improving milk production (*ARS 1995*)

Discuss the factors that aid and hamper the genetic response to selection. (*ARS 1984*)

***

# 7

# MEASUREMENT OF RESPONSE

## 7.1. PURPOSE OF MEASURING RESPONSE TO SELECTION

The response to selection is also known as the genetic change. The comparison of the mean performance of two successive generations under selection programme provides an estimate of the genetic change or response to selection. The response to selection is measured for the following purposes.

1. To know whether selection is likely to result in genetic improvement.
2. To compare the expected response to selection ($R=h^2S$) with that actually obtained in progeny generation (realized genetic change)
3. To compare the rate of genetic change under different sire selection schemes and different breeding programme viz. inbreeding, recurrent selection, hybridization or strain/line crossing

The measurement of response to selection has certain assumptions which are as under:

1. The genetic change is entirely due to selection and there is no change in environmental conditions.
2. The generation means should be free from the effects of random genetic drift arising from sampling of gametes in each generation.

## 7.2. PROBLEMS IN MEASUREMENT OF RESPONSE

The R depends on the $h^2$ of the parental generation and hence the R in later generations can not be predicted without predetermining the $h^2$ in each generation. The $h^2$ is expected to change in each generation under selection for the reasons that selection changes the gene frequencies and reduces the variance which in turn affects the $h^2$. However, the magnitude of change in gene frequencies and $h^2$ is very small unless only a few loci are involved. Thus the response is usually maintained with little change over several generations.

The measurement of response for more generation of selection is problematic. The response to selection varies from generation to generation and leads to the variability of generation means. The generation means do not progress in a regular fashion but fluctuate erratically and for this the response can not be measured with accuracy. The best is to measure the average response per generation.

**I. Variability of generation means:**

The different causes assigned to the variability of generation means are as:

- Population size which causes the random drift and the sampling errors in estimating generation means
- Variation in selection differential
- Effects of environmental factors

**(i) Population size:** The selected lines are small in size. Thus there will be genetic drift and sampling effect which will cause the changes in gene frequencies at random. This will consequently lead to change of generation means. The random drift has cumulative effect because any change in gene frequency in one generation act as the starting point for the change in the next generation. The increase in population size can help to reduce the variability due to random drift and sampling errors.

**(ii) Selection differential:** The selection differential in different generations is different. This happens due to the reason that different parents do not contribute equally to the offspring generation in terms of their number of progeny. The unequal contribution of different parents is caused by natural selection and artificial selection.

The artificial selection of parents separates the parental population in two groups viz. selected and culled. These two groups differ in gene frequencies. On the other hand, the natural selection exert its influence on change of gene frequency in two stages viz. differences of fertility among the parents and the viability of parents as well as among their progeny. Therefore, the change in gene frequency due to selection occurs at three stages viz. artificial selection among the parents, natural differences of fertility among the parents, and natural differences of viability among the parents and progeny generation. Depending upon the choice of breeder some parents are culled without having reproduced at all, some are culled after getting one or two progeny and others are not culled as long as they can reproduce in the herd. The consequence of these three stages of selection is that some parents contribute more offspring than others.

**Weighting the selection differential:** The problem of unequal contribution of parents (selected to produce the progeny generation) in terms of their different number of offspring that are available for measurement in the progeny generation necessitates the weighting of the selection differential of the parents according to the number of offspring from different parents measured. This weighted selection differential is really the effective selection differential which is more relevant to the response observed in the progeny mean. Thus, it requires to distinguish between two types of selection differential viz. effective (weighted) and the expected (unweighted). The expected selection differential is the superiority of selected parents taken as deviation from population mean as defined earlier. Whereas the effective selection differential is obtained by weighting the expected selection differential (deviation of parents from population means) according to the proportionate contribution of the progeny measured from each parent. Therefore, the effective selection differential is the weighted mean deviation of parents. The weights are given to each parent (pair of parents) according to their proportionate contribution of individuals measured in next generation. The weighted selection differential takes into account the effect of natural selection also. Natural selection will be taken to opposing artificial selection if selected individuals with better phenotypes have low fertility and viability. The joint effects of natural and artificial selection together can be measured by weighting the selection differential. The effect of natural selection can be determined by comparing the effective with the expected selection differential. The ratio of effective to expected S, if less than 1 indicates that natural selection is operative. However the effective selection differential does not cover the effect of differences of viability among the offspring. Thus the whole effect of natural selection is not accounted for in the effective selection differential.

Falconer (1955) compared the effective and expected selection differential in a two way selection experiment for 6 weeks body weight in mice for 30 generations in upward selection and for 24 generations in downward lines. He could not find any vertical difference between the effective and expected S in upward selection which indicated that natural selection was not operating to influence the response. On the other hand, in downward selection, the effective S was found less than expected particularly with the increase in generation number beyond 18. This indicated that natural selection hindered the artificial selection and reduced the observed response by reducing the effective S. The natural selection could not influence the fertility of mice in upward selection because large mice produced large litters than small mice and litters were reduced to 8 young at birth for standardization. Litters having less than 8 young in upward selection were very few and so differential fertility had no effect, while in downward line the litters with 8 young were very few. Thus, the effective selection differential in downward lines was reduced to fewer-young and further the smallest mice after 18 generations did not breed at all which further reduced the effective selection differential.

**(iii) Environmental differences:** The variability of generation means is created by a number of environmental factors like differences in climatic conditions, nutrition level of animals and differences in general managemental practices which changes over time. With the passage of time the environmental conditions (climatic conditions, nutrition, managemental practices) are changing. It is well known that the genotypic value of a quantitative character is modified and changed by the environmental factors. Therefore, any change in subsequent generation mean may also be due to change in environmental conditions. Thus, both the genetic and non-genetic factors contribute to the changes in performance traits in subsequent generations. Therefore, these changes in generation means reflect the phenotypic trend or phenotypic change in the character over time rather than only the genetic change. Thus, the direct comparison of generation means does not provide an estimate of the genetic change (genetic gain) but it provide an estimate of phenotypic change ($\Delta$P). Therefore, it requires partitioning the phenotypic change into its component parts viz. genetic change ($\Delta$G) and environmental change ($\Delta E$). The partitioning of $\Delta P$ is the main problem to measure the genetic change.

**II. Specific problems to measure response to selection in large livestock species**

Besides the problem of variability of generation mean in measuring the genetic change, a number of other specific problems also occur which are specific to large livestock. These are:

i) The generations are overlapping in large livestock
ii) The sires are compared in different herds, years and regions
iii) The selection intensities and also the selection criteria are different for the two sexes

**(i) Overlapping generation**

Large livestock species (dairy animals, sheep etc.) have overlapping generations. This means that the numbers of generations of selection are different for different animals. The older parents experience less cumulative selection than the younger parents. Consequently the progeny of younger parents are genetically superior to older parents. When the generation number of sire and dam of each offspring differ, the generation number of each offspring ($T_o$) is taken as:

$$T_O = 1 + \frac{T_S + T_D}{2}$$

The estimate of the $\Delta G$ per generation is obtained as the intra year regression of offspring performance on offspring generation number. This method also needs to adjust the performance record of offspring for dam's effect.

Another method to measure the response from selection is to compare the contemporary progenies produced by sires belonging to two different generations (Smith, 1962). This method involves the equal allotment of dams of each age and generation to the sires of the two generations. The annual genetic change can be estimated as:

$$\Delta G = 2\sum_{i=1}^{k} \frac{\bar{X}_1 - \bar{X}_2}{mk}$$

Where, K is the number of years for which the comparison is done,

m is the age difference in years between two groups of sires (older sires which are progeny tested, and younger sires which are non tested).

$\bar{X}_1$ and $\bar{X}_2$ are the average performance of progeny from younger and older sires, respectively.

**(ii) Comparison of sires in different herds**

The ranking of different sires and their comparison can only be made if all of them are tested in one herd or population, and also in the same year. This is because the herd differences and year differences are caused by both genetic and environmental factors. To overcome this limitation, the sires are compared after making adjustment of data for the environment factors viz. herd differences, year differences etc. The sires which have been tested with large number of progeny in two herds, two years etc. are taken as reference sires and included with new sires in progeny testing programme. The use of reference sires provides a genetic control as an aid to compare the different sires which do not have progeny in the same herd. The concept of reference sire is clear from the following example:

Suppose the two sires X and Z are progeny tested in one herd. The sire X ranked first by a difference of 30 units than sire Z and in another herd, two sires Y and Z are progeny tested and the sire z ranked first with a difference of 20 units than sire Y as shown below:

| **Herds** | **Sires and their ranking** | | |
|---|---|---|---|
| | **X** | **Y** | **Z** |
| I | + 30* | Not used | - 30 |
| II | Not used | -20 | + 20* |
| | Difference between X and Y = 30*+20* = 50 units | | |

In the above PT programme, a direct comparison of sires X and Y is not possible but they can be compared in reference to sire Z which has been progeny tested in both the herds. The two sires X and Y are expected to differ in progeny performance by 50 units.

## 7.3. MEASUREMENT OF RESPONSE

Considering the partitioning of the phenotypic superiority of parents into its component parts (genetic and environmental), the phenotypic change ($\Delta P$) between two generations can be partitioned into the corresponding changes – the genetic change ($\Delta G$) and the environmental change ($\Delta E$). The $\Delta P$ equals $\Delta G$ only when environmental change between generations ($\Delta E$) is zero. This is possible only when environmental effects on parents and progeny generations are exactly the same. However, the effects of environmental factors are beyond control and, therefore, response to selection of a population can be measured by partitioning the $\Delta P$ into its genetic and environmental parts:

$$\Delta P = \Delta G + \Delta E$$

The variation due to changes in environment can be reduced or eliminated by two methods in estimating the genetic change. The **first method** is the **control system** to estimate the environmental change using the control population whose genetic value remains unchanged over generations. The **second method** is to control the environmental change either in the experiment or in statistical analysis (phenotypic and genetic trend).

**7.3.1. Use of control population:** There are three ways of control system. These have been discussed here.

### (a) Unselected control population (Random bred control population)

The unselected control population is one in which there is no selection and the parents in each generation are taken (selected) entirely at random. As no genetic change between generations ($\Delta G_C$=O) is expected in control population, so the phenotypic change occurred will be caused by the environmental factors ($\Delta P_C = \Delta E_C$). The effect of environment will be the same in control and in selected population ($\Delta E_C = \Delta E_S$). The change in phenotype of the selected population will be caused due to change in genetic structure as a result of selection plus due to change in environment corresponding to $\Delta G_S$ and $\Delta E_S$ respectively. Thus

$$\Delta P_S = \Delta G_S + \Delta E_S$$

Therefore, the genetic change ($\Delta G$) can be estimated by difference in the mean phenotypic merit of the control and selected population as:

$$\Delta G = \Delta P_S - \Delta P_C$$

$$= \{\Delta G_S + \Delta E_S\} - \Delta E_C$$

$$= \Delta G_S \qquad \text{(since } \Delta E_s = \Delta E_C\text{)}$$

**Assumptions:** The expectation of control population for no genetic change ($\Delta G_C$ =0) is based on the following assumptions:

- The control and selected population are of the same genetic background so that both the populations respond equally to the same changes in environment.
- Both the populations (control and selected) should be raised under similar environments and management practices so that $\Delta E_C = \Delta E_S$.
- The size of control population should be large enough so that there is no genetic change due to sampling of gametes (genetic draught) or due to natural selection.
- There is no G x E interaction

This control system has certain **limitations**. (i) It is mostly used in poultry because it is easy to maintain control population. On the other hand, to maintain an unselected control population of large livestock is costly of space and capital investment. (ii) The second limitation to use this control system is that it leads to a biased estimate of $\Delta G$ in later-generations. This is because the selected lines and control lines becomes genetically different after several generations of selection and hence they respond differently to the same change in environmental effects. In order to overcome this problem it is better to take new unselected control population every generation by randomly choosing the individuals from selected population. In the absence of control population which is the situation mostly occurred in the improvement of domestic animals, it is difficult to decide the magnitude of the improvement due to selection because of the progressive change in the management conditions.

The control population provides a genetic constant (no genetic change) and reflects only variation caused by the environment. The control populations are the herds, flocks or lines which are bred continuously at random as a base or reference. The size of **control population** should be large enough to maintain effective random mating as well as to keep the inbreeding level low as far as possible. The increase in rate of inbreeding per generation depends upon the number of males and females in the population. The rate with which the homozygosity is increased is given by the following formula (Lush 1945, A.B. Plans):

$$\Delta F = \frac{1}{8M} + \frac{1}{8F}$$

Where, = the increase in inbreeding per generation

M and F = number of males and females in the population, respectively.

The factor $\frac{1}{8M}$ is more important because the males are less in numbers. This formula is used for the whole population regarding the rate of inbreeding in relation to population size. It is suggested that the population should contain about 25-50 males and 50-100 females. The control populations are mainly used in poultry. The control population size kept in Cornell (USA) is 50 cocks and 250 hens, for pigs the size is 12 boars and 12 gilts (USA) while it is 16 boars and 32 gilts in U.K., 10 rams and 250 ewes (UK) and 1 bull and 25 cows for Hereford cattle selection (USA).

Random change in gene frequency due to random genetic drift is the main problem in control population. The problem of random drift can be avoided to keep reconstituting the control population or to maintain at different locations so as to allow comparison between control populations and to have a check on random drift.

## (b) Two way selection or bidirectional selection

The entire population is divided in two groups – one for higher phenotypic merit and other for low phenotypic merit, and then selection is done in both the lines for increased and decreased performance. Both the lines are maintained contemporaneously under the same environmental and managemental practices. Thus both the lines are affected simultaneously to the same extent by the environmental changes and each of the two lines provides control for the other. This reduces the variation between generation means because the environmental changes affect both the population equally. The response is measured from the difference between the two lines which is about twice as great as that in the two lines separately as:

$$\Delta P_u = \Delta G + \Delta E$$

$$\Delta P_D = \Delta G + \Delta E$$

and the difference between two lines is:

$$\Delta P_u - \Delta P_D = (\Delta G + \Delta E) - (-\Delta G + \Delta E) = 2\Delta G$$

Therefore, the estimate of genetic change or genetic gain ($\Delta$ G) is half the difference.

This system has the following **limitations**:

- It has been observed that the response is not equal in the two lines (upward and downward lines) and it is called as asymmetry of response to selection.

The response is unequal for various reasons discussed in chapter 13.

- This system is expensive and not feasible for large livestock because the selection for decrease performance is not justified.

## (c) Repeat mating

This is another control system to estimate $\Delta G$ and $\Delta E$. The same parents are repeatedly mated in adjacent years to get full sibs. This leads to an expectation that the full sibs born in adjacent years will not differ genetically and the difference in the progeny of the same sire is due to environment. However, single pair of sibs related to the extent of 50% is expected to have only half of their genes in common and so will differ genetically. Therefore, the average of many pairs of full sibs should be taken with the expectation of their equal genetic merit. The average difference between the phenotypes of full sibs from adjacent years is taken as an estimate of environmental change ($\Delta E$) between two years.

$$\Delta E = \Delta P_{\text{I year}} - \Delta P_{\text{II year}}$$

The phenotypic change between two adjacent years is also obtained for the entire population which contained both the component parts of the phenotypic change ($\Delta P = \Delta G + \Delta E$). Therefore, an estimate of genetic change is obtained by substracting the environmental change (estimated from full sibs) from the phenotypic change estimated for the entire population between two years. Thus the genetic change ($\Delta G$) is obtained from the difference of phenotypic change in entire population ($\Delta P$=$\Delta G$+$\Delta E$) and the environmental change ($\Delta E$) of repeated progeny:

$$\begin{aligned}\Delta G &= \Delta P \text{ in entire population} - \Delta E \text{ in repeated progeny}\\ &= \Delta P - \Delta E\\ &= (\Delta G + \Delta E) - \Delta E\end{aligned}$$

The method of repeat mating has the advantage relative to control population method that there is no accumulation of drift variance and that there is little chance of G x E interaction.

However, several records from several years need to be analysed. In this case, an estimate of average phenotypic change per year ($\Delta P$/year) is obtained from the linear regression of phenotype on time and likewise an estimate of average $\Delta E$ per year is obtained from linear regression of cumulative $\Delta E$ on time. Now the estimate of average genetic change per year is obtained from the difference of the two regressions.

**Requirements:** This system has the following requirements

- This control scheme of repeat mating requires a sufficient number of repeat mating for each pair of adjacent years.
- Secondly, it requires the **adjustment of age effect of dams,** at least for traits which are affected by dam's age. The dams in different adjacent years will differ in their age and so the progeny of repeat mating (full sibs) will differ due to environmental differences plus due to the effect of differences in dams' age. Therefore, $\Delta E$ will be the biased estimate and so will be the $\Delta G$. To

overcome this biasness, the records for dams' effect are adjusted, or like-aged progeny from repeat mating in adjacent years (i.e. like-aged full sibs) are measured and compared.

**Advantages:** The repeat mating is more useful and restricted to poultry and pigs, and is not practicable for large livestock. This control **scheme is advantageous** because (i) it is less expensive even in a commercial herd/flock, (ii) it does not involve the problem of G x E interaction when there is divergence in the selected and control populations, (iii) the same genetic background is not an assumption and (iv) the population size is not a problem to avoid the effect of inbreeding.

## 7.3.2. Statistical analysis (Phenotypic and genetic trend)

### 1. Estimation of phenotypic trend

The change in mean over years is the phenotypic trend over time. It is estimated as regression of performance on time (year) as:

$$\Delta P = b_{P.T} = \frac{\sum Pt}{\sum t^2}$$

with its S.E. as $\left[\frac{\sum p^2 - b_{P.T}(\sum Pt)}{(\sum t^2)(N-2)}\right]^{1/2}$

Where, $b_{P.T}$ = linear regression of population performance (P) on time (year) of calving (T)

$\sum Pt$ = corrected sum of product for performance and time

$$= \sum PT - \frac{\sum P \sum T}{N}$$

$\sum P^2$ = correct SS of performance (trait)

$$= \sum P^2 - \frac{(\sum P)^2}{N}$$

$\sum t^2$ = corrected SS for time taken as deviation from its means

$$= \sum T^2 - \frac{(\sum T)^2}{N}$$

N = Total number of records

## 2. Estimation of genetic trend

The method of estimation of genetic change was developed by Smith (1962). This was based on the comparison of mean performance of paternal half sisters in different years. Therefore, it requires the continuity of the genotypes over different years. However, the changes in performance of trait of paternal half sibs in successive years reflect the genetic plus environmental trend as:

$E(b_{P.T}) = g + e$

$$E\left[b(P - \bar{P}).T/s = -\frac{1}{2}g\right]$$

Where, $b_{P.T}$ = linear regression of performance (P) on time (T)

$b(P - \bar{P}).T/s$ = intra sire linear regression of P on T, each record being taken as deviation from contemporaries

g = genetic trend

e = environmental trend

The genetic trend ($\Delta G$) was calculated as :

$$= \Delta G = -2b(P - \bar{P}).T/s$$

$$S.E.\ \Delta G = \sqrt{4^{V}\ b(P - \bar{P}).T/s}$$

This method eliminates year effect in environment and hence it is more precise.

The following expectations of regression have founded the method of Smith (1962) or some modification of it

$E(b_{P.T}) = g + e$

$E(b_{P.T/S}) = 0.5g + e$

$E[\,b(P - \bar{P}).T/s = -0.5\,g$

$E(b_{P.T/SD}) = e$

The $b_{P.T./s}$ is the regression within sire which gives e+0.5g because the sires did not vary and only dams contribute to genetic progress.

$$b(P - \bar{P}).T/S = (0.5\,g + e) - (g + e) = -0.5\,g$$

$b_{P.T/SD}$ = regression of performance on time within sire and dam = e because individuals being F.S. are expected to have same B.V.

The followings are obtained by combining above 4 equations

$$\hat{g} = 2(b_{P.T} - b_{P.T/S})$$

$$\hat{g} = b_{P.T} - b_{P.T}/SD$$

$$\hat{g} = -2[b(P - \bar{P}).T/S]$$

Smith (1962) estimated the rate of genetic change as $2(b_{P.T} - b_{S.T})$ (where, $b_{P.T}$ is the linear regression of population performance on time and $b_{S.T}$ is the within sire regression of progeny performance on time.

To avoid year effect, the expression 2b (P-S) T was suggested which is twice the pooled within sire regression on time of the difference between the population and individual sire means.

## 3. Environmental trend

This is taken as a difference of $\Delta P$ and $\Delta G$

Therefore, $\Delta E = \Delta P - \Delta G$

$$S.E.\ \Delta E = \sqrt{SE(\Delta P)^2 + SE(\Delta G)^2}$$

## 4. Genetic change by direct selection

The method given by Rendel and Robertson (1950) is used as a measure of genetic change of measuring the genetic superiority and generation interval from 4 paths of parents to offspring

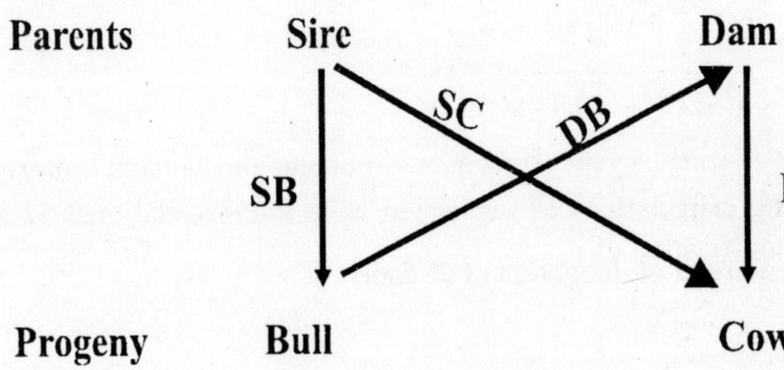


$$\Delta G/_{yr} = \frac{G_{SC} + G_{SB} + G_{DC} + G_{DB}}{L_{SC} + L_{SB} + L_{DC} + L_{DB}}$$

**1. Expected genetic gain by selection of sires to produce daughters ($G_{SC}$):** The genetic superiority of i[th] sire having n daughters is estimated as:

$$G_{SC_{(i)}} = \frac{2n_i h^2}{4 + (n_i - 1)h^2}(\overline{X}D_{(i)} - \mu)$$

$\overline{X}D_{(i)}$ = Average record of $n_i$ daughters of i[th] sire

$$G_{SC} = \frac{\sum_{i=1}^{S} n_i G_{SC(i)}}{\sum_{i=1}^{S} n_i}$$

**2. Genetic superiority of sires of bulls ($G_{SB}$) :** Expected genetic gain due to selection of B.V. on the basis of their sires performance is measured as :

$$G_{SB(i)} = \frac{2n_i h^2}{4 + (n_i - 1)h^2}(\overline{X}_D - \mu)$$

$\overline{X}_D$ = Average of records of n daughters of sire of i[th] bull

$$G_{SB} = \frac{\sum n_j . G_{SB(j)}}{\sum n_j}$$

Where, $n_j$ = Number of daughters of i[th] bull.

**3. Genetic superiority of dams of cows ($G_{DC}$):** Expected $\Delta G$ by selection of cows to produce daughters is taken as :

The genetic superiority of i[th] dam of j[th] cow was estimated as

$$G_{DC(i)} = \frac{n_i h^2}{1 + (n_i - 1)r}(\overline{X}_D - \mu)$$

Where, $n_i$ = no. of repeated records of i[th] dam

$\overline{X}_D$ = dams average

$G_{Dc} = m\ n_j\ G_{DC}\ (ij)$

Where $n_j$ = number of daughters of j[th] dam

m =total number of dams.

**4. Genetic superiority of dam's of bulls (GDB):** Expected genetic gain due to selection of breeding bulls on the basis of their dam's performance

The genetic superiority of dam of i[th] bull was computed as:

$$G_{DB(i)} = \frac{nh^2}{1 + (n - 1)r} \text{(Dam's average - } \mu)$$

where, $n_i$ = number of records of the dam of i[th] bull

$$G_{DB} = \sum_{i=1}^{S} n_i\ G_{DB(i)}$$

Where, S = Number of bulls

The $G_{DB}$ was estimated by weighted sum of $G_{DB(i)}$, weights being the number of daughters ($n_i$) sired by the son of i[th] dam.

**Generation intervals for each path**

$L_{SC}$ = Average age of sires when their daughters were born which entered in herd

$L_{SB}$ = Average age of sires when their sons (bulls) were born and used as breeding bulls

$L_{DC}$ = Average age of dams when their daughters were born which entered in herd

$L_{DB}$ = Average age of dams when their sons (bulls) were born and used as breeding bulls

## 7.4. SELECTION BETWEEN POPULATIONS – POPULATION COMPARISON

The selection exploits the genetic variation whether exists between and or within the population. The different breeds or strains are kept by different breeders for their particular preference even for the same purpose. However, selection between populations requires the information on the relative merits of various populations under any set of conditions for making comparison. This task is difficult for single breeder as it requires relatively long time and large number of animals. Therefore, the government, universities, breed societies having the resources necessary for comparison are involved in this work.

### Requirements for comparing population

- The most important requirement is that all stock should be treated equally and hence comparison is conducted in a manner that minimizes the chances of any population receiving favoured treatment.
- Each population should be represented by a random sample of animals or the method and extend of selection of animals should be similar for each population. In case of P.T., the mates must be selected at random from the tester population. Moreover, in case of comparison at more than one place, the stock from each population should be allocated at random to each place.
- The type of comparison is an important factor. There should be direct comparison which means that all populations under test for comparison should belong to the same location. Similarly, purebred progeny should not be compared with crossbred.
- The numbers of measurements made on each population under test also influence the efficiency of a comparison. In this context, there are two important points. The first is that it is the number of sires represented in each population rather than number of progeny per sire, which determine the efficiency of comparison. Thus each population under test should be represented by many sires. The comparison based on two or three sires per population does not give the true representation of the entire population. Secondly, it is better to measure a different set of progeny each season or year than to take repeated measurements on the same set of progeny, unless the characters have low repeatability.

- In view of the possibility of G x E interaction, it is better to conduct the comparison in all relevant environments.

## Random sample tests

The random sample tests are conducted in poultry. The samples are taken from various strains at regular interval, usually annual. The random samples of eggs from the hatchery of a number of breeders are taken and raised the chickens in well defined set of conditions. An independent body conducts the tests on performance measurements and publishes the results. The random sample test has now been started for pigs and sheep. In india there are 4 centres for random sample test in poultry. These are at Banglore, Bombay Bhuvneswar and gurgaon where 750 eggs for layers and 700 eggs for broilors are received for testing.

There are certain objectives of random sample tests; the first is that different breeders have different aims e.g. one strain may have been developed for a restricted feeding regime while another for one particular feeding regime, say *ad libitum*. Secondly, very large numbers of observations are often required to detect economically important differences between strains, especially for reproductive characters having high variability.

## 7.5. NUMERICAL SOLVED EXAMPLES

**Example 7.1:** Find out the expected and effective selection differential, taking the population mean 27.0 from the following data when 6 individuals were selected

| No. | 1 | 2 | 3 | 4 | 5 | 6 | Total |
|---|---|---|---|---|---|---|---|
| $x_i$ | 34 | 32 | 30 | 28 | 26 | 25 | 175 |
| $n_i$ | 16 | 36 | 50 | 38 | 35 | 45 | 220 |

**Solution:**

$$\overline{X}_P = 27.0$$

$$\overline{X}_S = \frac{176}{6} = 29.16$$

S = 29.16 – 27.0 = 2.16 units

Weighted (effective)

$$S = \frac{\sum X_i n_i}{\sum n_i} - \overline{X}_p = \frac{6327}{220} - \overline{X}_P = 28.75 - 27.0 = 1.75 \text{ units}$$

The ratio less than one indicates that natural selection was operating.

**Example 7.2** The selection was practiced for 10 generations in a flock for egg number upto 300 days of age together with maintaining a random bred control population. Estimate the average phenotypic and genetic response per generation from the given data

| Generation No. (x) | 1 | 2 | 3 | 4 | 5 | 6 | 7 | 8 | 9 | 10 |
|---|---|---|---|---|---|---|---|---|---|---|
| Selected line (s) | 62 | 64 | 64 | 66 | 66 | 68 | 71 | 71 | 76 | 75 |
| R.B.C. line (c) | 60 | 63 | 63 | 64 | 62 | 63 | 68 | 65 | 67 | 66 |
| Diff. (s-c) = d | 2 | 1 | 1 | 2 | 4 | 5 | 3 | 6 | 9 | 9 |

## Solution:

**(a) Av. phenotypic R per generation** $(\Delta P_S) = b_{sx} = \frac{Cov_{sx}}{\sigma^2 x}$

This is estimated as the regression of generation mean on generation number.

$\Sigma S = 680$ $\Sigma X = 55$

$$\Sigma x^2 = \Sigma X^2 - \frac{(\Sigma X)^2}{N} = 385 - 302.5 = 82.5$$

$$\Sigma XS - \frac{\Sigma X \Sigma S}{N} = 3856 - 3740 = 116$$

$b_{sx} = \Delta P_s = 116/82.5 = 1.40$ eggs

**(b) Average genetic R per generation** $= \Delta_G = b_{xd}$

or $\Delta G = \Delta P_S - \Delta P_C$

(i) This is estimated by the regression of deviation of generation mean of selected and control population on generation number.

$\Sigma d = 39$

$$\Sigma d^2 - \frac{(\Sigma d)^2}{N} = 213 - 152.1 = 60.9$$

$$\Sigma Xd - \frac{\Sigma X \Sigma d}{N} = 278 - 214.5 = 63.5$$

$$b_{d.x} = \Delta G = \frac{63.5}{82.5} = 0.77 \text{ eggs}$$

(ii) $\Delta G$ as the difference of $\Delta P_S - \Delta P_C$

$\Sigma C = 641$

$$\Sigma C^2 - \frac{(\Sigma C)^2}{N} = 41141 - 41088.1 = 52.9$$

$$\Sigma XC - \frac{\Sigma X \Sigma C}{N} = 3578 - 3225.5 = 52.5$$

$$b_{cx} = \Delta Pc = \frac{52.5}{82.5} = 0.63 \text{ eggs}$$

$$\Delta Gs = \Delta Ps - \Delta Pc$$
$$= 1.40 - 0.63 = 0.77 \text{ eggs}$$

Thus Δ Gs is same by two methods.

**Example 7.3: Estimate the genetic trend from the following date**

| Sire No. | Cow No. | Year | Milk yield | Cow temp. average | Deviation (d) |
|---|---|---|---|---|---|
| 1 | 1 | 1 | 2780 | 2202.8 | 577.2 |
| | 2 | 1 | 2720 | 2211.4 | 508.6 |
| | 3 | 2 | 2230 | 2466.3 | -236.3 |
| | 4 | 2 | 2624 | 2410.0 | 214.0 |
| 2 | 5 | 1 | 1580 | 2374.3 | -794.3 |
| | 6 | 1 | 1640 | 2365.7 | -725.7 |
| | 7 | 2 | 1540 | 2564.9 | -1024.9 |
| | 8 | 3 | 1600 | 2097.1 | -497.1 |
| | 9 | 3 | 1540 | 2105.7 | -565.7 |
| 3 | 10 | 2 | 2510 | 2426.3 | 83.7 |
| | 11 | 2 | 3070 | 2346.3 | 723.7 |
| | 12 | 3 | 1800 | 2068.6 | -286.6 |
| | 13 | 4 | 2420 | 2222.0 | 198.0 |
| | 14 | 4 | 2500 | 2206.0 | 294.0 |
| | 15 | 4 | 2100 | 2286.0 | -186.0 |
| | 16 | 4 | 1800 | 2346.0 | -546.0 |
| 4 | 17 | 1 | 1630 | 2367.1 | -737.1 |
| | 18 | 1 | 2850 | 2192.8 | 657.2 |
| | 19 | 1 | 3000 | 2171.4 | 828.6 |
| | 20 | 1 | 2000 | 2314.3 | -314.3 |
| | 21 | 2 | 1820 | 2524.8 | -704.0 |
| | 22 | 2 | 3100 | 2342.0 | 758.0 |
| | 23 | 2 | 2600 | 2413.4 | 186.6 |
| | 24 | 3 | 2900 | 1911.4 | 988.6 |
| | 25 | 3 | 2450 | 1975.7 | 474.3 |
| | 26 | 3 | 2520 | 1965.7 | 554.3 |
| 5 | 27 | 3 | 1870 | 2058.6 | -188.6 |
| | 28 | 3 | 1600 | 2097.1 | -497.1 |
| | 29 | 4 | 2310 | 2244.0 | 66.0 |
| | 30 | 4 | 2400 | 2226.0 | 174.0 |

## Solution

Contemporary averages = (year total – cow's yield)/n-1

| Years(X) | 1 | 2 | 3 | 4 |
|---|---|---|---|---|
| $n_i$ | 8 | 8 | 8 | 6 |
| Total M.Y. | 18200 | 19494 | 16280 | 13530 |

Herd Average = 67504/30 = 2250.13 kg

e.g. the contemp av. for cow No. 1 = (18200-2780)/7 =2202.8

Calculate for other cows in the same way

Years s.s. (sire wise) : $\Sigma X^2 - \dfrac{(\Sigma X)^2}{n}$

Sire No. 1= 10 – 9 = 1.0

Sire No. 2= 24 – 20 = 4.0

Sire No. 3= 81 – 75.6 = 5.4

Sire No. 4= 43 – 36.1 = 6.9

Sire No. 5= 50 – 49 = 1.0

S.P. (Year x deviated yield) = $\Sigma Xd - \dfrac{\Sigma X.\Sigma d}{N}$

Sire No. 1= 1040.8 – 1595.25 = -554.2

Sire No. 2= -6758.2 – (-7215.4) = 457.2

Sire No. 3= -151.0 – 981.7 = -1132.7

Sire No. 4= 6967.2 – 5115.18 = 1852.02

Sire No. 5= -1097.1 – (–1559.95 ) = 462.85

| Sire No. | N | SS years | SP (year x deviation) |
|---|---|---|---|
| 1 | 4 | 1.0 | -554.45 |
| 2 | 5 | 4.0 | 457.20 |
| 3 | 7 | 5.4 | -1132.70 |
| 4 | 10 | 6.9 | 1852.02 |
| 5 | 4 | 1.0 | 462.85 |
| Total | 30 | 18.3 | 1084.92 |

$$b = \frac{1084.92}{18.3} = 59.28 \text{ kg/year}$$

Thus genetic progress ($\Delta$G) = – 2b(P– S).T

= -2(59.28)

= -118.5 kg/year

The genetic gain in milk yield over the 4 years in the herd was negative at the rate of -118.5 kg/year

# QUESTIONS

**7.1.** What is response to selection? How is it measured? (*ARS 1976, 1981*)

**7.2.** Discuss the utility of random bred control population in poultry. Give an ideal size of flock for this purpose and technical programme to maintain such a population over generations. (*ARS 1985*)

***Or***

(i) What do you understand by random bred control population? How can this be developed and what are its uses?

(ii) How we evolved specialized sire and dam lines in poultry and why? (*ARS 1990*)

***Or***

(i) Describe random bred control population and its importance in poultry breeding. (*ARS 1987*)

(ii) Give briefly the role of random sample testing in India (*ARS 1985, 87, 78,81*)

***

# 8

# SELECTION OF SUPERIOR ANIMALS

The first step in designing a selection programme is to decide which characters should be improved. These characters are different in different type of animals viz. dairy animals, meat animals, wool and fur bearing animals and egg producing birds/ poultry etc. These characters under selection are called as **selection objectives**. Further the aims in designing a selection programme are to maximize response to selection (R) which is equal to $ir_{AP}\sigma_A/t$ and also to decide a minimum effective population size (Ne) in relation to inbreeding and random drift.

## 8.1. MULTI STAGE SELECTION

The selection involves the identification of the individuals which are superior and it is a complex process completed in different stages/ages of the animal and known as multi stage selection.

The process of selection starts with the birth of the animal. The new born animals are culled if they have off breed characteristics, anatomical and genetical defects. This is the first stage of selection.

Secondly, the animals are rejected if they have slow growth rate and late maturity. Similarly, the animals belonging to poor pedigree are culled which means the progeny of the parents with low performance are culled.

In case of male selection, the young males (dairy sires or rams or bucks or boars or cockerels) are culled based on poor libido, poor semen quality and poor semen freezability. Lastly the animals are selected or culled based on their breeding value for the character in which the improvement is required. This process of selection is thus completed in stages and hence known as multi stage selection.

Broadly speaking there are two stages of selection. The selection of the first sage is based on physical attributes of phenotypic performance and called as the initial selection or the **phenotypic selection**. The selection at the second stage is based on the breeding value of the animals which is the final selection and called as the **genetic selection**.

### 8.1.1. Phenotypic selection or initial selection

Before the animals are finally selected on the basis of their breeding value for the trait under improvement, it is most essential to have initial selection of the animal based on the followings:

(i) The selected animals should be free from any type of genetical or **congenital defect.**

(ii) Functional reproductive system: The reproduction organs of the animal to be selected should be normal viz. testis of bull should be normal (well developed and descended). The quantity and quality of semen should meet the minimum standard etc. Bulls with poor libido must be rejected.

(iii) Health: The selected animals should be healthy and free from serious genetic defects or diseases.

(iv) Dams performance: The young animals to be selected should be the progeny of better parents and preferably from the progeny of tested ones.

### 8.1.2. Genetic selection or selection based on breeding value

The final selection of an animal to be allowed to produce the next generation is based on the breeding value of that animal for the trait in which improvement is sought through selection. The selection based on breeding value is called genetic selection. The breeding value of an individual can be estimated either on the basis of individual's own performance (phenotypic value of the individual for the character) or on the basis of the performance of the relatives of the individual. The relatives of the individual may be its direct relatives (ancestors and the progeny) or its collateral relatives (full sibs, half sibs, aunts, niece etc). The sources of information based on which the breeding value of the individual is estimated are called as the **basis of selection** or **aids to selection** or **criteria of selection** which are the basis of estimating the breeding value. The breeding value so obtained is known as estimated breeding value (EBV) or probable breeding value (PBV) or predicted breeding value. The breeding value is really the genetic worth of an individual which is due to the sum of the average effect of genes carried by the individual for a trait and half of which is transmitted to its progeny as such. The accurate or erroneous estimation of breeding value of an individual affects the selection progress.

## 8.2. BASIS AND IMPORTANCE OF SELECTION FROM RELATIVES PERFORMANCE

The basis of estimating the breeding value of an individual from the phenotypic value of its relatives lies in the fact that the relatives also have some of the same genes possessed by the individual. The kind of genes an individual carries is expressed in the phenotypic value of the individual and of its relatives. The use of information from relatives (to estimate the breeding value of an individual) is very important and essential aspect of selection for some characters under the following conditions:

**(i) When the individual selection is not possible. The traits for which individual selection can not be applied are:**

- The **sex-limited traits** which are expressed in only one sex like milk yield, egg production are expressed only in females. Thus, breeding value is estimated based on the phenotypic value of the female relatives of the individual.
- The traits which cannot be measured in living animals like **slaughter traits, longevity**, and **lifetime production**. The performance records of relatives are used to estimate the breeding value of the individual.

(ii) When selection is required earlier but the trait is expressed in later life of the individual. Under such conditions the part records like part lactation milk yield in dairy animals to predict the lactation milk yield and the first lactation milk yield to predict the lifetime milk production, part year egg production to predict the annual egg production in poultry, birth weight to gain in adult body weight may either be used or the information from relatives may be used to predict the breeding value of the trait.

(iii) When the $h^2$ of the trait under selection is low. In this case the individual selection on single records is not effective. The use of multiple measurements (repeated records) on the individual or the mean value of a number of relatives (family members like sibs) gives a more reliable estimate of the breeding value of the individual compared to the indi dual's own phenotypic value.

## 8.3. DIFFERENT SELECTION CRITERIA : BASIS OF SELECTION

The different selection criteria to estimates the breeding value of an individual for single trait can be diagrammatically shown as below:

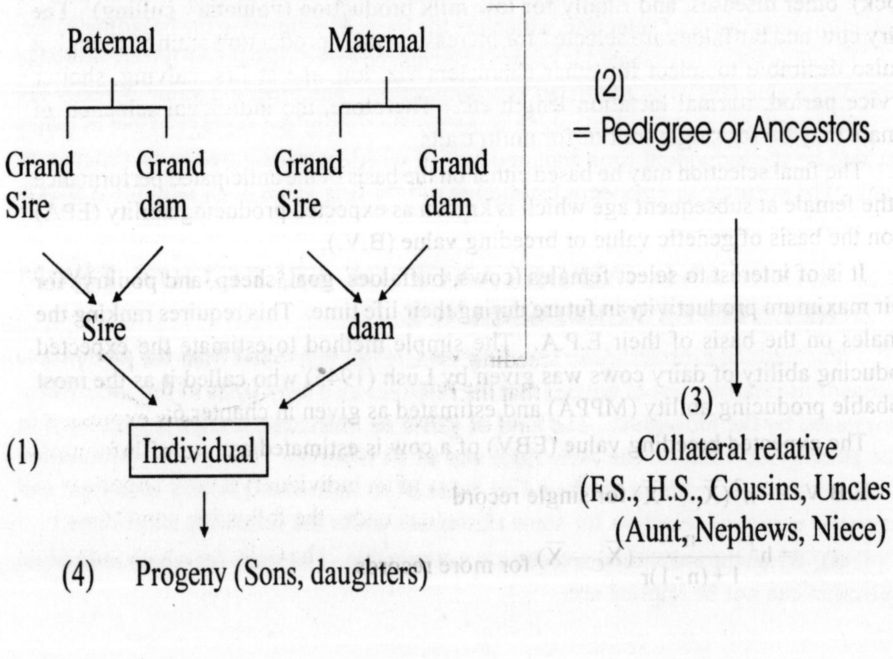

When the breeding value of an individual is estimated based on individual's own phenotypic value of that trait it is known as **individual selection**. When the improvement through selection is required for more than one trait and the individual's performance is the criteria of selection, then three different methods of individual selection are applied to estimate breeding value of the individual viz. tandem, independent culling level and the selection index.

The estimation of breeding value of an individual based on ancestors performance (parents and grand parents) is known as **pedigree selection** and based on collateral relatives which are commonly known as family members (sibs etc.) is known as **family selection**, whereas the estimation of breeding value of the individual based on its progeny performance is called as **progeny selection** or progeny testing.

## 8.4. SELECTION OF MALES AND FEMALES

The selection criteria for males and females are little different. These have been given here in brief.

The culling of low producing dams, selections of replacement young females born to high yielding dams and breeding them (replacements) by proven sires have been recommended. Therefore, genetic improvement can be made by selection of outstanding dams of future sire and by selection of males that will produce future cows and bulls.

### 8.4.1. Female selection

The adult female animals are culled for a number of reasons viz. late maturity, reproductive problems (anoestrus condition, repeat breeding), uterovaginal disorders (prolapse of uterus, retention of placenta, metritis), udder problems (mastitis, teat block), other diseases, and finally for low milk production (voluntary culling). The dairy cow and buffaloes are selected for increase in milk production mainly, though it is also desirable to select for other characters viz. low age at first calving, shorter service period, normal lactation length etc. Therefore, the individual selection of female may be for single trait or for multi traits.

The final selection may be based either on the basis of the anticipated performance of the female at subsequent age which is known as expected producing ability (EPA) or on the basis of genetic value or breeding value (B.V.).

It is of interest to select females (cows, buffaloes, goat, sheep, and poultry) for their maximum productivity in future during their life time. This requires ranking the females on the basis of their E.P.A. The simple method to estimate the expected producing ability of dairy cows was given by Lush (1945) who called it as the most probable producing ability (MPPA) and estimated as given in chapter 6:

The expected breeding value (EBV) of a cow is estimated as:

$$\text{E.B.V.} = h^2(\overline{X}_C - \overline{X}) \text{ for single record}$$

$$= h^2 \frac{n}{1+(n-1)r}(\overline{X}_C - \overline{X}) \text{ for more records}$$

The accuracy of selection is h based on single record and $\sqrt{nh^2/[1+(n-1)r]}$ based on more records.

The multi trait selection has 3 methods viz. Tandem selection, I.C.L. method and the selection index method. The details have been given in Chapter 9.

In case of female selection, the individual selection is advocated rather than based on the performance of its relatives.

### 8.4.2. Male selection

The individual selection is not possible in case of males. Therefore the males are selected on the basis of the performance of their relatives.

### Importance of sire selection

The males as well as females contribute equally to the inheritance of polygenic traits. Therefore, equal emphasis should be given for selection of males and females. However, selection of sire rather than of the dam is important. This is because of the followings:

- Dams leave limited number of progeny whereas sires leave more number of progeny. Thus sire has a greater impact on the herd for which it is said that sire is "half the herd". The use of A.I. and frozen semen technology has further extended the extensive use of a sire in many herds.
- Only few sires are needed for breeding a herd and hence selection can be made more intense among males than among females. This is because most of the female progeny born are selected to replace the old and unproductive ones. As a result of higher intensity of selection in case of males, the selection differential is larger.
- Sire selection is not only important within a herd or breed but is also equally important in grading up and crossbreeding programme. The male progeny produced by better dams mated to best sire, are selected for breeding and improvement programme.

### Sire selection criteria

The sire selection can be completed in three steps viz. selection of young bull based on pedigree, preliminary or phenotypic selection and sire evaluation based on progeny performance.

### (i) Selection of males based on pedigree

The expected predicted difference (EPD) of male calves/kids/lambs based on dam's performance is estimated as:

$$E.P.D. = 0.5 = h^2 \frac{n}{1+(n-1)r}(M - \overline{H})$$

Where, $h^2$ = heritability of trait

n = number of records of dam

r = repeatability

M = average of dam's record

$\overline{H}$ = Herd average or contemporary average

The accuracy of male selection based on dam' records will be as

$$\text{Accuracy} = 0.5\sqrt{\frac{nh^2}{1+(n-1)r}}$$

The E.P.D. based on the records of dam and paternal grand dam will be :

$$\text{E.P.D.} = 0.5h^2\frac{n_1}{1+(n_1-1)r}(M-\overline{H})+0.25h^2\frac{n_2}{1+(n_2-1)r}(G-\overline{H})$$

Where,

$n_1$ and $n_2$ = No. of lactation records of dam and paternal grand dam, respectively

G = Average of grand dam's records

## (ii) Preliminary selection of males

Once the males are selected on the basis of pedigree it is essential to examine those males for breed characteristics, any physical defect, body growth and health, maturity age, testicles, libido, semen production and quality as well as freezability of semen

## (iii) Progeny testing

The final selection of sire for further use in the herd is based on its progeny performance. In view of the small population size, the P.T. should be done in more than one herd. The E.B.V. of sires can be estimated by any method of sire indices.

## Problems in sire evaluation

There are certain problems/constraints in conducting a P.T. programme effectively. These are as under:-

**(i) Population size:** Most of the organized farms have small population due to the reason of having very limited capacity to maintain large populations. The genetic improvement is less in a herd of small size. Therefore, it is better to progeny test the sires in associated herds or farmers herd.

**(ii) Infrastructure:** To associate farmers herd in a P.T. programme has the problem that farmers do not keep the records. The reasons are that they are not educated and find no immediate use of record keeping.

**(iii) Generation interval:** The generation interval in dairy cattle and buffaloes is very long for the reasons of slow growth rate, delayed maturity and poor breeding efficiency. The generation interval can be reduced by using young bulls, replacing older cows by heifers, improving the plane of nutrition and proper management. The use of part lactation records will also help in proving the sire at an earlier age.

**(iv) Bull disposal:** A large number of sires remain idle over the years between test mating to the time the P.T. results are available. Keeping the bulls in store for such a long time is an expensive and moreover, some of the bulls either die or become sterile during this period. This problem has been solved to some extent by the frozen semen technology. It is now possible to dispose of the bulls after collecting and freezing the semen.

## 8.5. SELECTION AND BREEDING FOR DISEASE RESISTANCE

Animal breeders have given main emphasis to select animals for higher milk yield, meat, wool and egg etc. On the other hand, the genetic differences in resistance to various pathogens to develop highly productive and disease resistance strains have not been utilized. This field has been totally neglected, except very few attempts, for the inability to recognize its potentialities and lack of research rather than lack of resistance.

Hutt (1958), working on respiratory disease of White Leghorn, had mentioned that some birds need protection but others do not, while some hens die of these diseases or stop laying, others in the same pen of the same flock are completely unaffected and continue to lay well. It is not that the unaffected birds are not exposed but it is much more probable that they are able to tolerate the infectious organisms, to resist them in some way and thus to withstand a bit of environment that may be disastrous to other birds. Two strains of a breed housed together can differ significantly in resistance to a disease and, moreover, remarkable differences may be observed among sire families within a strain. There are many examples of genetic variation to many diseases and parasites in different species of farm animals, viz., mastitis, TB, FMD, John's disease, protozoan disease in cattle; respiratory disease in poultry; internal parasites in sheep. Thus, it is obvious that heredity play an important role in determining whether an individual will withstand a disease or succumb to it. Now the important point to be valued is about the identification/selection and multiplication of resistant individuals so as to produce a resistant strain.

Tomar (1984) also found genetic variability in the occurrence of certain diseases in Murrah buffaloes.

There are three possible methods to identify and select the individuals for differences in resistance/susceptibility to a certain disease/parasite, these are as under:

- occurrence of the disease under normal environmental conditions,
- inoculation of animals with pathogen causing the disease, and
- use of indicators of resistance.

The first method to identify the resistant animals on the basis of the incidence of the disease is not effective in the sense that under the changed environmental conditions the resistant become susceptible. The second method of inoculation is not likely to be applied because of the objections to deliberate infection with pathogenic organisms. The third one requires very great efforts and research to find a better indicator of genetic resistance; however, which do not require deliberate exposure to pathogens. **Some of the good indicators** are available in literature as given below:

(i) Adams and Rickard (1963) tested the bactericidal potencies of the lipid, sebum-like material from the **teat canal of the** udder that differed in susceptibility to *Str. Agalactiae* along with its composition for fatty acids. They found that material from udder quarters resistant to infection contained higher proportion of some fatty acids (myristic, palmitic and linoleic acids) than the material from susceptible quarters which contained significantly more palmitic acid compared to resistant quarters. Stovikova and Sojda (1975) found that of the 60 fatty acids constituting the neutral lipid fraction of the lactosebum, the levels of lauric and myristic acids were highest in cows resistant to mastitis and the variation in lipid composition of the lactosebum has genetic component. These evidences show that resistance is associated with a high level in the lactosebum of fatty acids that excel in bactericidal potency.

(ii) An indicator of resistance to ***eye cancer*** in Hereford cattle has been identified. The animals with pigmented eyelids have far less eye cancer than those with white faces and lids not pigmented. The incidence of lesions decreases steadily with the increase in pigmentation and a solid ring of pigment (at least half an inch wide) around the eye ensure pigmentation of the lids. It has been shown that the amount of coloured skin around the eye is influenced by heredity and hence is amenable to selection.

(iii) The differences among the chicks that are resistant and susceptible to *Salmonella pullorum* causing the **pullorum disease** were found that the resistant chicks have better control to maintain their body temperature. This was measured by determining the number of days the newly hatched chicks with their body temperature of 102°F (when they hatch) raise their temperature upto 105-107°F which is normal at ten days of age. The differences among them in this ability appeared by 6 days after hatching, the chicks most efficient in making transition are more resistant to pullorum. This ability is believed to accelerate the production of antibodies and other mechanisms of defence.

(iv) Briles et al. (1977) found that birds resistant for **Marek's disease** have RBC antigen $B^{21}$ whereas the susceptible one lacked this antigen but carry another antigen $B^{19}$.

(v) Crittenden et al. (1970) reported embryos lacking the antigen $R_1$ are resistant to infection by certain viruses causing **avian leucosis** and those carry the dominant allele for $R_1$ are all susceptible.

Falconer (1989) has discussed the efficiency of individual selection and family selection on the basis of the incidence of the disease with two visible classes. The effectiveness of selection depends on the selection differential which, in tern, depends mainly on the proportion selected. But in case of threshold characters, the selection differential depends on the incidence rather than on the proportion selected. Selecting all the resistant individuals or only a portion of them will give their mean as the mean of the resistant group. Thus, selecting a smaller proportion than the incidence, does not give an added advantage. It is, thus, evident that maximum selection differential is achieved when the proportion selected is equal to the proportion of resistant

**individuals. The individual selection is less effective when the difference between the two (incidence of resistance animals and proportion selected) is more. Further, the individual selection is less effective when the proportion of resistant individual is very low, but the family selection is more effective. An individual's phenotype as resistant or susceptible is not precisely known whereas the family is more precisely known for the proportion of affected members of the family. However, the precision depends on the family size and on the incidence of a disease in the family.**

# QUESTIONS

**8.1.** **What do you mean by multistage selection? Give the basis and importance of selection based on relative's performance.**

**8.2.** **Discuss the procedure of selection for males and females separately**

**8.3.** **Describe the various methods of enhancement of general disease resistance in a breeding programme.** (*ARS 1996*)

***

# 9

# SELECTION CRITERIA-INDIVIDUAL SELECTION

The animal itself is the smallest unit of selection and improvement. The animal's own phenotypic value of the character under selection is considered to estimate the breeding value of that character for that individual. The character may be any one either productive or reproductive or physical trait. When the breeding value of an animal is estimated based on the phenotypic value of the trait of that animal to select it for future breeding, the criteria is called the "**individual selection**" or performance testing because individual' own performance (phenotypic value) is taken as a measure of the breeding value (genetic merit) of the individual. Thus, individual selection is when the animal's own performance is considered as a measure of its genetic merit, and the individuals are selected only in accordance to their own phenotypic values. This is also known as mass selection instead of individual selection when the selected individuals are kept together en mass for mating e.g. Drosophila and Tribolium kept in a bottle without keeping records of individual mating. When the matings are controlled or records are maintained as in case of large animals, mice etc. the term individual selection is used.

## 9.1. EXPRESSION OF INDIVIDUAL SELECTION (ESTIMATION OF B.V.)

The phenotypic merit of the individual under selection is determined in comparison to the average of other individuals of the population. It should be kept in mind that the comparison is made with the average of other individuals kept under similar environmental conditions and that too of the same age and same time. Therefore, the individuals are ranked relative to others under similar conditions.

The breeding value (B.V.) of an individual is estimated from the phenotypic value of that individual as a deviation from the population mean (selection differential) times the heritability of the trait and known as the Probable breeding value (PBV) as

$$PBV = \overline{P} + h^2(P_i - \overline{P})$$

Where, $\overline{P}$ = population mean

$P_i$ = phenotypic value of the individual

$h^2$ = heritability of the character

The PBV so estimated is the genetic superiority or inferiority of the individual in comparison to the population mean. The non-additive gene effects and the environmental factors brings the PBV nearer to the population mean rather than phenotypic value of the individual.

The **accuracy of individual selection** to predict the breeding value depends on the correlation of breeding value and phenotypic value that how closely these two are related. The correlation between breeding value and phenotypic value ($r_{AP}$) is equal to the square root of heritability ($r_{AP}$= h). Therefore, the accuracy of predicting the breeding value of an animal based on its own performance will be increased with the increase in $h^2$ of the trait and the progeny performance will come close to the phenotypic value of the selected parent rather than population mean.

Thus, efforts must be made to get accurate and higher estimate of heritability by reducing the environmental variations. The accuracy of individual selection can further be increased by estimating the $h^2$ based on repeated records of the individual. The use of repeated records is helpful for traits of low $h^2$.

## Advantages of individual selection

1. The information on individuals to be selected are easily available. Thus, it is easy to use this method.
2. It can be applied earlier to progeny testing. This is used when pedigree information are not available.
3. The generation interval is shorter by this method compared to progeny testing.
4. This gives a direct estimate of B.V. and not on the basis of relatives and hence it is more accurate.
5. This allows a greater selection differential because the B.V. of all the individuals can be estimated while in case of P.T. only a few individuals may be progeny tested as parents.
6. This method minimizes the environmental effects because the individuals for selection are tested in the same environmental conditions.

## Limitations of individual selection

The individual selection can not be applied under the following conditions:

1. When the traits are not expressed by the individual (sex limited traits).
2. When the traits are expressed in later life of the individual or after death of the animal.

3. When the traits have low heritability individual selection is not effective. This is because the accuracy of individual selection depends on $r_{AP}$ which is equal to square root of heritability. The phenotypic value is a poor indication of B.V. if $h^2$ is low. Thus low $h^2$ reduces the accuracy of the selection.

In view of these limitations, the individual selection particularly for male selection is not applied in dairy animals because the most important economic characters are sex-limited (expressed only in females) and have low heritability estimates. The individual selection is applied when traits are expressed in the individual and when the $h^2$ of the trait is high.

## 9.2. AIDS TO INDIVIDUAL SELECTION

There are certain situations when the information of relatives is not available, and also the $h^2$ of character is medium to low. This embarrasses the situation making the selection more difficult based on individual information. Moreover, it may also happen that early selection is required before the final trait is expressed by the animal.

When the $h^2$ of a trait is low, the repeated records of the same animal can be used to improve the estimate of real breeding value or real producing ability. The use of part records and of genetic correlation among the traits will be helpful when earlier selection is to be practiced for the traits expressed later.

### (1) Additional records

Many traits are repeated several times in the life of the animals e.g. milk production, lactation length in dairy cattle and buffalo, egg production in poultry and fleece production in sheep. It is advantageous to predict the B.V. of an individual based on the mean of several records of that individual, if such records are available. This is because due to some environmental effects the genetic potential of the animal is not fully expressed in a single record. The mean of records will then give the better estimate of the real producing ability of the animal. The records on the same animal at different times may show variation due to changes in environment which prevail at the time the records are made, or sometimes due to error of measurement. The environment may include the internal conditions also e.g. endocrine functions of the animal, health of animal, as well as external conditions e.g. feeding, management and climate. The selection based on the mean of a number of records for each animal will improve the accuracy of estimate of real producing ability because temporary environmental influences tend to be balanced and disappear in the averages. This minimizes some of the differences between individuals due to temporary environmental effects and it will result in an increase of the $h^2$ and the B.V. is estimated more accurately on n records. The $h^2$ for mean of n records, with repeatability of records, r, is taken as:

$$h_n^2 = \frac{nh^2}{1+(n-1)r}$$

Thus the regression of B.V. of individual based on n records will be equal to

The accuracy of selection using n records will be equal to $h_n^2$

$$r_{A\overline{P}} = \sqrt{\frac{nh^2}{1+(n-1)r}}$$

Where $\overline{P}$ is the mean of n records on the same animal, and r is the repeatability. The relative efficiency can be obtained as the ratio of gain from selection on mean of n records over the gain from single record selection and it will be

$$= \sqrt{\frac{\frac{nh^2}{1+(n-1)r}}{h^2}} = \sqrt{\frac{n}{1+(n-1)r}}$$

Thus selection of repeated records is always more efficient than selection on a single record by the quantity $\sqrt{\frac{n}{1+(n-1)r}}$

(i) This quantity increases with n for fixed value of r. Therefore, the more the numbers of repeated records are used, the greater is the efficiency in terms of gain per generation.

(ii) Secondly, efficiency increases with decrease in the value of r, for any given value of n. Therefore, as r increases the use of more than one record in selection is not advantageous. This is because it indicates that the temporary environmental influences were not important and permanent effects are more important. As such if r is high there is no use waiting even for the second record.

(iii) The use of many records in selection is useful for the traits which are more variable from time to time in the individual's life i.e. more affected by temporary environmental effects. The use of mean of records in selection result much of the gain with the use of second record and if r is small the gain from using third or fourth record may be considerable. The main advantage of this method is that it is used for the traits which are more influenced by temporary environmental effects which are cancelled out in taking the average of more records.

This method based on n records has also some **disadvantages.**

(i) It results in increased cost because the animal has to be kept till more than one record is available.

(ii) It increases the generation interval and consequently will decrease the response (genetic gain) per unit of time in comparison to base on single record.

(iii) The selection differential is reduced because the variation decreases in calculating the mean.

(iv) The individuals with several records constitute a highly selected group, within which further selection will be comparatively ineffective, if continuous selection is carried out every time a new record is available. Thus, the final relative efficiency of the two methods must be based on the annual genetic gain which is obtained by dividing the genetic gain ($\Delta G$) by the generation interval. Thus, the increased generation interval by the method of using several records will reduce the annual genetic gain. Therefore, using n records for selection is less efficient in terms of annual genetic gain.

## (2) Most probable producing ability (MPPA)

When more numbers of records of animals are available and it is desired to cull some animals and to retain others, it is then problematic to evaluate properly the animals with varying number of records. Females in a herd/flock often differ in age in terms of parity order. The real estimate of producing ability of a female to rank them in the herd is required if there is a difference in the number of records of different females. The most probable producing abilities (MPPA) is calculated as given in chapter 6.

## (3) Use of part records

The part record selection is known as the use of production performance for part period (viz. 12 months growth, milk yield before lactation is completed). This method reduces the generation interval. The genetic gain ($\Delta G$) by use of part record will be: $\Delta G = b_{AP}\left(X_P - \overline{X}_P\right)$

Where, A is the B.V., p is the phenotype of part record, $b_{AP}$ is the regression of BV of total production on part record, $X_P - \overline{X}_P$ is the selection differential of part record. Thus, for greater gain by use of part record, it is important that $r_{AP}$ be positive and greater. Thus, the part production must be positively and highly correlated with total or full time production/record. If the genetic correlations is negative, net result of part record selection can be the reduction in total production.

# 9.3. MULTI TRAIT SELECTION (METHODS OF SELECTION)

The economic value of an animal depends upon several characters, known as overall performance of total breeding value (net merit) of animal. For example, a dairy cow will be more economical to maintain if she produces more milk with higher fat content for a longer period during lactation and remained dry for a shorter time between successive calvings. On the other hand, if a cow produces more milk daily of low fat content with shorter lactation length and goes dry earlier during the lactation, it will not be economical to maintain. Likewise, more profit from pigs depends on their fertility (litter size), mothering ability, growth rate, efficiency of food conversion, carcass quality, and also the resistance to various diseases. The economic production in poultry is affected by the annual yield of eggs, their weight, and age at which egg production starts etc. The traits of direct economic importance in sheep are wool clip, fertility and lamb weight. Thus, the net economic value of an animal depends upon several traits. It is, therefore, essential to estimate the total breeding worth (net merit) of an animal based on several characters. In practice, the breeding merit of an animal is often determined on several traits simultaneously and not by a single trait, to improve the overall economic value based on **simultaneous selection for several characters**, which is also known as **multi trait selection**.

## 9.3.1. Requirement and efficiency of multi trait selection

In order to select an individual as parent of next generation for improvement in several traits, the following information need to be known for each trait.

(i) The economic value of the traits. This is measured as the amount by which each unit of variation in it actually raises or lowers an individual's value, known as the relative economic value of the trait.

(ii) The genetic significance of the traits in terms of the heritability of the trait and genetic correlations among the traits.

(iii) The method of selection chosen and the number of traits to be included in selection criteria also influence the efficiency of simultaneous selection of several traits besides economic and genetic significance of the traits.

## 9.3.2 Methods of multi trait selection

Simultaneous selection for many traits can be applied based on individuals' own performance by adopting any of the procedure of selection. One may wish to adopt tandem selection or independent culling levels methods or one may evaluate the individuals on the value for each of the traits selected for and then sum up these values to give a total value (score) for all the traits (total score or index selection). The animal with the highest score is then selected. These procedures are known as methods of selection (Hazel and Lush, 1942).

## 1. Tandem selection

In this method of individual selection the individual traits are improved successively. The selection is practiced for one trait only at a time till the satisfactory improvement is achieved. After improvement in this trait the selection is started for improvement in the second trait till the goal is achieved to the desired level. Thus, trait A is improved first, then trait B, and so on.

(1) This method is less efficient than other methods. The genetic progress per unit of time by this method is less and that too for great efforts. The average genetic improvement per generation in each of n traits (which are independent and equally important) would be only 1/n times which would be made if it was the sole object of improvement over the entire period of selection.

(2) Secondly, it requires more time for improvement in all the traits because while selection is being done for one trait, the other traits must wait.

(3) The efficiency of this method depends on the genetic correlation among the traits under selection. A desirable genetic association would lead improvement in other trait while selection is made for one trait. The low

genetic correlation will decrease the efficiency of this method because there will be no correlated response in other trait. An undesirable genetic correlation between two traits, in which selection for an increase in desirable direction in one trait results in a decrease in the other trait, would neutralize the genetic progress made in any one trait.

## 2. Independent culling levels

This method of individual selection involves selection for two or more traits at a time. A minimum standard (level) for each trait is fixed and every animal to be selected must met this minimum level for each of the trait under consideration. An animal fails to meet the minimum standard fixed for any one of the trait will be rejected, irrespective of the fact that how good the animal was in other trait. Thus, an animal is rejected inspite of its being exceptionally good in one trait but if it was little poor in another trait.

The procedure of this method can be understood by the following table, taking an example in buffalo:

| Traits | Standard set | Buffalo No. | |
|---|---|---|---|
| | | 1 | 2 |
| AFC (months) | 42 | 40 | 44 |
| Milk yield (kg) | 1900 | 1950 | 2100 |
| Fat (per cent) | 7 | 7 | 6.5 |

Under the use of ICL method of selection buffalo No. 1 will be selected and no. 2 will be rejected because no. 2 fails to meet the standard for AFC and fat percentage, though it was much superior in milk production. Thus, the buffalo superior in milk production will be lost from the herd.

## Advantages of I.C.L.

**(i) Selection for more than one trait:** This method is superior to tandem selection because the selection is practiced for more than one trait.

**(ii) Culling at early age:** The practical and economic advantage of this method is that it allows to cull the animals earlier which are inferior in early expressed traits.

## Disadvantages of I.C.L.

**(i) No compensation for other traits:** The first disadvantage of this type of selection is that it does not permit superiority in some traits to compensate for deficiencies in others, and there is a possibility to cull genetically superior animals.

**(ii) Culling level:** The method involve a tedious work to determine the optimum culling levels.

**(iii) More emphasis to early expressed traits:** In case of early selection, the early expressed traits get more emphasis rather than actually more important trait which are expressed later

**(iv) Selection intensity:** The intensity of selection is reduced with increase in number of traits.

The **effectiveness of this method** depends on the level kept for each of the traits. In case of keeping low levels, very few animals are culled and it affects the genetic progress. On the other hand, if the standards kept are high, it results in gradual extinction of population because it will find difficult to have adequate replacements.

This type of selection is used in selection of cattle for show purposes. The animal is selected with excellence in type, colour and conformation traits ignoring its performance for economic traits.

## Selection intensity under I.C.L.

The ICL method decreases the selection intensity of the individual traits. The decrease is along the increase in number of traits. The genetic correlations among traits also influence the selection intensity. The negative genetic correlation among traits decreases more selection intensity in single trait because animals superior in one trait may be inferior in other trait. The effect of positive genetic correlation is less on the decrease of selection intensity because animals superior in one trait may also be superior in another trait. The decrease in selection intensity for including more number of traits suggests a restriction to a minimum number of traits. This is because animals superior in all or in most of the economic traits are rare. It is, therefore, that fancy traits like horn shape and coat colour should not be included in selection. Its effect is two fold. First is the decrease in intensity of selection for important traits. Secondly, if in dairy cattle fancy traits are considered in addition to economic traits, the work become more difficult and superior genotype for economic trait not associated with fancy trait of the breed will be rejected. The selection intensity is decreased by selection for more than one trait. The intensity of selection for n traits which are equally important and independent is equal to $\frac{1}{\sqrt{n}}$ compared to selection intensity for only one trait. Heavy culling for one trait limits the amount of culling which can be practiced for others. For example, if selection is for a single trait and p = 0.25, the selection differential is 1.27 standard deviations. When two independent and economically equal important traits are to be selected with the restriction that p= 0.25, the p will be obtained as $\sqrt{p} \times \sqrt{p}$ $\sqrt{0.25} \times \sqrt{0.25}$ 0.50 x 0.50 = 0.25. Thus $P_1 = P_2 = 0.50$, instead of 0.25. Thus, selection can only be among the best 50% of individuals for each trait instead among the 25%. The selection differential for p = 0.50 is 0.80 standard deviations instead of 1.27. Thus, the S is reduced. The simultaneous selection of equal intensity of n traits reduces the S from $i = Z/p$ to $i' = z'\sqrt{p}$ where, z is the ordinate of the point on the abscissa separating the best $\sqrt{p}$ per cent of the population. In this example, the i = 1.27 and i' = 0.80. Thus, $\Delta G$ per generation will be equal to $\Sigma\, i'\, h_j . \sigma_{Aj}$ instead of $\Sigma\, ih_j\, \sigma_{Aj}$.

Therefore, if the heritabilities and variances are equal for all n traits the $\Delta G = n\, i'\, h\sigma A$.

Maximum aggregate genetic gain is obtained by proper combination of culling levels determined by heritability, economic value (a) and proportion saved (P) for breeding. The genetic gain (H) expected from selecting independently for each of n traits which are uncorrelated is $H = a_i h_i^2 \frac{z_1}{p_1} \sigma P_1 + ........ + a_n h_b^2 \frac{Z_n}{P_n} \sigma P_n$

Where, the $P_1$'s refer to the fraction saved for each of n traits, making $p = p_1 P_2 ........ p_n$. For example, if there are two traits, the $p = \sqrt{p} \times \sqrt{p}$ and for n traits $p = n\sqrt{p}$

The values of a, $h^2$ and p which measures the importance of a trait, must be known to find the culling levels of various traits to make the H maximum. According to the restriction that $P_1 P_2 ........ P_n = P$ the different values of $P_i$ corresponding to Zi are substituted in the equation of H and best combinations of $P_i$'s are chosen which make the H maximum.

Hazel and Lush (1942) gave the following table of $p_i$ for each of two traits in order to make maximum genetic progress under ICL method for different values of p and when the importance of two traits varies:

| **Relative importance** | **Total fraction saved (P)** | | | | | |
|---|---|---|---|---|---|---|
| | **0.8** | | **0.50** | | **0.2** | |
| $\frac{a_1 h_1^2 \sigma p_1}{a_2 h_2^2 \sigma p_2}$ | $P_1$ | $P_2$ | $P_1$ | $P_2$ | $P_1$ | $P_2$ |
| 1. | 0.89 | 0.89 | 0.71 | 0.71 | 0.45 | 0.45 |
| 2. | 0.81 | 0.99 | 0.53 | 0.94 | 0.24 | 0.82 |
| 4. | 0.80 | 1.00 | 0.51 | 0.99 | 0.21 | 0.98 |
| 8. | 0.80 | 1.00 | 0.50 | 1.00 | 0.20 | 1.00 |

They indicated that when the traits are equally important, the same culling level ($P_1 = P_2 = \sqrt{p}$) for each trait is most efficient for every value of p (line 1 in table). When one trait is more important than the other, the culling proportions differ for the two traits in such a way that the culling proportion for less important trait is less to maximize H. In the above table, when first trait is twice as important as second trait, the culling level are 19 & 1 for p = 0.80, 47 & 6 for p = 0.50, and 76 & 18 for p = 0.20.

## 3. Total score or selection index

In this method of mass selection, the selection is practiced for several traits simultaneously. But this method differs from ICL in that (i) the culling levels are flexible, (ii) each trait is weighted by a score and these scores for individual traits are summed to a total score (index value) for each animal, which is taken as selection criterion (iii) superiority in some traits can make up deficiency in others, unlike ICL which discards an animal failing to qualify in one trait regardless of its superiority in other trait.

The selection index method of individual selection is an index of the net merit of an animal for many traits. This is constructed by adding the scores for each trait into one figure. The values for each of the trait being added give a total score for all the traits. Thus credits and penalties are given to each animal according to the degree of superiority or inferiority in each trait. The animal with the highest score is then selected for breeding. Some weightage is given to each trait due to their unequal economic importance and thus allows equal attention to each trait. The amount of weightage given to each trait in relation to other traits determines the influence of each trait on the final index. The amount of weightage depends upon the economic and genetic significance of the traits. Thus this method encompass all the advantages and disadvantages of an animal by permitting extra merit in one trait to off set slight defects in another.

## Efficiency of S.I. over other methods of selection

Index is a more efficient method of selection than others (tandem and ICL):

(i) It allows the individuals which are superior in some traits to be selected regardless of their inferiority in other traits and thus superior genotypes are saved for breeding.

(ii) All traits do not have equal heritability and so the same intensity of selection will not be expected to give the same proportionate improvement for each trait.

(iii) The traits are correlated with each other to which the index gives appropriate consideration. It also results in more genetic gain for the time and efforts made. The advantage of index method increases with the number of traits. Thus it requires less time to bring about an overall improvement.

## Use of discriminate function to construct index selection

Selection index method involves the technique of discriminant function originally developed by Fisher (1936) and used by Smith (1936). They developed an optimum linear discriminant function for multiple trait selection in self perpetuating varieties of crops. Hazel (1943) extended the application of this technique in animal improvement discussing the genetic basis for constructing selection index, when it is required to select individuals whose progeny will be of superior merit.

The use of discriminant function as a basis for making selection on several characters simultaneously is aimed at discriminating the desirable genotypes from undesirable ones on the basis of their phenotypic performance. Such a selection index should combine the different traits in a way that maximize the probability of progress in the aggregate economic value.

The index will take the form as:

$I = b_1 x_1 + b_2 x_2 + ............+ b_n x_n$

Where, $x_i$ represent the phenotypic value for the different traits

$b_i$ are the weighting factors (multiple regression coefficients) given to each of the trait.

## Genetic basis of selection index

The discriminant functions or selection index are obtained with the same principle as that of fitting a multiple regression equation for predicting a dependent variable from two or more known independent variables. The selection indices are constructed to bring about genetic improvement from phenotypic selection. Therefore, in order to select most efficiently, the observed phenotypic variation in the trait which represent differences in genetic make up that is heritable should be known.

The phenotypic value (X) is the combined result of genotype and environment, and thus X = G+E, where G represents the genotypic value (additive genetic value) and E the other effects including genic interaction and environmental deviations. The genetic improvement depends on the magnitude of genetic variability in terms of heritability of the trait ($h^2$). The overall net genetic improvement (H) for several traits should be the sum of the genetic gains made for several traits i.e.,

$$H = \sum_{i=1}^{n} G_i$$

But all the traits of an animal are not likely to be equally important economically. Therefore, economic value of a trait obviously is important for deciding how much consideration the trait deserves in selection. Economic value, denoted by a, is defined as the increment in profit occurring from improving the trait by one unit, independent of improvement in other traits, therefore, additive genotype of the total economic value is the sum of the breeding (genotypic) values of all the traits ($\overline{G}i$) weighted by their respective economic values ($a_i$). Thus, the aggregate genetic worth (H) of the individual or the average genetic superiority of a selected group was described by Hazel and Lush (1942) as:

$$H = a_1G_1 + a_2G_2 +...........+ a_nG_n$$

$$= \Sigma a_iG_i$$ = Genetic worth of animal or, aggregate genotypic value

Where, $a_i$ are the relative economic values which measures the amount by which profit is expected to increase for each unit change in $X_i$.

Gi are the expected values of $X_i$ due to additive gene effects.

The genetic worth or aggregate breeding value of an animal is H and the overall phenotype of an animal for multi traits determined by the discriminant function or index is I. Therefore, the index value (I) should be as closely correlated to the individuals composite breeding value (H) as possible.

The genetic gain or gain in aggregate genotype or response in H from selection ($\Delta H$) will be :

$$\Delta H = iR_{IH}\sigma_H = \frac{\sigma I}{\sigma H} i\sigma H = i\sigma I \left( Since \quad r_{HI} = \frac{\sigma I}{\sigma H} \right)$$

Where, $\sigma I = \Sigma b_i \sigma X_i = b_1 \sigma X_1 + b_2 \sigma X_2 + \ldots\ldots\ldots\ldots + b_n \sigma X_n =$

$\sigma H = \Sigma a_i \sigma g_i = a_1 \sigma g_1 + a_2 \sigma g_2 + a_3 \sigma g_3 + \ldots\ldots\ldots\ldots\ldots\ldots + a_n \sigma g_n$

$$r_{HI} = \frac{Cov_{HI}}{\sigma H \sigma I} = \frac{\sigma I^2}{\sigma I \sigma H} = \frac{\sigma I}{\sigma H}$$

The $r_{IH}$ should be as high as possible to make index selection more efficient. The $R_{IH}$ will depend upon the correct estimation of $b_i$ values of the index. Therefore, the $b_i$ which are multiple regression coefficients should be obtained so as to make $R_{IH}$ as high as possible. Thus the $b_i$ should be such that I may best discriminate the individuals with greatest genotypic economic value (H). Thus the selection based on I should be as accurate as based on H, if it was known.

The $b_i$ values are estimated by setting and solving the simultaneous equations whose number is equal to the number of traits under selection. The simultaneous equations use the economic value of each trait, genetic variances and co-variances for all the traits, and phenotypic variances and co-variances.

$b_1x_{11} + b_2x_{12} + \ldots\ldots\ldots\ldots + a_nx_{1n} = a_1G_{11} + a_2G_{12} + \ldots\ldots\ldots\ldots + a_nG_{1n}$

$b_1x_{n1} + b_2x_{n2} + \ldots\ldots\ldots\ldots + a_nx_{nn} = a_1G_{n1} + a_2G_{n2} + \ldots\ldots\ldots\ldots + a_nG_{nn}$

The equations in matrix from can be written as :

$bP = a\,G$, therefore, $b = P^{-1}aG$

Where, b is the column vector of coefficients to be calculated,

$p^{-1}$ is the inverse of phenotypic variance and covariance matrix,

a = column vector for economic weights.

G = genotypic variance and covariance matrix

The value of $b_i$ are obtained by the multiplying the aG with the inverse of P or $P^{-1}$ and then fitted in the mathematically description of the function (I) = $b_1 X_1 + \ldots + b_n X_n$. The fitted equation is called the selection index.

By using this function the selection criterion (index value) for each animal based on several traits may be determined. The animals are then arranged in order of merit to select those with the highest value.

## Requirements to construct selection index

The construction of a selection index requires:-

- the economic value or the relative net economic importance of each of the trait,
- the genetic and phenotypic variances of all traits

- the phenotypic and genetic covariances among all traits.

## Estimation of economic value

It is important to know the method of estimating the relative economic value (a) of the trait, by taking the example of cattle. The most important economic traits are age at first calving (AFC), milk yield, lactation length, peak yield, and milk yield per day of calving interval etc.

The economic value of AFC is estimated by taking actual cost of raising an animal from birth till first calving. Actual expenditure incurred on feed and fodders fed per day per head alongwith labour and miscellaneous charges are considered for finding the economic value of each day of AFC. The minor expenditure on housing, depreciation on capital and medicine charges are not included as these are considered to be balanced out by the income from dung, sale of skin and hides etc. To find out the cost per head per day till AFC, the monthly expenditure and the number of animals are considered. It is better to divide the period from birth to AFC in atleast 3 groups viz. calves (upto 6 or 9 months), young stock (6 or 9 months to 2 years of age) and heifers (2 years to AFC). The cost per head per day for each of the categories is calculated. The total cost per head per day of AFC is calculated by giving due weightage to the length of age in days for calves, young stock and heifers but multiplying the cost per day in the category with the number of days in the category and summing up over the three categories, and then dividing by the total number of days from birth to AFC.

Economic value of milk yield is the selling price of milk during different month of the year. From this the average cost of one Kg. of milk is calculated. The economic value of lactation length, peak yield, and milk yield per day of calving interval may be calculated as the regression of milk yield on these traits. This results in the value of a unit of the trait in terms of Kg. of milk. The value is subsequently multiplied with the selling price of milk to get in terms of rupees the economic value of one unit of trait.

Further in order to bring about similarity among different traits, the economic value of a standard unit of each trait is considered. A standard unit is taken as equal to one per cent standard deviation of the trait. Finally, keeping the economic value of milk as unity (one), relative values of other traits are calculated. This gives the vector of economic values when a proper sign is attached to the values. In this case positive sign to all the traits except AFC which is assigned a negative sign for the obvious reason to effect a decrease in AFC for economic reasons.

## Construction of selection index

Selection index is constructed in the following steps:-

### 1. Estimation of genetic and economic parameters

The following genetic and economic parameters of the traits included in selection for improvement are estimated:-

(i) The genetic and phenotypic variances of all the traits.

(ii) The genetic and phenotypic covariance among all the traits.

(iii) The economic values for all the traits based on price data and profit.

## 2. Estimation of partial regression coefficients

The selection index (I) is:

$I = \Sigma bi\ xi = b_1 x_1 + b_2 x_2 + \dots\dots\dots\dots\dots\dots + b_n x_n$

Where, bi are the partial regression coefficient of each trait

xi are the phenotypic values of the traits.

The regression coefficients are estimated by setting and solving the normal simultaneous equations for n traits under selection as follows:-

I $\quad b_1 V_{P1} + b_2 \text{ Cov } P_{12} + \dots + b_n \text{ Cov } P_{1n} = a_1 V_{A1} + a_2 \text{ Cov } A_{12} + \dots + a_n \text{ Cov } A_{1n}$

II $\quad b_1 \text{ Cov } P_{21} + b_2 V_{P2} + \dots + b_n \text{ Cov } P_{2n} = a_1 \text{Cov}_{A21} + a_2 V_{A2} + \dots + a_n \text{ Cov } A_{2n}$

N $\quad b_1 \text{ Cov } P_{n1} + b_2 \text{ Cov } P_{n2} + \dots + b_n V_{Pn} = a_1 \text{Cov} A_{n1} + a_2 \text{ Cov } A_{n2} + \dots + b_n VA_n$

The above equations are solved for bi values. The variances and covariances (both genetic and phenotypic) and economic values are first determined and put into the above equations to solve for bi values.

## Selection index

The selection index (I) = $b_1 x_1 + b_2 x_2 + \dots\dots\dots + b_n x_n$

The bi and xi values are put up in the index to obtain the index value for each animal and the animals with top highest index value are selected.

## Practical problems in constructing selection index

There are certain practical problems in construction of selection index and to recommend in general for all herds and even in the same herd over time

The information required is not available or accurate enough. The relative economic importance of traits varies from time to time and in different locality and relative economic value of each trait is difficult to establish. It requires information on the long time price average and cost of production of the traits. Sometimes the economic value changes due to change in market demand.

To find the genetic and phenotypic parameters is not an easy job particularly when the number of traits included in the index exceeds three or more.

Moreover, the selection index constructed can not in general be recommended because the genetic and phenotypic parameters differ in different populations due to different genetic constitution of the herds and different management practices. The genetic correlations have large sampling errors mainly due to small herd size. Because of these problems, an index constructed for one herd can not be widely applied in general. The different management practices and environmental conditions at different places may cause the variability of the traits.

The net merit (aggregate genetic worth H) of an animal has been assumed as an additive linear combination of characters each weighted by its relative economic value. This assumption may not true always, and the economic value of a character either may not be linear or may not be independent of the other character. The example of milk yield and fat content may be taken. The net return for increate in milk production is not linear and fat content depends on milk yield of the animal. It is, therefore, advisable to use a model which covers both additive and non–additive functions:-

## 9.3.3. Comparative efficiency of different methods of selection

Hazel and Lush (1942) compared the efficiency of these three methods in terms of genetic gain, assuming that traits under selection were independent, and had equal heritability, economic weight and variance. They discussed that in all three methods there is always the danger that selection will fall below its maximum efficiency because too much attention is paid to some characters and too little to others. In tandem method the selection may be for unimportant characters in the beginning of first few generations and selection for more important characters may be for a brief period. In ICL method, the culling levels may be set too high for one trait and too low for other. In selection index method there may be mistakes in estimating genetic parameters and economic value. Moreover, the value of Z/P (intensity of selection) is not properly taken because the value of i is taken from Statistical Tables based on normal curve which are not possible always in biological data that show little skew ness. If the curve is skewed with long tail of distribution towards low merit, the progress is faster with mild selection and less rapid with intense selection than in a truly normal curve. On the contrary, if the curve is skewed towards high merit, the progress is less with high selection but more with intense selection. Lastly, the selection progress is also affected by animal health which affects p, and also by the breeders ability to record the observations properly.

The expected genetic gain due to one generation of selection of one trait alone by tandem selection ($H_1$), for ICL method ($H_2$), and for total score based on traits ($H_3$) has been given as:

$$H_1 = ah^2 \sigma_p \frac{Z}{p}$$

$$H_2 = n\, ah^2 \sigma_p \frac{Z_3}{p}$$ where $Z_3$ is fixed by q the common level for all traits, and

$$q = \sqrt[n]{p}$$

$$H_3 = \sqrt{n}\, ah^2 \sigma_p \frac{Z}{p}$$

The ratio of gain from index to tandem = $\frac{H_3}{H_1} = \sqrt{n}$

This showed that index selection based on equally important and uncorrelated traits is times as efficient as the single trait or tandem method, regardless of intensity of selection. The progress in any one trait is only $\frac{1}{\sqrt{n}}$ times as efficient by the index selection as if selection was applied for that trait alone. ICL method is more efficient than tandem selection for each trait at a time, the relative efficiency increases with the number of traits and intensity of culling. But ICL method is less efficient than index selection except in some cases of earlier selection. Thus ICL method is always intermediate in efficiency between tandem and index selection method. However, the p value influences the efficiency of all the three methods. The lower value of p leads to more progress by all the 3 methods and the increase in progress is more rapid with ICL than other two methods. With mild selection the relative efficiency of ICL method is closer to that of tandem method but tends to be close to the total scores method when the selection is very intense. Thus, Hazel and Lush (1942) concluded that index method was most superior and tandem selection least, whereas the efficiency of ICL method was intermediate:-

(i) The index is more efficient than tandem, the relative efficiency of the index increase with n.

(ii) The index is more efficient than ICL, its superiority rises with increasing n but falls with increasing i.

(iii) The ICL is more efficient than tandem selection, the superiority of ICL rises with increase in n and i.

Youg (1961) and Finney (1962) compared the efficiency of three methods of selection under general conditions of correlation among traits and their unequal importance.

Young (1961) concluded that:-

**(i)** The index is never less efficient than ICL in all the circumstances, though in some cases it is no more efficient; ICL is never less efficient than tandem but in some cases no more efficient than tandem selection.

**(ii)** The superiority of the index over tandem and ICL increases with an increase in n but decreases with increasing differences in relative importance. Its superiority is maximum for equal importance of traits. An increase in selection intensity decreases the superiority of index over ICL but the superiority of index over tandem is independent of intensity.

**(iii)** An increase in selection intensity or an increase in number of traits increases the superiority of ICL over tandem selection but decreases with increasing differences in relative importance of traits.

**(iv)** Since the changes in correlations among traits affect the genetic gain, the phenotypic and genetic correlation may affect the relative efficiency of selection methods. The relative efficiency of the index over other methods is higher when $r_p$ is low or negative when the traits are of equal importance.

## Restricted Selection index

Under certain conditions, the breeder may like to effect change in the means of certain traits (say, r) out of p traits while keeping the means of p – r traits unchanged. This is the case of restricted selection which has been dealt by Kempthorne and Nordskog (1959) with the constraints that some linear functions of genotypic values would remain constant (unchanged).

Now the question that what are those conditions which compels the breeder to impose restrictions? Some times it is restricted because one trait is at an optimum level of performance beyond which no improvement can be made because of physiological optima, or one does not want to reduce the means of a certain trait which is expected because of its negative genetic association with other economic traits under selection. Reports appeared in the literature (Salisbury and Van demark, 1961 and Swanson, 1967) suggested that the physiological optima to age at first calving and calving interval exist, below which the economic value of the animal decreases. Secondly, fat percentage is negatively genetically correlated with milk production and similarly egg production with egg weight and so an improvement in milk yield and egg production will lead to an associated decrease in the fat percentage in milk and egg weight, respectively, which will not be desirable. Therefore, the problem is, for example, to allow a change in milk yield only and no change in the fat percentage.

The problem of index construction with restriction requires to maximize the correlation between H and I such that $\Delta G_j = 0$, i.e., the genetic gain in character $x_j$ (the character under restriction) is zero. A solution to this problem was given by Kempthorne and Nordskog (1959) imposing restrictions equal to the number of traits that were not allowed to change their phenotypic value. They proposed that the usual index equations be solved subject to the simultaneous conditions that the covariance between the index and the linear function of the genotypes involved be zero, thus preventing selection on the index from causing any genetic change in this function.

For example, take two traits, $x_1$ and $x_2$ , with a condition to impose restriction on $x_2$. To impose restriction that the new index shall produce no change in $G_2$, the index equations are solved subject to the condition that cov. $(G_2, I) = 0$. The aggregate genotype (H) for 2 traits is $H = a_1G_1+a_2G_2$ but when restricted no change in $X_2$, $H = a_1G_1$. Thus select for $H = a_1G_1$ by $I^* = b^*_1x_1+b^*_2x_2$ where * indicates the restricted selection index (RSI) – restricted in that the index is to maximize H with the restricted selection that $\Delta G_2 = 0$. Mathematically, it can be shown that the covariance between $G_2$ and I is $b^*_1x_1G_2+b^*_2x_2G_2$ which must be zero. In addition the equation for the $b_1$ to maximize $R_{HI}$ are

$$b^*_1x_1+b^*_2x_1x_2 = x_1H$$

$$b^*_1x_1x_2+b^*_2x_2 = x_2H$$

Thus, there are three equations including the restriction but only two unknowns. In order to find a solution we must add a dummy unknown, the so called **Lagrange multiplier**. The equations can now be solved and are :

$$\begin{aligned}
b^*_1x_1 &+ b^*_2x_1x_2 &+ \lambda G_1G_2 &= x_1H \\
b^*_1x_1x_2 &+ b^*_2x_2 &+ \lambda G_2G_2 &= x_2H \\
b^*_1x_1G_2 &+ b^*_2G_2G_2 &+ O &= 0
\end{aligned}$$

or

$$\begin{vmatrix} b_1 \\ b_2 \\ \lambda \end{vmatrix} = \begin{vmatrix} V_{P1} & + Cov_{P12} & + Cov_{G12} \\ Cov_{P21} & + V_{P2} & + V_{G22} \\ Cov_{G12} & + V_{G2} & + 0 \end{vmatrix}^{-1} \begin{vmatrix} V_{G11} \\ Cov_{G12} \\ 0 \end{vmatrix}$$

These can be solved for $b_1$* to get the restricted selection index.

The $b_i$ estimates can also be obtained by the formula:

$b = [I\text{-}P^{-1}GC\ (C'CP^{-1}GC)\text{-}C'G]P^{-1}Ga$

Where I is the identity (unit) matrix,

G is the genotypic variance convariance matrix,

$P^{-1}$ is the inverse of phenotypic variance and covariance matrix

G is the coefficient vector matrix, and

C' is the transposed coefficient matrix, which is defined as:

(i) For $\Delta G_1 = 0$ and other ($\Delta G_2$, $\Delta G_3$ and $\Delta G_4$) unrestricted, C' = (1 0 0 0) is a vector

(ii) For $\Delta G_2 = 0$ and other ($\Delta$ $G_1$, $\Delta G_3$ etc.) unrestricted, C' = (0 1 0 0) is a vector

(iii) For $\Delta G_1 = \Delta G_2 = 0$ and other ($\Delta G_3$ & $\Delta G_4$) unrestricted, C' $\left[\frac{1000}{0100}\right]$

Cunningham (1970) explained the method of calculating the genetic cost of the restrictions. It is known that there is always a genetic cost attached to maintaining a restriction. The response in selecting according to I* can be compared with the response in selecting directly without restriction. Such a cost has been calculated to be as followed.

$$\text{Genetic cost \%} = 100\left[1-\sqrt{[(b'\ Pb - b^2 / W_{ii})\ b'\ Pb]}\right]$$

Where, Wii is the corresponding diagonal element of $P^{-1}$,

$b^i$ is the weighing factor for the variate being evaluated,

and b pb' is thevariance of the index.

**Role(uses) of R.S.I.:** The R.S.I. are of special use when the breeder wishes to keep the means of a certain trait unchanged which is otherwise expected because of association among the economic traits. In case the traits are positively correlated, the intermediate optimum in some traits(s) having arrived, the method of R.S.I. can help in improvement of some traits without affecting the average value of others, like age at first calving and weight of the calf. Likewise, if the traits are negatively correlated, viz., milk yield and its fat percentage, egg size and production, the improvement in milk yield and egg production is possible without allowing a reduction in fat percentage and egg size, respectively, by the use of R.S.I.

The technique, of R.S.I. is not effective/applicable when the traits are either uncorrelated of having perfect correlation. Considering that the population have reached plateau after intensive selection for a long time, high selection intensity for further improvement is no more desirable. The main reason is that the traits negatively correlated e.g. egg weight and production will be affected adversely. It is reasonable to reduce the selection intensity for such traits. In such a case R.S.I. methodology makes possible judicious reduction in selection pressure of such traits resulting into best desirable improvement.

**Selection experiments on R.S.I. :** Very few reports are available in the literature regarding the use of R.S.I. Applanalp et al. (1963) selected turkeys for 7 generations using an index calculated to produce maximum gains in 9 week weight while holding 24 week body weight constant. The results were in fair agreement of prediction, except a little negative response in 24 week body weight. Okada and Hardin (1967) designed R.S.I. to increase 14 day larval weight without increasing 30 days adult weight of Tribolium, using the technique developed by Kampthorne and Nordskog (1959). They found that R.S.I. was effective for increasing larval weight while holding adult weight constant. Scheinberg et al. (1967) also confirmed the biological validity of the R.S.I. model working with *Tribolum castaneum* for 10 generations. They compared uni-stage tandem selection with R.S.I. for high larval weight, short development time and high pupal weight imposing restriction on two traits at a time in each experiment.

Some selection experiments using the technique of R.S.I. have also been conducted with mice (Putledge et al., 1973 and Eisen and Bandy, 1977). They considered 6 week body weight and tail length at 6 week of age. They found that the index selection was effective and in agreement with theory. Eisen (1977) also designed a R.S.I. on mice with the aim to maximize genetic change in post-weaning weight gain from 5 to 6 weeks of age while keeping genetic response in feed intake at zero. He found the R.S.I. to be as:-

Ir = Pg-0.067 Pf where Pg and Pf are phenotypic values for post weaning gain and total feed intake from 3-6 weeks of age, resp. The result supported the validity of R.S.I. theory.

A number of selection indices with and without restrictions have been given by Gurnani et al. (1977) for selection of dairy cattle. However, they only utilized already available data of Tharparkar herd of NDRI – on the first and second lactation yield, the age at first calving and first calving interval. They observed that restriction on age at first calving did not reduce the gains while restricting the mean genotypic value of calving interval resulted in halving the gains.

## Assumptions and conditions in constructing and using R.S.I.

1. Relative weights are known without error. This can be achieved and would change over time and with region.
2. Relative economic weights remain constant over the range of variation likely to occur for the different traits. This is doubtful because of too good and too poor kind of cattle/buffaloes. These relative economic weights do not change through time, however, new indices may be constructed in due course.
3. Genetic and phenotypic variances are known without error.

4. The traits under consideration are heritable and the genetic correlation between the two traits is not perfect or absent.
5. Aggregate genotype and index are normally distributed.

**Practical situations for using RSI in farm animals:** The main selection trait in sheep is fleece weight, besides other features. The S.I. is required to increase the fleece weight of the flock as much as possible while stabilizing staple length and number of crimps at optimum level.

In cattle it is required to :

(i) Increase the birth weight of calf.
(ii) Increase the average monthly growth rate in the first year of life
(iii) Increase the weight at first calving
(iv) No change in the age at first calving
(v) Increase the first lactation production
(vi) No change in the fat test of milk.

It is known that all these six traits, (i) through (vi), are heritable, more or less, and that there exist correlations, phenotypic as well as genetic, positive or negative amongst them. Thus any change in one trait would bring about an undesirable correlated change in other traits when classical selection index incorporating all the traits is used. It is here that the restricted selection index is of use and involves the imposition of restrictions on the mathematical model that traits (iv) and (vi) do not change in value.

In poultry the situation arises when one wants to increase the egg production without affecting the egg size which are negatively correlated. Egg size is kept constant while using an index to maximize progress in genetic economic value based on egg weight, body weight and production.

## Multitrait – multisource selection index

The selection index is obtained for individual selection for many traits simultaneously. However, the different traits may not have equal heritability estimates but some may have low heritability. Thus it may not be possible to make improvement in the lowly heritable traits. The accuracy of selection for such traits (with low $h^2$) can be increased by using the information from other sources (individual's relatives records) for such traits. The selection index for two or more traits is obtained from individual and its relative's records. Such a selection index is known as multi trait – multi source index which is constructed on the principle of selection index theory (Hazel, 1943). The presentation by Ronningen and VanVleck (1990) given in «General and Quantitative Genetics» edited by A.B. Chapman may be referred by the readers.

## 9.4. NUMERICAL SOLVED EXAMPLES

The breeding value of an individual can be estimated based on single record in a herd, in many herd, as contemporary deviation and with average of multiple records of the individual

## (i) Single record in a herd

Probable Breeding value = $\overline{H} + h^2(P_i - \overline{H})$

Where, $\overline{H}$ = herd average, $P_i$ = Individual's record

**Example 9.1:** A herd of Tharparkar cows had an average milk production of 6.0 kg with an $h^2$ estimated of 0.25. The average milk production of 4 cows is 9.0, 5.0, 8.5 and 6.0 kg. Estimate the B.V. of these cows

## Solution

| | | |
|---|---|---|
| Cow No. 1 | PBV = 6.0+0.25 (9-6) | = 6.75 kg |
| Cow No. 2 | PBV = 6.0+0.25 (5-6) | = 5.75 kg |
| Cow No. 3 | PBV = 6.0+0.25 (8.5-6) | =6.62 kg |
| Cow No. 4 | PBV = 6.0+0.25 (6-6) | = 6.0 kg |

## (ii) Single record in many herd

$$\text{P.B.V.} = \overline{H} + h^2(P_{ij} - \overline{H}_i) + h_H^2(\overline{H}_i - \overline{H})$$

Where,

$\overline{H}$ = Population mean (all herds)

$h^2$ = $h^2$ of the character

$P_{ij}$ = $j^{th}$ individual of $i^{th}$ herd

$\overline{H}_i$ = $i^{th}$ herd mean

$h_H^2$ = $h^2$ of the herd difference within population

**Example 9.2** A population comprising two herds had average milk production of 1900 kg whereas the herd average of two herd was 2000 kg and 1800 kg. Considering 3 cows in each herd with their milk production as 1900, 2000, 2100 for one herd and 1700, 1800, 1900 for second herd, $h^2$ of milk production as 0.25 and $h_H^2$ as 0.12 find out the PBV of all the cows and rank them.

## Solution

$$\text{P.B.V.} = \overline{H} + h^2(P_{ij} - \overline{H}_i) + h_H^2(\overline{H}_i - \overline{H})$$

Cow no. 1 of herd 1 = 1900+0.25 (1900-2000) +0.12 (2000-1900)

= 1900-25+12 = 1887 kg

Likewise the P.B.V. of all other cows can be estimated and their ranking may be done.

## (iii) Single record with contemporary deviation

It is better to use the contemporary deviation to estimate the P.B.V. so as to remove the effects of year or season of calving. Thus

P.B.V.= $\text{P.B.V.} = \overline{H} + h^2(\overline{P}_i - \overline{P}_C)$

Where, is the contemporary average

The contemporaries are those cows which calved within ± 2 months of the cow whose P.B.V. is to be estimated

## (iv) Average of multiple records

When $h^2$ of a trait is low, it is better to select on the basis of family mean to increase accuracy but F.S. families are not available and thus the accuracy of individual selection can be increased by using multiple records on the same individual. This reduces the environmental effects and hence increases the accuracy of P.B.V.

$$\text{P.B.C.} = \overline{H} + \frac{nh^2}{1+(n-1)r}(\overline{P}_i - \overline{H})$$

Where, n = No. of records, r = Repeatability of the trait, = Average of n records of $i^{th}$ individual, $\overline{H}$ = Herd average

**Example 9.3** The average milk production of a flock of goats is 400 kg. The milk production of 4 outstanding goats in different lactation is as under:-

| Goat No. | $L_1$ | $L_2$ | $L_3$ |
|---|---|---|---|
| 1 | 460 | 480 | - |
| 2 | 390 | 400 | 450 |
| 3 | 480 | - | - |
| 4 | 400 | 380 | - |

Taking the $h^2$ as 0.25 and repeatability as 0.35, estimate the B.V. of all the 4 goats and rank them:

## Solution

$$\text{PBV} = \overline{H} + \frac{nh^2}{1+(n-1)r}(\overline{P}_i - \overline{H})$$

Goat NO. 1: $\text{PBV} = 400 + \frac{2 \times 0.25}{1+0.35}(470-400) = 425.92 \text{ Kg}$

Goat No. 2: $\text{PBV} = 400 + \frac{3 \times 0.25}{1+(2 \times 0.35)}(413.3-400) = 404.8 \text{ Kg}$

Goat No. 3: $\text{PBV} = 400 + \frac{1 \times 0.25}{1+0.0}(480-400) = 420 \text{ kg}$

Goat No. 4: $\text{PBV} = 400 + \frac{2 \times 0.25}{1+0.35}(390-400) = 396.2 \text{ kg}$

Therefore, the ranking of 4 goats for their P.B.V. is

| Goat No. | 1 | 2 | 3 | 4 |
|---|---|---|---|---|
| Rank | 1 | 3 | 2 | 4 |

## Estimation of MPPA

Culling of low producers is essential to increase the productivity next year. This is done by estimating the 'Most Probable Producing Ability'. The estimation of MPPA is also essential under the situation where the $h^2$ estimate can not be made for non availability of the information on pedigree of the individual. The MPPA is estimated as :

$$\text{MPPA} = \overline{H} + \frac{nr}{1+(n-1)r}(\overline{P_i} - \overline{H})$$

The contemporary deviations are used instead of herd average ( $\overline{H}$ ) in order to reduce the seasonal variation

**Example 9.4:** The average milk production in a lactation of Tharparkar herd is 1800 kg. The milk production of 4 cows in different lactations is given as under:

| Cow No. | Lactation 1 | Lactation 2 | Lactation 3 | Lactation 4 |
|---|---|---|---|---|
| 1 | 1820 | 1860 | - | - |
| 2 | 1810 | 1836 | 1860 | 1840 |
| 3 | 1830 | 1850 | 1870 | - |
| 4 | 1840 | - | - | - |

Taking the repeatability of milk yield as 0.40, estimate the MPPA of all the cows and rank them.

**Solution**

$$\text{MPPA} = \overline{H} + \frac{nr}{1+(n-1)r}(\overline{P_i} - \overline{H})$$

Cow No. 1: MPPA = $1800 + \frac{2 \times 0.40}{1+0.4}(1840 - 1800) = 1822\ Kg$

Cow No. 2: MPPA = $1800 + \frac{4 \times 0.40}{1+(3 \times 0.4)}(1816.5 - 1800) = 1812\ Kg$

Cow No. 3: MPPA = $1800 + \frac{4 \times 0.40}{1+(2 \times 0.4)}(1850 - 1800) = 1813\ Kg$

Cow No. 4 MPPA = $1800 + \frac{1 \times 0.40}{1+0}(1840 - 1800) = 1816\ Kg$

Ranking of the cows is as under

| CowNo.= | 1 | 2 | 3 | 4 |
|---|---|---|---|---|
| Rank= | 1 | 4 | 3 | 2 |

**Example 9.5:** Construct an index to selection for fast growth and lean beef percentage from the information given below:

| Traits | $h^2$ | a | $\sigma_p$ | $r_g$ | $r_p$ |
|---|---|---|---|---|---|
| Average daily gain | 0.43 | 1.5 | 80.0 | 0.3 | -0.1 |
| Lean beef % | 0.30 | 0.5 | 7.0 | | |

## Solution:

The first step is to work out the genetic and phenotypic variance and covariance as under:-

$$\sigma^2_{p(1)} = (80)^2 = 6400 \qquad \sigma^2_{p(2)} = (7.8)^2 = 51.84$$

$$\sigma^2_{A(1)} = h^2\,\sigma^2_{p(1)} = 0.43 \times 6400 = 2752$$

$$\sigma^2_{A(2)} = h^2\,\sigma^2_{p(2)} = 0.30 \times 51.84 = 15.552$$

$$Cov_{P(12)} = r_p \sigma_{P(1)} \sigma_{p(2)} = -1 \times 80 \times 7.2 = -57.6$$

$$Cov_{A(12)} = r_g \sigma_{A(1)} \sigma_{A(2)} = 0.3 \times \sqrt{2752} \times \sqrt{15,552} = 0.3 \times 52.46 \times 3.94 = 52.064$$

=0.3 x 52.46 x 3.94 = 52.064

The bi values will now be estimated as under

$$\begin{vmatrix} b_1 \\ b_2 \end{vmatrix} = \begin{vmatrix} V_{P(1)} & Cov_{P(12)} \\ Cov_{P\,(12)} & V_{P(2)} \end{vmatrix}^{-1} \begin{vmatrix} a_1 V_{A(1)} + Cov_{A(12)} \\ a_1\, Cov_{A(12)} + a_2 V_{A(2)} \end{vmatrix}$$

Now putting the values, the equations will be:

$$\begin{vmatrix} b_1 \\ b_2 \end{vmatrix} = \begin{vmatrix} 6400 & -57.60 \\ -57.60 & 51.84 \end{vmatrix}^{-1} \begin{vmatrix} 1.5(2752) + 0.5(62.064) \\ 1.5(62.064) + 0.5(15.572) \end{vmatrix}$$

$b_1 = 0.74$ and $b_2 = 2.695$

(ii) The $b_1$ value can also be estimated by setting the two simultaneous equations and solving them as

$$b_1 V_{P(1)} + b_2\, Cov_{P(12)} = a_1 V_{A(1)} + a_2\, Cov_{A(12)}$$

$b_1\ Cov_{P\ (12)} + b_2\ V_{P(2)} = a_1\ Cov_{A(12)} + a_2\ V_{A(2)}$

Now putting the values, equations will be

$6400b_1$ -57.60b2 = 1.5 (2752)+0.5(62.064)

$-57.60b_1 + 51.84b_2$=1.5 (62.064) + 0.5(15.552)

Now multiply eq. 1 with 51.94 and eq. (2) with -57.60 and adding two equations will cancel the $b_2$. Thus $b_1$ value can be obtained. Then the value of $b_2$ can be estimated.

The selection index (I) will be:

$1.0674\ X_1 + 2.695\ X_2$

$0.674(X_1 - \overline{X}_1) + 2.695(X_2 - \overline{X}_2)$

or $1 = X_1 + 3.998\ X_2$ by dividing with 0.674

$= (X_1 - \overline{X}_1) + 3.398(X_2 - \overline{X}_2)$

The accuracy of index ($r_{ai}$) will be

$$r_{AI} = \sqrt{\frac{\sum b_i b_{ij}}{d_a^2}}$$

$$= \sqrt{\frac{0.674(2752) + 2.695(62.064)}{2752}} = \sqrt{\frac{1854.848 + 167.26248}{2752}}$$

$$= \sqrt{\frac{2022.1105}{2752}} = 0.857$$

**Example 9.6:** Given the following information construct a selection index to maximize genetic gain in aggregate genetic rate. (ARS 1984)

$h^2_x = 0.5,\ h^2_y = 0.1,\ a_x = 1,\ a_y = 4,\ r_{g(xy)} = 0.4,\ r_{P(xy)} = 0.4$

**Solution:** The variances and covariances can be estimated with the given information:

$$h^2 = \frac{\sigma_A^2}{\sigma_P^2} \text{ and hence } \sigma_P^2 = \frac{\sigma_A^2}{h^2} = 1.0$$

or the $h^2$ itself is an indicator of additive genetic variance ($\sigma_A^2$)

Therefore, $\sigma_X^2 = \sigma_{A(x)}^2$ and $h_Y^2 = \sigma_{A(y)}^2$

$\sigma_{P(x)}^2 = 1.0$ and also $\sigma_{P(y)}^2 = 1.0$

$$r_{xy} = \frac{Cov_{xy}}{\sqrt{\sigma_x^2 \sigma_y^2}} \text{ and hence } Cov_{xy} = r_{xy}\sqrt{\sigma_x^2 \sigma_y^2}$$

$Cov_{p(xy)} = r_{P(xy)} \sqrt{\sigma^2_{P(x)} \sigma^2_{P(y)}}$

$0.4\sqrt{1 x 1} = 0.4$

$Cov_{A(xy)} = r_{A(xy)} \sqrt{\sigma^2_{A(x)} \sigma^2_{A(y)}}$

$= - 0.4\sqrt{0.5 \times 0.1} = - 0.4 \times 0.2236 = 0.0894$

The selection index (I) = $b_1 X_1 + b_2 X_2$

Where, $b_1$ are the partial regression coefficient estimated by setting and solving the following simultaneous equation as:-

$b_1 V_{P(X)} + b_2 Cov_{P(XY)} = a_1 V_{A(X)} + a_2 Cov_{A(XY)}$

$b_1 Cov_{P(XY)} + b_2 V_{P(Y)} = a_1 Cov_{A(XY)} + a_2 V_{A(Y)}$

Now substituting the values of genetic and phenotypic variances, genetic and phenotypic covariance and economic values in the above equations, the following two equations will be obtained:-

$b_1 + 0.4b_2 = 1 x 0.5 + 4(-0.0894)$

$0.4 b_1 + b_2 x 1 = 1 x (-0.0894) + 4(0.1)$

Multiplying the equation (i) by o.4 and substracting equation (ii) from equation (i),

$0.4b_1 + 0.16b_2 = 0.0569$

$0.4b_1 + b_2 = 0.3106$

-- -- --

---

$-0.84b_2 = -0.2537$

$b_2 = 0.302$

Substituting the value of $b_2$ in equation (i)

$b_1 + 0.1208 = 0.1424$

$b_1 = 0.1424-0.1208$

$= 0.0216$

Therefore, I $= b_1 X_1 + b_2 X_2$

$= 0.0216 X_1 + 0.302 X_2$

$= X_1 + 13.98 X_2$

**Example 9.7:** Based on first lactation milk yield (kg) and age at first calving (months) using the following statistics, the selection index can be numerically constructed as follows:

| Traits | Economic value (a) | Genetic variance(VA) | Phenotypic variance (VP) | Covariance Cov. A | Cov. P |
|---|---|---|---|---|---|
| Milk yield ($X_1$) | 1.00 | 84687.21 | 125423.41 | -42.26 | 111.989 |
| AFC ($X_2$) | -5.84 | 13.678 | 17.498 | | |

The following two simultaneous equations to be set are:-

$b_1 V_P(x_1) + b_2 \text{ Cov P } (x_1 x_2) = a_1 V_A(x_1) + a_2 \text{ Cov }_A (x_1 x_2)$ .........(1)

$b_1 \text{ Cov P } (x_1 x_2) + b_2 V_P(x_2) = a_1 \text{ cov A } (x_1 x_2) + a_2 V_A(x_2)$ ........ (2)

Putting the values given in the table we get the following two equations:-

$125423.41\, b_1 + 111.989\, b_2 = 1.00(84687.21)+(-5.84)\,(-42.26$ .........(1)

$111.989\, b_1 + 17.498\, b_2 = 1.00(-42.26) +(-5.84)\,(13.678)$ ................(2)

Multiplying equation (i) with 17.498 and equation (ii) with 111.989, we get

$2194654.1\, b_1 + 1959.58\, b_2 = -122.1395 \times 17.498$ ................(3)

$12541.54\, b_1 + 1959.58\, b_2 = -84934.06 \times 111.989$ ................(4)

Substracting equation (4) from equation (3) we get

$2182112.6\, b_1 = 1499853.6$ $b_1 = 0.687$

substituting the value of $b_1$ in equation (2) we get

$111.989 \times 0.687 + 17.498\, b_2 = -122.139$

$76.97 + 17.498\, b_2 = -122.139$

$$b_2 = \frac{122.139 - 76.97}{17.498} = -11.378$$

The index, $I_1 = b_1 x_1 + b_1 x_2$

$= 0.687\, X_1 - 11.378\, x_2$

$= X_1 - 16.56\, X_2$

## Solved example 9.8 : Restricted S.I.

Using the data of solved example 9.5 construct an index to improve the aggregate genotype for fast growing lean cattle with no change in lean percentage

## Solution:

The equation for the index are

$$\begin{vmatrix} b_1 \\ b_2 \\ \lambda \end{vmatrix} = \begin{vmatrix} p_{11} & p_{12} & p_{12} \\ p_{21} & p_{22} & g_{22} \\ g_{21} & g_{22} & 0 \end{vmatrix}^{-1} \begin{vmatrix} g_{11} \\ g_{12} \\ 0 \end{vmatrix}$$

$$\begin{vmatrix} b_1 \\ b_2 \\ \lambda \end{vmatrix} = \begin{vmatrix} 6400 & -57.60 & 62.064 \\ 57.60 & 50.80 & 15.552 \\ 62.064 & 15.552 & 0 \end{vmatrix}^{-1} \begin{vmatrix} 2572 \\ 62.064 \\ \end{vmatrix}$$

Solving the equations:

$b_1 = 0.325$, $b_2 = -1.1.303$

$$I = 0.325(X_1 - \overline{X}_2) + (-1.303)(X_2 - X_2)$$

$$r_{AI} = \sqrt{\frac{\sum b_i g_{ij}}{\sigma_a^2}} = \sqrt{\frac{0.325(2752) - (-1.303)(62.064)}{2752}} = 0.544$$

The imposition of restriction on any trait in the index never increases the efficiency of index but usually reduces it.

## QUESTIONS

**9.1.** Discuss the genetic and other parameters that are required as prerequisite for selection index for production traits. *(ARS 1976)*

**9.2.** Wh at is selection index? What are its prerequisites for its calculation? What are its merits over other methods of selection? Give one example each in dairy and poultry. *(ARS 1978)*

**9.3.** Discuss in detail the method of construction of selection index. Give its definition and prerequisites *(ARS 1982)*

**9.4.** Compare the relative efficiency of the three methods of selection. What are the advantages of R.S.I. *(ARS 1984)*

**9.5.** Define three methods of selection. How they differ particularly to their relative efficiency for

Correlated traits *(ARS 1990)*

Uncorelation traits *(ARS 1983)*

Different selection pressure and $h^2$ *(ARS 1987, 1990)*

9.6. Compare the efficiency of different methods of selection for average genetic gain. How the numbers of traits affect efficiency of index selection? *(ARS 1995, 1999)*

9.7. Describe that selection for more than one character at a time reduces the intensity of selection for each

9.8. What is concept of selection index? What are the parameters required for constructicn of S.I.? Given the following information construct a S.I. to maximize genetic gain in aggregate genetic rate: *(ARS 1984)*

$h^2_1 = 0.5$, $a_1=1$, $r_p=0.4$ $h^2_2 = 0.1$, $a_1=4$, $r_g=-0.4$

***

# 10

# SELECTION CRITERIA–Pedigree and Collateral Relatives

The performance records of ancestors and collateral relatives of the individual are also used as selection criteria to estimate the breeding value of an individual for the trait under selection.

## 10.1. PEDIGREE SELECTION

The pedigree is a list or record of ancestors in the past few generations of the individual. The ancestors are the parents, grand parents, great grand parents etc. The pedigree having information on the economic characters of the ancestors is useful in selection of an individual. The B.V. of an individual is estimated on the basis of the performance of the ancestors. The selection criteria based on ancestors performance is called as the pedigree selection

### 10.1.1. Basis of pedigree selection

An individual receives genes from his ancestors. The percentage of ancestral genes is halved in each generation. This decides the genetic relationship between an individual and his ancestor(s). This relationship is reduced to half in each generation. It is thus important to consider more recent ancestors (parents) rather than distant ancestors (great grand parents) for pedigree selection. The inclusion of more remote ancestors results only in marginal gain in accuracy of selection due to the halving process and sampling nature of inheritance. The pedigree selection adds very little to the accuracy of estimating the B.V. of an individual if the information on individual are available. The significance of pedigree is decreased when information are available either on the individual or its family members (sibs and progeny).

### 10.1.2. Guides to pedigree selection

The following factors determine that how much attention is to be given to pedigree selection.

- The degree of genetic relationship of the individual with its ancestor – more closely related ancestors should be given more emphasis.
- Heritability of the character – the pedigree selection is more accurate for traits of high heritability.
- Environmental correlations among animals used in the prediction.
- Information available on ancestors.

### 10.1.3. Practical difficulties to use pedigree selection

- The ancestors' records are always not available.
- The records may be faulty due to stray mating.
- The pedigree records are destroyed with passage of time.
- Most of the characters have low heritability

### 10.1.4. Merits of pedigree selection

- It is less costly as only compilation of pedigree is required.
- Allows selection at younger age and provides first hand information.
- It is helpful in multistage selection.
- It is useful for sex limited traits and traits expressed in later life or after death of animal.
- It is helpful when two individuals have similar performance but one belongs to a better pedigree.

### 10.1.5. Demerits of pedigree selection

- There is a disadvantage of using pedigree selection that all animals of similar pedigree are culled out inspite of the fact that an individual may be of good merit and free from recessive allele causing defect.
- Some pedigree gets undue emphasis and favoured irrespective of the true merit of the individual. Better environment is provided to the progeny of favoured pedigree.
- It introduces non random biases because pedigree records are for different environmental conditions.
- Pedigree selection provides no basis of selection among individuals which are descendants of the same ancestor.

### 10.1.6. Breeding value based on pedigree records

The B.V. of an individual from its pedigree records is estimated by the selection differential of its relations $(\overline{P})$ from their contemporary $(\overline{P}_c)$ times the regression of the genotype of the individual on the phenotypic mean of the relatives ($b_{AP}$) and added to the mean of the contemporary group as :

P.B.V. = $\overline{P}_c + b_{AP} (\overline{P} - \overline{P}_c)$

The $b_{AP}$ is taken as $rh^2$ where r is the coefficient of relationship between the individual and its relative. In estimating the PBV of an individual the record (s) of one parent or both parents or parents and grand parents can be sued. The regression coefficients based on the record (s) of either parent or both parents for single and multiple records and the accuracy of selection will be as :

| Ancestor | Regression coefficient | Accuracy of selection |
|---|---|---|
| **A. For single record:** | | |
| Dam | $0.5\ h^2_{\ D}$ | $0.5\ h_{\ D}$ |
| Sire | $0.5\ h^2_{\ S}$ | $0.5\ h_{\ S}$ |
| Mean record of both parents | $\frac{1}{\sqrt{2}} h^2$ | $\frac{1}{\sqrt{2}} h$ |
| Parents and grand parents | | $\sqrt{\frac{3-2h^2}{4-2h^4}}\ h$ |
| One grand parents | $0.25\ h^2$ | $0.25\ h$ |
| **A. For more record:** | | |
| Dam | $0.5\ h_D^2 \frac{n}{1+(n-1)r}$ | $0.5\sqrt{\frac{nh_D^2}{1+(n-1)r}}$ |
| Sire | Same as for dam | Same as for dam |
| Both parents | $\frac{1}{\sqrt{2}} \frac{nh^2}{1+(n-1)r}$ | $\frac{1}{\sqrt{2}} \sqrt{\frac{nh^2}{1+(n-1)r}}$ |
| Parents and grand parents | | $\sqrt{\frac{3-2h^2\ h_n^2}{4-2h^4\ h_n^2}}\ h_n$ |
| One grand parents | $0.25\ \frac{nh^2}{1+(n-1)r}$ | $0.25\sqrt{\frac{nh^2}{1+(n-1)r}}$ |

The information on ancestors (parents and grand parents) combined with individual's own record increases the accuracy of selection than based on individual's own record (Table 10.1)

The B.V. of an individual can be estimated by combining information from all sort of relatives whose records are available. This is done by giving weights to different relatives by the technique of multiple regression coefficients. Thus the weights are partial regression coefficients of B.V. of the individual on each kind of relative's phenotype. The B.V. is then estimated by an index of the weighted sum of the records of different relatives. This index is used as the selection criteria.

The records of different ancestors can also be used in combination of individual's own record and the P.B.V. of individual can than be estimated. In this situation the partial regression coefficients are used because the records of two or more relatives are used. The partial regression coefficient for the individual is multiplied by the selection differential for the individual and this is added to the product of the partial regression coefficient and selection differential for each ancestor to predict the P.B.V. of individual, as shown below:

$$PBV = \overline{P}_{ic} + b_1 (P_i - \overline{P}_{ic}) + b_2 (P_p - \overline{P}_{pc})$$

Or

$$\overline{P}_{ic} + b_1 (P_i - \overline{P}_{ic}) + b_2 (P_p - \overline{P}_{pc}) + b_3 (P_{gp} - \overline{P}_{gpc})$$

Or

$$\overline{P}_{ic} + b_1 (P_i - \overline{P}_{ic}) + b_2 (P_s - \overline{P}_{sc}) + b_2 (P_d - \overline{P}_{dc})$$

Where,

$\overline{P}_{ic}$ = mean of individual's contemporaries

$\overline{P}_i$ = Individual's own record

$\overline{P}_p$ = Parents record

$\overline{P}_{PC}$ = Parents' contemporaries mean

$\overline{P}_s$ and = $\overline{P}_d$ Sire and dam's record

$\overline{P}_{sc}$ and $\overline{P}_{dc}$ = Average of sire and dam contemporaries

$b_I$= Partial regression coefficients

$p_{gp}$= Grand parent record

## 10.1.7. Accuracy of pedigree selection

The regression coefficients obtained indicated that the selection based on the performance of one parent is half as effective (accurate) as that based on individual's own performance. The values of $b_i$ are further reduced by half for each ancestor further back to the individual. The information on records of both the parents plus all of the four grand parents give lesser accuracy of selection which does not exceed 0.71 than based on individual's own record. However, the information on ancestors combined with individual's own performance give little higher accuracy of selection than based on individual's own record. The accuracy of selection based on single parent never exceed to 0.50 and that based on either two parents or on parents and grand parents to 0.70 (Table 10.1)

**TABLE 10.1 : ACCURACY OF INDIVIDUAL AND PEDIGREE SELECTION BASED ON SINGLE RECORD**

| Heritability values | 0.1 | 0.2 | 0.3 | 0.4 | 0.5 | 0.6 | 0.7 | 0.8 | 0.9 | 1.0 |
|---|---|---|---|---|---|---|---|---|---|---|
| Individual | 0.31 | 0.44 | 0.54 | 0.63 | 0.70 | 0.77 | 0.84 | 0.89 | 0.95 | 1.0 |
| One parent or all 4 G.P. | 0.16 | 0.22 | 0.27 | 0.32 | 0.35 | 0.39 | 0.42 | 0.45 | 0.47 | 0.50 |
| Two parents | 0.22 | 0.32 | 0.39 | 0.45 | 0.50 | 0.55 | 0.59 | 0.63 | 0.67 | 0.71 |
| Parents and grand parent | 0.27 | 0.37 | 0.43 | 0.49 | 0.53 | 0.57 | 0.61 | 0.64 | 0.67 | 0.71 |
| Individual+ one (p) | 0.34 | - | 0.58 | - | 0.73 | - | 0.84 | - | 0.95 | 1.0 |
| Individual + one (p) + one grand (p) + one great grand (p) | 0.37 | 0.51 | 0.61 | 0.69 | 0.75 | 0.81 | 0.86 | 0.90 | 0.95 | 1.0 |

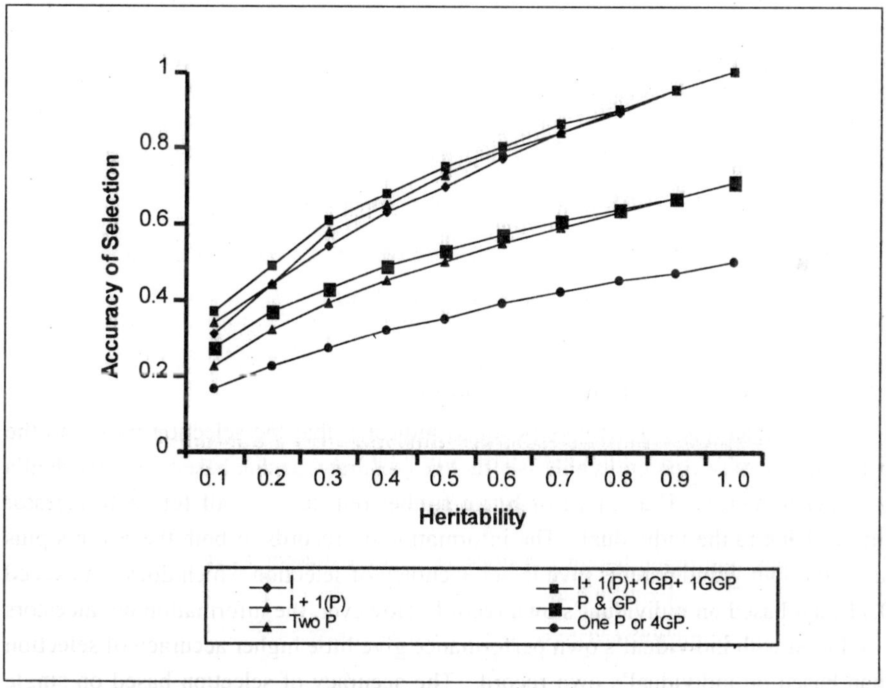


**Figure 10.1: Comparison of accuracy of individual selection and of various types of pedigree selection.**

It can be concluded that pedigree selection is really only useful to select the individual before its own record is available. The pedigree selection is less accurate than individual selection or P.T. based on 4 or more progeny

The accuracy of pedigree selection is expressed by the correlation of the genotype of the individual with the phenotypic mean of the ancestors used in selection. The ancestors records add little to the individuals own record for the traits of low heritability because the accuracy is increased with the increase of $h^2$ of the trait. Thus, for such traits with low $h^2$ the information from ancestors without individual's own record results in low accuracy than individual selection. The accuracy of pedigree selection is generally low because of the followings.

(i) The different possibilities of combinations resulting from segregation of genes.

(ii) It is not possible to predict as to which half of the dam's genes (better or inferior) are transmitted to the offspring because of the halving process and sampling nature of inheritance. Thus, the best lactation performance of the dam in sire evaluation is not a correct method.

(iii) The different environmental conditions prevail at the time of taking records of ancestors and the individual.

## 10.2. COLLATERAL RELATIVES – FAMILY SELECTION

The selection criteria to estimate the B.V. of an individual may be the information (performance records) of its collateral relatives. An individual's collateral relatives are those which are not related with the individual on direct genes donor – recipient basis but receive common genes from their common ancestor (s) e.g. full sibs, half sibs, cousins, uncle/aunt, and nephew/niece. The collateral relatives should be more closely related to the individual and these are full sibs and half sibs. The more closely related collaterals to the individual are likely to have more common genes possessed by the individual and can provide more accurate information about the individual. The more closely collaterals can be grouped as full sib families and half sib families. The family mean of these collateral relatives then form the basis to select the superior individual. The procedure to estimate the B.V. of an individual on the basis of family mean is called the **family selection** or **sib selection** depending upon the inclusion or exclusion of individual's own record in estimating the family mean. The selection criteria is called as family selection when the individual's own record is included to estimate the family mean but the selection criteria is called as the sib selection when the individual's own recorded is not included in estimating the family mean.

### 10.2.1. Sib selection

It is the selection of an individual based on its sibs performance. The sibs may be full sibs or maternal half sibs or paternal half sibs. Thus sib selection is of two types viz. Full sib selection and half sib selection. The sib selection is practiced for the following traits for which the measurements on the individual are not available or recorded –

- Slaughter traits
- Sex limited traits
- Threshold traits like disease resistance
- Traits with low heritability in species with high reproductive rate so as many sibs are measured in short time

The full sib (F.S.) selection is more accurate than half sib (H.S.) selection. However, the H.S. selection is favoured for the following reasons:

- Half sibs are easily available in more numbers than F.S.
- The rate of inbreeding is more for F.S. selection than H.S. selection. The inbreeding counter balance the effect of selection.
- The F.S. correlation is more likely to be increased by c-effects (common environment shared by F.S.). The intra class correlation (t) is $rh^2$ for H.S. and $rh^2+c^2$ for F.S. where $c^2$ is the added contribution of maternal or common environmental effects. This reduces the accuracy of F.S. selection.

The breeding value (B.V.) of an individual based on sibs performance can be predicted from multiplying the regression coefficient of the genotype of the individual on the average phenotypes of the sibs by the selection differential of the sibs as :

$$\text{P.B.V.} = \overline{P}_c + rh^2 \frac{n}{1 + (n-1)t}(\overline{P}_s - \overline{P}_c)$$

Where

$\overline{P}_c$ = average of contemporaries

$\overline{P}_s$ = average of sibs

n = number of sibs

r = coefficient of relationship between sibs and individual
= ½ for FS and ¼ for HS, if no inbreeding

t = Intra class correlation among sibs
= $rh^2$
= ½ $h^2$ for FS and ¼ $h^2$ for H.S., if C-effects are not considered

$h^2$ = heritability of the trait

$$h^2 \frac{n}{1 + (n-1)t} = h_s^2 = \text{heritability of sibs}$$

The expected response to sib selection is:

$$R_S = i\sigma_p h^2 \frac{nr}{\sqrt{n(1 + (n-1)t]}}$$

The accuracy of sib selection is taken as the correlation between the genotypes of the individual and the phenotypic average of its sibs and estimated as:

$$\text{Accuracy} = rh\sqrt{\frac{n}{1 + (n-1)t}} = r\sqrt{\frac{nh^2}{1 + (n-1)t}}$$

## 10.2.2. Family selection

The selection criteria are known as family selection when based on the performance of the sibs plus the individual's own record. The family selection like the sib selection is of two types depending on the type of sibs viz Full sib family selection and Half sib family selection.

The family selection is also taken in another way viz. as a unit of selection. Based on the family mean the whole of the family is selected or rejected as a unit of selection.

The B.V. of individual based on family mean is estimated as (Lasely, 1972)

$$\text{P.B.V} = \overline{P}_s + h^2\left[\frac{1-r}{1-t}(P_1 - \overline{P}_S) + \frac{1+(n-1)r}{1+(n-1)t}(\overline{P}_s - P_{Cs})\right],$$

Where, $h^2 \dfrac{1+(n-1)r}{1+(n-1)t} = h^2$ of family mean

$h^2 \dfrac{1-r}{1-t} = h^2$ of within family mean

The accuracy of family selection (after Lasely, 1972) is estimated as:

$$\text{Accuracy} = \frac{h[1+(n-1)r]}{\sqrt{n[1+(n-1)t]}}$$

The expected response to family selection ($R_f$) is estimated as (Falconer, 1965)

$$R_f = i\sigma_p h^2 \frac{[1+(n-1)r]}{\sqrt{n[1+(n-1)t]}}$$

## Common environment (c – effects)

The environmental effects which are different for different families but same for all members of one and the same family are known as common environmental effects denoted as c-effects (Lerner, 1950). The family members share common environment during pre and post natal stage. The c-effects thus create resemblance within family members over and above the resemblance due to having common genes and this contributes to the variance between families. This increases the intra class correlation (t) among family members. The c-effects are more for F.S. than for H.S. The F.S. are affected by maternal effects viz. liter mates in swine and full sibs have the same intra uterine environment in any species. To some extent the half sibs also share common environment viz. all the daughters of a sire being born almost at the same time and being reared together are likely to be subjected to similar environmental conditions like climatic conditions, feeding regime and managemental practices etc.

When environmental similarities (c-effects) are present among family members, the intra class correlation among the phenotypic values of family members (t) is increased equal to the amount of c-effects as $(t+c^2)$ where $C^2$ is the portion of the total variation caused by differences in c-effects among families. This makes the denominator larger and hence the regression is deceased. Thus the c-effects decrease the accuracy of sib and family average.

## Factors affecting accuracy of sib and family selection:

The perusal of the formulae of the accuracy of sib selection and family selection it is clear that the accuracy depends on the $h^2$ of the trait, coefficient of relationship between sibs and individual (r) , number of sibs (n) and the degree of correlation (t) between the phenotypes of sibs. The values of r and t are affected by inbreeding and common environments, respectively.

(i) The accuracy of sib selection and family selection is more for traits of low heritability. The relative efficiency of family and sib selection compared to individual selection decreases with increase in heritability. The family selection is superior at low heritability. The accuracy of family and individual selection is equal at low $h^2$ values. The accuracy of sib selection compared to individual selection decreases along increase in $h^2$. When $h^2$ is greater than 0.5 the selection on any number of FS is never as accurate as individual selection and same is true for HS selection when $h^2$ is greater than 0.25.

(ii) The accuracy of sib selection based on one FS is 0.5 h and based on one HS is 0.25 h. The accuracy of HS and FS selection as well as family selection is increased with increase in **n** but never exceeds more than 0.5 for HS $(\sqrt{0.25})$ and 0.71 for FS $(\sqrt{0.50})$ selection irrespective of **n** and $h^2$ of the trait. The family and sibs selection based on large families result in greater response. However, family size (n) is limited due to breeding space, available facilities and intensity of selection. The space and other facilities can be exhausted in two ways viz. more number of families with their small size and lesser number of families with their large size. The optimum family size for HS families has been proposed by Robertson (1957) as:

$$N = 0.56 \sqrt{T / Nh^2}$$

Where, T = Total number of individual to be measured (nN)

N = No. of families

n = Family size

The large size family brings the mean phenotypic value close to the genotypic value. The effect of family size (n) on the relative efficiency of family and sib selection compared to individual selection is more when **t** is low. The accuracy of sib selection just equals that of individual selection based on 5 FS and 26 HS when $h^2$ is 0.1.

(iii) The type of family viz. HS and FS families in terms of **r** between sibs also affects the accuracy of selection. The more close family members (FS and

HS) provide more reliable information for selection compared to remote families. In other words, the accuracy of family selection decreases when **r** among family members decreases. Thus FS selection is more efficient than HS selection.

(iv) The degree of correlation between the phenotypes of sibs (t) affects the accuracy of selection. The family selection is better (even better than individual selection) when the phenotypic correlation (t) is low. When **t** is low, the $h^2$ will be low with little resemblance due to common environment. This makes the denominator smaller and consequently the regression is increased. Thus with low values of **t** the accuracy of family selection is increased or say that c-effects decrease the accuracy of family average. Family selection is preferred to individual selection for characters of low $h^2$ and when c-effects are not important. Individual selection is better than family selection when **t** is larger than 0.25 for the reason that family selection acts only on the variance between family means while the individual selection operates on whole of the additive genetic variance.

## Advantages of family selection

- The family selection can improve the characters of low heritability in species with high reproductive rates (pig, poultry) so as to get many sibs in a short time.
- The family selection does not allow the generation interval to increase
- Family selection is a support to individual selection because it is better to select an individual from a superior family

## Disadvantages or limitation of family selection

The family selection to be effective requires large family size and more number of families to avoid inbreeding as well as to increase the intensity of selection. In view of this it can be inferred that –

- Family selection is costly of space particularly when the breeding space and testing facilities are limited. The limited facilities reduce the intensity of selection.
- The family selection as a unit of selection results in inbreeding and thus limits the genetic diversity. This is because only few families represent the next generation.
- The F.S. family selection can only be applied in species with high reproductive rates to get large family size.

## 10.2.3. Within family selection

It is the selection criteria when individuals are selected on the basis of their performance expressed as deviation from their family mean. The individuals that exceed their family mean by the greatest amount are selected. Thus it is opposite to family selection because family mean is given no weight.

This selection criteria is preferred when c-effects are important i.e. when a large component of environmental variance is common to all members of a family. A large component of environmental variance common to members of a family arises when the different families differ in the environment to which they are exposed. Thus the families differ largely due to differences in environment and hence whole family get good or poor environment. The best example is the pre weaning growth in pigs and mice wherein a large part of the variation in weaning weight is due to mother and hence common to all members of a family. The selection within family eliminates the environmental differences among families.

The within family selection economizes the breeding space and minimizes the rate of inbreeding. In within family selection, each family contributes equally to the parents of next generation, when single pair matings are made and two individuals from each family are selected as replacement of the parents.

The within family selection is better than individual selection when the sib correlation (t) is very high and caused largely by environmental effects. The within family selection operates on a large amount of additive variance within families.

The $h^2$ of within family deviations is : $h_W^2 = h^2 \dfrac{1-r}{1-t}$

with accuracy of selection as square root of this heritability. The expected response (Rw) to this selection is:

$$Rw = i\sigma ph^2 (1-r) \sqrt{n - 1/n(1-t)}$$

The within family selection is rarely applied to HS families because c-effects are not important in case of HS families. Thus within FS family selection is more practicable.

## 10.2.4. Combined selection

The selection of an individual on the basis of two or more sources of information is called as the **combined selection** or **index selection**. It is better to select on the basis of an index combining information from various relatives (dam, sibs and or progeny) with or without individual's own record. This is done by the technique of multiple regression. These multiple regression coefficients are to be used as the weighting factors. All information available about each individual's breeding value combined into an index of merit is the optimal procedure for selection.

## 1. Family mean and within family deviation

Considering the family mean and within family deviation of the phenotypic value of an individual, it is obvious that the phenotypic value of an individual (P) is composed of two parts viz. $P_f$ which is the deviation of its family mean from the population mean and $P_w$ which is the deviation of the individual from the family mean called as the within family deviation. Thus

$$P = P_f + P_w$$

The weight given to these two parts decides the procedure of selection. When equal weight is given to both the parts it is known as **individual selection**. When family mean is considered as a basis of selection giving no weight to the within family deviation (Pw), it is known as **family selection** whereas the selection, on the basis of the within family deviation (Pw) alone giving no weight to the family mean (Pf), is known as **within family selection** and the best individual from each family is selected. Lastly, when the two components (Pf and Pw) are given different weights, the selection is known as **combined selection** or **index selection.**

The best estimate of an individual's breeding value on the basis of its phenotypic value is $h^2P$ where $h^2$ is the regression of breeding value on phenotypic value. Now considering the two parts of the phenotypic value (Pf and Pw) which are uncorrelated and give independent information about the B.V., the expected breeding value of an individual can be estimated from multiple regression equation as:

$$\text{E.B.V.} = h^2_f\, P_f + h^2_w\, P_w$$

Where the two heritabilites ($h^2_f$ and $h^2_w$) are the weighting factors (partial regression coefficients of family mean and within family deviation). Now substituting the values of two hertitabilities the E.B.V. becomes as:

$$\text{E.B.V.} = \left(\frac{1-r}{1-t}\right)P_W + \left(\frac{1+(n-1)r}{1+(n-1)t}\right)P_f$$

after omitting the term $h^2$ which is common to both the weighting factors and hence will not affect the relative weighting. Lush (1947) had proposed the following index of merit after rearrangement of the appropriate weighting factors and taking the individual values in place of within family deviations (which is more convenient) after assigning them a weight of 1:

$$I = P + \left[\frac{r-t}{1-r} \times \frac{\text{n}}{1+(n-1)t}\right]P_f$$

Where P is the value of the individual.

The expected response to this combined selection is generally higher to about 10-20% than individual selection, family selection and within family selection.

$$R_C = \text{i}\sigma_P h^2\sqrt{1 + \frac{(r-t)^2}{(1-t)} \times \frac{n-1}{1+(n-1)t}}$$

The quantity under the under root is the combined efficiency of family average and individual mean.

## 2. Combining information from individual and all sort of relatives

There are situations when information from the individual, its parents, FS, HS etc. are available and when the character on the individual is not measured (like sex limited characters). The individual can be selected to combine all information with an index. This involves the **matrix method** and takes the form of a multiple regression of B.V. on all the sources of information. The index so constructed is the best linear prediction of an individual's B.V. The index can be represented as:

$I = b_1P_1 + b_2P_2 + b_3P_3 + .....$

Where b's are the weighting factors whose values are to be estimated so as there is maximum correlation between index and B.V. ($r_{IA}$).

P's are the phenotypic values of different selection criteria.

The maximization of $r_{IA}$ means to minimize the sum of squared deviations of index value from linear regression of I and A like $\Sigma$ (I-A)$^2$. The b's values so obtained are the partial regression coefficients of individual's B.V. on each source of information. The maximization leads to a set of simultaneous equations equal to the number of sources of Information.

If the sources of information are three viz. the individual, the parents (dam) and paternal half sibs, then three simultaneous equations will be as follows.

$b_1 V_{P1} + b_2 Covp_{12} + b_3 Covp_{13} = V_{A1}$

$b_1 Covp_{21} + b_2 vp_2 + b_3 Covp_{25} = Cov_{21}$

$b_1 Covp_{31} + b_2 Covp_{32} + b_3 Vp_3 = Cov_{A31}$

Where 1 = Individual, 2 = parents and 3 = PHS

The b's can be estimated after putting the values of variances and covariances.

## Osborne Index

Osborne ('1957) developed a selection index based on combining information of records of the individual and its family members (sire family and dam family average) by giving proper weights in poultry for improving egg production. This is known as Osborne Index. The indices were developed for two sexes separately as:

$$I_F = (P - \overline{P}) + W_2 (F_D - \overline{P}) + (F_S - \overline{P})$$

$$I_M = W_2 (F_D - \overline{P}) + (F_S - \overline{P})$$

Where, P is the individual's own records

$\overline{P}$ is the flock mean

$F_D$ and $F_S$ are the dam and sire families average

$$W_2 = \frac{2n(1 - h^2)}{4 + (n - 2)h^2}$$

$$W_3 = \frac{4\bar{n}d(1 - h^2)(2 - h^2)}{[4 + (\bar{n} - 2)h^2]\,[4 + \{\bar{n} + \bar{n}d - 2\}h^2]}$$

n is the no. of pullets per dam

$\bar{n}$ is the average number of pullets per dam

d is the number of dams mated to a cock

$h^2$ is the heritability of the character

## Abplanalp Index

Another index of combined selection was proposed by Abplanalp (1974) for selection of pullets and cockerels as:

$$I_F = b_1 (P - P_{DF}) + b_2 (P_{DF} - P_{SF}) + b_3 (P_{SF} - \overline{P})$$

$$I_M = b_4 (P_{DF} - P_{sF}) + b_5 (P_{SF} - \overline{P})$$

Where, P is the individual record

$P_{DF}$ and $P_{SF}$ are the dam and sire family averages

$\overline{P}$ is the flock mean

$b_i$'s = weights given to different selection criteria as

$$b_1 = \frac{G_1}{P_1} \textit{ where, } G_1 = \frac{\sigma_G^2}{2}\left(\frac{n-1}{n}\right)$$

$$P_1 = \sigma_W^2\left(\frac{n-1}{n}\right)$$

$$b_2 = \frac{G_2}{P_2} \textit{ where, } G_2 = \frac{d-1}{d}\left(\frac{\sigma_G^2}{2n} + \sigma_D^2\right)$$

$$P_2 = \frac{d-1}{d}\left(\frac{\sigma_W^2}{n} + \sigma_D^2\right)$$

$$b_3 = \frac{G_3}{P_3} \textit{ where, } G_3 = \frac{S-1}{S}\left(\frac{\sigma_G^2}{2nd} + \frac{\sigma_D^2}{d} + \sigma_s^2\right)$$

$$P_3 = S - 1\left(\frac{\sigma_W^2}{nd} + \frac{\sigma_D^2}{d} + \sigma_s^2\right)$$

$$b_4 = G_4 + P_4 \textit{ where, } G_4 = \frac{d-1}{d}\sigma_D^2$$

$$P_4 = P_2$$

$$b_5 = G_5 + P_5 \textit{ where, } G_5 = \frac{S-1}{S}\left(\frac{\sigma_D}{d} + \sigma_s^2\right)$$

$$P_5 = P_3$$

n = no. of progeny per dam

d = no. of dams per sire

s = no. of sires

Expected response = $\Delta G = \frac{i}{\sigma_1}(b_1G_1 + b_2G_2 + b_3G_3)$

$$\sigma_1 = (b_1^2P_1 + b^2{}_2P_2 + b^2{}_3P_3)^{\frac{1}{2}}$$

i = intensity of selection

## 10.3. NUMERICAL SOLVED EXAMPLE : SINGLE RECORD OF INDIVIDUAL AND RELATIVES

**Example 10.1:** The phenotypic value of a trait recorded on a calf, its sire and dam are 900, 800 and 450 units respectively. Taking the $h^2 = 0.43$, $\sigma p = 80.0$, estimate the B.V. of the calf.

## Solution

$$V_{P1} = V_{P2} = V_{P3} = (80)^2 = 6400$$

$$V_{A1} = h^2\sigma^2_{p1} = 0.43 \times 6400 = 2752$$

$$Cov_{P\,12} = \frac{1}{2}\sigma^2_P = \frac{1}{2}(2752) = 1326$$

$$CoV_{P\,13} = Cov_{P\,12} = 1326$$

$$CoV_{P\,23} = 0$$

$$Cov_{A\,12} = CoV_{p\,13} = \frac{1}{2}\sigma^2_A = 1326$$

Now putting the values the equations will be:

$$\begin{vmatrix} b_1 \\ b_2 \\ b_3 \end{vmatrix} = \begin{vmatrix} V_{P1} & Cov_{12} & Cov_{13} \\ Cov_{21} & V_{P3} & Cov_{23} \\ Cov_{31} & Cov_{32} & V_{P3} \end{vmatrix} = \begin{vmatrix} V_{P1} \\ Cov_{12} \\ Cov_{13} \end{vmatrix}$$

Now the values

$$\begin{vmatrix} b_1 \\ b_2 \\ b_3 \end{vmatrix} = \begin{vmatrix} 6400 & 1326 & 1326 \\ 1326 & 6400 & 0 \\ 1326 & 0 & 6400 \end{vmatrix}^{-1} = \begin{vmatrix} 2752 \\ 1326 \\ 1326 \end{vmatrix}$$

After solving these equations we get

$b_1 = 0.372$, $b_2 = 0.135$ and $b_3 = 0.135$

Therefore, $I = b_1 X_1 + b_2 X_2 + b_3 X_3$

$0.372\ X_1 + 0.135 X_2 + 0.135\ X_3$

$= 0.372\ (900-\mu) + 0.135\ (800-\mu) + 0.135\ (450-\mu)$

$$\text{Accuracy} = \sqrt{\frac{0.372\,(2757) + 0.135\,(1326) + 0.135\,(1326)}{2752}}$$

$= 0.712$

**Example 10. 2 : Mean records of individual and relatives:**

When mean of groups of individuals are taken, there n in the group is also required. The between group and within group variances are estimated as:

The intra class correlation between members of families (t)

$t = \sigma^2_B/\sigma^2_P$ and hence $\sigma^2_B = t\sigma^2_P$

like wise, within group component $(\sigma^2_w) = (1-t)\ \sigma^2_P$

So that $\sigma^2_P = t\sigma^2_P + (1-t)\ \sigma^2_P$

$= V_P$ between families + $V_P$ within families

Now, if the average of first 2 lactations of a cow is 230 units and the mean of its 5 half sisters with 2 lactation is 300 units. Estimate the B.V. of the cow taking $h^2 = 0.25$, $t = 0.5$ and $\sigma p = 34$ units.

## Solution:

$$V_{A1} = \sigma^2_A = h^2\sigma^2_P = 0.25(34^2) = 289$$

$$CoV_{A12} = CoV_{HS} = \frac{1}{2}\sigma s^2_A = \frac{1}{4}(289) = 72.25$$

$$V_{P1} = V_{\bar{P}_1} = t\sigma^2_P + \frac{1}{n}(1-t)\,\sigma^2_P$$

$$= \left(t + \frac{(1-t)}{n}\right)\sigma^2_P$$

$$= \left(0.5 + \frac{(1-0.5)}{2}\right)(34)^2 = 867$$

$$V_{P2} = Var_{\bar{P}_2} = \sigma^2_B + \frac{1}{n}(\sigma^2_W)$$

$$\text{Where } \sigma^2_W = \frac{1}{4}\sigma^2_A = \text{Bet. cow variance}$$

$$\sigma^2_w = V_{\bar{P}2i} - \sigma^2_B$$

Taking $V_{\bar{P}2i}$ = mean of first 2 lactation of cow i

Since all 5 cows each with 2 records, $= V_{\bar{P}2i} = V_{P_1}$

Thus

$$\sigma_W^2 = \left(V_{P_1} - \frac{1}{4}\sigma_A^2\right)$$

$$\frac{1}{n}\sigma_W^2 = \frac{1}{2}\left(V_{P_1} - \frac{1}{4}\sigma_A^2\right)$$

So $$V_{P2} = \frac{1}{4}\sigma_A^2 + \frac{1}{n}\left(V_{P_1} - \frac{1}{4}\sigma_A^2\right)$$

$$= \frac{1}{4}(289) + \frac{1}{5}\left[867 - \frac{1}{4}(289)\right] = 231.2$$

Now substituting the values in equations and solving them as

$$\begin{vmatrix} b_1 \\ b_2 \end{vmatrix} = \begin{vmatrix} 867 & 72.25 \\ 72.25 & 23.12 \end{vmatrix}^{-1} \begin{vmatrix} 289 \\ 72.25 \end{vmatrix}$$

$b_1 = 0.316$, $b_2 = 0.213$ and $b_3 = 0.135$

Therefore, $I = b_1 X_1 + b_2 X_2$

Accurcay of index = = $\sqrt{\dfrac{0.316\,(289) + 0.213\,(72.5)}{289}} = 0.61$

## QUESTIONS

**10.1.** (*a*) What do you men by pedigree selection and its basis?

(*b*) Give the merits and demerits of pedigree selection.

**10.2.** (*a*) What are the guides and practical difficulties in using the pedigree selection?

**10.3.** (*a*) Write about the accuracy of pedigree selection.

(*b*) Give reasons for low accuracy of pedigree selection.

**10.4.** Give different forms of family selection. Discuss the factors affecting accuracy of sib and family selection.

**10.5.** (*a*) What is combined selection? Give examples.

(*b*) What do you mean by within family selection and under what condition it is preferred?

***

# 11

# SELECTION CRITERIA–Progeny Selection

The selection criteria for evaluating an individual based on his progeny performance is known as Progeny Selection or Progeny Testing (P.T.). The P.T. is the most important basis of selection. The selection criteria are the mean phenotypic value of the individual's progenies compared to the mean phenotypic value of the contemporaries. The P.T. is regarded as a form of family selection because progenies are the family members of each other.

## 11.1. GENETIC PRINCIPLES OF P.T.

The P.T. stems on the principle of like begets like. The progeny of an individual is the index of parents' genetic worth. Each progeny inherits one-half of the genes from each parent due to the halving nature of inheritance. This is taken as the transmitting ability of the parent and hence the breeding value (B.V.) of the parent is twice the mean deviation of the progenies from the population mean.

Second, is the sampling nature of inheritance. Chance at segregation may result in any one or few progenies receiving a good or poor than average sample of genes from its parent. Different genes are transmitted by a parent to its different progenies due to segregation of genes during gamete formation and the probability to receive exactly the same set of genes by its progenies is very low for polygenic traits. This segregation is called the Mendelian error. Therefore, the estimation of B.V. of an individual (parent) based on one or few progenies may be misleading. Moreover, the polygenic traits are influenced by environmental factors and the different progenies of the same parent do not get same environment. Thus the environmental factors cause differences in the performance of different progenies. Therefore, chance at segregation and environmental factors cause greater deviation from true B.V. of a parent. The effect of these two factors are balanced out by estimating the B.V. based on many progenies so that the progeny mean give more reliable/accurate estimate of B.V. with the increase in progeny size.

## 11.2. SUPERIORITY OF P.T. OVER OTHER SELECTION CRITERIA

The **individual selection** is not possible for traits of low $h^2$, sex limited traits and the traits expressed after death of the individual. Most of the traits in farm animals have low $h^2$ and are sex limited. Thus these can not be improved through individual selection and hence the B.V. is estimated based on the performance of relatives (dam, sisters and progeny).

The **pedigree selection** based on the performance of dam is not a good selection criterion for the reasons of halving process and sampling nature of inheritance. It is not possible to know as to which half (better or inferior) of dam's genes are transmitted to the progeny (male). Moreover, the pedigree selection is effective for traits of high $h^2$. In pedigree selection, only one sample is tested.

The accuracy of **sib selection** is also low due to sampling nature of inheritance. Every individual receives different set of genes from its parent and the probability to set same get of genes by the individual and its sibs is very less.

**Finally**, the performance of many progenies (progeny testing) gives the best and most reliable information about the genetic merit of parent (individual). This overcomes the limitation of Mendelian error of gene segregation and hence provides the true estimate of B.V. of an individual

## 11.3. SOURCES OF ERROR IN P.T.

The various sources of error in P.T. and the ways to correct them can be grouped as:

- Randomly distributed sources of variation – caused by Mendelian segregation, environmental effects and the error in measurement of data. These errors can be reduced by increasing the number of progenies to estimate the B.V.
- Systematic error – arises by age and weight effect of cows, parity number, lactation length, days open, dams belonging to selected group, herd differences and period effect. These can be reduced by adjustment of data for these effects.

## 11.4. PRECAUTIONS IN P.T.

In view of the various sources of error in P.T., the following precautions need attention:

- The adult females should be allotted randomly to all the sires under test to avoid the effect of production level of the dam on the progeny. Allotment of superior dams to a particular sire overestimates the B.V. of that sire.
- Different sire groups should be raised and compared under similar environmental conditions viz. same nutrition regime and management practices. The progeny should be born in the same season and year as well as should be recorded at the same age/lactation.

- All the healthy progeny should be included and excluded those which could not complete the lactation either due to their death or culling during lactation or due to disease or abnormal calving.
- The data recorded should be adjusted/corrected for environmental effects such as age, year, season, lactation length etc.
- More number of progeny per sire should be recorded to cancel out the randomly distributed sources of error.

## 11.5. REQUIREMENTS FOR P.T.

In addition to the above precautions, there are several requirements for an effective large scale P.T. programme.

- It is always better that more than required number of males must be kept for P.T. so as to have an opportunity of selection among the P.T. sires. About 4-5 males should be progeny tested for each required progeny tested sire for future breeding.
- The facilities should exist for frozen semen, and to record information on progeny. Moreover, a large population is also required.
- The progeny should be tested in several herds and stations and comparison should be made with contemporaries from other sires. This increases the accuracy.
- No progeny should be culled until the end of the test.
- The P.T. should be completed as early as possible in the life of the males.
- All precautions mentioned above should be kept in mind

## 11.6. CONSTRAINTS IN P.T.

There had been mainly two constraints for effective results of P.T. in the past. These had been small population size and unplanned mating to get required number of daughters from all the bulls under test.

The problem of **small population size** can be solved if the sires are tested simultaneously in different associated herds and the field progeny testing. This will allow to test more number of sires and that too in different herds with more number of progeny. This will result higher accuracy of selection.

The **unplanned mating** results in wastage of the breeding data and also the non-orthgonality of data. The non-orthogonality in terms of unequal number of daughters for different sires had been the intense at most of the animal farms in India, varying from one to several hundred daughters per sire. This results in loss of breeding data and that all the sires under test are not evaluated, besides creating the problem in data analysis and biasness in predicting the breeding value. Based on a number of studies at NDRI Karnal during 1985-2001 by Tomar and his students, the data of about 40 per cent of the total sires under test could be used in estimating the B.V. and the data on rest of the sires were wasted. This puts restriction to P.T. of a large number of sires under test. Therefore it is proper to prepare a calculative mating plan to obtain nearly equal progenies from different sires. The studies conducted on this aspect by Tomar and his students (1985-2001) have indicated that 5 pregnancies are required to get one replacement daughter. Therefore to run a P.T. programme effectively, it is required to get 100 inseminations or 50 pregnancies from each bull to get about 10 daughters to be performance recorded.

## 11.7. METHODOLOGY OF P.T.

In view of the requirements and constraints experienced earlier, a sound technical programme is required to be formulated.

- In order to overcome the problem of population size the P.T. programme should be carried out in the associated herds.
- About 4-5 males should be kept under test for each required progeny tested bull for future breeding.
- About 50 pregnancies should be settled from each bull so as about 10 daughters of each bull must be performance recorded.
- It is better to complete one set of bulls within a period of 2 years.
- In each set of bulls, about 8-10 males should be tested so as atleast 2 top ranking bulls are selected on the basis of their B.V. estimated from their daughter's performance.
- Taking a set of 10 males, 2 tested and 8 under test, it will require 500 pregnancies in a period of 2 years. Now taking into consideration that only 66% of the breeding females will calve each year, 250 pregnancies will be settled in one year from 375 breedable females.
- The 2 best proven bulls should be used on about 60 best yielding cows to get a set of young males for testing in a later batch and the remaining 8 which are the sons of 2 best proven bulls of an earlier batch should be used on the remaining cows. It should be kept in mind that no male is to be kept from the bulls under test.
- The B.V. of bull based on its progeny performance is estimated by multiplying the regression of B.V. of parent on the phenotypic performance of its progeny with the selection differential of the progeny of $i^{th}$ sire from the mean of the contemporaries $(\overline{P}_i - \overline{P}_c)$. The regression (b) is taken as

$$b = rnh^2/[1+(n-1)t]$$

$$= 0.5nh^2/[1+(n-1)t]$$

$$= 2nh^2/[4+(n-1)h^2] \quad \text{since } t = 0.25h^2$$

Where r = coefficient of relationship between individual and his progeny

t = Intra class correlation among progeny with is ¼ for H.S.

n = No. of progenies

Thus the B.V. is estimated as

$$\text{R.B.V.} = \overline{P_c} + \frac{2nh^2}{4+(n-1)h^2}(\overline{P_i} - \overline{P_c})$$

## 11.8. ACCURACY OF P.T.

The accuracy of P.T. is expressed as the correlation of genotype of parent with the average phenotype of its progeny (half sibs) and hence it is estimated as $r_{G\bar{P}}$ which is

$$r_{G\bar{P}} = r_{A\bar{P}} = 0.5\sqrt{\frac{nh^2}{1 + (n-1)t}}$$

The accuracy of selection based on one progeny is the same as that based on one parent or one FS and it is 0.5h. The accuracy increases with increase in number of progeny and the increase is much larger than for sib selection. The accuracy of P.T. with about 5 progeny gives as high as that of individual selection for traits of moderate heritability and it is more effective if n exceeds 5 in number. The accuracy of P.T. quickly reaches a level higher than that of individual selection and tends towards 100% for any value of $h^2$. Thus P.T. gives a higher accuracy than any other selection criteria.

The relative accuracy of P.T. and individual selection is estimated as :

$$0.5\sqrt{\frac{n}{1 + (n-1)t}} / h = \sqrt{\frac{n}{4[1+ (n-1)t]}} = \sqrt{\frac{n}{4 + (n-1)h^2}}$$

The P.T. compared to individual selection is relatively more accurate at lower values of $h^2$. In comparison to family selection the P.T. is almost twice as effective as the selection based on H.S. families and about 1.4 times that based on F.S. family mean for any value of $h^2$.

There are a number of factors which influence the results of P.T. like selection of dams mated to sires under test (contemporary dam average) and common environment (c-effects) which cause similarity between progeny. The presence of c-effects reduces the accuracy of P.T. (i.e. $r_{A\bar{P}}$) . The c-effects can be caused by season differences in lactation milk yield and when cows are from different herds. The $C^2$ is environmentally determined correlation which exists between daughters of a bull\. The $c^2 = t = 0.25h^2$ for season differences and $c^2 = h^2 = 4t$ for cows belonging to different herds. In estimating the true B.V. of a male based on P.T. require some correction in order to minimize the effect of level of dams production etc. These corrections have been discussed under sire evaluation.

## 11.9. ADVANTAGES OF P.T.

- The P.T. is a better method for sex limited traits, the traits with low $h^2$, and slaughter traits in meat animals.
- The P.T. is useful to prove a sire whether he is free from any recessive

gene. To identify the carrier individual for harmful gene, it is mated to its sibs or progeny.

- The main feature and principal advantage of P.T. is the increased selection intensity. This is because the progeny are also used as parent and await selection at the time of testing their own parent. Thus P.T. is a modified form of family selection.
- Its accuracy increases with increase in progeny number.

## 11.10. LIMITATIONS OF P.T.

- The time and cost required is the main limitation. It increases the generation interval.
- Due to larger generation interval the genetic gain per year is low.
- P.T. is effective on adequate number of progeny
- It requires to progeny test and compares many sires to find which one is superior. Thus selection is needed among sires under test.

## 11.11. SIRE EVALUATION

The result of P.T. are expressed in the form of an index which is the index of the genetic worth of the sire and such an index is known as sire index. Based on sire index a numerical value is obtained which indicates the production ability of the sire. Since a number of sires are progeny tested, it requires to rank all sires for their genetic worth so as to select the best sire.

### 11.11.1. Biasness in sire evaluation

The biases in obtaining the accurate estimate of sire's B.V. arise due to genetic and environmental differences. The genetic biasness is created by genetic differences among herds and due to the differences in genetic merit (production level) of the mates of the sire. The major environmental biases are introduced by the different environmental conditions (feeding, management, climatic factors etc.) of different herds whereas the year and season of calving create minor biasness. In order to eliminate or reduce these biases, it is better to adjust the data before estimating the B.V. of sires. Considering all these a number of sire indices have been proposed by different workers.

### 11.11.2. Methods of indexing sires

The different indices developed are for two purposes viz. indices which simply rank the sires and the indices which provide the estimates of breeding value of sires. The B.V. is estimated for indexing in a single herd as well as for indexing in many herds.

**Notations used in sire indices:** The following notations have been used in the construction of various sire indices.

$\overline{D}$ = Average of all daughters of a sire under test

$C_D$= Average of contemporary daughters of the sire

$\overline{M}$ = Average of the mates of the sire or dam's average

$C_M$ = Average of contemporary mates

= $\overline{H}$ = Herd average

n = Number of daughters

b = 0.5h$^2$, the intra sire regression of daughters on dam

### (i) Simple daughter average index

Edwards (1932) proposed this sire index as:

$$I_I = \overline{D}$$

This index is the simplest measure in a single herd under same environment. It provides a sound basis of evaluation but it does not take into account the production level of the mates of the bull (dams of the daughters) and hence it is subjected to the bias when production level of mates allotted to different sires are different.

### (ii) Equi-parent or intermediate index

Hansson (1913) proposed this index and it is also known as Yapp's index (Yapp, 1925) or Mount Hope Index because it was first used at Mount Hope Farm in 1928. This index is:

$$I_2 = 2\overline{D} - \overline{M} = \overline{D} + (\overline{D} - \overline{M})$$

This index makes adjustment for the variation in production level of the dam (Mates). However, it over corrects the production level of mates allotted to different sires. If inferior dams (than average) are allotted to a sire, there is over estimation of sire's B.V. but in case superior dams than average are allotted, it then underestimate the sire's B.V. This index is based on the assumption that the dams and daughters are raised under similar conditions so that the daughter dam difference reflects the sire effect otherwise it will reflect managemetnal practices in the herd.

### (iii) Corrected daughter average index

Krishan (1956) gave the following index

$$I_3 = \overline{D} - b\ (\overline{M} - \overline{H}) = \overline{D} - 0.5\ h^2\ (\overline{M} - \overline{H})$$

This index is superior to $I_1$ and $I_2$ as it corrects for the production level of dams allotted to the sire over herd average. Thus daughters average is corrected for the differences in the production level of their dams. The correction factor is b $(\overline{M} - \overline{H})$. This factor substracts the genetic superiority of the dam from daughters average and hence the genetic potentiality of the daughters is stepped up over the herd average. On the contrary, if the dams allotted to a sire are inferior than herd average, the genetic potentiality of the daughters will be reduced and hence the quantity b $(\overline{M} - \overline{H})$ is added in the observed daughters average.

Searle (1964) compared records of daughters with those of their herd mates in the same year and referred to as contemporary comparison or stable mate comparison. The sire's merit was estimated as:

$$I \equiv \overline{H} + 0.5\,h^2 \frac{n}{1 + (n-1)0.25h^2}(\overline{D} - \overline{H})$$

$$= \overline{H} + \frac{2nh^2}{4 + (n-1)h^2}(\overline{D} - \overline{H})$$

Where, n = no. of daughters.

## (iv) Contemporary daughter average index

The herd mate or contemporary comparisons reduce the environmental variation due to herd, year and season. The records of the daughters of a sire are compared with the daughtes of all other sires in the same herd calved in the same month or ± 2 months.

The sire index proposed by Sunderasan et al. (1965) is:

$$I = \overline{H} + \frac{n}{n+k}(\overline{D} - C_D)$$

Where, n = no. of daughters

K = constant based on sire error variance

The following sire index also takes into account the number of daughters and the environmental conditions

$$I = \overline{H} + 0.5h^2 \frac{n}{1 + (n+1)t}(\overline{D} - C_D)$$

## (v) Corrected contemporary daughter average index

The following 2 sire indices as an extension of the contemporary daughter average indices have been proposed. These indices besides adjusting the number of progeny and period to period variation also adjust for the differences in production level of dams allotted to different sires.

These indices are:

$$I = \overline{H} + 0.5\,h^2 \frac{n}{1 + (n-1)0.25\,h^2}[(\overline{D} - C_D) - b(\overline{M} - C_M)]$$

$$I = \overline{H} + \frac{n}{n+12}(\overline{D} - C_D) - b(\overline{M} - C_M)]$$

The second index was proposed by Sunderasan et al. (1965) and known as Dairy Search Index.

## (vi) Least square constants

The sire constants are obtained by least squares techniques which adjust the data for all the environmental effects including the non orthogonality in data. These sire constants are used in getting the sire index as

$$I = \frac{2nh^2}{4 + (n - 1)h^2}(S_i)$$

Where, $S_i$ is the sire constant for $i^{th}$ sire

### (vii) Maximum likelihood method and REML

The least squares method minimizes the error variance whereas the maximum likelihood (chance) method estimates the parameters by maximizing the logarithm of the likelihood function. The likelihood function is the likelihood of simultaneous occurrence of observation and is generally the product of the density function of the observations (variables). However, the ML estimates are biased because no account is taken of the degree of freedom in estimating the variance components. The ML method was improved by a method known as restricted maximum likelihood (REML) which takes care of the bias in estimates as well as avoids negative estimates of component of variance (Searle et al, 1992). The variance components by REML are estimated based on residuals calculated after fitting by ordinary least squares from the fixed effects part of the model. This maximizes a marginal likelihood function. This is also called as the residual maximum likelihood or marginal maximum likelihood.

### (viii) Best linear unbiased prediction method (BLUP)

The BLUP method of estimation was developed by Henderson (1949, 1973). This method is more powerful than the conventional selection index approach. This provides directly comparable estimates of the average breeding value of groups of animals born in different years. It takes into account the complications of non random mating, sires from more than one herd, environmental trends over time, herd differences for B.V. of dams and bias due to selection. Thus BLUP takes account of the fixed effects such as herd-year-season and it is applicable when mixed models are used whereas BLUE is applicable when all effects are fixed. The BLUP eliminates the non genetic biases in estimating B.V. Not only has this but it also removed the genetic biases taking into account the effects of non-random mating, genetic merit of dams and selection.

### (ix) Other methods for multi herds

Some methods for evaluation of sires used in more than one herd have also been proposed. These are Stable-Mate Daughter Average Index, Contemporary Daughter Average Index and Corrected Stable-Mate Daughter Average Index.

## 11.11.3. Efficiency of sire indices

The following criteria may be used to judge the efficiency or accuracy of various methods:

(i) Repeatability of the index-taken as the correlation between an index based on n daughters and an index based on n' future daughters.

(ii) Regression of a sire's future daughters on the average performance of number of present daughters. This was given by Robertson and Rendel (1950) as:

$$b = \frac{0.25\ nh^2}{1 + (n - 1)0.25\ h^2} = \frac{nh^2}{4 + (n - 1)h^2}$$

(iii) Error variance or within sire variance

(iv) Rank correlation

(v) Coefficient of determination ($R^2$) of fitting the model:

$$R^2(\%) = \frac{\text{S.S. of fitting the model}}{\text{T.S.S.}} \times 100$$

## 11.12. SOLVED EXAMPLE

**Example 11.1:** The average milk production of Sahiwal herd comprising 150 progenies of 6 sires is 2000 kg with $h^2$ of milk yield as 0.30. The average milk production and number of progenies per sire is given below:

| **Sire no.** | **1** | **2** | **3** | **4** | **5** | **6** |
|---|---|---|---|---|---|---|
| N | 30 | 20 | 25 | 15 | 10 | 50 |
| $\overline{X}$ | 1600 | 2250 | 1840 | 2200 | 2300 | 2100 |

Rank each sire based on their breeding value

### Solution

(i) Mean of contemporaries of all sires will be

$$(1)\ \frac{300000 - 48000}{120} = 2100 \qquad (2)\ \frac{300000 - 45000}{130} = 1961.5\text{kg}$$

$$(3)\ \frac{300000 - 46000}{125} = 2032\ \text{kg} \qquad (4)\ \frac{300000 \quad 33000}{135} = 1977.7\ \text{kg}$$

$$(5)\ \frac{300000 - 23000}{140} = 1978.5\ \text{kg} \qquad (6)\ \frac{300000 - 105000}{100} = 1950\ \text{kg}$$

(ii) Regression of B.V. of sire on his progeny ($b_{AP}$)

$$b_{AP} = \frac{2nh^2}{4 + (n - 1)h^2}$$

| Sire No. | n | $h^2$ | $\frac{2nh^2}{4+(n-1)h^2}$ | |
|---|---|---|---|---|
| 1 | 30 | 0.3 | 18/12.7 | = 1.41 |
| 2 | 20 | 0.3 | 12/9.7 | = 1.24 |
| 3 | 25 | 0.3 | 15/11.2 | = 1.34 |
| 4 | 15 | 0.3 | 9/8.2 | = 1.09 |
| 5 | 10 | 0.3 | 6/6.7 | = 0.89 |
| 6 | 50 | 0.3 | 30/18.7 | = 1.60 |

(iii) Breeding value of sires

$$\left(\overline{H} + \frac{2nh^2}{4+(n-1)h^2}(\overline{P}_i - \overline{P}_c\right)$$

Sire 1. 2000 +1.41 (1600-2100) = 1295.0 kg

2. 2000 + 1.24 (2250-1961.5) = 2354.7 kg

Like wise, the B.V. of other sires can be estimated.

**Example 11.2:** From the following data on milk yield construct the sire indices by different possible methods

| Sire No. | Daughters records | Dam's average | Contemporary Daughters | Contemporary Dams |
|---|---|---|---|---|
| 1 | 1252, 1858, 2343, 1880, 1532, 1743,1274, 1806, | 1600 | 1930 | 1550 |
| 2 | 1780, 1510, 1781, 1561, 1744 | 1340 | 1710 | 1310 |
| 3 | 2455, 1498 | 1680 | 2200 | 1590 |
| 4 | 1581, 2051, 2100, 1583, 2155, 2178 | 1500 | 2000 | 1490 |
| 5 | 1258, 1616, 1424 | 1315 | 1510 | 1300 |

$h^2$ of milk yield = 0.28, population mean = 1660

## Solution

(i) Simple daughter average index ($I_1$) as I = $\overline{D}$

| Sire No. | 1 | 2 | 3 | 4 | 5 |
|---|---|---|---|---|---|
| Index () | 1711 | 1675.2 | 1976.5 | 1941.3 | 1432.6 |
| $n_i$ | 8 | 5 | 2 | 6 | 3 |

(ii) Equi-parent index ($I_2$) = $2\overline{D} - \overline{M}$

| **Sire No.** | **1** | **2** | **3** | **4** | **5** |
|---|---|---|---|---|---|
| | 1822 | 2010.4 | 2273.0 | 2382.6 | 1550.2 |

(iii) Corrected daughter average index ($I_3$)

Krishnan Index = $\overline{D}$ $-0.5h^2$ $(\overline{M} - \overline{H})$

Sire No. 1 : 1711.0-0.5)0.28) (1600-1660)=1719.4

Sire No. 2: 1675.2 -0.5(0.28) (1340-1660) = 1720.0

Sire No. 3: 1976.5 -0.5(0.28) (1680-1660) = 1973.7

Sire No. 4: 1941.3 -0.5(0.28) (1500-1660) = 1741.3

Sire No. 5: 1432.6-0.5(0.28) (1315-1660) = 1720.0

(iv) $I_4 = \overline{H} + \dfrac{2nh^2}{4+(n-1)h^2}(\overline{D} - \overline{H})$

Sire No. 1: $1660 + \dfrac{2 \times 9 \times 028}{4 + (7)0.28}(1711 - 1660) = 1698.3$

Sire No. 2: $1660 + \dfrac{2.8}{5.12}(1675.2 - 1660) = 1668.3$

Sire No. 3: $1660 + \dfrac{1.12}{4.28}(1976.5 - 1660) = 1742.8$

Sire No. 4: $1660 + \dfrac{3.36}{5.4}(1941.3 - 1660) = 1835.0$

Sire No. 5: $1660 + \dfrac{1.68}{4.56}(1432.6 - 1660) = 1576.0$

(v) Dairy Search Index ($I_5$) = $\overline{H} + \dfrac{n}{n + 12}(\overline{D} - C_D) - b(\overline{M} - C_M)$

Sire No. 1: $1660 + \dfrac{8}{20}(1711 - 1930) - 0.5 \times 0.28\,(1600 - 1550)$

$= 1660 - 87.6 - 7.0 = 1565.4$

Sire No. 2: $1660 + \dfrac{5}{17}(1675.2 - 1710) - 0.14\,(1340 - 1310)$

$= 1660 - 10.2 - 4.2 = 1645.6$

Sire No. 3: $1660 + \dfrac{2}{14}(1976.5 - 2200) - 0.14\,(1680 - 1590)$

$$= 1660 - 31.9 - 12.6 = 1615.5$$

Sire No. 4: $1660 + \frac{6}{18}(1941.3 - 2000) - 0.14\,(1500 - 1490)$

$$= 1660 - 19.5 - 1.4 = 1639.1$$

Sire No. 5: $1660 + \frac{3}{15}(1432.6 - 1510) - 0.14\,(1315 - 1300)$

$$= 1660 - 15.5 - 2.1 = 1642.4$$

## QUESTIONS

**11.1.** Draw a progeny testing (P.T.) programme for evaluating dairy crossbred bull. (*ARS 1984*)

**11.2.** Give an appropriate plan of P.T. programme for sire evaluation of 20 sires in each generation for milk production in buffaloes. (*ARS 1985*)

**11.3.** What are essential requirements for an ideal P.T. programme in improving milk production? (*ARS 1984*)

**11.4.** Define selection. What is difference between selection and mating system? What kind of a selection procedure would you recommend for improving productivity of : (*ARS 1992*)

(*a*) Cattle for milk production

(*b*) Poultry for egg production upto 40 weeks of age

**11.5.** Discuss the genetic principle of P.T. and its superiority over other selection criteria.

**11.6.** Discuss the sources of error, precautions and constraints with their solution in P.T. programme.

**11.7.** What are the advantages and limitations of P.T.?

**11.8.** What are the modern approaches in sire evaluation? To what extent can these be used in cattle improvement programme in India (*ARS 1987*)

**11.9.** Describe four methods of sire evaluation giving appropriate models. Which one you consider best and why? What is the importance of secondary traits like dystocia, mastitis etc. in sire evaluation? (*ARS 1995*)

**11.10.** Discuss the various techniques used in the estimation of sire's breeding value. Which one is more efficient and why? (*ARS 1997*)

***

# 12

# SELECTION FOR DIFFERENT KINDS OF GENE ACTION

It has been mentioned earlier that for the development and expression of quantitative traits, neither genes nor environmental influence can be solely responsible but it is the cooperative result of heredity (genes) and environmental influences. The genotype determines the genotypic value for each individual and the environment modifies the genotypic value before the character is expressed.

## 12.1. TYPES OF GENE ACTION

The genes carried by an individual for a particular trait (i.e. the genotype) act in different ways to produce their effect. The gene action may be additive (individual effect of each gene) or non-additive (interaction effect or combination effect of genes). The additive effect of all genes which influence the character is called the additive genetic value or the breeding value. The non-additive gene action (gene interaction) may be allelic i.e. interaction between genes within locus (dominance and over dominance), or non-allelic i.e. interaction of genes between loci present on the same or on different chromosomes (epistasis). Thus the total value of a given genotype (G) is determined by its additive value, denoted by A. together with interaction effect of genes i.e. deviations caused by dominance (D) and epistasis (I), thus, the genotypic value can be indicated as $G = A+D+I$. The dominance and epistatic effects are known as gene's non additive effects. As a result of these non-additive effects of genes an individual in certain mating combinations has a special breeding value. When the phenotype of an individual say Aa is exactly at the mid point of the two homozygotes, it is then said that the effect of substituting A gene for a or vice versa is due to additive gene action in that the change of a single gene adds that much value to the phenotype to bring it to the mid point. But if the phenotype of Aa individual deviates in any direction other than mid point, the effects are said to be non-additive which may be either dominance or overdominance.

However, the quantitative traits are controlled by polygenes. The genes present at one locus may interact with genes present at other locus (Loci) of the same chromosome or of the different chromosomes. This type of inter-allelic interaction is called as epistasis which is a type of non additive gene action. It is the properties of the quantitative traits that they are influenced by many gene pairs (polygenes) most of which have individually small effects and expresses all forms of gene action (additive or non-additive), and are also greatly influenced by non genetic (environmental) factors. However, certain traits are more influenced by the additive gene action (AGA) while for others the non-additive gene action (NAGA) is more important. It is important to identify that which type of gene action is more responsible for trait. The type of gene action can be identified by the population performance for a metric trait in terms of the mean, variance and covariance.

## 12.2. SELECTION FOR ADDITIVE AND NON-ADDITIVE GENE ACTION

The sole purposes of selection is for the improvement of the trait to increases the frequency of the desirable genes controlling the trait with additive effects in particular but at the same time genes with non additive effects can not be ignored.

The selection theory for each type of gene action is different. Thus once the kind of gene action is identified the selection system which should maximize the effects of both types of gene action may be followed.

### 12.2.1. Selection methods (theories) for additive gene action

An effective selection is one which lead to genetic improvement in a trait in the next generation. The amount of genetic progress in traits controlled by additive gene action depends upon the amount of additive genetic variability (expressed in terms of $h^2$ of the trait) times the selection differential. Therefore, the genetic gain ($\Delta G$) = $h^2$x selection differential. The selection may be for one or more traits.

### Single trait selection

The success of any selection programme depends upon the ability of identifying and selecting the individuals with superior inheritance. The genetic superiority is indicated by the phenotypic merit of the individual in case of additive gene action. Thus, it is an important aspect to estimate the breeding value of the individuals selected as parents of the next generation. The basis of estimating the breeding value may be individual's own phenotype (called as individual selection) or the phenotypic value of individual's. relatives which may be the parent and grant parents of the individual (called pedigree selection) or its progeny (called as progeny testing) or its collateral relatives constituting its family (viz. half sibs, full sibs, aunts, uncles, nephews, niece etc) called as the family selection. These sources of information which are used to estimate the breeding value are called as selection criteria. The discussion on the relative merits of these criteria of selection has already been made in chapter 9-11.

### Multi trait selection

The net value of an individual is dependent upon several traits rather than on a single trait. Therefore, multi trait selection is taken as the goal of the selection programme. The methods of multi-trait selection are the tandem selection, independent culling level selection and index selection (total score method). The procedure and relative merits of these selection methods has also been discussed already in chapter 9.

### 12.2.2. Selection methods (theories) for non-additive gene action

The selection methods to get success in improving a trait due to non additive gene effects are: crossbreeding, recurrent selection, and reciprocal recurrent selection.

The **crossbreeding** refers to the crossing of two different breeds or strains that have been long established. The crossbreeding is practiced to take advantage of hetrosis (hybrid superiority) and of the good qualities of both the breeds/strains in complementary combinations.

The **recurrent selection** includes the crossing of a large number of individuals with a tester line (which is highly inbred) and to evaluate the progeny. Those individuals giving the best results are selected and intermated. This process is repeated over and over. Consequently the line being selected become homozygous for genes different from those in the tester lines provided the heterosis is due to over dominance.

In applying the **reciprocal recurrent selection**, randomly selected individuals from each of two non inbred strains are progeny tested in crosses with each other. Those individuals giving the best results in crosses from the two strains are intermated to continue their respective strains.

The recurrent selection and reciprocal recurrent selection results in improved cross performance whether the trait is due to over dominance, epistasis or additive effects. However, these are effective only for those traits which are affected by non-additive gene action (NAGA) because of increased generation interval the progress is slow for the traits controlled by additive gene action. A detailed discussion on these methods has been given in succeeding section.

## 12.3. GENETIC PRINCIPLE TO EXPLOIT NON ADDITIVE GENETIC VARIANCE

The selection response gradually declines and finally ceases as a consequence of continuous selection for several generations applied to closed lines. This is explained due to the exhaustion of additive genetic variance. However, in some cases the lines continue to show genetic variation, which is partly or mainly of non-additive nature. The non-additive genetic variation in some traits like viability and fertility is very important in all species of farm animals, and for this the inbreeding depression to a large extent has been observed in these traits. In order to exploit the non-additive genetic variation, some procedures based on combination of selection and crossing have been suggested, and found their greater application in improvement of maize and have also been used in pigs and poultry.

The application of inbreeding to produce inbred liens and their crossing play a major role to exploit heterosis for improvement. A breeder is interested to produce crossbred or $F_1$ individuals which should be superior not only to the inbred lines but also to the base population from which the lines were produced. To achieve this objective the selection is important besides inbreeding and crossing. Though natural selection play its role but to a lesser extent because it only eliminates lethal and severely deleterious genes during inbreeding.

The production of inbred lines and their crossing without selection or selection alone can not bring desired improvement. The crossing of inbred lines originating from base population produce no genotype that could not occur in the base population and therefore the mean of all crosses will not differ from the mean of base population.

The crosses made at random between lines which are inbred without selection gave the mean value equal to that of the base population. However, the line crosses, highlight some valuable gene combinations which can be multiplied. The selection is practiced with the aim to find those lines that cross well. The combination of both, i.e. developing inbred lines, their evaluation and selection is advantageous over straight forward selection applied to base population. Through inbreeding and crossing the desired and best genotypes present only in certain individuals of base population can be replicated in every individual of a certain cross. And after evaluation of the crosses the best genotype can be produced further to the required number by repeating the cross. This is the merit of the method and principle to take advantage of the existing genetic variability in base population or to say the genetic principle to exploit heterosis. However, there is a practical difficulty to find those lines which combine best and, therefore, it is necessary to produce many lines to cross them with each other in order to find which one give rise to superior genetic combinations.

The replication of the genotype in a cross has an additional advantage to allow the genotypic value to be measured with little error. The measurement of genotypic value by its phenotypic value in the base population is not as much accurate. It is the breeding value which can be reproduced by selection of individuals in a base population (non-inbred), whereas in the cross the genotypic value can be measured and reproduced till inbred lines exist. Therefore, selection alone, without inbreeding, to the base population can take advantage of the additive genetic variance to improve the character. While inbreeding and crossing combined with selection provide a better means to improvement when non additive genetic variance in a character exist in substantial amount. Therefore the selection is made for combining ability of the lines.

## 12.4. SELECTION FOR COMBINING ABILITY : ADDITIVE AND NON-ADDITIVE GENE ACTION

The inbred lines are evaluated in crosses and selected those which give the best cross. The procedure of crossing the inbred lines to produce hybrids has been utilized in the improvement of some plants, particularly the maize. Highly inbred lines of farm animals are not available due to reduction in fertility and survivability among inbreds. Therefore, crosses are made between different breeds or mildly inbred lines of farm animals.

The amount of variation between the crosses and the intensity of selection determines the amount of improvement through selection. A large number of crosses are required in order to get higher intensity of selection. A preliminary selection of lines is required to save time and space. This can be done by selecting the lines based on their own performance which is correlated with its performance in crosses to some extent. The additive genetic variance present in base population determines the amount of improvement by preliminary selection of the lines for their general combining ability (GCA). The GCA of the lines can be tested without the necessity of making all possible crosses. On the contrary, selection for specific combining ability (SCA) for further improvement utilizes the non-additive genetic variance. This needs to make crosses and select the best cross. In order to select for SCA to gain much improvement, the lines must have reached a high level of inbreeding because the variance of SCA is proportional to square or higher powers of inbreeding coefficient.

The relative magnitude of improvement due to GCA and SCA is proportional to their variances provided the intensity of selection is same for each. Further for fully inbred lines the variances of GCA and SCA equals to the additive variance and non-additive variance in the base population, respectively. Thus the relative amount of improvement from GCA and SCA can be estimated if the variance components in the base population are known. The additive variance of number of Kernels in barley was 77.2% of the total and rest 22.8% was the non-additive genetic variance. Thus 77% of the improvement, through inbreeding and crossing and selection of crosses, is expected to come from GCA and 23% from SCA. Thus the largest part of improvement comes from GCA i.e. additive variance in base population.

### 12.4.1. Selection for GCA : Breeding plans for additively genetic differences

The additive gene action (AGA) is responsible for differences of GCA. The AGA is indicated when the trait has high $h^2$ and show little or no heterosis or inbreeding depression. This means that the average values for the parental, $F_1$ and $F_2$ generation are all the same with some individuals being superior over others. These best individuals are best because they have more contributing or plus genes that act additively and not because of heterozygosity. It is therefore, essential to find the genetically superior individuals and select them for breeding. Thus selection should be based on the individuals breeding merit, this is because the correlation between performance of parental inbreed lines and the crossbred progeny is generally high for traits with large additive gene effects. To make selection effective for AGA, the environmental variance should be minimized by keeping the environment standard as much as possible equal for all individuals. The superior individuals then must be mated with superior. It is, therefore, better to select the superior individuals from superior relatives. Thus the selection for the improvement of GCA is through individual selection with pedigrees, progeny tests or family selection without inbreeding as a supplement to make selection more accurate. Mass selection alone is more reliable when $h^2$ is higher. It is usually more important then any other basis of selection if $h^2$ is much higher than 0.25 and if the trait can be measured early enough on the individuals which are to be selected or rejected. But when $h^2$ is low or when the trait is sex limited or when the trait can not be measured early, and when the trait can not be measured on living animal, the other basis of selection are more important. The selection without inbreeding is effective because the variation in GCA is attributable to additive variance in the base population from which the lines or families are derived. The GCA of all the available lines can be measured and some selection can be applied so that a portion of lines can be discarded on the basis of their own performance before crosses are made. This is possible because there is some degree of correlation between a line's performance as an inbred and its GCA. The selected individuals are mated to individuals of their own population to produce the next generation. The selection for GCA is repeated and thus it is known as recurrent selection for GCA (Jenkins, 1940).

For the traits with low heritability, the inbred lines are evaluated on the basis of their GCA which is measured by their performance in top crosses with base population from which the inbred liens are derived. In top crossing schemes the males of various lines are tested by crossing them with females of randomly bred population of test for GCA. The mean performance of the progeny so produced, measure the GCA of the line. Some selection among the lines is practiced and the lines with good GCA be finally tested in crosses.

## 12.4.2. Selection for SCA: breeding plans to exploit NAGA

The selection for SCA means to take advantage of hybrid vigour when NAGA is important. The causes of NAGA for difference in SGA of the lines in crosses are dominance, over dominance or epistacy. Selection on the basis of individuality is not effective when traits are largely affected by NAGA but the improvement in such traits depends upon heterozygosity through cross breeding resulting in the expression of heterosis. Thus the ultimate goal is to produce breeds or varieties each of which is homozygous which will produce the desired phenotypic merit when crossed with each other. This is important when epistatic effects and overdominace is important. The seed stock lines which are homozygous (produced by inbreeding) are selected and crossed with each other to get some special combination of genes which produce the desired phenotypic merit. The non-additive genetic variation is very important for viability and fertility in all species of farm animals. Several methods of exploiting non additive genetic variation have been suggested based on a combination of selection and crossing and have been utilized in maize breeding and also in poultry and pigs.

**(i) When the SCA is caused by dominance:** The dominance gene action can be exploited by two ways. One is by producing homozygous dominant individuals for the pairs of genes which affect the trait, and secondly by producing heterozygous individuals. There are two difficulties to use the first method viz. to distinguish homozygous dominants from heterozygotes, and that the quantitative traits are polygenic which reduces the probability of getting all dominant genes into one homozygous strain. The second method uses the production of heterozygous individuals which can be achieved by producing two complementary homozygous lines. Though the production of two complementary homozygous lines is problematic but can be achieved by directed process of selection during inbreeding. This will create maximum differences of gene frequency in two complementary lines. These lines are then crossed to obtain hybrids. However, for polygenic traits it is not possible to determine the genotype from phenotypes i.e. which individuals are complementary homozygous. To identify the complementary homozygous individuals (i.e. those which are homozygous in opposite ways) is by the method of finding the lines or breeds that combine and nick best when crossed. This method is used for production of hybrid seed corn. 1) The first step is to increase homozygosity of all pairs of genes by inbreeding and forming several inbred liens. 2) The next step is to cross these liens and test their combining ability that which produce the best line cross progeny. 3) The lines producing most superior progeny will be homozygous in opposite ways for many pairs of genes and will give greater heterozygosity in the progeny. 4) The progeny are sold and not kept for further breeding, and these liens are kept pure to cross again and again to produce further line cross progeny.

**(ii) When SCA is caused by over dominance and epistasis:** The most of practical procedure of utilizing the SCA is the formation of different families, or lines and crossing them to find those which result in greatest hybrid vigour. Two breeding systems have been proposed when heterosis is largely dependent upon over dominance. The first is the recurrent selection proposed by Hull (1945) and the second is reciprocal recurrent selection proposed by Comstock et al. (1949). Both these methods involve progeny testing to take advantage of overdominace.

**(a)** The **recurrent selection** proposed by Jerkins (1940) for improving GCA in plant breeding was modified by Hull (1945) to utilize SCA as well as GCA. As such this is also called as Hull's modification of recurrent selection or recurrent selection to inbred tester lines because it produce stock which combine best with inbred tester line or recurrent selection for SCA. This method has been sued in poultry breeding. In this method a highly inbred line is selected as a tester, "tester line" and a large number of individuals of a line under testing are tested in crosses with this tester line known to have good GCA. Therefore, in animals the females are selected on performance of their test cross progeny giving best results. The selected females are then mated with males of their own line to produce next generation of parents to be tested with inbred tester line. The crossbred progeny are not used for breeding and the selected individuals from source population are mated again and again among themselves to produce next generation of complementary stock to the tester inbred line. This cycle is repeated to several generations. The complementary stock will be homozygous recessive. Thus their test cross progeny will show greater heterosis. By this method the GCA of only one line and SCA of cross is improved and the GCA of inbred tester is already determined. This method has also a practical difficulty or limitation to produce and maintain the highly inbred tester line. Therefore, usually less inbred tester line is used which goes on changing genetically in subsequent generations and thus the optimum gain is not achieved. Therefore, another method of selection is required.

To measure the SCA of a cross requires to make and test that cross. Further a large number of crosses are required to be made and to be tested in order to have a reasonably high intensity of selection for SCA. To exploit heterosis (non additive genetic variance) the pre requisite is that the pair of lines should differ widely in gene frequencies at all loci affecting the trait and showing dominance. The differences of gene frequency can be produced by selection or by the process of inbreeding. It is more effective and more economical to produce differences of gene frequencies by the directed process of selection, and it will lead simultaneous selection for both GCA and SCA. This procedure of selection of combining ability is known as reciprocal recurrent selection proposed by Comstock et al. (1949) to make maximum use of both GCA and SGA.

**(b)** The **reciprocal recurrent selection** implies progeny testing of each of the two lines by crossing with each other. The crosses are made reciprocally viz. $M_1XF_2$and $M_2XF_1$ and the parents are evaluated on crossbred progeny performance. The best parents of both lines are selected and the rest parents as well as all the cross bred progeny are culled. The crossbred progeny are used only to test the combining ability of parents. The selected parents are remated to members of their own line to produce the next generation of individuals which are to be tested by mating them with individuals of the second line produced in the same way. They are evaluated based on their crossbred progeny and the best parents of both lines are selected to produce next generation of parents to be tested. Thus RRS is a kind of progeny selection. This cycle is repeated over and over.

The initial difference of gene frequency between the two lines is a pre-requisite of this method (reciprocal selection). Thus the start is made with the two breeds, lines or varieties. Secondly, deliberate inbreeding is avoided as far as possible. This can be done by using all of the females as parents in their own lines and to intensify the selection among males. The disadvantage of this method is that the performance of the lines for the character under selection is reduced. This is because this method is used for the characters which respond to inbreeding depression and heterosis i.e. to those which have directional dominance. Thus the change of gene frequency by selection is towards the extremes and so the mean value of the lines declines. That is to say the selection is made to make both the lines homozygous for individual genes for loci which exhibit over dominance. However, with reciprocal recurrent selection, the decline in performance is not so deleterious as the effect of deliberate inbreeding because the inbreeding affect all loci and so mean value of all characters showing directional dominance declines whereas in reciprocal selection only the character under selection decline.

The selection progress by reciprocal selection is more or less uniform over a number of generations, and depends on the initial gene frequency and the relative amount of AGA and NAGA. If the two lines have more or less similar gene frequency the change in gene frequency is slow in the beginning and so the initial genetic change is low. And the rate of progress increases after a certain difference in gene frequencies is reached. The reciprocal selection also changes the gene frequencies of additively acting genes which changes rapidly at the start of selection than later due to the reduction in additive variance later. Thus these two trends balance out each other to some extent and so the progress is more or less uniform over a number of generations.

Comparing the recurrent selection and reciprocal selection, the recurrent selection is superior at the beginning. This is because of more differences in gene frequencies of inbred tester and reference or source population to be tested, than between the two segregating populations used in reciprocal selection. But the recurrent selection is inferior if the loci with additive or semi-dominant gene action prevail. This is because it is difficult to differentiate between homozygous dominant and heterozygous in test cross progeny if one allele is dominant over others. Thus the desirable dominant gene can not be accumulated in the segregating population.

Both these systems are inferior to **pure line selection** or **within line selection** (WLS) for traits governed by additive gene effects with high $h^2$.

The present day is the era of crossbreds for the reason that they show heterosis that indicates the existence of non-additive gene effects. The performance of crossbreds can be improved by R.R.S. However, the suitability of within line selection (WLS) and RRS is decided by the genetic correlation between purebred (P) and corssbred (C) half sib's performance ($r_{PC}$). A moderate to high positive $r_{PC}$ favours WLS but when $r_{PC}$ is low or negative, RRS is said to be more efficient over WLS (Bell, 1982). This is for the reason of existence of non additive gene effects and that two populations under RRS do not have identical gene frequencies which causes the covariance to be smaller or negative

$$r_{PC} = \frac{Cov_{PC(Sires)}}{\sqrt{\sigma^2 \text{ s(P)} \sigma^2 \text{ s(C)}}}$$

The RRS is more efficient than WLS to improve the heterotic traits. In the presence of over dominant genes the response to selection is highest under RRS.

At later stage of using reciprocal methods of breeding, the performance of pure lines shows negative correlation with the crosses. This is because the continuous selection for combining ability improves the cross but the parent lines deteriorate due to increased homozygosity at heterotic loci. It is only the heterotic loci which show further segregation after most of the loci showing additive gene effects become fixed.

The RRS is used for egg production in poultry and also encouraging results were obtained with maize. The comparison of the two methods of selection has been shown diagrammatically below:

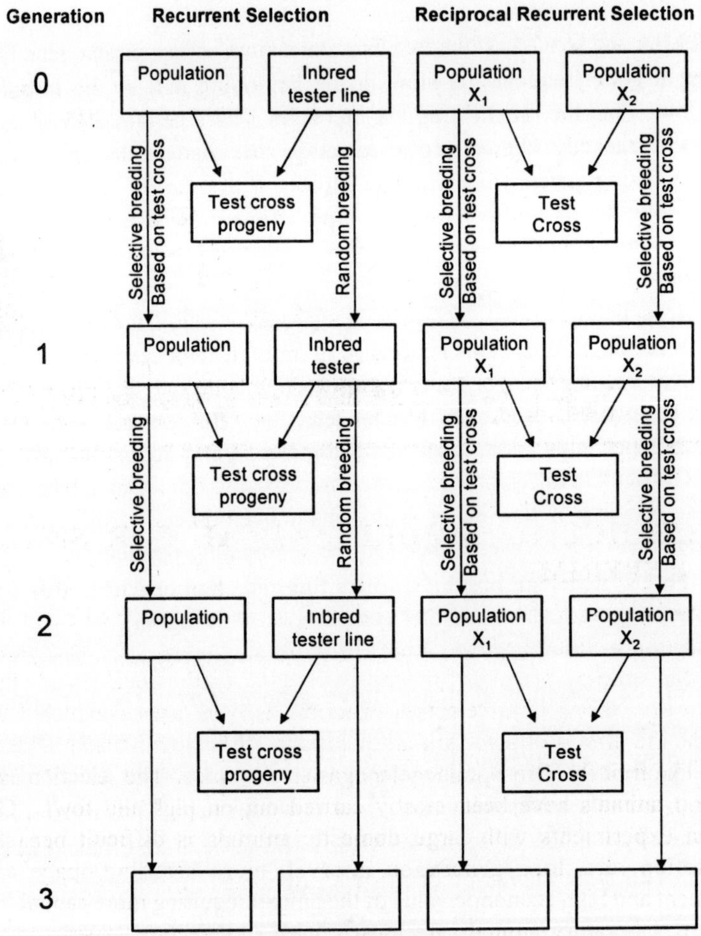


**Fig. 12.1. Showing comparison of R.S. and R.R.S.**

## QUESTIONS

**12.1.** Explain fully how additive genetic variance in poultry can be beneficially used for increased production. (*ARS 1976*)

**12.2.** What is non-additive genetic variance? Discuss various breeding plans for its profitable exploitation in poultry production. (*ARS 1978, 1981*)

**12.3.** Define GCA and SCA. Give briefly the methods of selection for traits mainly affected by NAGA. (*ARS 1982*)

**12.4.** Give a suitable breeding plan for utilization of GCA and SCA (*ARS 1985*)

***Or***

Give various breeding plans for utilizing GCA and SCA in poultry for egg production. (*ARS 1995*)

# 13
# SELECTION EXPERIMENTS

## 13.1. CHOICE OF MODEL ANIMAL FOR SELECTION EXPERIMENT

Improvement of livestock to meet the human needs started since the days of domestication without the knowledge of genetic principles. The science of genetics helped the animal breeder for improvement of livestock more rapidly and economically. Long term selection experiments have been conducted in order to determine the effects of selection on quantitative traits particularly with laboratory animals like fruit fly (Drosophila melanogaster) and mice. The selection experiments with farm animals have been mostly carried out on pigs and fowl. Conducting selection experiments with large domestic animals is difficult because of low reproduction rate, long generation interval, more breeding space and labour requirement and high economic value of the animal requiring more capital investment. Therefore, laboratory animals are mostly used in selection experiments. This is because of their rapid high reproduction rate, short generation interval, ease of handling more numbers, and less breeding space, labour and capital requirement. These factors make the Drosophila, Tribolium and mice favourable for test material. The generation interval in fruit fly and mice is about 2 weeks and 8-12 weeks, respectively.

Recent studies have shown that the science of genetics has no species barrier and the basic genetic principles are applied to all. Therefore any experiment carried out to know the basic genetic principles is relevant to animal breeding. There are reasons to undertake the experiments with lab animals on quantitative genetics. The relevance or contribution of lab experiments to large animals can be viewed for two reasons viz. how far the conclusions drawn in such lab experiments are true for large animals and the usefulness of lab experiment to large animals improvement.

Correct selection or **choice of model lab animal** is more important to maximize the relevance of lab experiments for farm animals. It should be kept in mind that choice of model lab animal should be based on the basis of the genetic theory involved rather than the availability of the model animal or the available facilities to conduct the experiment or the availability of trained personal. Conducting experiment on **Drosophila** is advocated for genetic studies like genetic basis of chromosomal theory, as it contained only 4 pairs of chromosomes. **Tribolium** is the best species/ model animal to test the existing breeding methods for non additive genetic variance or to find the genotype environment interaction because the Tribolium can sustain the changes in temperature and culture etc. **Mice** being closer to domestic mammals are more suitable for studying the specific problems of animal breeding and particularly the lactation studies, and maternal effects etc. Likewise, the **Japanese quail** is mostly useful for breeding experiment related to poultry.

## 13.2. RELEVANCE OF LAB EXPERIMENTS TO LARGE LIVESTOCK

(i) The lab experiments provide prior information which can be tested with large livestock. Any attempt to try some idea like to explore the causes of heterosis, genotype-environment interaction, and efficiency of breeding methods (reciprocal recurrent selection etc.) on large animals without sound evidence based on lab experiments will be merely wastage of time and resources. Any genetic theory can be further checked on large animals after it is established on lab animals. But testing of the adequacy of theory developed on lab animals posses a problem. The results obtained on lab experiments are not straight way applied to large animals. There may be some different factors working on lab animals and farm animals. However, based on the results of lab experiments it may lead to develop refined theories. It requires an experimental test of the population which will indicate whether the theory is adequate for the population under test. For example, Hammand (1947) recommended that animals should be best selected for a trait under the environment which favours its fullest expression and that once a superior line is developed it can be used in other environment. This theory of Hammand was later on criticized and a new theory was developed by Falconer (1952) suggesting that the breed should be selected in the environment in which it has to live.

(ii) The genetic theory developed on lab animals fully supported with experimental proof creates confidence, thinking, an aptitude to learning and understanding the problem.

(iii) The lab experiments help to know the correct population size for estimation of a particular parameter and accuracy of its estimation. The genetic control is essentially required in selection experiment to know the comparative effect of selection and genetic drift.

(iv) Lab experiments help to examine, understand and in establishment of basic genetic concept like Mendelian inheritance, sex linkage, gene frequencies, number of genes affecting a trait, origin of new variation by mutants, rate of inbreeding depression etc. This help to understand the genetic structure of population and properties of a population which can not be from a general theory.

(v) The lab experiments are also helpful in testing the validity of the theories of quantitative genetics like theory of additive and non-additive gene action, correlated response theory, asymmetry of response, limit of response to selection, theory of response to selection, theory of maternal effects, genotype environment interaction etc.

Roberts (1965) has reviewed the contribution of the lab mouse to animal breeding research, citing the various lab experiments conducted by various workers which demonstrated the followings:

- Additive genetic nature of variation in body weight;
- Correlated response by shortening ears, feet and tail, and higher ovulation rate as a result of selection for weight;
- Assymesty of response in body weight due to maternal effect, directional dominance and inbreeding;
- Limit to selection for body weight due to loss or exhaustion of additive genetic variance
- Genotype – environment interaction for body weight;
- The significance of non additive genetic variance in body weight, and
- The existence of maternal effects

The results of selection for thorax length in Drosophila indicated that the response was assymetrical and that selection ceased to have an effect (Robertson and Reeve, 1952). Experiment for increased shank length in the mature fowl was conducted by Lerner (1958) with making additional observations on the correlated changes in vigour and body proportions. The selection resulted in a rapid increase in shank length in the first seven generations after which there was no consistent progress. The selection for increased shank length had a detrimental effect on the vigour of the birds, and after the selection was ceased and the shank length decreased, there was an improvement in vigour. Body conformation, length of spinal column and posture of the birds were also altered as a result of increase in shank length.

(vi) The extrapolation of results of genetic studies from any experiment of a population is not definitely justified for other population or species. But when the traits of different species are governed by the same kind of gene action, the results obtained with one species can be extrapolated to another. The additive gene action largely determines the bristle number in Drosophila, bodysize in mice and pupal weight in Tribolium and responds to selection, and hence these can be easily extrapolated from one species to another. It is, therefore, not important that the species have analogies with respect to phenotype, economy and taxonomy but the extrapolation should be based on similar genetic parameters.

The findings of selection experiments with Drosophila, mice and fowl can be concluded in general the followings:

(i) Selection can rapidly change the traits which show additive genetic variation.
(ii) The continued selection over many generations showed that response is more in the first few generations, then declining and finally ceases reaching limit to selection.
(iii) Two way selection experiments indicated asymmetry of responses in two lines and that the difference between the means of the two lines at the selection limit considerably exceeds to that of the original population.

## 13.3. CONSEQUENCES OF SELECTION EXPERIMENTS

The basic effect of selection is to change the gene frequencies and consequently the genetic properties of population which determine the effect of further selection. The population mean is changed as a result of selection without having the idea of the effect of selection on individual loci affecting the quantitative trait. Therefore, it is not possible to predict the changes of gene frequencies. Thus the response to selection can be predicted only when the genetic properties remain unchanged. The selection experiments can only discover and explain the consequences of selection.

The selection theory states that:

1. The realized or observed response to selection in progeny generation should agree with that expected theoretically on the basis of equation $R = h^2$. Sd. Obtained from information on parental population.

2. Long term selection should lead to fixation of alleles with the consequent loss/exhaustion of genetic variance at selection limit. The reduction in genetic variance will also reduce the phenotypic variance and at last selection will not result in any response.

The validity of selection theory can be tested from experimental studies of selection. The observations that have emerged from selection experiments regarding unexpected consequence of selection theory are:

- **Insufficient response:** The observed or realized response obtained from the selection experiment should agree to the expectation based on the $h^2$ estimate and selection differential. But it has been observed that the realized response deviates and generally falls short than expected based on selection theory. This disagreement between expected and observed (realized) response to selection is called as the insufficient response.

- **Asymmetry of response:** The selection in opposite direction, known as bidirectional selection or two way selection, should lead to equal response in the two lines selected for increased performance (upward selection) and selected for decreased performance (downward selection). But it has been observed that the response is not equal in upward and downward lines. This is called as inequality of selection progress or the asymmetry of response to selection.

### 13.3.1. Insufficient response

The causes of variation in theoretical (predicted or expected) response and actual obtained (realized) response to selection (genetic progress) or the factors which potentially reduce the net response to selection can best be explained from the component factors affecting the response. These are $\Delta h = h^2.S$

**1. Heritability:** The heritability is the function of the trait and population, besides being affected by some other factors.

**(a) Low and wrong $h^2$ estimates:** The maternal effects and other common environmental effects called as C-effects such as herd differences, seasonal influences etc. prevent an accurate estimate of $h^2$. The other factors which cause wrong $h^2$ estimates are inaccurate measurement of data, scale effect, unadjustment of data, violation of the assumption in $h^2$ estimation. In view of these factors the actual genetic merit can not be known. As a result the accuracy of B.V. falls short of expectation and the realized genetic progress is less than expectations.

Similarly when $h^2$ of a trait is low, the $r_{AP}$ (i.e. h or accuracy of selection) is low and hence most of the variation in the character is of environmental in nature. This will lead more deviations from expected phenotypic merit of the progeny. It has been observed that the $h^2$ estimates of most of the economic traits of farm animals are of low magnitude.

**(b) Gene interaction:** The long term prospects of selection can be seriously over estimated in the presence of gene interaction (additive x additive). This is due to the over estimate of $h^2$ in the presence of gene interaction. The contribution of genes, which interacts, towards genetic progress can be much larger if such genes are linked. The epistatic interactions disintegrate if selection is discontinued and gain in performance due to interaction effect disappears.

**(c) G-E interaction:** The G x E interaction may also decrease genetic progress. Such interactions change the ranking of bulls in different environments and thus the genetic gains obtained in one environment will not be consistent but will only be partly or not at all repeatable in another environment depending on the magnitude and direction of genetic correlation between performances in different environments. The interaction between breeding value and the environment in different years was suggested in poultry by Dickerson (1955). When the correlation ($r_G$) between performances in two environments is zero the selection progress is zero for which the term genetic slippage was given by Dickerson for the reduction of the breeding value when populations perform in environment other than that in which they were selected.

In this context the G-X interaction is important because the environmental conditions at the time of predicting the response on the basis of information on parent generation are different when the response to selection is measured on the performance of the progeny generation. This time gap creates the environmental differences. Thus there is a possibility of G-E interaction which if exist will influence the genetic progress.

**2. Selection differential :** This influences the R in the following ways -

(a) The selection progress is also influenced by the **artificial and natural counter selection**. The accidental loss of selected parents (through viability, fertility or longevity) reduces the selection differential and thus it results in low progress i.e. the progress falls short than expected. This is because the R depends on S of the selected parents and if the selected parents will differ in fertility and viability then they will not contribute equally to the progeny of next generations and hence due to unequal number of progeny of different parents, the contribution of their genes to next generation will differ. The R depends on the realized (effective/weighted) selection differential rather than the attempted selection differential. Thus the actual response obtained will not be equal to the predicted response. The situation arises for the traits which genetically correlated to fitness i.e. the traits under selection which influence viability or fertility. The selection experiment for change in shank length (Lerner, 1959) in fowl was found to have a detrimental effect on vigour of the birds. The selection resulted in an increase in shank length in early (upto 7) generations after which the progress was not consistent. The ratio of actual to expected response decreased. But after the selection was stopped, the shank length decreased and there was an improvement in vigour and reproduction.

The natural selection may aid or hamper the artificial selection and it depends upon the genetic correlation between the traits under selection and fitness. The natural selection hampers the artificial selection when attempts are made to change the optimum performance level. The reproductive rates of selected individuals with extreme phenotypes are lower and thus the realized Sd is lower than expected. This makes the actual response to fall short than expected.

**(b)** The female progeny of culled animals or of the low rank P.T. bulls remain in the breeding herd and cause insufficient response.

**(c)** The bulls are selected on pedigree performance before P.T. The bull from superior dam may not be superior due to sampling nature of inheritance. However, if the bull is superior, it may not transmit its genetic superiority to his progeny because of sampling nature of inheritance.

**(d)** Practically, the selection directed towards the characters other than milk yield (primary character) also causes the insufficient response to selection.

**(e)** The realized selection differential is reduced if additional traits are included in the selection goal. This reduces the actual superiority than the S if the selection is only for one trait.

**3. Population size:** It is an important factor, when selection lines are small the sampling errors will be more frequent and larger in magnitude. This will contribute to the variability among lines for response to selection. This can be explained as:

**(a)** The true genetic merit may not be reflected from the phenotypic merit of the selected individuals when the sample size is small and it will result low $r_{AP}$. Thus the observed response will fall short of predicted. The low $r_{AP}$ means low $h^2$ which indicate that most of the differences among individuals are caused by environmental effects and therefore the deviations from expected phenotypic merit of the progeny from selection errors as well as from environmental variations will be larger.

(b) Second way of causing the variability in R by small number of parents per generation is through the inbreeding. The inbreeding causes fixation of alleles at random which means that different lines may undergo fixation for different alleles having different effects. The inbreeding depression counterbalances the effect of selection.

(c) Thirdly the effect of sampling variation depends upon the initial gene frequencies in the base population as well as during the course of selection. The effect of sampling variation is very less when the genes affecting a trait under selection are at intermediate frequencies than when they are at low frequencies. The effect with low gene frequencies is more because in some lines the genes will be present while in others may be absent. Thus it will affect the response because of the presence or absence of genes with large effect.

A substantial amount of difference in response between lines starts appearing in later generations than in early generations. The response in early generations is mainly due to the genes which have major effects and are at intermediate frequencies. The response is consistent in all lines till these genes are fixed after which these genes do not contribute to genetic differences among individuals. In later generations the selection is emphasized for the numerous loci with initially low frequencies and with small effect on the trait.

## 13.3.2. Asymmetry of response

The different magnitudes of response in opposite direction have been observed in many two way selection experiments. It is the second surprising feature of the unexpected result of selection experiment. This disappoints a breeder when the selection progress falls short than expected. In a series of experiments, Falconer observed the phenomenon of asymmetrical response for most of the traits in mice when selected in opposite direction, particularly for body weight of mice. The response was more in downward line than in upward line. Similar observations were made by Robertson and Reeve (1950) in thorax length of fruit fly. The total change was greater for decreased length.

Falconer mentioned that the realized heritabilities in the two directions must be significantly different if the asymmetry is real. Many factors may cause selection response to differ in two directions. These main causes which may create asymmetrical response are discussed below:

**1. Population size:** The population size is an important factor. The lines under selection are not very large in size. This causes the random drift, inbreeding and reduction in genetic variance.

The **random drift** can easily result the asymmetry of response if there is only one selection line in each direction. The effect of random drift can be assessed only by replication of the selection.

The inbreeding is unavoidable in small population and hence the inbreeding depression occurs which reduces the mean performance. This results into less response in upward line but higher response in downward line. The progress for increased performance is counteracted by the effect of inbreeding for the traits affected by inbreeding depression and hence the net genetic gain is less than expected. On the other hand, the progress due to selection is more in downward line by the effect of inbreeding depression. Therefore, the effect of selection and inbreeding is antagonistic in upward line but synergetic in downward line. This results the genetic gain to fall short in upward line because of opposite (antagonistic)) effect of two forces while the inbreeding depression augment the effect of selection in downward line and hence asymmetry of response occurs.

**2. Correlated characters:** The milk production often called as mothering ability particularly in small mammals (mice) affects the growth of young one upto weaning age. Selection for low weaning weight at 6 weeks in mice brings simultaneous change in mothering ability. The mothering ability, for which there is no selection, is reduced when selecting for low weaning weight. The selection for weaning weight has thus different effect in two lines. The decrease in weaning weight due to selection is more in small mice due to reduction in their mothering ability and hence the rate of genetic progress is more compared to an increase in weaning weight in larger line (upward selection)

**3. Selection favouring heterozygous:** The heterozygotes are superior to either homozygote in case of over dominance. In this case the heterozygotes are selected in upward line. This results the equilibrium to be reached gradually in the upward line because heterozygotes produce two alleles in equal frequencies to the next generation. At equilibrium state the genetic variation still exists but there will be no response to selection. Thus as the gene frequencies approach equilibrium when selection favours heterozygotes, the response is slow. In downward line the response is more till the favoured alleles approach fixation.

**4. Genetic differences:** The asymmetry of response to selection may be due to any following form of genetic differences in the initial population. These are:

**(i) Directional gene frequency** – Some alleles affects the trait in one direction while others in other direction. The frequencies of these two types of alleles may be different. This is called as the directional gene frequency which indicates the differences in the frequencies of the alleles affecting the trait in two opposite directions. The frequencies of the alleles affecting the trait in one direction may be high, which expects to cause a more rapid response in the direction of the less frequent alleles and low response in the direction of the most frequent alleles. The frequencies of less favourable alleles are low due to natural selection, particularly the alleles related to fitness. This causes a more rapid response in the direction of greater loss of fitness when the selection in one direction reduces fitness more than selection in other direction.

**(ii) Directional dominance of genes** – There may be unequal distribution of genes which are increasing and decreasing the value of a trait. The directional dominance occurs when most of the genes are dominant in one direction (either to decrease or increase the value of the trait). It is a situation when genes dominant in one direction are more in number or have large effect than those which are dominant in other direction. When the frequencies of alleles acting in one direction are already high, further progress will be slow than the progress in opposite direction.

The dominance of alleles masks the true B.V. of heterozygotes and of dominant homozygotes. Thus selection is not effective or accurate when made to increase the frequency of dominant alleles. On the other hand, the response to selection for recessive alleles is not affected by the masking effect of dominant alleles. However, the effect of neither of the two genetic symmetry is immediately observed in first few generations but after the gene frequencies become differentiated in two lines.

**5. Selection differential:** The selection differential of the two lines may be different for the following reasons – (a) Antagonistic or synergetic effects of the natural and artificial selection, (b) differences in fertility of two lines and c) scale effect. When the S will be different, the R will also be different in two lines.

The use of wrong scale may be a cause of asymmetry. The scale effect causes differences in skewness, of the genetic and environmental variation, in opposite direction. The difference in skewness may also be due to G-E interaction. The individuals of upward line are of high genetic value and receive better environment than the individuals of downward line. The genetic variation is fully exploited or expressed in better environment than in poor environment and hence the genetic variation is less among individuals receiving better environment. The example of school education may be cited here. Secondly, the individuals with high genetic value are more prone to environmental variation compared to those having low breeding value. The example is the intelligence. Both result in low $h^2$ of upward line than of the downward line.

## 13.4. LIMITS TO ARTIFICIAL SELECTION

### 13.4.1. Concept:

The selection acts on additive genetic variance which goes on diminishing in future generations as a result of continuous selection. The response to selection, therefore, diminishes. The quantitative characters are controlled by polygenes which segregate in the population. These genes are brought to fixation by the selection or inbreeding or random drift due to small population size or also they may reach equilibrium in case of over dominance. Thus due to continuous selection there will be no genetic variance and hence there will be no response to further selection. When there is no response to selection it is said that selection limit has reached and such a population is called at selection limit or plateaued population. This is also known as selection **plateau**. Thus the phenotypic level of a trait at which the response ceases is termed the **selection limit**. The selection limits have been noted under long term selection experiments in laboratory animals (mice, Drosophila) and poultry.

Some of the examples of selection limits due to long term selection experiments are:

- Drosophila – Thorax length, wing length and abdominal bristle numbers obtained by Robertson and Reeve (1952), Reeve and Robertson (1953), Robertson (1955), Clayton and Robertson (1957).
- Mice – Body weight and litter size obtained by Falconer (1955, 1965, 1971, 1973), Roberts (1966), Falconer and King (1953)
- Poultry – Egg production and shank length obtained by Lerner and Dempster (1951), Dickerson (1955).

Most of the above selection experiments were bidirectional and the selection limits reached between 20-30 generations. The selection had resulted the mean at the limits far beyond the range of variation present in base population.

## 13.4.2. Total response and its determinants

The observed range of response or total response ($R_T$) is taken as the difference between the upper and lower limits and expressed in relation to the initial genetic variance or phenotypic variance as $R_T/\sigma_A$ or $R_T/\sigma_P$. The determinants of total response are the number of gene loci affecting a trait, population size and mutation.

(i) The **numbers of genes** affecting a character have inverse relation with the magnitude of their effect but have direct relationship with the response to selection that can be achieved. The genes few in number affecting a character have large effects but if the genes are many in number controlling the character their effects will be small. The $R_T$ in relation to $\sigma_A$ depends on the number of gene loci affecting a trait and hence contributing the genetic variation in the trait. The larger the number of loci, the larger will be the response in relation to the original variance. This is because the number of genotypes formed depends upon the number of loci affecting a trait and the frequency of the most extreme genotype is getting reduced with the increase in number of loci viz. ¼, 1/16, 1/64, 1/256, 1/1024 and 1/4096 for one through six loci affecting a trait The most extreme genotype represents the selection limit. Therefore, selection limit is expected within the range of variation in base population. Since extreme genotype is rarer in the base population for larger number of loci, so the selection limits are far away from the original mean.

The total response is related to the additive variance in the base population. The additive effect of a gene is taken as the average of the difference of two homozygotes and represented by 'a'. The total difference between homozygotes is thus 2a and by summing over all loci is $\Sigma 2a$. Assuming the equal effect of all loci on the character, the range of difference which also represents the total response ($R_T$) becomes as $R_T$=2na with n as the number of loci each having a homozyote difference of 2a. Further assuming the equal gene frequencies of 0.5, the additive variance in the base population is

$$\sigma_A{}^2 = 2pq[a+d(q-p)]^2 = 2pqa^2 = 0.5\ \Sigma a^2 = 0.5na^2$$

The degree of dominance does not make any contribution for the case of equal gene frequencies. Squaring the range of response develop the relation with additive variance as

$$\frac{R_T^2}{\sigma_A^2} = \frac{(2na)^2}{0.5na^2} = \frac{4n^2a^2}{0.5na^2} = 8n$$

In the presence of large number of genes, the response that could be achieved in the theoretical maximum response which sets an upper limit to expectation. This is the total response what would be attained when genetic variance is caused by an infinite number of loci. Robertson (1960) has shown the theoretical maximum response ($R_{max}$) as :

$$R_{max} = 2n_e\ i\ h^2\ \sigma p$$

This may be more with favourable recessive genes of low initial frequencies.

The ratio of observed to theoretical maximum response gives an indication of whether the character is influenced by very large number of genes having equal effects. The long term experiments on thorax length and abdominal bristle number of Drosophila and the 6-week body weight and litter size in mice for which selection limits have reached, showed the ratio of observed to theoretical maximum response ranging from 0.21 to 0.36. This means that observed response had fallen short of the maximum response which indicated that none of these characters were controlled by a very large number of genes having equal effects.

(ii) The **population size** also influenced the total response. Selected lines are often small in size and hence random drift causes fixation of some unfavourable alleles inspite of selection against them. This results the response to fall short than expected. The limit to selection is then decided by the chance of fixation of favourable alleles. The selection and inbreeding interacting together decide this chance of fixation. The inbreeding depends on population size whereas the selection on the selection coefficient (s) or intensity of selection (i). Therefore, the chance of fixation can be taken as a function of effective population size (Ne) and the selection coefficient as NeS or Ne i. The coefficient of selection depends on the gene effect ($2a/\sigma p$) and intensity of selection as $S = i(2a/\sigma p)$. The quantity $2a/\sigma p$ is the difference of value between two homozygous relative to phenotypic standard deviation and hence called as the standardized effect of a locus. In view of the above, the total response is expected to be more in a population of large size under more intense selection. This was confirmed by Jones et al. (1968) who found that total response was greater for increased abdominal bristle number in drosophila in the selected lines of larger size with high intensity of selection.

The fixation of alleles either by inbreeding or selection can be tested from the results of repeated experiments i.e. different replicate lines are subjected to selection. The fixation due to inbreeding is indicated by reaching the different replicate lines to different selection limits because different alleles at many loci are fixed in different replicates. This causes the response to show on crossing these lines. In case of fixation of alleles by selection, the different lines have the same selection limits because the same alleles at most loci are fixed and these lines will not respond to selection.

(iii) The **mutation** seems to be important in affecting the selection limits in long term response. The mutation give rise to new genetic variation, though new mutants have very small effect in next or in next few generation for their low frequencies which is 1/2N where N is the population size. The frequency of new mutants increase in case of their favourable effect on the character under selection. The continued increase in the frequency of favourable mutant increases the genetic variance and hence contributes to response to selection. The new mutants arise in every generation and have their cumulative effect to the response but after about 20 generations. The response should then continue without approaching selection limit when there is mutation.

## 13.4.3. No selection limit

Some long term selection experiments have shown no selection limits and the response continued over many generations of selection. The examples are:

- Oil content and protein content in maize. The high line did not reach the selection limit upto 78 generations of selection.
- Pupal weight of Tribolium increased continuously upto 75 generations.
- One of the 3 replicates for increased abdominal bristle number in Drosophila continued responding upto 88 generations.
- The important livestock species also do not seem to be at selection limit because there is continuous improvements in traits of most economic importance viz. milk yield and body weight in cattle, body weight and litter size in pigs and sheep, weight gain in broilers and egg number in layers are showing improvement though these species have been under continuous selection for many generation. The rate of genetic improvement ranged from 1 to 2% per year of the mean.

## 13.4.4. Nature or expectation of limit : Genetic properties of lines at plateaue

The quantitative characters are controlled by many genes. The response to selection continues over a number of generations with gradual diminution of the rate till a limit is reached. The selection acts on additive genetic variance. The effect of long term selection experiment on variance can be explained as under

(i) Theoretically it is expected that selection should lead to fixation of alleles (homozygosity) with the consequent loss or exhaustion of genetic variance. Consequent upon the absence of genetic (additive) variance, the heritability estimate should be zero and relaxation or reversed selection will bring no change in the level of the performance i.e. response should cease.

(ii) As a consequence of the decline in genetic variance as the limit is reached there should be a decline in phenotypic variance

## Evidence from selection experiments

The evidence from selection experiments on these expectations of selection limit are given here:

Selection experiment on abdominal bristle number in Drosophila indicated that the phenotypic variance in the large line remained at the same level upto about 25 generations when the limit is reached. The comparison with the control line indicated that the variance did not decrease at all, whereas in the small line a sudden and large increase was observed (Clayton and Robertson, 1957)

Long term selection experiments on abdominal bristle number in Drosophila conducted by Clayton and Robertson (1957) and Jones et al. (1968) have shown that the phenotypic variance increased very much during selection in both directions (high and low lines) than in base population.

Selection for thorax length in Drosophila (Robertson 1955) showed that the population at selection limit respond to selection in reversed direction, respond rapidly and returned to the unselected level when the reverse selection was made in upward line but the low line (for reduced thorax length) did not respond to reversed selection. Similar results were reported by Robertson and Reeve (1952) for two way selection of thorax length of fruit flies following selection for increased and decreased length (selection in opposite direction) after the selection limit had been reached, resulted in a rapid return in the lines selected for longer thorax but this did not happen in the lines selected for shorter thorax. Therefore the two lines behaved differently to reverse selection and indicated the presence of genetic variance after the selection ceased to have an effect. It may be probably that the genes for shorter thorax had been fixed in the homozygous condition but in the larger thorax lines the genes must have been still quite heterozygous.

The evidence from selection experiments about the nature of the selection limit do not confirm the simple theoretical expectation of reduction in phenotypic and genetic variance. The phenotypic variance fails to decline and the genetic variance of some kind still remains after the selection limit reached.

The increase in phenotypic variance instead of its declining as expected may be due to the following reasons:

1. The selection limits represents the fixation of alleles concerned leading to an increase of the frequency of homozygotes which are more sensitive to environmental effects as compared to heterozygotes and it will increase the environmental variance. This increase of environmental variance not only compensates the decrease in genetic variance but the variance is increased.
2. This depends on the character under selection. Scale effect may be a cause for the characters for which the variance changes along change in mean through selection (the variance is not independent of the mean for some characters). The selection changes the mean and the variance is changed with it automatically.
3. The genetic variance may not be completely exhausted. The existence of additive genetic variance at selection limit may be tested by two way selection experiment and applying reversed selection. The presence of additive genetic variance is indicated if the selected line responds to reversed selection. Inbreeding of selected line provides the evidence of the presence of non-

additive genetic variance. However, some lines lose all additive genetic variance as per expectations but others retain at selection limit. The existence of additive genetic variance at limit may be due to

(i) The selection limit is not reached in reality
- due to reduction in fertility in selected lines which reduces the selection differential and
- due to low frequencies of unwanted recessive alleles which may remain unfixed. Further reduction of frequencies of such alleles is very low by selection for they contribute the non additive genetic variance.

(ii) When the selection favours heterozygous, there is genetic variation due to genes at selection limit. Under this situation the natural selection prevents the fixation of the alleles because the homozygous are sterile for some traits e.g. pygmy gene in mice which control the body size (Faloner, 1960). Reversed selection shows immediate and rapid response. This situation is very common, when the natural selection acts through lethality or sterility.

(iii) The nature of the trait or its scale of measurement may impose the limit. There are measurement limits in score traits like 0 to 5, 0-10 etc. which are attained through selection before the genetic variance is fully exhausted. Thus a false limit is reached.

## 13.4.5. Factors affecting selection limits

It is essential to understand the genetic basis of limits to selection and the methods to overcome the limits to selection when planning for improvement of economic traits. The selective breeding has been in practice since long for the improvement of farm animals. As a consequence of this, the limit to selection may have reached and it is not possible to get further response to selection. Al Murrani (1974) published a review on the limits to artificial selection regarding the genetics of limit and attempts to overcome the limits to selection. There are many factors which cause the cessation of response and leads to the limits to selection.

**(1) Exhaustion of genetic variance:** Many loci control the quantitative traits. As a result of continuous selection for long time, it is expected that the genes will get fixed and there will remain no genetic variance. This will lead zero $h^2$ estimates and thus no change in population mean for the selected trait is expected even with relax selection or reversed selection. Experimental evidences for body weight in mice (Falconer and King, 1953; Roberts 1966), for thorax length in Drosophila (Robertson, 1955) and for fecundity in Drosophila (Brown and Bell, 1961) have shown that the exhaustion of additive genetic variance was the cause of selection limit. The loss of genetic variance as a cause of limit to selection is based on the theory that new variance and renewed response should occur in crossbred population produced by the two lines selected in two directions (high and low expression of the trait) and have reached limit to selection.

The absence of additive variance and the fixation of all loci affecting a character are distinct. One is over dominance when selection favour heterozygotes for their superiority over both homozygotes and some loci segregate without showing any additive variance. This results in gene frequency equilibrium at an intermediate level. The second is the opposition of artificial selection by natural selection. One homozygote may be rejected for having low value of the character while other homozygote may not contribute due to its inviability or infertility under natural selection and thus heterozygote becomes superior. The additive variance will be exhausted for overall fitness but not for the character under selection.

**(2) Reasons of failure to respond in the presence of genetic variance**

**(i) Overdominance gene action:** Some form of overdominance when heterozygotes are at advantage may be a barrier to further advance. The heterozygotes may be superior than the homozygotes or the homozygotes may be less fit than heterozygotes and thus the genetic variance exists at the limit. Heterozygote superiority may lead to an equilibrium gene frequencies and $h^2$ at equilibrium should be zero because all the genetic variance is non additive type. Under the situation the reverse selection will be effective to decrease the performance level of the population for trait under selection.

The overdominance as a cause of plateauing for wing length (Reeve and Robertson, 1953) and bristle number (Clayton and Robertson, 1957) in Drosophila has been observed. There was an increase in variance as the response diminished at the limit and response to reverse selection was observed in bristle number. For wing length also the variance and $h^2$ estimate was greater, at the limit, than in the unselected stock. Natural selection may favour heterozygotes. The recessive lethal genes may be the factor in the maintenance of heterozygosity and the selected individuals may be heterozygous carrier of lethal genes. Thus the heterozygotes have the selection advantage.

The pygmy gene in mice, selected for small size, appeared due to mutation (McArthur, 1949). The mice homozygous for pygmy gene are small but sterile and hence the gene could not fixed due to natural selection against homozygotes. The, mice heterozygous for pygmy genes were favoured in selection because they are smaller in size. Thus there existed the genetic variance due to the gene but without further progress. In case of reversed selection there is a joint synergetic effect of artificial and natural selection in the same direction and hence there is immediate and rapid response.

**(ii) Low frequency of recessive genes:** The selection reduces and eliminates the recessive genes until they become rare in the population. Thus the unfavourable recessive genes are brought to low frequency. The variance caused by recessive genes at low frequencies is non additive. In this situation, the mean will change in unfavourable direction on inbreeding. Therefore the genetic variance may persist at the selection limit due to the segretation of recessive genes which are at low frequency. This makes the further selection ineffective. Litter size and body weight in mice threw some light on this matter.

**(iii) Negative genetic correlation:** There are some traits in farm and lab animals showing negative genetic correlation. The continued selection may develop the negative genetic correlation. The examples are: egg production and egg weight in poultry, milk production and fat % in milk, shank length and hatchability in poultry. As a result of continuous selection for two traits simultaneously, there will be no response due to the high negative genetic correlation (Lerner and Dempester, 1951)

**(iv) Genotype –environmental interaction:** The combined effect of genes for maximum value of the character are changed in different environments and also in subsequent generation. Dickerson (1955) pointed that the combination of gene effects changes under different environments or successive generations. The loss in performance (genetic slippage) occurs if the environment is changed. The slippage between generation may occur simply because the response obtained in one environment is irrelevant to the changed environment. For example, a strain may be resistant to some disease in one environment but not in other.

**(v) Natural selection:** The natural selection through differential viability may oppose artificial selection. In this situation, the effective S is less than expected due to the effect of fertility and viability of selected parents. In mice selected for low body weight (small mice), at selection limit, it was observed that $h^2$ was positive and the reverse selection for increased weight showed the response (Roberts, 1966). Thus the additive genetic variance existed at the limit. The fertility and viability of the small mice was affected adversely naturally. Low fertility in selected line reduces the S in later generation and so there was no further response. On the other hand, the large mice reached at selection limit due to exhaustion of additive genetic variance (Roberts 1966, Falconer and King 1953). In case of Drosophila the situation was found reverse by Robertson (1955).

**(vi) Nature and scale of character:** The selection limit is imposed by the nature of the character and its unit of measurement. There are certain characters measured in scores or percentage or in number like bristle number in Drosophila which have their lower limit of zero. The limits of measurement of the character may be reached without fixation of genes concerned.

**(vii) Linkage:** The linkage of loci is not an important cause of limit to selection and it works in combination with some other causes of limits. The linkage affects the limit only when the linked loci have equal effects on the character and maximum effect will be when the chance of fixation of these loci was between 0.7 and 0.8. The linkage is not an important cause of limits to selection for quantitative traits because their inheritance is polygenic and the polygene are distributed among many pairs of chromosomes. This makes the linkage effect very small. However, when the two loci are linked they will be inherited together without producing recombination. The progress under selection with no recombination (i.e. no crossing over or with linkage) is less (about 70 to 80%) than with usual amount of recombination. The linked genes may have opposite effect on the trait under selection and thus the response obtained due to selection of favourable gene at one locus will be offset by the loss associated due to selection of undesirable allele at the linked locus. Under the situation of linkage the population mean should not change by relaxed selection but the reverse selection will bring a change. The relaxed selection for several generations may allow crossovers to break up the unfavourable linkage and show further response to upward selection.

### 13.4.6. Methods to overcome the limits to selection

It is difficult to overcome the limits to selection for the reason that it is difficult to know the actual reason of limit and secondly it is not feasible in terms of time required and the expenses to meet the testing facilities. However, the limit to selection reached due to exhaustion of additive genetic variance can be overcomed by introducing new genetic material either through mutation or through out crossing.

To induce **mutation** is not advantageous. This is because the effects of mutagenic agents are not selective but random. That is to say that there is no surety that the induced mutation will be favourable. Moreover in case of farm animals the dose of mutagenic agents is beyond the animals' tolerance. However, attempts have been made to induce mutation as a source of new genetic variance but the results are contradicting and inconsistent. Some advance was achieved after crossing the irradiated male mice at selection limit without the establishment of the effectiveness of the method (Roberts, 1967). This method is thus not promising.

The **out crossing** may be done in two ways viz. crossing of two selected strains at limit and crossing of selected strain at limit to an unselected strain.

The first system includes the crossing of two selected strains which attained selection limits and then to select the crossbred progeny. This method resulted heterosis for large body weight in mice (Falconer and King, 1953). The cause of heterosis was the dominance effect of genes controlling the skeletal dimensions and fatness – one strain being long bodied but not very fat and the other strain was not large but was very fat. Both these strains were selected for large size over a period of more than 30 generations and attained the limits due to the exhaustion of the additive variance. The crossbreds of these two strains had significant rate of response to selection in both directions. In other experiment this method of crossing selected strains in mice was also found successful to increase the body weight but not to decrease it (Roberts, 1967). However, the large mice developed fertility problem.

The crossing of a selected strain which approached limit to selection with an unselected strain and then selecting the crossbred progeny to break the limit in body weight in mice was found successful. It required many generations of selection first to recover the selected level and then some more generations of selection to obtain the progress. Thus the period is very long. Therefore, crossing of two selected strain is superior than crossing with an unselected strain.

In both these mating systems, the superiority of the crossbred progeny is due to over dominance which results heterosis. In order to exploit maximum heterosis in a trait and to utilize the non additive genetic variation, two methods are used. These are recurrent selection to a tester line (RST) for specific combining ability and reciprocal recurrent selection (RRS) for specific combining ability. Both these methods are efficient only when over dominance is important. It is better that all the selected strains are tested in all possible combinations including reciprocals to find out the superior progeny.

The above methods to break the limit to selection can not be applied in farm animals because mainly one strain is only available. The **inbreeding combined with selection** was tried for improvement in litter size in a strain of mice at a selection limit (Falconer, 1971). In all 9 lines of independent origin from the plateaued strain were chosen and inbreeding by full sib mating was used. Five lines were eliminated upto seventh generation. The selection within each of 4 remaining line was practised. The inbreeding reduced the litter size. All the 4 lines were crossed when F = 89% and repeated cross when F = 99 %. Heterosis in $F_1$ and $F_2$ of the first cross was above the selected level of the strain and thus the improvement gained from inbreeding and crossing proved the success of the system in breaking the limit for litter size. This method was tried for body weight in mice for a strain which reached to a selection limit due to exhaustion of most of the additive variance due to fixation of favourable alleles affecting body weight. The breeding method with relaxation, selection and inbreeding was not proved successful to change the 6-week body weight. The inbreeding with selection and the subsequent crossing of the best inbred lines when F = 0.50 did not produce any improvement in body weight. This failure was due to lack of directional dominance and also of the lack of differentiation in gene frequencies between the lines when they were crossed. Thus no method will be effective, unless it introduces more genetic variance, in the absence of directional dominance and the lack of differentiation of gene.

Selection within an inbred line is effective to minimize the inbreeding depression and also to increase the combining ability of the line. But the results are inconsistent regarding the effect of selection in inbred line on the rate of inbreeding depression. However, the increased genetic variability of the lines crossed leads to increased heterosis.

## Relevance of limit to selection

The farm animal breeders remain interested with genetic progress in short time and hence the long term selection experiments are not relevant. Selection is practiced since long in various breeds of livestock. The limit to selection in broiler chickens under intense selection has not been reached so far.

The important species of livestock do not seem to attain the selection limit as they are responding to selection and continued improvement is being made. Therefore, the understanding of the nature of selection limits and methods of overcoming those to make further progress is not relevant at present in case of large livestock species.

## QUESTIONS

**13.1.** What is plateaued population? What are its merits and demerits? How they may be used or corrected? (*ARS 1976*)

**13.2.** In domestic animals undergoing selection, plateaue or diminution of progress has been recorded, yet considerable variation remains.

(*a*) There are a number of genetic situations when either separately or in combination could account for this condition, give five and discuss possible corrective breeding measures

(*b*) Give atleast one known instance of apparent plateau and one in which there seems no obvious plateau. (*ARS 1990*)

**13.3** Describe the response of selection in a polygenic trait, reasons for genetic slippage and limits of genetic progress to selection. (*ARS 1990*)

**13.4** (*a*) If a character of economic importance is selected in one direction only, the response may be disappointing. (*ARS 1987, 1992*)

(*b*) What is asymmetry of response? Describe the causes of asymmetry of response. (*ARS 1976, 1981, 1990, 1992*)

**13.5** It is often stated that observed response to selection fall short of the expected rate, Justify. (*ARS 1981*)

***Or***

Discuss the factors responsible for insufficient response to selection. How these can be improved? (*ARS 1987*)

**13.6** Describe a two way selection experiment on animal, where asymmetry of response has been found. Explain the various causes. (*ARS 1995*)

**13.7** Describe the various kind of information you would like to collect in order to interpret results of selection experiment. (*ARS 1996*)

***

# 14
# INBREEDING

The mating systems besides selection are also important tools of an animal breeder for bringing genetic improvement of livestock. The mating systems have been based on the genetic relationship of the mates viz. whether the mates are genetically related or not. The mating systems can also be classified on the basis of phenotypic similarity or dissimilarity of the mated individuals. However the two systems of mating based on alikeness or unlikeness either due to pedigree or phenotype have opposite effect to each other. The opposite effects are the homozygosity and heterozygosity. When mated individuals are alike in pedigree or phenotype there is an increase in homozygosity but on the other hand when the mated pairs of individuals are unlike in pedigree or phenotype, there is an increase in heterozygosity, the reason is that the genetic make-up of the zygotes produced by mating of alike or unlike mates is influenced.

## 14.1. DEFINITION OF INBREEDING

Inbreeding is a mating system when the mates are more closely related than the average members of the breed. The mated individuals should have one or more common ancestor in their pedigree upto 4-6 generations. This means that inbreeding is the mating of related animals within 4-6 generations. This is because the contribution of ancestral genes to the total genetic constitution of the descendent of seventh generation is less than one per cent on the basis of the halving nature of inheritance. Thus the maximum limit of considering an ancestor/common ancestor in the pedigree of an animal is upto 6 generation.

## 14.2. TYPES OF INBREEDING

The inbreeding, depending upon the extent of relationship of the mated animals, can be said as close breeding and line breeding. The close breeding is the mating of more closely related individuals like parent-offspring mating (sire –daughter, son-dam), full sib mating. Sometimes the half sib mating is also taken as close breeding. The close breeding is done for some specific purposes which are –

- To develop highly inbreed lines.
- To discover undesirable recessive genes with the help of parent-offspring mating.
- To get more uniform progeny

However, the close breeding has some disadvantages like inbreeding depression and intensification of undesirable characteristics.

The **line breeding** is taken in two ways. The first way is the mating of animals which are more distantly related like cousins mating. In this system the rate of inbreeding is less than close breeding and hence the inbreeding depression is less. The second way is the mating of animals in such a way that their descendants are kept closely related to an outstanding animal. In other words, the descendants are mated to outstanding animal (sire) upto 3-4 generations. In this system the mating is between a fixed sire and his daughters, grand daughters and great grand daughters as shown below-

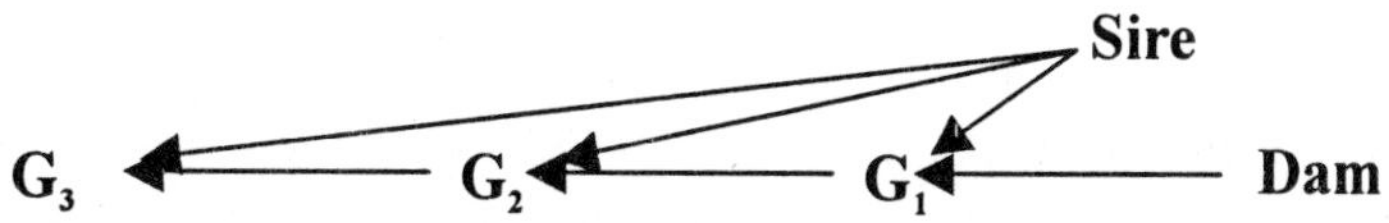


**Fig. 17.1: Line breeding (mating of a sire to his offspring in successive generations). This develops the sire line.**

The line breeding causes rapid increase in homozygosity. The aim of line breeding is to perpetuate the special character of an outstanding animals or strain. This system is followed by selecting the best and culling the poor animals.

The prime aim of line breeding is to maintain a high relationship to an outstanding ancestor for retaining it's a goodly proportion of the genes. The line breeding based on this logic can take various forms like parent-offspring mating in one generation or in subsequent generations continuously or after one-two generation as shown below-

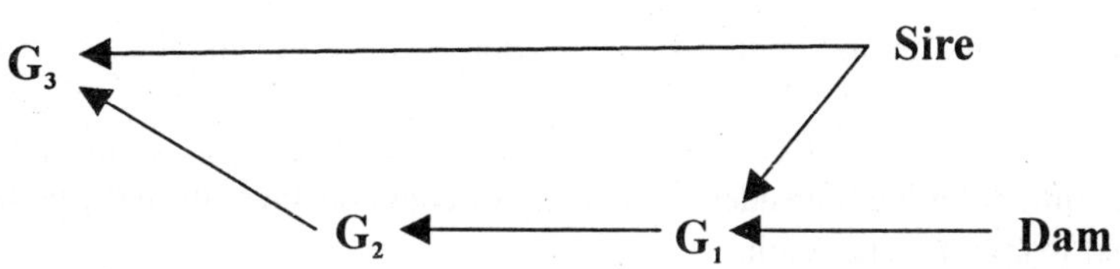


**Fig. 17.2 Line breeding (mating of sire to grand daughter)**

In view of the various forms of line breeding, it is difficult to classify some matings either as close breeding or line breeding, e.g. sire-daughter mating is taken as close breeding but it effectively concentrates the hereditary material of the sire and hence logically should be called as line breeding. Half sib mating is also considered as line breeding.

Half sib mating among the offspring of a sire is practiced to avoid intense inbreeding. Another reason to use half sib matings as a system of line breeding is that line breeding is often used when the ancestor is either dead or not available for breeding. In this situation half sib mating is the closest possible mating for line breeding. Below are given some of the pedigree to illustrate line breeding

| Sr. No. | Pedigree | $F_X$ | $R_{AX}$ | Parent A inheritance |
|---|---|---|---|---|
| 1 |  | 0.031 | 0.06 | 25% |
| 2 | 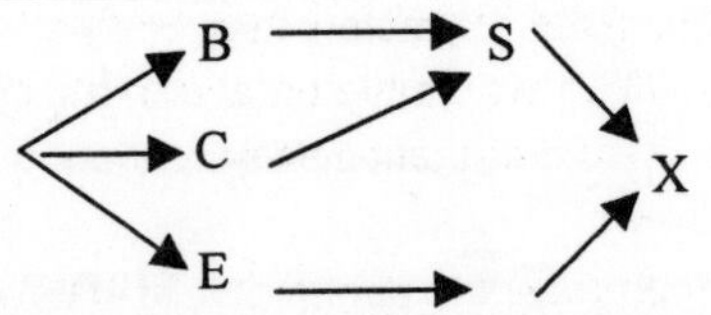 | 0.0625 | 0.36 | 37.5% |
| 3 | 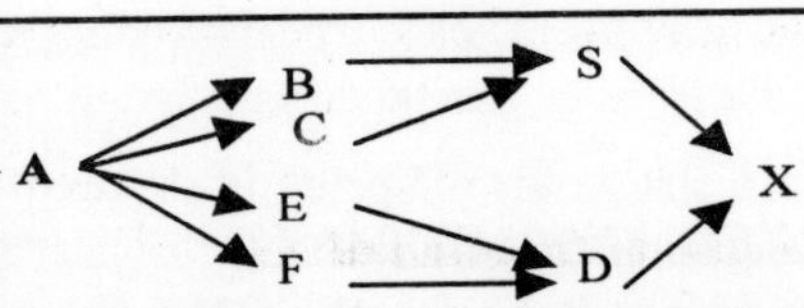 | 0.125 | 0.47 | 50% |
| 4 | 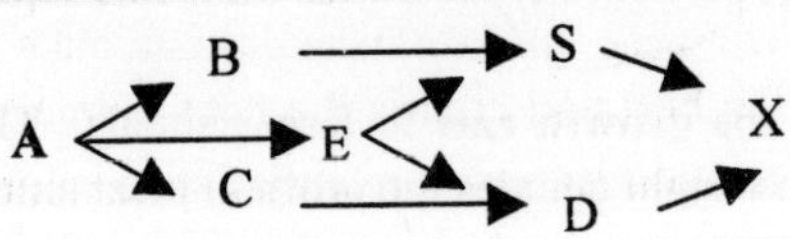 | 0.219 | 0.45 | 50% |
| 5 | 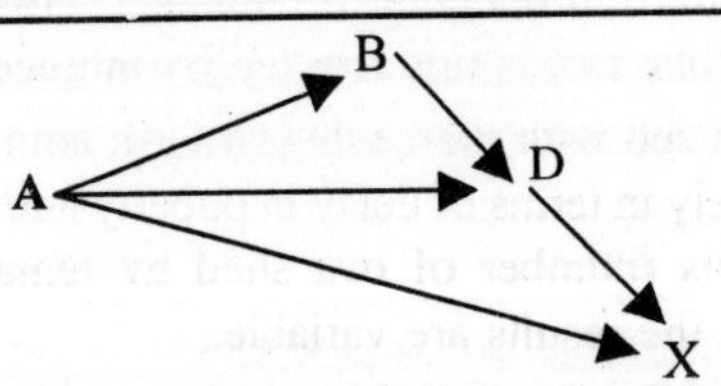 | 0.375 | 0.78 | 87.5% |

As line breeding is practiced to retain or concentrate the genes of an outstanding animal, it should be carried out in better than average herds particularly when it is not possible to get good quality sires from outside. Secondly, there should be atleast two sires in the herd in which the line breeding is practiced. It should not be used in grade or commercial herds producing animals for the market.

## 14.3. GENETIC EFFECTS OF INBREEDING

The foremost effect of inbreeding is that it increases the homozygosity at the expense of heterozygosity without affecting the gene frequency. However, the inbreeding has some effect on fluctuation of gene frequency depending on the size of population. In small population the gene frequency fluctuates more extreme and certain genes may be lost while some are fixed. But in large size population the fluctuation in gene frequency is less extreme and few of the alleles would be lost. The large population is differentiated into sub populations which are likely to be homozygous for different alleles under continuous inbreeding without selection and mutation.

There are many hidden recessive genes in outbred population. They are hidden by being paired with dominant genes. The inbreeding brings them to light by increasing homozygosity. Thus inbreeding increases the frequency of recessive traits in the population. Therefore, inbreeding requires more intense selection by culling less desirable individuals from the herd and thus a large number of animals should be produced in developing a line.

As a consequence of increased homozygosity the characters are fixed in an inbred population due to gene fixation. These fixed characters may be favourable or unfavourable. It requires the culling of animals in which the unfavourable character is fixed. The homozygous animals particularly for dominant genes are more prepotent than non inbreds.

The inbreeding changes the genetic structure of the population by changing the genotypic frequencies without changing the gene frequencies. The inbreeding reduces the genetic variability within inbred line but leads to genetic differentiation between lines.

## 14.4. PHENOTYPIC EFFECTS OF INBREEDING

The inbreeding has adverse effect particularly on fitness traits like reproduction, vigour (vitality) and growth traits.

The inbreeding tends to depress the **growth rate** in farm animals. This results in small margin of profit when the live weight decides the profit in meat animals. The growth rate also affects the production and reproduction of animals. However the growth rates in some laboratory species like rats is not affected by inbreeding.

The **reproductive efficiency** is reduced with inbreeding in farm animals. The reproductive efficiency is affected adversely in terms of delay in puberty and testicular development, reduction in gametogenesis (number of ova shed by females), and increase in embryonic losses. However, the results are variable.

Inbreeding results into an increase in death rate and hence **loss in vigour**. The inbred animals are more susceptible to environmental conditions. However, the results are not consistent.

The inbreeding also causes the appearance of **genetic defects** which are mostly recessive in inheritance and remain hidden in outbred animals. The inbreeding brings them in homozygous state and hence the abnormalities are expressed and identified.

The **phenotypic uniformity** among inbred animals within an inbred line is increased for the characters which are monofactorial. However, it is not true for polygenic traits. The variations within inbred lines are more due to environmental than to genetic causes.

The **productive traits** show inbreeding depression which means a decrease in performance records of the inbred animals.

## 14.5. DISADVANTAGES OF INBREEDING

- The frequency of undesirable recessive genes is increased
- It results in inbreeding depression which causes reduction in growth, reproductive efficiency, vigour in terms of vitality.
- The inbred animals are more prone (susceptible) to environmental changes

## 14.6. APPLICATIONS OF INBREEDING

The inbreeding is a useful tool in animal breeding. Though inbreeding results in inbreeding depression but there are certain cases when inbreeding is advantageous.

- Inbreeding is used to test for recessive alleles the sire may have. The inbreeding unhidden the undesirable recessive genes by bringing them in homozygous state. This is done by mating a sire to his 20-25 daughters. This results 25% inbreeding in one generation. This mating system also gives some indication of the better genes the sire is carrying. Inbreeding thus can be used to select against a recessive gene after it is unhidden. Thus it helps to **eliminate the undesirable genes**.
- Inbreeding is used to **produce distinct families** within a breed. The selection between families for traits of low $h^2$ is more effective than individual selection.
- The inbreeding is used to **develop inbred lines** as a seed stock which can be crossed according to their combining ability. This has been done for hybrid seed corn. The highly inbred lines are used in bioassay and other research work related to genetics, nutrition and physiology. The inbreeding with selection had helped in the past **to develop several breeds of livestock** viz. long horn cattle, Leicester sheep and Shire horse of Robert Bakewell and later on Merino, Rambouillet and South Down breeds of sheep were developed. Some strains of lab. animals (mice, rabbit, guinea pigs) had also been developed.
- Inbreeding also helps to know the type of **gene action** affecting a trait. The traits governed by additive gene action do not show inbreeding depression.
- Inbreeding increases the **prepotency** which is the ability of an individual to stamp its characteristics on the progeny. The propotency depends on the homozygosity of dominant genes.

## 14.7. WAYS TO MINIMIZE INBREEDING

The level of inbreeding primarily depends on the mating plan, number of sires used for breeding and the population size. Keeping these factors in mind, the level of inbreeding can be minimized.

**Mating Plan:** The mating should be among the unrelated animals. This requires calculating the coefficient of relationship of a bull with all the breedable females in the herd. It is easy to monitor the mating plan by use of computer. The packages of mating plan are now available suggesting that which male should be used on which female to avoid inbreeding. The pedigree of males and females is generated on computer which enlists the bulls related to a given female. The inbreeding is reduced by mating females from one sire line to males from another sire line.

**Population size:** In India the population size of organized herds is small. The inbreeding is inevitable in a closed herd of limited size having about 100 females and 5-10 sires. An increase in herd size is not possible for the reason of limited resources etc. Further, it is the effective population size (Ne) which decides the level of inbreeding. The rate of inbreeding (ΔF) with respect to Ne for unequal number of two sexes is :

$$\Delta f = \frac{1}{2Ne} = \frac{1}{8Nm} + \frac{1}{8Nf}$$

The Ne depends more on the sex with small numbers and hence on males in animals. The Ne is reduced with decrease in the number of males used for breeding and consequently the ΔF is increased. Therefore, Ne should be such that ΔF is not more than 1.0% per generation. It is thus essentially required to use more number of males.

**Purchase or exchange of sires:** In a single herd, the ΔF is increased by use of limited number of males. The way to reduce ΔF is to introduce new breeding males in the herd from outside. This can be done either by purchasing the males or by exchanging the males with other herds. The advent of frozen semen technology has made it easy.

## 14.8. GENETIC BASIS OF INBREEDING EFFECTS

The inbreeding increases the homozygosity and affects the phenotype depending upon the kind of gene action involved in affecting a trait.

The additive gene action means that there are no dominant or recessive genes and also there is no interaction between alleles or pairs of genes. The inbreeding depression does not occur when there is additive gene action. The reason is that each allele has equal and similar effect.

On the other hand, when there is dominance-recessive relationship among alleles, there will be a decline in mean phenotypic value of a trait on inbreeding. This is because the inbreeding increases the proportion of homozygous recessive loci. Secondly, the over dominance is also responsible for the harmful effect of inbreeding. In case of over dominance the heterozygotes are superior to either homozygote. The dominance and over dominance make impossible the development of highly productive inbreds. Thirdly, the epistasis, which is the interaction of genes that are not alleles, may also be responsible for harmful effect of inbreeding. This is because the combinations of some genes are favourable whereas other combinations may not be favourable.

## 14.9. INBRED LINES

Inbreeding is useful for certain specific purposes. It is then important to know the method of development, use and improvement of inbred lines and also the problems faced by a breeder to develop inbred liens.

Inbreeding should be more intense to observe the effect of recessive genes hidden in parental stock. Thus, it is important to know the method of developing inbred lines. For maximum intensity of inbreeding in the first generation, two types of matings are done. First is parent offspring mating which includes mating of a sire to his own daughter, or mating a dam to her own son. Such matings produce progeny having about 75% inheritance of the parent mated to its own offspring. This will give an indication of the number and kind of recessive genes that a parent carries when it is mated to several off-springs. The second kind of mating is the mating of full sibs which results in 25% inbreeding in the first generations. The parent-offspring and full sib mating both produce 25% inbred progeny. In FS matings two different individuals (both grand parents) instead of one contribute to the inbreeding but in parent-offspring mating only one individual, which is parent as well as grand parents of the inbred individual, is responsible for all of the increase in homozygosity which is 25%. Thus a specific recessive trait is more likely to be expressed in the parent-offspring mating than in FS matings. This is because the degree of homozygosity is due to a single parent. However, the more intense form of inbreeding is more likely to express the recessive traits regardless of the kind of mating because more intense inbreeding identify more quickly the lines having detrimental genes. The lines with more recessive genes may be discarded and the superior inbred lines may be developed.

The highly inbred lines developed posses **problems** besides that development of inbred lines in animals is expensive, time taking, and show inbreeding depression in performance traits. The main problem is the loss of their fertility and survivability. The inbred lines have poor fertility and survivability and thus such lines become incapable to reproduce and maintain. Most of the inbred animals which die before weaning age probably have defective recessive genes. However, the lines with better performance and normal vigour should be selected to propogate further.

## Use and improvement of inbred lines

The inbred lines are developed mainly for crossing them to take advantage of hybrid viogour. This is the main use of inbred lines. The best combining lines based on the performance of their line bred progeny are selected. The parents whose progeny show better performance are said to have superior combining ability. In case of animals, the inbreeding is not possible to the extent of 100% as in case of plants. It is therefore advisable to start crossing lines when inbreeding is 40 to 50%. However, higher degree of homozygosity increases the repeatability of performance in recurrent crosses of the same lines.

As has been mentioned repeatedly about the inbreeding depression shown by inbred lines, it is therefore needed to correct for the inbreeding depression i.e. to say how to improve the inbred lines. The **improvement of inbred lines of corn** is done by several methods, some of which can also be used to improve inbred lines of animals. The improvement of lines may be done by crossing two lines which are superior in one trait and inferior in other trait, e.g. one line is superior in growth rate and inferior or mediocre in carcass trait whereas the reverse is true for second line. In this situation, these two lines are crossed to combine the two qualities, the line cross progeny is backcrossed to the first as well as to the second line. The back cross progeny are selected for better growth rate and carcass trait, and inbreeding in each line produced by back crossing is continued. The back crossing is continued combined with selection within each line for each trait as shown below taking two lines A and B.

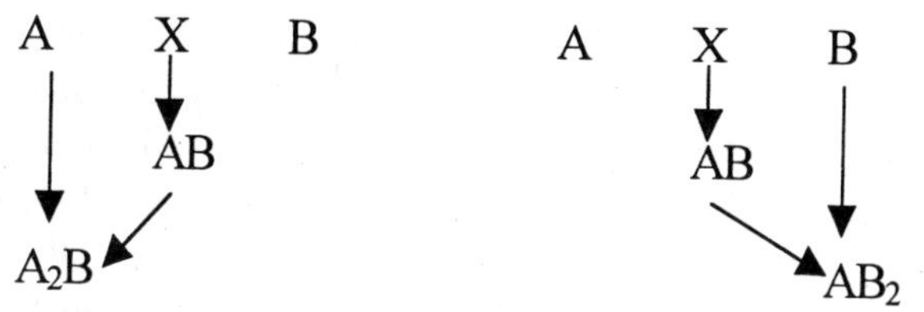


Selection & inbreeding

Back crossing and selection within each line is continued. This method incorporates new desirable additive genes into an inbred line.

It is not always necessary to cross two inbred lines to combine their best qualities. This can be done by mating of several outbred females having desirable quality with males of an inbred line. The inheritance of some of these females producing superior progeny can be incorporated into the inbred line by continued back crossing of her descendants with the original inbred line. Similarly, outbred males may also be used to introduce new genes into an inbred line.

The development of superior inbred lines and crossing those with the best combining ability is one of the methods to increase the efficiency of livestock production. But this method is not suitable for small herds. In large purebred herds the inbred lines may be developed for commercial use. The use of inbreeding for commercial production is being exploited in poultry and pigs.

## QUESTIONS

**14.1.** (*a*) Explain and illustrate with suitable examples the genetic and phenotypic consequences of inbreeding. How is inbreeding utilized for livestock improvement by breeders of different species in India?

(*b*) Explain different kinds of gene action responsible for deterioration effect of inbreeding (*ARS 1982*)

**14.2.** Explain the followings-

(*a*) Outbreeding decreases variation whereas inbreeding increases variation between lines/strains. How and where is each to be used for animal improvement?

(*b*) In a closed small dairy herd of high merit, there is likelihood of deterioration due to unavoidable inbreeding. Can this be avoided? How? (*ARS 1982*)

**14.3.** (*a*) Define inbreeding. Give its genetic and phenotypic effects. (*ARS 1990, 92*)

(*b*) In what situations this breeding approach is used for the benefit of the species and mankind. (*ARS 1990*)

**14.4.** Give the differences between inbreeding and outbreeding. What are the uses of these breeding systems? In our country which system need to be used for enhancing overall productivity in goat and why? (*ARS 1993*)

**14.5.** Indicate the exotic sheep with their superiority in various traits that are being used in the country for crossbreeding of Indian sheep. What is the progress achieved? (*ARS 1976*)

**14.6.** Briefly review the crossbreeding work in sheep with special reference to improvement in production of wool, meat and pelt. (*ARS 1981*)

***

# 15
# OUTBREEDING

## 15.1. DEFINITION

The mating of unrelated individuals is called as out breeding or genetic disasortative mating which is opposite or complementary to the inbreeding. The unrelated individuals may not necessarily belong to the same herd or different herds of the same breed (out crossing), but may also belong to different breeds (crossbreeding) or even to different species (species hybridization or species crossing).

## 15.2. FORMS OF OUT BREEDING

Out breeding can occur in several ways. The different forms of out breeding have been given as under:

### 15.2.1. Out crossing

This is the mating system when the matings occur among the unrelated individuals of the same breed. The progeny produced by out crossing are called out-cross. The outcrossing system is to use the selected best available sires on the females of a herd. This is the most common breeding system practiced by breeders and has been responsible for most of the changes in livestock breeds. The outcrossing system is effective to bring marked changes in livestock characteristics for the reason that genetic variability exists within breed. The outcrossing within a herd by use of selected sires is also called as **selective breeding.**

The selection of sires and their use on the females of the same herd results in close herd and hence the replacements come from the same herd. An opinion is prevalent about the close herd that inbreeding increases rapidly in close herd. However, the increase in homozygosity within a herd or pure breed is reduced by use of selected sires and sometimes there is a selection of females too. The animals selected for breeding purposes are having less than average homozygosity because the performance of the selected animals is superior. This is because the inbreeding results in an increased homozygosity and tends to depress the performance. Therefore, the selected animals being superior in performance are expected to be less homozygous. Thus out crossing with selection is capable for genetic change and improvement.

This system of selection and out crossing is very effective for characters governed by additive effect of genes having high heritability. The out crossing is practiced to exploit intra herd genetic variability. This system is also effective that it does not allow the fixation of undesirable genes and hence brings improvement. However, the selection combined with out crossing have an effect that the response to selection after 10-15 generations starts declining and in some cases after 20-30 generations of continuous selection the response is ceased. Thus a point of selection limit is reached. This point or level at which there is a failure to respond is often called as a **plateau** and the population is called **plateaued population.** Thus plateau is a phenomenon when selection is not effective. The effectiveness of selection determines the usefulness of out crossing. However, in large farm animals hardly any economically important trait has reached the point when selection is not effective system for genetic improvement particularly for traits which are largely under the control of genes with additive effects. The out crossing combined with selection is effective to offset the adverse effect of inbreeding.

## Top crossing

This mating system is a form of out crossing and is like grading up system. It is the mating of females to the last male in the top side of the pedigree. It is also used to refer the mating of purebred (inbred) males with unrelated females. The concept of top crossing can better be understood with the help of an example. Suppose a new strain has been developed by crossbreeding (like Karan Fries) and further improvement is required in this newly developed strain. It is then advisable to introduce pure Friesian inheritance in the herd of new strain developed earlier. Therefore, the mating of females of new strain (Karan Fries) with purebred sire of Holstein Friesian breed will be known as "top crossing"

## 15.2.2. Crossbreeding

The mating of animals from different established breeds is called crossbreeding. The progeny produced is called crossbred. This system has major role in livestock improvement by developing new breeds of livestock. It is rightly said that purebreds of today were the crossbreds of yesterday.

**Purpose of crossbreeding:** The crossbreeding is practiced for the purposes mentioned below:

**(i) Commercial purposes:** The crossbreeding is done for commercial production of livestock for two reasons:

**a. To take advantage of heterosis:** The two breeds differ genetically and hence the crossbreds are expected to show heterosis or hybrid vigour. This makes the crossbred more productive and better than either of the parental breeds. The crossbreeding has become quite common in pigs and poultry.

**b. To combine good qualities of two or more breeds:** The distinct breeds have different good qualities. One breed may be superior for one or more traits than the other breeds(s) while other breed(s) may be superior for some other desired traits. For example, exotic breeds of cattle from European origin are better for high milk production but have low disease resistance whereas the zebu breeds of cattle are poor for milk production but have better disease resistance. The crossbreeding may combine these good qualities of the two species in one breed. This is known as the **complementarity** in crossbreeding.

**c.** The crossbreeding is effective for traits that can not be improved by selection within a breed due to less genetic variability. New breeds of livestock can be evolved/developed by crossbreeding.

**(ii) Genetics of characters:** The crossbreeding is also used to study the behaviour of characters in hereditary transmission. The crossing of inbred line is particularly more useful in this respect.

## Types of crossbreeding

The mating of individuals from different populations of strains, breeds or species is known as crossing. The crossing of different breeds (cross breeding) can be practised in different ways depending upon the number of breeds used and the manner of their crossing. The major forms are the regular crossing and composite crossing.

## 1. Regular or systematic crossing

This is making of the same cross on regular basis to take the advantages of heterosis and complementarity. The crossing exploits non-additive gene effects through heterosis and the additive gene effects through complementarity when two or more characters complement each other. The amount of heterosis depends on the environment, genetic variability between two populations involved in crosses and the non-additive gene effects. The heterosis may be parental (maternal or paternal) referring to the performance of animals as parents and the individual heterosis referring to non-parental performance of the individual.

There are two basic methods of regular crossing known as specific crossing and the rotational crossing.

**A. Specific crossing:** This can be further grouped into the following forms.

**(i) Two breed crosses:** Two pure breeds are crossed together. This may be restricted with crossing of only the purebreds (purebred crosses) or may be extended to crossing the crossbreds ***(interse* mating)** or with males of pure breed **(back crossing or criss crossing).**

**a. Two pure breed crosses:** When two purebreds are mated together and their crossbred progeny are not used in breeding programme. This produces offsprings which are 100 % heterozygous showing 100% individual heterosis but no parental heterosis because the parents are not crossbreds.

***b. Inter se* mating:** This is the crossing of crossbred progeny having the same level of inheritance of two breeds like crossing of $F_1$ with $F_1$. This creates a number of genetic groups.

*c.* ***Back crossing:*** It is the mating of crossbred animals to purebred animal of either breed used to produce the crossbred progeny of first generation ($F_1$) like $F_1$ x $P_1$ or $F_1$ x $P_2$ where $P_1$ and $P_2$ are two purebreds used to produce $F_1$ animal. This cross is made to exploit maternal or paternal heterosis. As the maternal heterosis is generally of more importance, the crossbred parents should be the females ($F_1$ females). The back crossing between crossbred female and purebred males shows 100% maternal heterosis. The back cross progey are, on an average, 50% less heterozygous (or say 50% homozygous and 50% heterozygous) than $F_1$ and hence they show only 50% of individual heterosis.

*d.* ***Criss crossing:*** It is similar to back crossing except that both the parental breeds ($P_1$ and $P_2$) are used alternately in each generation as shown below:-

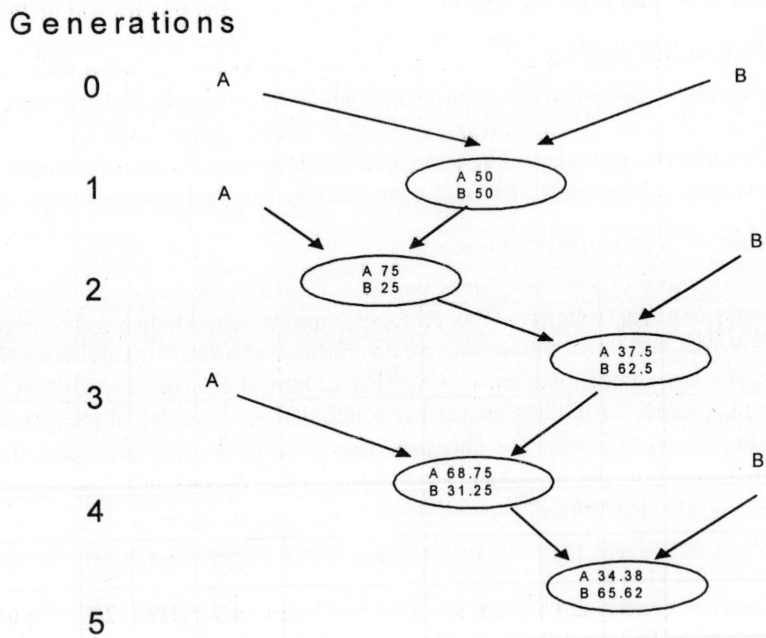


**(ii) Three breeds cross** or **triple crossing:** In this system of crossbreeding three breeds are used. The first cross animal ($F_1$) is mated to an animal of a third breed like (AB) female x C male.

This results in full utilization of maternal heterosis because the dam is 100% heterozygous being crossbred as well as of individual heterosis because the progeny are also 100% heterozygous.

The first cross and three breed cross show full utilization of individual heterosis because they are both 100% heterozygous but the amount of heterosis may not be the same for the reason that different crosses are involved and the amount of heterosis is greater with some crosses than others.

**(i) Four breed crosses** or **double two breed crosses**: This involves the crossing of crossbred females produced by crossing two breeds (A and B) with crossbred males produced from crossing another two breds (C and D). Thus, mating is between (AB) x (CD). This is used to produce commercial progeny. This enables full exploitation of both maternal and paternal heterosis as well as individual heterosis for the reason that both parents are crossbred.

**B. Rotational crossing:** The males of two or three breeds are used in regular sequence (rotation) in successive generations on crossbred females of the previous generation. Thus it is called as the rotational crossing which may involve two or three breeds. The proportion of genes of two or three breeds and the average heterozygosity in different generations will be as shown below:-

| **Two breeds** | **Proportion of genes** | | **Average heteroz-ygosity@** | **Three breeds** | **Proportion of genes** | | | **Average hetero-zygosity** |
|---|---|---|---|---|---|---|---|---|
| | A | B | | | A | B | C | |
| A x B | | | | A x B | | | | |
| {AB}xA | 1/2 | 1/2 | 1 | {AB}xC | 1/2 | 1/2 | | 1 |
| [(AB)A]xB | 3/4 | 1/4 | ½ | [(AB)C]xA | 1/4 | 1/4 | 1/2 | 1 |
| [{(AB)A}B]xA | 3/8 | 5/8 | ¾ | [{(AB)C} A]xB | 5/8 | 1/8 | 1/4 | 3/4 |
| Equilibrium of generation | | | | | | | | |
| T | 1/3 | 2/3 | 2/3 | | 1/7 | 2/7 | 4/7 | 6/7 |
| T+1 | 2/3 | 1/3 | 2/3 | | 2/7 | 4/7 | 1/7 | 6/7 |
| T+2 | 1/3 | 2/3 | 2/3 | | 4/7 | 1/7 | 2/7 | 6/7 |

@ The average heterozygosity of animals in square brackets, relative to $F_1$

The major disadvantage of rotational crossing is that it does not allow any exploitation of complementarity. Thus, it is good to use when the population show little or no complementarity but show heterosis. However, it produces less benefit from heterosis. The advantage of rotational crossing is that all female replacements are obtained from crossing programme itself and do not therefore have to be specifically bred in a separate population as they do in case of specific crossing.

The summary of fraction of different types of heterosis as indicated by average heterozygosity from different forms of crossbreeding is given as under:-

| Type of crossing | Fraction of heterosis | | |
|---|---|---|---|
| | Individual | Maternal | paternal |
| Straight bred | 0 | 0 | 0 |
| Two breed cross | 1 | 0 | 0 |
| **Back cross** | | | |
| Cross breed female x pure male | ½ | 1 | 0 |
| Pure bred female x crossbred male | ½ | 0 | 1 |
| **Three breed crosses** | | | |
| Cross breed female x pure male | 1 | 1 | 0 |
| Pure bred female x crossbred male | 1 | 0 | 1 |
| Four breed cross | 1 | 1 | 1 |
| **Rotational crossing** | | | |
| 2 sire breeds | 2/3 | 2/3 | 0 |
| 3 sire breeds | 6/7 | 6/7 | 0 |

## 2. Composite crossing to produce synthetic breed

This is alternate to regular crossing. It is done by producing one or few crosses between two or more populations to produce a single population having genes from each of the population. This single population of a mixture of various crossbred populations is called a synthetic or composite. This synthetic population is improved by selection within it. In the past, this crossing system with selection has resulted in the development of new breeds e.g. Santa Gertrudis, Jamaica Hope, AMZ, Australian Friesian Sahiwal, Norwegian Red and White and Belmout Red breeds of cattle which were developed by selection within a synthetic. Similarly synthetic populations of cattle to evolve new breeds have been produced by crossing of **Bos taurus** and **Bos indicus** with the objective to combine the high production of Bos taurus breeds with heat tolerance and tick resistance of Bos indicus breeds.

The theoretical expectation about heterosis is that 1-1/n of the heterosis persent in $F_1$ is retained in $F_2$ and in subsequent generations (Dickerson, 1973) where n is the number of different populations contributing equally to the synthetic.

## 15.2.3. Grading up

This is one type of crossbreeding. The sires of a pure breed are mated to the females of non-descript, scrub or native (deshi) type. This mating system is called grading up. The crossbred females are back crossed to the pure bred sires to produce the progeny with 75% genes from the pure breed. Thus after six generations of crossing the graded females with the purebred sires produce the progeny which have 98.4% genes of the purebreed. Thus upgrading system of mating changes the genetic composition without creating new genes but by transmitting good quality genes of an improved breed.

Grading up is useful to produce purebreds after a few generations. Secondly it is less expensive. Thirdly, this system helps to prove the genetic potentialities of the sire. However, this system has certain limitations. The most important is that the genotype-environmental interaction puts a limit to use this system. This is because the purebred sire which gives good results in one environment may not give similar results in other environment.

### 15.2.4. Species hybridization

The crosses between two species are the widest (extreme) possible type of outbreeding. This is known as species hybridization. The following are the example of species hybridization:

| Species hybrid obtained | Species crossed |
|---|---|
| 1. Mule | Male ass (Jack) x females horse (mare) |
| 2 Hinny | Female ass (Jennet) x Male horse (Stallion) |
| 3. Zebroid | Zebra-horse hybrid |
| 4. Asbra | Ass x Zebra (in Africa) |
| 5. Pien niu | Cattle-Yak cross in Tibet |
| 6. Cattalo | American buffalo bull (B. bison) x Domestic cow (B. taurus) |
| 7. Jatsa ($F_1$ male) | Mithun x Cow |
| 8. Jatsamin ($F_1$ female) | Mithun x Cow |
| 9. Jechha ($F_1$ males) | Mithun x siri cow |
| 10. Jessam ($F_1$ females) | Mithun x siri cow |

## 15.3. GENETIC AND PHENOTYPIC CONSEQUENCES OF OUT BREEDING

The out breeding is opposite to inbreeding and hence its effects on the genetic structure of population as well as on population performance are also opposite to inbreeding.

### 15.3.1. Genetic effect

The out breeding tends to increase heterozygosity because the mated pairs are genetically unrelated having different alleles. The important and peculiar characteristic of out breeding is that the maximum heterozygosity is attained in first generation outcrosses and goes on decreasing in subsequent generations produced by random mating of outbreds. The decrease in heterozygosity in subsequent generation is due to the segregation of genes which consequently increases the homozygosity. The two parents are homozygous (AA and aa) and their $F_1$ progenies are all heterozygous (Aa) while the $F_2$ progenies are produced in a ratio of 1AA : 2, Aa : 1aa. Further the crossbreds of $F_1$ generation are likely to be uniform in traits related to physical fitness particularly when the parents are homozygous for different alleles of a particular pair. However, the outbreds can not breed true because of heterozygosity and hence the selection is less effective among outbreds.

## 15.3.2. Change of mean on crossing – Heterosis

The outbreds are heterozygotes in which the effects of undesirable recessive genes are hidden by the effect of favourable genes (dominant). Therefore, the outbreds are superior to the average of their parents. This superiority of outbreds/crossbreds over the average of their parents is called the **heterosis** or **hybrid vigour**. The hybrid vigour is the opposite to the phenomenon of inbreeding depression.

The heterosis is the measure of the effect of out breeding and is defined in terms of the difference of outbred animals/plants from the average of purebred parents. Thus heterosis may be positive or negative. The positive heterosis is often called as hybrid vigour. This is the phenomenon by which crossbred progenies are better than the average value of the two purebreds used to produce crossbred progeny. In some cases, the crossbred progeny exceed even the better parent. The heterosis is caused by heterozygosity created due to crossing two purebred populations with different gene frequencies. The cause of heterosis, like inbreeding depression is the non-additive gene action (dominance, over dominance and epistasis) to be discussed in subsequent section. No heterosis is observed for traits governed by additive gene action. The traits showing heterosis are called often as **heterotic traits**.

## Estimation of heterosis

The amount of heterosis is estimated by comparing the mean value of purebred and crossbred animals as follows:

**Heterosis = mean of $F_1$ progeny – Mean of parental breeds**

This can also be expressed in terms of percentage as:

$$\% \text{ heterosis} = \frac{\text{Mean of } F_1 \text{ progeny - mean of parent breeds}}{\text{Mean of parent breed}} \times 100\%$$

**Example 14.1** Calculate the heterotic effect in $F_1$ and $F_2$ progeneis considering the milk yield in 300 days of Sahiwal and Holstein Friesian cows as 1600 and 5600 kg respectively and of their $F_1$ crossbreds as 3900 kg.

$$\text{Heterosis } F_1 = \overline{M}_{F1} - \overline{M}_P = 3900 - 1/2\ (5600 + 1600)$$

$$= 3900 - 3600$$

$$= 300 \text{ kg}$$

$$\text{The heterosis in } F_1\ (\%) = \frac{300 \times 100}{3600} = 8.3$$

$$\text{Heterosis } (F_2) = 1/2 \text{ heterosis in } F_1 = \overline{M}_{F2} - \overline{M}_P$$

$$= 1/2 \times 300 = 150 \text{ kg}$$

## Genetic basis of heterosis

When additive gene action affects the character the mean of $F_1$ progeny is exactly the same as the mean of the parents if environmental variations are not taken into account. Thus this type of gene action is not responsible for heterosis. The mean of the $F_1$ progeny differ from the mean of the parents, if non-additive gene action is important. In this case the mean of the $F_1$ may even be higher than the better parent or lower than the inferior parent. When $F_1$ exceed the better parent it is called useful heterosis.

**(i) Dominance hypothesis:-** The degree of heterosis depends upon the type of trait and type of mating. The early expressed traits, like survival and growth rate to weaning are more influenced. The traits which are more adversely affected by inbreeding also show greatest degree of heterosis. The mating of unrelated individuals (mating of inbred lines, two purebreds) show heterosis in their offspring. There are two reasons for this.

a. The mated unrelated individuals are homozygous for different alleles. The animals of one purebred will be homozygous for some loci and the animals of other group (lines, purebreds) will be homozygous for other loci. When lines or breeds homozygous for different genes (lines or breeds with different gene frequencies) will be crossed they will produce heterozygous offspring. The favourable dominant genes in the offspring will mask the unfavourable recessives. Thus the performance of the hybrid offspring will exceed to that of the average of the parents and sometimes exceed even to that of better parent. This is because each purebred will be homozygous for some loci (for favourable genes at some and for unfavourable genes at other). In case if one line or breed complements the other, the hybrid progeny will have more favourable genes than either parent. The effects of favourable genes are generally dominant to those of unfavourable genes. Thus the performance of the hybrid progeny is superior to that of parental line. For example, for polygenic traits, one line or breed may be homozygous dominat for some pairs and homozygous recessive for another like AA, bb, CC and DD whereas the other breed may be respectively homozygous recessive and dominant at other loci like aa, BB, cc, dd. On crossing them the resulting progeny ($F_1$) will carry dominant alleles at all loci and would be superior to both parents for that trait.

b. The crosses between two lines or breeds having different gene frequencies (p and q) produce a lower frequency of recessive than the average of the two parents. This is because the frequency of the recessive in the cross will be qq instead of $\frac{1}{2}(q^2 + q'^2)$. For example if $q = 0.2$ and $q' = 0.6$, then $qq' = 0.12$ and $\frac{1}{2}(q^2+q'^2) = \frac{1}{2}(0.04 + 0.36) = 0.20$. This is always true except for equal gene frequencies.

**(ii) Overdominance theory:-** The overdominace is the interaction between genes that are alleles and it results in the heterozygous individuals being superior to the best homozygous parent. The crossbreeding results in superior animals if overdominance is important for the reason that the animal produced by crossbreeding has a maximum number of heterozygous loci. For example, for a gene locus, there will be three different genotypes such as $A_1A_1$, $A_1A_2$, and $A_2A_2$. If overdominance is present, the alleles $A_1$ and $A_2$ coming together ($A_1A_2$) produce a reaction which is not produced by them separately. The overdominance may be an important factor in heterosis for some characters and in some species. Crow (1952) suggested that the dominance hypothesis can account for only 5% of the increase in performance in crosses of lines of corn. Thus the dominance theory appears to be insufficient to explain heterosis in corn. However, heterosis observed in corn can be only due to overdominance at least at few loci affecting corn yield.

**(iii) Epistatic effects:-** The epistasis is a phenomenon of interacting genes which are not alleles. The epistasis is the effect of genes resulting from the new combination of genes from different loci. The different genes coming together in the hybrid interact with each other and produce greater effect than when they are alone in different parents. For example in plant, one dominant gene governs the length of internodes (long) and the other dominant gene governs the number of internodes. When these two dominant gene pairs are present in a single hybrid, they show their multiplication effect and results in offspring taller than expected from the average height of parental types having few but long internodes and having many but short internodes.

### Physiological basis of heterosis

It has been concluded on the basis of some studies that crossbreds have a more efficient metabolic system.

## 15.4. RESULTS OF CROSSBREEDING IN DIFFERENT SPECIES

In India, the crossbreeding has been done in different species by mating the females of native breeds with the sires of exotic breeds. The important findings have been given here.

### 15.4.1. Crossbreeding zebu cattle with exotic breeds

The crossbreeding of dairy cattle in India was started as early as 1875 and **Taylor** breed of cattle was evolved around Patna using Short horn bull on native cows.

The first Military Dairy Farm (MDF's) was started at Allahabad in 1886 and the crossbreeding was started in 1891 using Jersey, Ayrshire, Short horn and Friesian sires initially but in 1922 stopped using Ayrshire whereas HF was used extensively. The crossbred cows were maintained at different MDF's. The criss crossing had been the breeding policy prior to 1952 and later on back crossing with Sahiwal bulls was started at MDF's. The Friesian crosses performed better than Ayrshire and Shorthorn (Kartha, 1934).

At Allahabad Agriculture Institute, the crossbreeding was started using HF, BS, Guernsey and Jersey sires on Zebu cattle during 1924-1934 earlier to which from 1910 to 1924 the selective breeding was used to improve Sahiwal, Gir, Hariana and Kankrej breeds and in 1923 the Red Sindhi was also included. The crossbreeding was restricted to Red Sindhi with Jersey since 1934 having 3/8 to 5/8 Jersey inheritance and a strain named as **'Jersind'** was developed.

The crossbreeding was started in 1919 at Hosur Cattle Farm under erstwhile Madras Govt. with the objective to evolve a new crossbred cattle by crossing Ayrshire and Red Sindhi with interbreeding among $F_1$s. The crossbred cows had better production performance over Red Sindhi. The crossbreeding of cattle using exotic sires was also carried out in Nilgiri area of Madras State but there was no success due to the use of inferior and graded bulls without any selection.

Indo-Swiss crossbreeding project was started in 1963 in Kerala using Brown Swiss and Jersey semen on local non descript and Red Sindhi x non descript graded cattle. A new breed of cattle **'Sunandini'** was evolved.

At Bangalore, Tharparkar cows were crossed with Jersey bulls and a new breed **'Jerthar'** was developed

The crossbreeding work was initiated in 1963 at NDRI, Karnal involving BS as exotic breed with Red Sindhi and Sahiwal as Zebu breeds and various crossbred groups were produced which did not show significant evidence of non additive gene action for growth, milk yield and AFC. The various crossbred groups were merged and selective breeding was practiced. The creation of synthetic population following selection resulted into a new breed in 1980 named as **'Karan Swiss'**.

Another crossbreeding project was also started at NDRI Karnal in 1971 which involved HF, BS and Jersey semen on Tharparkar cows. A number of crossbred groups were produced and it was observed that two and three breed crosses did not show significant manifestation of heterosis for growth and milk yield. All the crossbred groups forming the synthetic population were merged in 1980 and the selective breeding was practiced in this population which resulted into a new breed of cattle named as **'Karan Fries'**.

The ICAR started AICRP on cattle in 1968 at 5 centres viz. IVRI, HAU, MPKVV to involve Hariana breed, JNKVV for Gir and Lam for Ongole breed. The exotic breeds used were HF, BS, Jersey. Later on during 1973 Haringhata Farm (West Bengal) was also included where the crossbreeding was already going on since 1957-58.

The ICAR also started financing Military Dairy Farms since 1985 to evolve a national crossbred cattle involving HF and Sahiwal to evolve **'Frieswal'** breed of cattle stabilizing at 5/8 HF level.

**Impact of crossbreeding:** The crossbreeding had the following impacts:-

- Crossbred cattle population was increased.
- There had been an increase in milk production and hence an increase in per capita of milk availability.
- An increase in growth rate and reproductive efficiency in terms of age at puberty, AFC, calving interval.

**Conclusions:** The following conclusions can be drawn on the basis of the results of crossbreeding dairy cattle:-

- Significant increase in milk yield and reproductive efficiency of crossbreds.
- HF crosses and Jersey crosses proved superior over other exotic breeds for plane and high areas, respectively.
- Regarding level of exotic inheritance, the optimum was found between 50 to 62.5% for better growth, production and reproduction.
- There was a decline in milk yield of $F_2$ over $F_1$ due to use of poor quality crossbred bulls.
- The crossbreds gave 30-60% higher milk yield under challenged feeding than controls given ration as per NRC requirement. This suggested to re-examine the feed requirement for crossbred cattle so as the production potential can be fully exploited.

**Constraints of crossbreeding cattle in India:** There had been some of the following constraints of crossbreeding:

- Higher initial investment and maintenance cost.
- Non-availability of proven exotic bull semen.
- Less availability of quality green fodder.
- Higher disease incidence among crossbreds and lack of optimum veterinary care.
- Non-acclimatization of crossbreds to widely varying climatic conditions in India.
- A myth that crossbred male calves are not fit for draft purpose
- High culling rates in crossbred bulls (upto 40-70%)
- No well defined breeding policy for $F_1$'s under field conditions.
- Problem of proper milk disposal of crossbreds.

**Realization:** The crossbreeding experiences had made the animal breeders to make the following realizations:-

- The indigenous recognized breeds should be maintained and not involved in crossbreeding with exotic breed.
- There should be balanced feeding of crossbred cattle.
- There is a need of proper health management to control mastitis and other infectious diseases.
- Realistic approach should be followed for culling of inferior/diseased animals.

## 15.4.2. Crossbreeding buffaloes

The genetic diversity among two types of buffaloes (river and swamp) exists to the extent of different number of diploid chromosomes. The riverine buffaloes have 50 chromosomes whereas the swamp buffaloes have 48 chromosomes. However, crossbreeding of two types of buffaloes produce fertile hybrids ($F_1$) with diploid number of chromosomes equal to 49. The crossbreeding of buffalo has been done to improve milk and meat potential of swamp buffaloes with river buffaloes in other countries like China, Vietnam, Malaysia, Thailand, Indonesia, Brazil and Philippines.

The crossbreeding between riverine breeds of buffaloes has also been carried out. As a result two new breeds of buffaloes (**Mehsana** and **Godavari**) have been developed by crossing of Surti and local buffaloes with Murrah bulls, respectively. The Murrah x Surti crossbreds at NDRI had shown increase in milk production and reproduction traits, the milk yield per day of calving interval was higher in crossbreds (3.4 kg) than Murrah (3.2 kg).

In Bulgaria, the Murrah x Bulgarian crossbreds were found close to Murrah for body weight at different ages whereas the milk yield and fat in crossbreds were close to mid parent value.

### 15.4.3. Crossbreeding sheep

The crossbreeding of Bikaneri (Magra) ewes with Australian Merino rams was started at GLF, Hissar and a new breed of sheep '**Hissardale**' was developed. It has 75% exotic inheritance. Similarly, '**Kashmir Merino**' breed was developed by crossing Gaddi, Bhakarwal and Poonchi ewes with Merino and Rambouillet rams. This has 50 to 75% exotic inheritance.

As a result of crossbreeding at CSWRI Avikanagar, two new synthetics (chokla and Nali synthetics) for fine wool have been developed. These new synthetics produce more wool of fine quality having desirable medulation percentage and fibre diameter. The crossbreeding of indigenous breeds (Gaddi at Tal in HP, Patanwadi at Dantiwada in Gujrat and Nilgiri at Sandynallah in TN) with Soviet Merino and Rambouillet showed improvement for wool production and quality together with a improvement in body weight. Three diverse native breeds (Chokla, Malpura and Jaisalmeri) were crossed with Rambouillet at CSWRI Avikanagar. The results of crossbreeding have shown that any exotic fine wool breed can be used in crosses with native breeds, for improvement in wool quality and quantity, with 50 to 75% exotic inheritance depending on the climatic and nutritional conditions.

Almost 60% of the total export of wool and woolens from India is obtained through the export of carpets. The Indian carpets are cheaper compared to that made in Iran, Afghanistan and China. This may be due to low quality of wool used or due to low labour charges in India. The important carpet wool breeds in India are Nali, Chokla, Bikaneri (Magra), Marwari, Pugal, Jaisalmeri, Malpura, Sonadi, Deccani, Patanwadi and Bellary. But of these, Chokla, Nali and Patanwadi produce finer wool.

The indigenous carpet wool breeds have been crossed with exotic fine wool, mutton and dual purpose breeds. Malpura breed was crossed with Rambouillet, Suffolk and Dorset; Sonadi with Suffolk; and Muzaffarnagri, Coimbatore, Nellore and Bellary with Corriedale. The results showed improvement in wool quantity and quality (in terms of low medullation percentage and low fibre diameter).

Among the native sheep breeds, the North Indian Carpet wool breeds are heavier than South Indian mutton breeds. The native breeds viz Malpura, Sonadi, Muzaffarnagri, Mandya and Nellore were crossed with Dorset and Suffolk whereas Coimbatore, Nellore and Bellary were crossed with Corriedale. The results showed better combining ability of Suffolk with Sonadi and Muzaffarnagri . Three new synthetic mutton strains were developed by crossing of Malpura and Sonadi with dorset and Suffolk at CSWRI Avikanagar, crossing of Nellore and Mandya breed with Dorset and Suffolk by stabiliszing 50% exotic inheritance. These new strains were named as **Avimaans**, **Mandya synthetic** and **Neelore synthetic**, respectively.

In India Malpura breed of sheep is used by some people of Rajasthan (Khatik) to produce lamb pelts on small scale. In 1975, 200 ewes and 50 rams of Karakul were imported in India from USSR. These were distributed to CSWRI and Khumbathang in Kargil district (J&K). The Karakuls adapted well to hot arid conditions of Rajasthan (Bikaner) as well as in the cold arid region. The native breeds of India (Chokla, Nali, Malpura and Sonadi) were crossed with Karakul at Avikanagar. The Malpura and Sonadi crosses performed better than Nali and Chokla crosses for pelt quality. Further, Malpura lambs produced better pelts than Sonadi but the results of karakul crossbreds were reverse (Sonadi Karakul half breds produced better pelts than Malpura Karakul crosses). The results indicated that crossing of coarse carpet Indian breeds with Karakul had good potential for pelt production.

## 15.4.4. Crossbreeding goats

The crossbreeding of goats has been made between native breeds as well as with exotic breeds. The bucks of Jamunapari and Beetal breeds were used to mate the Bengal does. These two crosses showed an improvement of 70 and 90%, respectively in the milk production over purebred Bengal. This improvement was due to large genetic differences between the breeds crossed. But the reciprocal crosses i.e. when high yielding dams of Jamnapari were crossed with low yielding bucks (Bengal), did not show heterosis. The crossing of Sirohi with Beetal showed imperceptible (very slight) improvement because the genetic divergence between the two breeds was less. There was considerable increase in milk production when Black Bengal was crossed with Barbari over the Black Bengal.

For meat components three large size indigenous breeds (Jamunapari, Barbari and Black Bengal) were crossed and 3 breed crosses were produced to study the meat parameters at B.R. College, Agra.

The crossbreeding of Indian breeds of goats with exotic breeds was done for milk (Alpine and Anglo-Nubian), for meat (Boer and Toggenberg) and for fibre (Angora) to assess the production potential of the crosses for various products during pre and post independence period. However, this programme was discontinued after short term experiment for certain reasons of high mortality and mobidity.

During fifties, the state Governmetns imported few Angora goats for use in M.S., HP and UP. The flocks at Pipalkoti (UP) could not adapt whereas the flocks in MS and HP performed better. Three-fourth and seven-eighth crosses of Angora x Deccani produced 0.183 and 0.454 kg mohair respectively. Whereas purebred Angora, and half, ¾ and 7/8 Angora x Gaddi crosses in HP produced 0.475, 0.105, 0.192 and 0.369 kg mohair respectively.

Later on, AICRP on goats by ICAR was initiated for genetic improvement of goat breeds at CSWRI, Avikanagar and then shifted to CIRG Makhdoom, Mathura. The exotic breeds included Alpine, Saanen for milk and Angora for Mohair for production of crossbreds. The different crosses made were – Half and three-fourth Saanen x Beetal, and half and three-fourth Alpine x Beetal at NDRI Karnal; half and three-fourth Alpine x Malabari, and half and three-fourth Saanen x Malabari at KAU, Mannuthy (Kerala). The Beetal crosses were found superior than Malabari crosses. Secondly, the Saanen crosses were superior to Alpine crosses. Milk yield of crosses increased upto 75 % exotic inheritance. However, the higher crosses of Malabari did not prove better than half breds. The $F_2$ and $F_3$ generations had low milk production than $F_1$.

The crossbreeding with Saanen of Local Deccani goats at Pune and with Alpine of Sirohi at Ajemr was started.

Under AICRP on goats at Rahuri (MS), the half bred Angora x Sangamneri could not produce Mohair but ¾ crosses produced finer fibres whereas 7/8 crosses produced 1.1 kg mohair per clip. White Marwari goats were crossed with Angora at CSWRI, Bikaner. The results obtained were similar to those at Rahuri. Indian Mohair strains have been evolved at Rahuri and Bikaner.

### 15.4.5. Crossbreeding results of poultry

Desi fowl were crossed with White Leghorn and RIR at Izatnagar and Nagpur. This increased the egg production upto 186 and 170 eggs for the two graded lines with egg weight of 60 gm for both lines at Izatnagar. Similarly there was an improvement in egg production and egg weight at Nagpur.

The cross of WL and RIR with desi fowls at Hisar showed heterosis for body weight at all ages, egg production and feed consumption. Similar performance of WL and RIR crosses was observed at Udaipur. The egg production in two lines increased by about 38 eggs over purebred desi but in reciprocal crosses using desi males over WL and RIR females decreased egg production.

The European community sanctioned an International Collaborative Project in 1992 on evaluation of Poultry Genetic Resources. Four native chicken breeds (Aseel, Kadaknath, Naked Neck and Frizzle Fowl) alongwith their $F_1$ and $F_2$ crosses with Dahlem Red were evaluated for their growth, egg production and quality, feed efficiency, genetic distance and disease resistance. In all 29 genetic groups comprising purebreds, $F_1$ and $F_2$ were produced and evaluated. The crossbred males of all the genetic groups were heavier than purebreds at all ages and there was heterosis in body weight. The heterosis was observed upto 15$^{th}$ week of age. The sexual maturity of various $F_1$ and $F_2$ crossbreds ranged from 180 to 212 days against the range of 194 days (Kadaknath) to 218 days (Dahlem Red) of purebreds. The egg production of crossbred $F_1$ showed significant increase but slightly lowers for $F_2$ than $F_1$. The egg weight also showed drastic increase in crossbred eggs. The albumen quality was better for the eggs from crossbred pullets and there was further improvement in albumen quality of the eggs from $F_2$ compared to $F_1$. The albumen height and yolk index also improved for crossbred eggs. The eggs from crossbred $F_1$ had comparatively higher shell thickness which is desirable. Regarding disease resistance status, it was observed that high producing stocks were less efficient for immune system probably due to the production stress and hence the native breeds were more resistant to general diseases. The Aseel x Dahlem Red and Kadaknath x Dahlem Red crosses were recommended for back yard poultry production for their better immuno competence. The Aseel and Frizzle assorted together genetically and then Naked Neck whereas Kadaknath was most distant from other ecotypes.

## QUESTIONS

**15.1.** Explain genetically I.D. and heterosis. What it is so and how these can be beneficially used? *(ARS 1976)*

**15.2.** Define the 'agro-climatic conditions' and discuss briefly this component with significance of their influence on production traits of various crossbreds produced in the country. What kind of research is needed in this connection? *(ARS 1976)*

**15.3.** When, where and with which exotic breed the crossbreeding in dairy cattle was first started in India? *(ARS 1978)*

**15.4.** Discuss different kinds of heterosis. What breeding system will you use for exploiting heterosis in broiler production? *(ARS 1987)*

What do you understand by selection and mating system? Discuss the condition under which each of these methods separately and jointly may be used for animal improvement. *(ARS 1990)*

***

# 16

# LIVESTOCK BREED IMPROVEMENT PROGRAMMES

The sire is said to be "half of the herd". It is true because a few sires are used in a herd of hundreds of females and that the inheritance is a halving process. Therefore, the genetic improvement is possible only when the sires used in the herd are of high genetic merit. But it is not remunerative for the farmers to keep the bull for the reason of small herd size. Therefore, the Govt. on the recommendation of the Royal Commission on Agricultural, established the livestock farms to produce and keep purebred indigenous animals for improving nucleus herds of different breeds and to produce bulls of superior genetic merit of known pedigree and performance. The Govt. of India had started a number of livestock improvement programmes from time to time. The brief description of these programmes is given here in chronological order of their starting year.

## 16.1. POST INDEPENDENCE MILESTONES OF ANIMAL BREEDING POLICIES AND PROGRAMMES ON DAIRYING IN INDIA

* ICAR (1949) emphasized on the following:
  - Preservation of general utility animal combining draft and milch quality;
  - improvement of well defined breeds by selective breeding;
  - Improvement of milk production from recognized milch breeds and propagation of milch breeds in underdeveloped area.
* Dept. of Agriculture (1960) constituted a committee to review cattle breeding policy in the country, grading up of non-descript cattle with pure milch, dual or draft breeds to improve milk yield without imposing draft capacity.

### First Five Year Plan (1951-56)

- Central Council of Gosamvardha set up a central coordinating agency on cattle development (1952);

- Key village schemes were launched (1952);
- NDRI came into existence and shifted to Karnal (1955);
- Rs. 77.8 million were allotted towards dairying.

## Second Five Year Plan (1956-61)

- Animal Husbandry Wing recommended crossbreeding for possible research and commercial exploitation (1958);
- Some crossbreeding work was started at Haringhata (1957-58);
- Rs. 120.5 millions were allotted for livestock sector.

## Third Five Year Plan (1961-66)

- More emphasis was given on milk production in breeding tracts of draught breeds, replacing one or other existing draught breeds with dual purpose breeds;
- Grading up of non-descript cattle with recognized dual purpose or dairy breeds;
- ICDP was launched in 15 centres of 10 states (1965);
- Crossbreeding with exotic breeds in hilly areas using Jersey exotic bull;
- Rs. 336 millions were allotted for dairying.

## Fourth Five Year Plan (1969-74)

- AICRP on cattle was launched (1968);
- Launching of Operation Flood I (July, 1970); P.T. programmes sponsored by Agr. Ministry for production of superior bulls;
- Propogation of superior germplasm of recognized breeds by financing the State Govt. alongwith BAIF, NDDB, KLDB;
- Rs. 787.5 million allotted to A.H. and Dairying.

## Fifth Five Year Plan (1974-79)

- Operation Flood-II launched (1979);
- Rs. 944.5 million allotted for A.H. and Dairying.

## Sixth Five Year Plan (1980-85)

- ICAR started financing Military Dairy Farms to evolve a national crossbred cattle "Frieswal" in 1985.
- Two cattle strains namely Karan Fries and Karan Swiss were developed by NDRI in 1980.
- Rs. 4362.9 million allocated to A.H. & Dairying.

## Seventh Five Year Plan (1985-90)

- Project Directorate on Cattle, Meerut came into existence (Nov. 1987).
- National level ETT project of Deptt. of Biotechnology was started in 1988 at NDDB, IVRI, NDRI and NII.

- Rs. 5887.9 million allocated to A.H. and Dairying.

**Eighth Five Year Plan (1992-97)**

- Center of Advance Studies in different disciplines at different SAU's and ICAR institutes including Animal Genetics and Breeding at NDRI were started by ICAR.
- Deptt. of A.H. and Dairying came into existence (Feb., 1991).
- Rs. 13075.1 million allocated to A.H. and Dairying.

**Ninth Five Year Plan (1997-2002)**

- Emphasis on crossbreeding non-descript cattle with establishment of 60000 A.I. centres as target.
- Conservation of recognized breeds.
- India produced 74.7 MMT milk during 1999 and became the number one milk producing country.
- HF crossbred cows produced peak yield of 44.2 kg and 52.5 kg milk at NDRI and PAU, respectively.
- Rs. 1965 crores allocated to A.H. and Dairying.

## 16.2. CATTLE AND BUFFALOES IMPROVEMENT PROGRMME

### 16.2.1. Central Herd Registration Scheme

An international convention on registration of cattle was held in Oct. 1936 in Rome, with its main recommendation that there should be only one herd book for a single breed in each country so as to avoid the conflicting standards and methods of performance recording. The herd book contains a list of animals qualifying the breed characteristics and production standard and thus purebred animals of high merit are enlisted in the book. This helps the owners in sale and purchase of the breeding stock. In India the herd books were started by 1949 for Sahiwal, Red Sindhi, Gir, Tharparkar, Ongole, Hariana, Kankrej and Kangayam breeds of cattle and Murrah breed of buffaloes. During Third Five Year Plan the breeding tracts of important breeds were covered to organize breeder's societies for taking up this work.

The animals to be registered should meet its breed characteristics like type, colour etc. In addition to producing minimum amount of milk in a lactation of 300 days, depending on the breed of the animals viz. Sahiwal 1700 kg, Red Sindhi and Tharparkar 1400 kg, Gir and Hariana 1100 kg. Kankrej and Ongole 700 kg, Kangayam 500 kg and Murrah 1400 kg. However, these criteria had been subjected to change over time depending on the utility of the breed and the improvement in production levels.

The CHRS was reviewed in 1998 and made the following recommendations:

- To register only elite animals which should be purchased by National Semen Grid or its state components for breeds improvement. The criteria for declaring the elite animals were revised for Gir (3500 kg & above), Hariana (2700 kg & above), Kankrej (3000 kg & above), Ongole (2500 kg & above), Murrah (3800 kg & above), Jffarabadi (4000 kg & above), Mehsana (3300 kg & above), and Surti (2900 kg & above).

- To give incentives to the farmers for maintaining the elite calves and dams as : Rs. 1000 per year for the dam for 4 years, Rs. 2000 for male calf for first year
- To register the bulls used for natural service in the area.

### 16.2.2. Key village scheme

This scheme was launched in 1951 (First Five Year Plan) on all India scale taking a key village unit covering an area having a population of 1000 cows and buffaloes. The objectives of this KVS were to use superior germ plasm (bulls) together with increased production of feeds and fodder, to provide prophylactic measures against contagious diseases, management and marketing facilities for selling of produce, and to contact farmers for advising them. A key village block comprising 6 to 10 key village units was set-up with A.I. station to supply semen to the key village units. Presently there are 550 key village blocks.

### 16.2.3. Intensive cattle development project

Another large scale programme, Intensive Cattle Development Programme (ICDP) was started in 1966 for increasing milk production as an area development approach and taking care of every aspect of cattle improvement viz. breeding, feeding, health care, extension activities and marketing facilities. The ICDP was located in the breeding tract of indigenous breeds of cattle and buffaloes. Each ICDP was linked with a dairy project for processing and marketing of milk. Each project covered upto one lakh breedable cows and buffaloes. At present about 130 ICDP's exist.

### 16.2.4. Progeny testing schemes

**(i) Single Herd P.T. Scheme:** In the Third Five Year Plan, a progeny testing scheme was started with the aim to identify and produce the bulls of high genetic merit on the basis of their progeny performance instead of their dam's yield, to achieve higher genetic gain through use of the tested/proven bulls with A.I. The P.T. scheme was started in the beginning at GLF Hisar for Hariana and Murrah breeds. During Fourth Five Year Plan, the scheme was started for other breeds viz. **Sahiwal** at State Cattle Breeding Farm, Chakgangaria (Lucknow), SCBF Durg (MP); **Red Sindhi** at SCBF, Hosur (TN); **Gir** at SCBF, Junagarh (Gujarat); **Hariana** at SCBF, Bharatpur (Rajasthan); **Murrah** at SCBF, Banvasi (AP) and Alamadi Farm (Madras), Govt CBF Anjora,GLF Hisar now under CIRB and for **Surti** breed at GLF Dhamrod.

**(ii) Associated herd P.T. Scheme:** The progeny testing scheme at none of these farms could yielded the desired results mainly for small herd size and hence a few sires could be tested. To overcome this problem of small herd size, it was thought to associate different herds and testing the sires simultaneously based on the data of all herds. This can allow to test more number of sires and that too in different herds. This also increases the accuracy of selection. However, this posses the problem of G-E interaction which can be taken care of. The associated Herd Progeny Testing Programme has been started for 3 breeds namely Sahiwal, Hariana and Ongole. The lead institute for running this programme for Sahiwal breed is the NDRI Karnal (Haryana) by associating 3 herds of NDRI Karnal, SCBF Durg and SCBF Chakganjaria (Lucknow). This programme is being run through frozen semen technology i.e. freezing of semen and distribution among different herds. The P.T. of 6 bulls in each set is the target and 2 best bulls to be selected for nominated mating for improvement.

The Project Directorate on Cattle, Meerut has initiated the associated herd P.T. Programme for Hariana and Ongole breeds through associated herds in their breeding tract viz. for Hariana breed, the associated herds are located at GLF Hisar, Gaushala at Bhiwani, Jind and Kurukshetra whereas for ongole breeds, the associated herds are located in Andra Pradesh at Lam (Gantur), Chintaladeri (Nellore), Ramtheertham (Parkasam) and Mahanandi (Kurnool). The breeding plan involve for each breed is the mating of 75 breedable females with 4 to 5 superior proven bulls for production of future young bulls. About 8 to 10 bulls to be selected at maturity based on their expected breeding values and to freeze about 3000 doses of semen of each bull: About 1000 to be used for sire evaluation in associated herds and 1000 maintained for germplasm unit and PDC, each bull to be mated with 60 to 70 females in associated herds to get at least 20 daughters per bull. The herd strength of germplasm unit was 76 cows and 24 bulls for Hariana breed and 55 cows and 11 bulls for ongole breed. The total breedable females in associated herds for Hariana and Ongole breed were 1069 and 845 respectively.

The other important breeds of cattle are Tharparkar and Gir on which this programme will be started by the PDC Meerut. A similar programme for improvement of Rathi, Deoni and Kankrej breeds is under consideration under NATP at 3 centres viz. RAU Bikaner for Rathi, Marthwada Agri. University Parbani for Deoni and Dudhsagar Research and Development Association Mehsana for Kankrej.

**(iii) Field P.T. Scheme:** The PDC Meerut has also taken up the Field Progeny testing of crossbred bulls during VIII Five Year Plan at 3 stations viz. BAIF Urlikanchan (MS), PAU Ludhiana (Pb) and Kerala Agri. University, Mannuthy. The Holstein Friesian crossbred bulls having 50 to 75% exotic inheritance with a minimum of 4500 kg dam's milk yield are to be tested in batches for a period of 15 months and each batch will comprise 30 crossbred bulls. Atleast 40 daughters will be reached per bull spread over different units.

## 16.2.5. All India Coordinated Research Project (AICRP)

The Indian Council of Agricultural Research (ICAR) had launched a coordinated research project with the objective of evolving high yielding breeds of different species for different utility viz., cattle and buffalo for milk production, sheep for wool and mutton production, goat for milk, meat and mohair production, pig for meat production and poultry for egg and meat.

**(i) Cattle**

The AICRP on cattle involved the crossing of indigenous cattle breeds (Hariana, Ongole, Gir, Tharparkar, Sahiwal, Red Sindhi and Local) with superior exotic breeds (H.F., Jersey, Brown Swiss). The objective of AICRP on cattle was to know the optimum combination and level of exotic inheritance based on assessing the production and reproduction performance of the crossbreds in different agro-climatic regions. A control frozen semen bank was also established at Hessarghata (Karnataka) for collection, processing, storage and distribution of frozen semen. On the basis of the results obtained it was found that crossbreds with ¾ exotic inheritance did not do better than half breds due to disease problem, availability of required input and management problems etc. The better performance had been of those having 50 to 62.50% level of exotic inheritance than all other crossbreds.

**(ii) Buffalo**

The AICRP on buffaloes was started in 1970-71 by ICAR for two buffalo breeds viz. Murrah and Surti at two centres for each breed. The centres for Murrah were NDRI Karnal and PAU Ludhiana whereas for Surti the centres were university of Udaipur at Vallabhnagar (Raj.) and UAS Dharwar. The objective was the progeny testing to identify the bulls of high genetic merit and to distribute the young bulls, produced from mating of elite buffaloes with proven sires, to various farms in the country. Later on during V Plan the field units were attached to each of the centres for testing of sires under transfer to technology.

The breeding plan for all the 4 centres was to maintain 220 breedable females and a separate elite herd of 70 buffaloes. It was decided to evaluate 8 bulls at each centre and finally selecting only 2 bulls out of these 8 bulls for mating with elite buffaloes. But in 1980 the technical programme was changed to test 12 sires in testing herd every 2 years in the two herds of Murrah as well as Surti breed and finally selecting 2 bulls for mating in elite herds of both centres as one unit for both the breeds. Coverage of 3000-4000 breedable females in field units attached to each centre was also recommended. The semen of each bull had to be used in testing herds and 2 field units. Further, it was recommended to freeze a minimum of 2000 doses of semen of each bull and to distribute 700 doses from each bull to the 2 herds and other associated herd.

In 1985, the technical programme was changed as:

- To keep Surti breed at Dharwad and Vallabnagar
- To keep Murrah at NDRI Karnal and to associate CIRB Hisar
- To change over to Nili Ravi buffaloes at PAU Ludhiana and its associate herd of Nabha (Pb) centre of CIRB. Under P.T. programme 68 bulls in 9 sets at CIRB Hisar, 53 bulls in 8 sets at PAU and 47 bulls in 8 sets at NDRI were evaluated till 1993. Three sets of Surti buffalo bulls at Vallabhnagar and 5 sets at Dharwad were progeny tested.

**Network Project on Buffaloes:** During VIII plan period efforts were made to collaborate the various institutional and organized buffalo farms under the **Net Work Project on buffaloes** w.e.f. 1.4.1943. The participating units taken for Murrah buffaloes were: CIRB Hisar with its substation Nabha, PAU Ludhiana, NDRI Karnal, HAU Hisar, IVRI Izatnagar and CBBF Alamadi (TN) while those for Surti buffaloes were : RAU Vallabhnagar, GAU Navsari and Anand, CCBF Dhamrod and UAS Dharwad. A total of 147 dams of Murrah breed and 56 of Surti breed from Various units were selected as elite dams. All male calves born from elite matings to be saved for breeding and kept at their respective units till 12 months of age. The bull rearing and semen producing units for Murrah were taken at CIRB, PAU and NDRI. In 1998 new centres added for Murrah buffaloes were GLF Hastinapur and Majhra in Meerut (UP), Banvasi and Mamnoor (AP).

During IX Plan, the Network Project included the improvement programme on:

- Murrah buffaloes at institutional farms of PAU, HAU, NDRI, IVRI, CIRB and CCBF Alamadi (TN).
- Murrah buffaloes under field conditions around CIRB, PAU and NDRI
- Institutional centres including field testing for different breeds were:
    - Jaffarabadi buffaloes at GAU Junagarh
    - Nili Ravi buffaloes at CIRB substation Nabha
    - Bhadawari at IGFRI Jhansi
    - Pandharpuri at MPKV Kohlapur
    - Godavari buffaloes at BRS, ANGRAU
    - Surti at LRS Vallabhnagar
    - Murrah at NDUAT Faizabad
    - Swamp at AAU Khanapara

## 16.2.6. Military Dairy Farms

The first Military Dairy Farm (MDF) in India was started in 1889 at Allahabad (UP) to supply the milk to the British troops and their families. Later on, some other MDF's were set up and there were 24 MDF in 1975 with 9835 animals comprising 7231 cows and 2604 buffaloes. The crossbreeding of Zebu cattle with European breeds was started on large scale first time in the country at MDF in 1907 with first importation of Ayrshire stock for the reason of low productivity and breeding efficiency of Indigenous cattle. Later on other breeds were imported. The crossbreeding at MDF's was discontinued in 1952 for the reason of dependence on foreign countries for importing exotic bulls. The crossbred females were mated with bulls of indigenous breeds. The cows of indigenous breeds (Sahiwal, Red Sindhi, Gir, Tharparkar and Hariana) were introduced at MDF's. But again the ban on crossbreeding at MDF's was lifted in 1958 and the crossbreeding was undertaken with Friesian bulls. The breeding policy for MDF's was as under:

- Pure breeding of Sahiwal and Red Sindhi cows yielding 2000 kg or more milk in a lactation and crossbreeding to low yielders of these breeds, and that of Tharparkar, Gir and Hariana cows with Friesian breed.
- Forward crossing of crossbred cows with 62.5% or less exotic inheritance with superior breed (Friesian) and backcrossing of crossbred cows with over 62.5% exotic inheritance with inferior breed (Sahiwal).
- To develop a herd of purebred Friesian cows at MDF Meerut by use of Friesian bulls of high merit.

The main objective was to evolve a strain of Holstein-Sahiwal crossbred cattle. At present the MDF's has collaboration with PDC Meerut to fulfill the objective of evolving a new strain named as 'Frieswal' since 1985 which could yield 4000 kg of milk in a lactation. Cows with 5/8 Friesian inheritance have been designated as Frieswal.

The MDF's has also a programme of selective breeding of buffaloes. As a result of culling level of replacement stock, which was set 1350 kg for the first lactation and subsequently revised to 1600 kg in 1966, 1800 kg in 1968 and 2400 kg in 1978, the lactation milk yield of buffaloes has increased from 1443 kg to 2080 kg.

## 16.2.7. Project Directorate on Cattle (PDC, Meerut)

The PDC Meerut came into existence in Nov. 1987 with the mandate as:

- To evolve a new breed of cattle 'Frieswal' and other crossbred genotypes for high milk production.
- To improve indigenous breeds of cattle for milk and draught through progeny testing in collaboration of already existing organized herds and farmer's animals.

For improvement of indigenous breeds in their breeding tracts, so far Ongole and Hariana breeds have been taken up. The Gir and Tharparkar breeds will be taken up in the next phase.

## 16.2.8. Gaushalas

The Gaushalas are mostly in existence in Northern states of the country for the last two centuries based on religio-economic considerations. There is a great scope of improving the livestock of Gaushalas if proper assistance and guidance is provided. These can be used as a source of *in situ* conservation of indigenous breeds and can also be associated in progeny testing programme. In fact, some of the Gaushalas are already participating in Associated Herd Progeny Testing Scheme. Moreover, Gaushalas which maintain non-descript animals, can be engaged in crossbreeding programme so as to enhance the milk production. There are about 1020 organized Gaushalas in 21 states maintaining about '130000 cattle and 1400 breeding bulls giving the employment to about 11000 persons. Some of the Gaushalas have very good resources and facilities viz. a Gaushala on an average possessing about 60 hactor of grazing area and 25 hactor of cultivable land.

The Animal Husbandry wing of the Board of Agriculture and Animal Husbandry considered the resources available with Gaushalas and recommended their reorganization for improvement of cattle. The Govt. of India in 1949 set up a central Gaushala Development Board for development of Gaushalas as centres for cattle breeding. Later in 1952 the Govt. of India established the Central Council of Gosamvardhana (CCG) to act as the coordinating and advisory body on cattle development. The CCG, after conducting a survey on the resources of Gaushalas, sponsored an ad-hoc scheme for their development and proper functioning. The technical assistance and guidance was extended to the Gaushala managements by appointing Gaushala Development Officers by some of the states. The assistance was given to 242 Gaushalas against the target for the development of 346 Gaushalas during Second Plan. This scheme continued under Third Plan to develop more Gaushalas. But the scheme was transferred to state sector from Fourth Plan but allocation of funds received low priority. Due to paucity of funds, these gaushalas could made little impact on the improvement in milk production except very few Gaushalas located at Nasik, Urli Kanchan, Indore, Ahmednagar and Amritsar.

## 16.2.9. Milk Producer Cooperatives

Milk production in India is mostly in the hands of small farmers and landless people who keep small number of milch animals. Thus there had not been any cooperative among milk producers and the marketing of milk has been dominated by middlemen who used to get the major share of the benefit. Sardar Vallabh Bhai Patel, the iron man realized this and he encouraged the small dairy farmers of Kaira district of Gujarat to form the milk cooperative in 1946. This also led the foundation of NDDB in 1963 and Operation Flood in 1969.

### (i) AMUL (Anand Milik Producer's Union Ltd.):

The first attempt, to form the dairy cooperatives by rural milk producers under the chairmanship of Sardar V.B. Patel was made to directly reach the urban market without middlemen. The milk producer's cooperative societies were formulated at village levels which were federated into a district union and this founded the AMUL with the **objective** to extend the help and guidance in milk production and marketing to the rural dairy household. The headquarter of AMUL was located at Anand, a district town of Kaira district. The district union (AMUL) represented all the village societies and hence it was a 2-tier dairy cooperative structure viz. village societies and district union.

In 1948, the union had only 924 members of 13 village milk societies whereas in 1994-95 the union had 532670 members of 954 cooperatives with a collection of 229210 tonnes of milk. The Kaira union in 1964 set up balanced cattle feed plant and started to provide the facilities of animal health care and breeding by running a semen production centre to make the A.I. facilities to the milk producers.

### (ii) Operation Flood:

The Anand pattern dairy cooperatives had been successful in organizing the milk production, procurement, processing and marketing. The Govt. of India realized the importance of dairy cooperatives for enhancing milk production and related aspects and established in 1966, the National Dairy Development Board (NDDB) at Anand in Gujarat as an autonomous body to extend the milk producers cooperatives in major milk sheds of the country. The NDDB in 1969 formulated the programme of Operation Flood for the development of dairy industry in India. The **objective** of the Operation Flood was to create a flood of rurally produced milk with remunerative price to the farmers and to supply the milk to urban consumer at stable and reasonable price. The Operation Flood was implemented in three phases as:

**Operation Flood-I (1970-80):** It was launched in July 1970 following an agreement with the World Food Programme which provided skim milk powder (124000 tonnes) and butter oil (40000 tonnes) as an aid to finance. The emphasis was to set up the Anand Pattern rural milk producer's cooperatives for procuring, processing and marketing of milk together with providing technical input services for milk production. About 13300 Dairy cooperative Societies in 27 milk sheds with membership of 1.8 million farmers were organized.

**Operation Flood-II (1980-85):** This was for the Sixth Plan Period and launched on October 1979 with an outlay of Rs. 2730 million and designed to build on the foundation of Operation Flood-I with the following objectives.

- To build a viable self sustaining dairy industry involving about 10 million rural milk producer's families.
- To develop a National Milch Herd of about 14 million crossbred cows and upgraded buffaloes.
- To develop link of rural milk sheds with major demand centres of urban population of about 150 million by eracting a National Milk Grid.

During this OF-II, the number of village cooperative societies increased to 34500 enrolling 3.6 million farmer members in 136 milk sheds.

**Operation Flood-III (1985-96):** It was launched in 1985 with major emphasis to consolidate the achievements gained during the earlier phases by improving the productivity and efficiency of the cooperative dairy sector. It also provided the animal health and breeding facilities for improving milk production. During OF-III 72744 Dairy Cooperative Societies in 170 milk sheds of the country with 94 million members were organized.

The OF had contributed to sustained increase in milk production because of:

- Assured market of milk,
- Remunerative price for raw milk to producers,
- Technical input services including A.I., balanced cattle feed and emergency veterinary health services to the dairy farmers.

## 16.2.10. Nucleus Breeding Schemes

The genetic improvement in productivity per animal in the shortest possible time with nominal cost is the main aim of the animal breeder. The conventional breeding programmes viz. selection and mating systems have made significant contribution in the genetic improvement of livestock in developed countries by large scale field progeny testing schemes but the rate of genetic improvement had been low in developing countries like India. The main reasons have been the non availability of sires of high genetic merit in required numbers, poor spread of A.I. due to lack of infrastructure, small size of farmer's herd, high cost of data recording and the selling of animals before time in field whereas in organized herds the main reasons had been the less intense selection particularly for female side, small population size and putting emphasis on non productive traits etc.

A **new concept**, considering the above situations, for changing the breed structure so as to increase the overall genetic merit of the breed is discussed here. This has been named as **Nucleus Breeding Scheme** which may be closed or open depending on the direction of gene flow. A nucleus herd is created which is used entirely for production of males for breeding in the population. It is known through the effect of selection that mating of best with the best (selective breeding) is effective in bringing genetic improvement. Under Nucleus Breeding Scheme, a breed is structured in such a way that all the animals are not allowed to make contribution for genetic improvement but very few are given this opportunity. In India, a breed of livestock is kept at organized/institute farms known as **organized herd**(s) and kept by farmers known as **commercial herds/flocks** or village herds/flocks which are very small to the extend of 1-2 animals per farmer but collectively the village herds constitute more population of animals of a breed. However, the genetic improvement can be made in organized herds/flocks for obvious reasons. An organized herd under conventional P.T. programme is treated as single herd but under Nucleus Breeding Scheme the herd is divided in two groups' viz. **Nucleus herd and test herd** (multiplier). The nucleus herd is constituted of elite females of high genetic merit and is of a size of about 10-15% top ranking females of the total herd. The aim is to maximize the genetic gain in nucleus herd to pass on to the test herd and village herds. The nucleus herd breeds its own male and female replacements and occasionally introduces a sire or dam from another nucleus herd. The test herd or multiplier takes the males and sometimes the females from the nucleus herd to produce sufficient breeding stock to meet the demand of commercial herds. Thus the genetic gain achieved in nucleus herd is passed on from nucleus herd to multiplier and then to village herds. The NBS are of the following two types depending upon the direction of gene flow.

## (i) Closed Nucleus Breeding Scheme (CNBS)

There is one way gene flow only with the direction from top to down herds i.e. Nucleus $\Rightarrow$ Multiplier $\Rightarrow$ commercial/village herds. The improvement is made in nucleus herd and passed on to multiplier and then to the commercial herds. Thus the only source of cumulative genetic progress in village/commercial herds is that occurred in the nucleus herd. This improvement in nucleus is thus must (essential) otherwise there will be no improvement in other two herds (multiplier and the commercial) because the improvement in nucleus herd is transmitted to other herds.

The time taken in transfer of genetic progress from one herd (nucleus) to the next, known as improvement lag, can be reduced by adopting any of two practices viz. transferring of males and females of nucleus herd directly to the commercial herds and keeping the males and females in the lower herd for short time before replacing them with younger stock.

As there is no gene flow to the nucleus, it is so called as the closed Nucleus Breeding Scheme which is mainly used in pigs and poultry to avoid the risk of introducing diseases in the nucleus flock.

## (ii) Open Nucleus breeding scheme (ONBS)

In this scheme, the gene flow is both ways viz. downward from nucleus to other lower herd (multiplier and commercial) and upward from lower herd to upper herd (nucleus) by introduction of superior animals from other herds. Therefore, the superior animals from commercial herd are introduced into nucleus herd. This reduces the rate of inbreeding in the nucleus herd and increases the genetic progress because the superior animals are also available with farmers. This scheme is mostly used in cattle, buffalo, and sheep.

The ONBS can run in an organized (pedigreed) herd at institutional (Govt.) farm or by farming breed societies. The scheme is run by a group of breeders or breed societies and hence require a close cooperation between breeders. They cooperate in forming and running of ONBS for getting breeding bulls in turn from nucleus herd. This is called as **cooperative breeding scheme**.

The progeny generation of nucleus herd is reared, recorded and the males are evaluated on the basis of the performance of their sibs, paternal half sibs and their own performance. The males with high genetic merit for trait under selection can be used in the base population (multiplier) for genetic improvement through natural service or A.I. The ONBS can be operated without E.T.T. as well as by using E.T.T.

## NBS using MOET or MOET Nucleus scheme

The NBS can run with or without using the MOET (Multiple Ovulation and Embryo Transfer). When MOET is used in NBS, it is called the MOET Nucleus Scheme.

In developed countries like USA, UK, France, the MOET has given a new era to the cattle improvement programmes. The MOET is a composite technology which involves a number of processes viz. super ovulation, estrus synchronization among recipients, A.I. of donor, embryo recovery from donor, and finally embryo transfer in the recipient females. Generally fresh embryos are transferred but these can also be cryopreserved for future use in case the recipients are not available on the day of embryo flushing or for the purpose of preservation of gene pool.

The MOET augment the reproductive potential of donor females, which are of high genetic merit and are given hormonal treatment. This results in shedding of more number of ova (eggs) which are fertilized by A.I. The embryos so formed are recovered from uterus of donor by flushing and transferred to the recipient cows of low genetic merit. In this way, more than one progeny (about 8) from donor cows per year can be obtained. In one flush about 4 good quality transferable embryos can be obtained and 4 flush can be taken in one year from one donor cow. The conception rate of transferred embryos in recipient (the successful rate of implantation) is about 50%.

## Common features of MOET-Nucleus scheme

An elite herd (or a few elite herds) of males and females is set up and the selection is made at an early age based on family information (sibling test from the information of full and half sisters).

The generation interval is considerably reduced for the reason of sibling test for selection and not using the performance of the daughters. Thus the accuracy of selection is less under sibling test but this loss in accuracy is outweighted by the reduced generation interval.

The selection and testing is done within elite or nucleus herd(s) under controlled environment. By controlling environment, $h^2$ should increase and so improves the accuracy of B.V. estimation. This makes possible the greater degree of control on intensity of selection, generation interval and rate of inbreeding. This is the major advantage of MOET nucleus breeding scheme.

The rate of twinning can be increased by transferring two embryos. There are then increased chances of freemartin which can be reduced by embryo sexing. Thus more number of progeny per donor can be obtained without increasing the herd size of recipients.

The problem of getting offspring from high yielding cows that are infertile due to disease or injury may be overcome using E.T. For example, it may allow brucella positive donors to have brucella negative offspring.

The females carrying harmful recessive genes causing diseases can be detected by progeny testing of females with E.T.

## Variants (Types) of MOET nucleus scheme

The MOET nucleus schemes are of 3 types based on the criteria and age of selection. These are as under:

**(i) Juvenile MOET:** In this scheme the selection of bulls and cows is done at an early age before first breeding. The selection criteria are the ancestor's performance only i.e. dams, dam's ancestors and sibs of dams and sires. The generation interval in this scheme is less.

**(ii) Adult MOET Scheme:** in this scheme the selection of males and females is done on different criteria viz. males are selected on the basis of ancestor's performance (dam, sibs of sire and dam) plus their full and half sisters records whereas the females are selected on the basis of ancestors performance plus their own sibs and their own performance. The generation interval in this scheme is longer than juvenile MOET scheme. The bulls have to be kept for longer time in this scheme till the records of their sibs is collected and the cost of keeping bull is high.

**(iii) Mixed or Hybrid MOET:** In this scheme the progeny testing of males required for nucleus replacement is carried out in nucleus herd. The mixed MOET can be juvenile mixed MOET or adult mixed MOET.

## 16.3. SHEEP IMPROVEMENT PROGRAMMES

Sheep development programme was started by the East India Company in 19th century by importing exotic breeds of sheep for crossbreeding of indigenous sheep breeds. The exotic sheep breed imported was Cape Merino and crossbreeding was started around Poona. Crossbreeding of indigenous sheep with Romney Marsh was undertaken in the beginning of 20th century in plains and hilly areas. Crossbreeding with Southdown and Cape Merino was also undertaken in Punjab, Bengal, Madras and Mysore. Bikaneri ewes were crossed with Merino rams at GLF Hisar and a five wool breed with ¾ exotic inheritances was evolved and it was given the name Hisardale.

The research work on sheep improvement was taken up on regional basis by ICAR after the country attained independence. The emphasis was on selective breeding within native stock and the crossbreeding with exotic fine wool breeds. The regional centres were set-up in the hilly areas of UP, Rajasthan and Deccan plateau to conduct crossbreeding trials during the First Five Year Plan. Three sheep breeding farms were established during 2nd Five Year Plan with the aim to produce stud rams along with wool extension centres in some states so as to improve the field flocks by providing breeding rams of superior merit. During 3rd Five Year Plan, the action taken were the strengthening of the existing sheep breeding farms, establishment of more number of sheep and wool extension centres, initiating a large scale sheep shearing and wool processing programmes in Rajasthan and other states of Northern and Western parts of the country, and establishment of central Sheep and Wool Research Institute, Avikanagar (Malpura-Tonk Distt), Rajasthan under Central Govt. in 1962. The aims of establishing CSWRI were to undertake the fundamental and applied research in sheep production and wool utilization, and to provide post – graduate training in sheep and wool sciences. Later on, during 1965 the CSWRI was transferred under the administration control of ICAR. There were 84 sheep breeding farms, 52 supplementary sheep breeding centres, and 602 sheep and wool extension centres in the country during 4th Five Year Plan.

An ad-hoc committee on Sheep Breeding Policy was constituted by G.O.I. in 1970. This committee suggested the importation of 20000 exotic sheep of fine wool breeds to produce breeding rams in order to meet the shortage of stud rams. Therefore Indo-Australian (now central) Sheep Breeding Farm, Hisar was set up with 3000 ewes and 300 rams of Corriedale breed to meet the objective of producing and distribution of Corriedale stud rams to different states for crossbreeding work of improving wool and mutton production since the Corriedale is a dual purpose breed. Later on, the Corriedales were replaced by Rambouillet. Two sheep breeding farms in private sector one in Maharastra and one in Gujarat were set up to produce purebred and crossbred rams. Seven Central Sheep Breeding farms in J&K, UP, MP, AP,

Bihar and Karnataka were established for same purpose of producing pure and crossbred rams. During 5th Five Year Plan, some more breeding farms were established. Efforts were made for intensive sheep development through genetically upgrade the stock, providing health care, pasture improvement, machine shearing and wool processing.

**AICRP on sheep breeding:** The AICRP on sheep breeding was started in 1971 for fine wool and for mutton. The objective was to achieve by crossbreeding of native breeds with rams of exotic breeds. The two coordinated research projects were merged into one project on sheep breeding in 1974 with the following objectives.

1. Fine wool component – 2.5 kg GFW/year with average fibre diameter of 22 microns and medulation percentage below 5.
2. Carpet wool component – 2 kg GFW/year with average fibre diameter of 30 microns and medulation per cent 25.
3. Mutton component – 30 kg live weight at 6 months of age with 50% dressing percentage and feeding efficiency of 15-20 per cent.

The native and exotic breeds used at different centres of AICRP and the new breeds/strains developed were as:

| Name of centres components Fine wool | Breeds used | | Breeds developed | Exotic inheritance |
|---|---|---|---|---|
| | Native | Exoitc | | |
| CSWRI Avikanagar (Raj.) | Chokla, Nali | Rambonillet Merino | Bharat Merino, | 75 50 |
| TNVASU Sandynallah (TN) | Nilgiri | Meriono | Nilgiri Synthetic | 62.2-75 |
| GAU Dantiwara (Guj.) | Patanwari | Merino, Rambouillet | Patanwadi Synthetic | 50 |
| **Mutton** | | | | |
| CSWRI Avikanagar | Mulpura, Sonadi | Dorest, Suffolk | Avimaans | 50 |
| APAU Palammer | Nellore, Mandya | | Nellore Synthetic | |
| MPKV Rahuri (MS) | Deccani | | Deccani Synthetic | |
| **Carpet wool** | | | | |
| RAU Bikaner | Magra | | | |
| CSWRI Avikangar | Malpura | Rambouillet | Avikalin | 50 |
| **Pelt Production** | | | | |
| CSWRI sub station Bikaner | Malpura, Sonadi, Marwari | Karakul | Indian Karakul | 75 |

**Net work project:** In 1990, all the ongoing units of AICRP on sheep breeding were converted into Network Project on Sheep Improvement (NWPSI). The mandate of NWPSI is survey, genetic evaluation and conservation of sheep genetic resources of the country. The breeding policy for NWPSI is the selective breeding in indigenous sheep. The NWPSI is functioning at 5 farm based cooperating units and 2 field based cooperating units. These are as under:-

Farm based units:

CSWRI Avikanagar using chokla for carpot wool

CSWRI substation Bikaner using Marwari for carpet wool

CIRG Makhdoom using Muzaffarnagri for wool and mutton

MPKV Rahuri using Deccani for wool and mutton

APAU Palamner using Nellore for mutton

**Field based Units:**

RAU, Bikaner using Magra for carpet wool

TNVASU, Kattupakkam using Madras Red for mutton.

In addition to NWPSI, the state Agric. Universities and state sheep breeding farms are involved in genetic improvement of sheep but with the major constraint of small population size. Some NGO like Nimbkar Agr. Research Institute, Phalton (MS) are also involved in sheep Improvement programme. This institute is working on Garole sheep.

The CSWRI have also the breeding programmes for indigenous sheep in addition to the breeds (Chokla and Magra) under NWPSI. These are as:

- Genetic improvement of Magra Sheep under field conditions
- Improving Malpura sheep for mutton production.
- Improvement of Awassi and Garole sheep for mutton, milk and prolificacy

In the state of Jammu and Kashmir, a new breed Kashmir Merino was evolved by crossbreeding of Gaddi and Bhakarwal breeds with rams of Delaine Merino, Soviet Merino and Rambouillet. This had 50-75% exotic inheritance.

## 16.4. GOAT IMPROVEMENT PROGRAMMES

All India Coordinated Research Project (AICRP) on goats was initiated in IV Five Year Plan (1971) with its basic theme to improve the production performance of Indian breeds of goats through crossbreeding with exotic breeds of temperate countries. Two separate projects were incepted viz. AICRP on goats for milk and AICRP on goats for fibre (Pashmina and Mohair) production, each at 3 centres. The centres for milk were NDRI Karnal (Beetal goat); KAU, Trichur (Malabari gaots) and MPKVV Rahuri (Black Bengal) for crossing these breeds with Alpine and Saanen. The 3 centres for fibre were : 2 for Pashmina at IVRI Mukteshwer (Chegu) and Upesi Farm, Leh (Changthangi) and one for Mohair at MPKVV Rahuri (Local Deccani) to cross with Angora goat.

The third component of meat was included in 1974 under AICRP on goats for meat. All the 3 AICRP on goats were merged into one project as AICRP on goats (for milk, meat and fibre production) in 1974. The coordinating unit of AICRP on goats remained at CSWRI Avikanagar upto Oct. 1976 and later on shifted at National Govt. Research Centre (IVRI), Makhdoom (UP). The number of units increased to nine in VI Plan period (1980-85) which declined to six in VIII Plan period.

**Net work Project:** The AICRP on goats was transformed in 1990 into Network Project in VIII Plan with its mandate to define, characterize and improve the productivity of native goat breeds incorporating farmers flock in the home tract through selective breeding based on progeny performance. All the ongoing six centres of AICRP on goat were converted into the centres of Net work Project on Goat Improvement (NWPGI). These centres were CSWRI Avikanagar (Sirohi); RAU Bikaner (Marwari); KAU Mannuthi (Malabari); MPKVV Rahuri (Synthetic Angora); Birsa Agric Univ., Ranchi (Black Bengal) and JNKVV, Mhow (Malwa goats). In 1993 the centres at BAU Ranchi, JNKVV Mhow, MPKVV Rahuri and KAU Trichur were delinked. The existing centres at Bikaner for Marwari goats in their home tract and Avikanagar for Sirohi goat in the farm flock were allowed to continue and 3 new centres were opened during VIII Plan for Jamnapari and Barbari farm units at CIRG Makhdoom in addition to Jamnapari field unit at Chakarnagar (Etawah, UP).

The summary of centres under AICRP on goats for different components alongwith the breeds used and breeding policy is as under:-

| Location | Breeds used | | Breeding Policy | Plan (Period) | |
|---|---|---|---|---|---|
| | Native | Exotic | | Starting | Discontinue |
| NDRI Karnal | Beetal | Alpine, Saanen | CB | IV | VII |
| KAU Trichur | Malabari | -do- | CB | IV | VIII |
| MPKVV Rahuri | B.Bengal | Beetal, Jamnapari | GU | IV | |
| RAU Bikaner | Jhakrana | | SB | VII | |
| **Pashmina** | | | | | |
| IVRI Mukteshwar | Chegu | Angora | SB | IV | VII |
| Upesi, Leh | Changthangi | Angora | SB | IV | VII |
| MPKVV Rahuri | Local Deccani | Angora | CB | IV | VIII |
| AAU Brunihat | Assam Local | Beetal | GU | IV | VII |
| **Meat** | | | | | |
| CSWRI Avikanagar | Sirohi | Beetal | CB | V | |

| Location | Breeds used | | Breeding | Plan (Period) | |
|---|---|---|---|---|---|
| | Native | Exotic | Policy | Starting | Discontinue |
| BAU Ranchi | B.Bengal | Beetal, Jamnapari | GU | V | VIII |
| AAU Guwahati | Assam local | Beetal | CB | V | |
| AHD Sikkim | Local Shingari | Beetal, Jamnapari | GU | VI | VII |
| Bikaner | Marwari | - | SBFF | VII | |
| JNKVV Mhow | Malva | Nutrition & Physi.Project | | VII | VIII |

CB = crossbreeding, SB = Selective breeding, GU = Grading up , SBFF = Selective Breeding in Farmer's Flock.

## 16.5. POULTRY IMPROVEMENT PROGRAMMES

The poultry improvement was first initiated by missionaries at Etah (UP) and Katpadi (TN) during 1920's by importing exotic breeds from UK, America and Australia.

A poultry development research scheme at Nagpur was undertaken by State Govt. in 1950's for evaluating the native chickens. The breeds evaluated were Aseel, Kadaknath, Black Bengal, Naked Neck and Haringhatta Black. The exotic breeds used for grading up/crossing were White Leghorn, Rhode Island Red, Black Australorp and New Hampshire. The final report of the scheme was published in 1957.

Selective breeding of indigenous fowl was started in 1940 at IVRI Izatnagar (UP). The crossbreeding was also initiated at the same time using exotic breeds.

The ICAR started the improvement programme of native breeds like Aseel, Chittagong, Punjab brown and Desi. During the last phase of First Five Year Plan, the major work of poultry research was started. This involved the upgrading of indigenous breeds with exotic breeds. In 1960's, the ICAR initiated a number of projects on improvement of poultry for egg production by family selection, breeding and hybridization; improvement of broilers by selection and crossbreeding; and the improvement of native chickens.

In late 1960's, the evaluation and improvement of indigenous fowl was started under PL-480 project at two centres viz. HAU Hisar and college of Agric. Udaipur.

Govt. of India had also started poultry breeding on a systematic basis at four central poultry breeding farms for eggs (Bangalore, Bombay, Bhubaneshwar) and meat (Chandigarh).

In 1960's, some private sector viz. Arbor Acre, Hi-Breed, Rani Shaver and Unichix entered into foreign collaboration of Canada, Czechoslovakia and USA for commercial production of genetically superior chicks. The poultry business had also attracted some other poultry farmers viz. Venketeshwara hatcheries, Kegg farms, CSR Ross breeders, Poona Pearls etc. The other leading international brand names available in India are Hy-line, Hypeco, Anak, Hubbard, Tegel, Dekalb, Bovans, Vencobb, H & N etc. The commercial egg type stocks are the result of three/four way crosses of White Leghorn whereas the meat stock involved the crosses of Cornish, Plymouth Rock and synthetic broilers strains.

AICRP on poultry breeding for eggs and meat was started by ICAR in 1971. The programme for egg production was to test 13 layer strains at different centres with 3-4 strains at each centre, as purebreds and inter crosses together for their improvement through combined selection. Eight strains of broilers were tested, at different centres each with 3-4 strains, as purebreds as well as crosses and intra population selection based on 8 weeks weight.

The ICAR had established Central Avian Research Institute, Izatnagar (UP) in 1980's and Project Directorate on Poultry at Hyderabad (AP) for improvement of poultry.

## 16.6. BIO-TECHNIQUES FOR ANIMAL IMPROVEMENT

The convention on Biological Diversity defines **biotechnology** as any technological application that uses biological systems, living organisms or derivatives thereof, to make or modify products or process for specific use.

The genetic variation in a population and the methods to exploit the genetic variability decides the magnitude of genetic improvement of livestock species. The traditional breeding programmes based on performance recording and crossbreeding have made genetic improvement in animal production. During the last two decades, newer technological breakthrough in the field of reproduction, genetics and related aspects have opened the new area of animal improvement.

### 16.6.1. Reproductive biotechnologies

The biotechniques in reproduction have made significant contribution in increasing the reproductive efficiency, global transport and multiplication of genetic material, and conservation of unique genetic material for use in future. These techniques are A.I., E.T., embryo production and preservation, semen and embryo sexing, embryo splitting and cloning.

### (i) Artificial insemination (AI)

The AI has played a valuable role to bring genetic change in animal populations. The specific advantages of A.I. are:

a) Dissemination of superior germplasm by widespread use of outstanding males.
b) Introduction of new genetic material by importing semen instead of live animals.
c) Progeny testing under different environments so as to increase the rate and efficiency of selection.

d) Use of frozen semen in future even after the death of sire.

e) Reduction in spreading the sexually transmitted diseases

## (ii) Frozen semen technology

It is also a valuable technique whereby the semen is stored for longer time without loss of viability for use in A.I. This may promote conservation of endangered genotype, though it requires cryopreservation facilities.

## (iii) Embryo transfer technology (ETT)

It is a composite technology involving superovulation, estrus synchronization, A.I., embryo recovery, embryo transfer and sometime cryopreservation and micro manipulation of embryos. This augments the fertility of females and brings faster genetic change.

**Super ovulation and AI:** The donors selected are those which are genetically superior whereas the recipients are those having low production. The donors are super ovulated by injecting gonadotrophins mainly FSH and ECG between days 8 and 12 of oestrus cycle. FSH is injected for 4-5 days daily twice whereas ECG is injected only once. The donors are inseminated during super oestrus with semen from fertile and high genetic merit bulls.

**Embryo recovery:** The uterine horns of the super ovulated donors are flushed using phosphate buffer saline solution containing antibiotics and serum using a 2-way Rusch catheter. The outflow is passed through an embryo filter.

**Embryo transfer:** The embryos are transferred to the recipients. The successful pregnancy (implantation) rate is about 50%.

The ETT has certain advantages:

- Rapid multiplication of rare genotype
- Low cost in transporting embryos instead of living animals which also require quarantine.
- Rapid improvement of livestock to produce elite herd
- Twinning rate can be increased
- Prenatal sex determination
- Control on sexually transmitted diseases
- Animal conservation programme

## (iv) In vitro produced (IVP) Embryos

The embryos can also be produced *in vitro* which involves the *in vitro* maturation (IVM) of oocytes, followed by fertilization (IVF) with the use of *in vitro* capacitated spermatozoa. The newly formed zygotes are cultured in suitable media to develop upto the transferable stage. Therefore, the *in vitro* production (IVP) of embryos technology requires the following steps:

- Collection of immature oocytes- Following a local anesthesia, an ultra sound probe is inserted into the vagina to puncture the follicle> 2 mm diameter using a transvaginal curvilinear transducer. This is known as ovum pick-up (OPU)

- Maturation of oocytes (IVM)-in culture medium preferabley TCM 199
- Sperm capacitation-by use of Heparin
- *in vitro* Fertilization (IVF)- in fertilization medium
- Culture of embryos – In culture media
- Embryo sexing, freezing and transfer to the uterus

The IVP technology has the several advantages over the conventional ET. Two techniques can be compared as under:

| **OPU + IVF = IVP embryos** | **Embryo transfer (ET)** |
|---|---|
| Donors need no hormonal stimulation | Required |
| IVP embryos can be obtained from | Nearly 30% animals do not produce viable embryos |
| Prepuberal donors can be used | Not |
| Infertile animals can be used for OPU | Not |
| No information on reproductive status | Require |
| of donor is required | |
| Pregnant donors upto third month of pregnancy can be used for OPU | Only non-pregnant donors are used |
| Aspiration of follicles can be done twice a week over a long period | Flushing can be repeated after 2 months |
| Once flushing gave about 14 transferable embryos or 6 pregnancies | Only 5 transferable embryos with 3 pregnancies |
| Oocytes of same donor can be fertilized individually with semen of any bull | Only one sire is used on a donor at one time |

The IVP embryos technology thus allows the repeated collection of oocytes for bulk production of high quality embryos from livestock of high economic value or unique genotype or endangered genotype so as to propagate such genotype at a much faster rate.

## (v) Embryo cryopreservation

Like freezing of semen, the freezing of embryos is possible and is a practice. It is useful as a conservation programme for endangered or unique genotype so as to propagate such genotype at a faster rate.

## (vi) Embryo splitting

The embryo splitting is a beneficial technique in which the embryo is divided into halves to have two embryos or into one quarter to get 4 embryos or sometimes to get 16 embryos from single embryo. The aim of embryo splitting is to obtain greater number of offspring from a given donor. The halving or quartering of embryos increases the intensities of selection for females nearly to that of males. The identical twins can be thus produced which will facilitate sire testing, reduction in insemination cost, testing of maternal traits, to study the genotype-environment interactions and to have information on carcass traits of other twin in meat animals by sacrificing one twin. However, the survival rate of split embryos is less.

## E.T. work in India

The E.T.T. has been adopted successfully in cattle by many institutions in India. APAU Tirupati had produced first E.T. calf (cattle) in 1986 in the country. The National Institute of Immunology (NII) also had ET calf (cattle) in January 1987 and Sabarmati Ashram Gaushala, Bidaj, in December 1987 produced first buffalo calf through E.T.

Govt. of India initiated in 1987 a National Service and Technology Project on E.T.T. to be operated through Deptt. of Biotechnology with NDDB as the lead implementing agency at Sabarmati Ashram Gaushala, Bidaj as the main E.T. laboratory. This project had also four collaborating centres/agencies viz. IVRI Izatnagar, NDRI karnal, NII New Delhi and Central Frozen Semen Production and Training Institute Hessarghatta. It had also four required ET centres viz. Sree Nasik Panchwati Pinjarapole, Nasik, with donor animals of pure Gir, HF and crossbreds of HF and Jersey; Buffalo Breeding Centre, Nekorikallu (Guntur, AP) exclusively to work on buffaloes; Animal Breeding centre, Salon (Rai Bareli, UP) to produce HF and its crossbreds; Centreal Frozen Semen Production and Training Institute, Hessarghatha (Karnataka) to work on Hallikar, Amritmahal and HF crossbreds.

## 16.6.2. Genetic biotechniques

More recent biotechniques in the field of genetics have demonstrated the potential for genome analysis and manipulation of genome.

## (i) Genome analysis

This includes the study of chromosomal karyotyping, chromosomal aberrations and genetic characterization of population to know the variation in blood groups, biochemical polymorphism and DNA markers.

The genetic characterization by use of DNA markers is the recent approach which has made possible the study of animal variability at basic level i.e. the genetic material itself, the DNA. There are two parts of DNA viz. Coding part (about 3 to 5%) and rest non-coding which is non functional and 'junk' DNA. The coding part is responsible for protein synthesis and has lesser variability among individuals. This minor part of the gene-coding DNA has been subjected to evolutionary forces among which mutation is more important, though random but maintained if useful otherwise lost. The non coding regions of DNA are not governed by these processes for so long they do not affect the survival of the individual. Therefore, the accumulation of mutations creates genetic variability within non-coding regions of DNA. In other words, the non-coding regions of DNA accommodate changes leading to a high level of polymorphism. Each of the polymorphisms serves as a genetic marker. Polymorphisms in DNA sequences are detected by means of certain enzymes (called restriction enzymes) which cleave double stranded DNA molecules.

The recombinant DNA technology has brought revolutionary changes and it has become possible to a large number of genetic polymorphisms at the DNA sequence level to use them as markers for genetic evaluation/characterization. A marker is usually considered as a constituent that determines the function of a construction. Likewise, a **genetic marker** can be defined as any stable and inherited variation which is measurable or detectable by a suitable method and can be used subsequently to detect the presence of a specific genotype or phenotype other than itself, which otherwise is non measurable or very difficult to detect. Such variations which are morphological, chromosomal, biochemical and DNA level can serve as genetic markers. The markers revealing variations at the DNA sequence level are referred to as **molecular markers**.

The methods of examining DNA polymorphism may be divided into two categories as under:

(a) **Site directed polymorphism:** This involves the techniques to search known sequences or genes for polymorphism. These include restriction enzyme polymorphism (RFLP), sequence polymorphism, sequence – specific oligonucleotides and conformational polymorphism.

**Sequence polymorphism:** All methods of describing differences between the DNA of animals depend upon detecting differences in the neucleotide sequence. This method is more efficient to determine the sequence of a specific gene.

**Restricted fragment length polymorphism (RFLP):** These are the fragments of DNA produced by cutting with restriction enzymes. There exists a large battery of restriction enzymes which cut DNA at specific sequences; these recognition sites may be 4-8 bases long. If an enzyme cuts the DNA of some but not all animals at a particular site then a polymorphism is inferred in atleast one of the bases in the recognition site.

**Sequence specific oligonucleotides:** These are sets of PCR (Polymerase Chain Reaction) primers which function in an allele specific manner.

**Conformational polymorphism:** They are used to detect polymorphism in specific locations which relies upon detecting sequence-specific mobility of PCR products under electrophoresis

**(b) Anonymous polymorphis:** Which covers the methods which reveal arbitrary polymorphism i.e. polymorphism which are developed on a purely random basis. These includes minisatellite, microsatellite, RAPD (Random Amplified Polymorphic DNA) markers.

**Minisatellite and Microsatellites:** They are the regions of repeatitive DNA and are highly polymorphic spots on non-coding regions characterized by repeating DNA blocks each of which contains upto several hundred of base pair in size. The **minisatellites** are tandom repeats of short sequences (15-60 bp long), interspread in the most chromosomes. The changes in the number of repeats casued by unequal crossing over between homologous tandom repeats or due to gain/loss of repeat units at a particular locus as a result of slippage during replication create hyper variability of minisatellites. This change continues over many generations and hence each such locus represents a variety of alleles with different number of tandom repeats. Therefore, in the population these loci have Variable Number of Tandom Repeats (VNTR) and hence called as VNTR loci. The VNTR define the length of the individual-specific 'alleles' which can be examined by Southern Blot or PCR techniques.

The term **microsatellite** was coined by Litt and Luty (1989) to characterize the simple sequence repeats amplified by PCR. These are tandemly repeated motifs of 1-6 nucleotides length distributed densely and evenly throughout the genome showing variation in number of repeats. These are also called as simple sequence repeats (SSR), short tandem repeats (STR) and sequence tagged microsatellite repeats (STMR). The short length of microsatellites makes them emenable to amplification by PCR and subsequent separation on PAGE (Poly acrylamide gel electrophoresis). They occur at a high frequency (one/10kb DNA) with their abundant number (50000-100000) in mammalian genome and display a high degree of polymorphism (PIC value of 0.6 or more) in eukaryotic genome. Polymorphism arises from differences in number of times the simple sequence motif is repeated. The microsatellites are now considered the most powerful genetic markers for biodiversity evaluation for their high heterozygosity.

**Random Amplified polymorphic DNA (RAPD):** This is another form of variation useful in DNA polymorphism analysis with high level of detectable polymorphism. It is the polymorphic DNA which is amplified randomly by PCR analysis. Randomly designed single primer is used to amplify a set of anonymous polymorphic DNA fragments. When the primer is short, the priming may take place at several sites in the genome that are located within amplifiable distance. The polymorphism detected by this method is called RAPD. This does not require any prior sequence knowledge.

The molecular markers are also classified on the basis of techniques used for detection. The techniques of DNA analysis may be PCR based (Polymerase chain reaction) or non –PCR (hybridization) based.

## Hybridization based markers

The techniques include RFLP analysis. The DNA is digested with restriction enzymes and the resulting fragments are separated by gel electrophoresis, transferred to a filter by Southern blotting, probes are hybridized to the filter and sequences in genome bound with hybridized probe are then visualized as hybridization bands. The individuals carrying different allelic variants for a locus will show different banding patterns. The hybridization can be carried out with genomic probes (cDNA, cloned genes, genomic DNA sequence) and with genome derived cloned probes of different families of hypervariable repeatitive DNA sequences (minisatellites, VNTR, microsatellites) and synthetic oligonucleotides.

The probe is a suitably labeled nucleic acid molecule which can be used to detect another nucleic acid molecule that has a homologous sequence by complementary base pairing. The probes may be single locus or multilocus. Three types of DNA probes are available. These are cloned cDNA or genomic fragments, synthetic oligonucleotides and PCR generated probes. The cDNA is the DNA copy of a mature mRNA. It is not a naturally occurring molecule of a cell but obtained artificially by enzymatic synthesis in an *in vitro* system.

## PCR based markers

The PCR process was invented by Kary Mullis (1985). It is a simple ingenious primer mediated enzymatic method of amplifying short, specific segments of longer DNA or cDNA template. It requires very little amount of biological material (0.1-0.5 μg of DNA or RNA) and it can amplify the template DNA many thousand or million fold. It is very easy and quick process and it has become the method of choice of people. The entire amplification can be performed *in vitro* as opposed to standard cloning procedure.

The primers used for PCR may be the primers of specific sequences targeted to a particular region of a genome or primers of arbitrary sequences. Thus the PCR based methods are sequence specific PCR assays and the arbitrary PCR assays. The arbitrary primers can be purchased from commercial companies, have the benefit of not requiring prior genetic or biochemical information, amplify several anonymous polymorphic discrete DNA fragments and produces multiple arbitrary amplicon profiling (MAAP) which includes RAPD, Arbitrary Primer PCR (AP-PCR) and DNA amplification fingerprinting (DAF). The AFLP (Amplified fragment length polymorphism) is an intermediate technique between RFLP and RAPD.

## Applications of molecular markers

The polymorphisms observed at the DNA sequence level have been playing a major role in human genetics for the following aspects.

- Parentage determination
- Individual identity
- Genetic distance estimation and evolution
- Determination of twin zygosity and freemartinism
- Identification of disease carrier (heterozygous) animals
- Gene mapping
- Marker assisted selection (MAS)
- Sex determination
- DNA fingerprinting
- Transgenic breeding

## Gene mapping

The gene mapping is a method to identify the genes responsible for specific traits. Mapping any genome requires genetic markers which may be any mandelian character. The gene maps are of two types viz. genetic map or linkage map and physical map.

The **genetic map** is constructed from linkage relationship based on the frequency of meiotic exchange (amount of recombination) among linked traits. These genetic maps locate the genes responsible for traits and they show the relative orders and distances between loci on the chromosome. Linkage analysis requires the segregation of alleles for which there should be 100% heterozygosity in parental generation like the $F_1$ generation in crosses between inbred lines or different breeds. All genetic markers can be used for linkage mapping. There are two approaches for genetic mapping viz. saturation or random mapping and targeted mapping. The saturation involves the generation of large number of markers to cover the whole genome so that the trait of interest lie near to atleast one marker. This is done by using either of the technique of RAPD, STS (Sequence Tagged Sites), AFLP,RFLP, SSCP (Single stranded conformational polymorphism) and the microsatellite analysis. The targeted mapping method involves the isolation of markers in a specific region or for a specific trait. This is carried out by different techniques including EST (Expressed Sequence Tags), subtractive hybridization.

The **physical maps** relate genes and markers to the actual location on a specific chromosome. In other words, they relate traits to actual chromosomal location. These maps can be cytogenetically or molecularly based. Physical mapping is done using the techniques such as somatic cell hybridization, radiation hybrids, fluorescence in situ hybridization (FISH).

Some useful traits affected by major genes have been identified in different species like –

**Cattle:** - Horn development gene on chromosome 1,
- muscular hypertrophy gene on chromosome 2, and
- obesity gene on chromosome 6.

**Sheep :** - Booroola fecundity gene on chromosome 6,
- obesity gene on chromosome 4 and
- muscular hypertrophy gene on chromosome 18.

**Goat:** - Horn development gene on chromosome 1,

**Pig:** - Dominant white coat colour gene on chromosome 8,
- RN gene with major effect on muscle glycogen content
- meat quality on chromosome 15, and
- calcium release channel gene on chromosome 6.

The gene mapping in humans contains a broad array of technologies and aims to understand the genome organization and identification of genes. In farm animals the gene mapping is used to detect genes controlling diseases and quantitative trait loci (QTL) so as to develop more efficient breeding strategies. The gene mapping has also significant role in the study of evolutionary divergence of mammalian species.

## Marker assisted selection (MAS)

The MAS is a form of indirect selection of superior breeding stock. MAS depends on identifying associations between genetic markers and linked QTL (quantitative trait loci) with useful effects. The association between the markers and the QTL depends on the distance between the markers and target traits. The genetic marker for a trait is a DNA segment associated with the trait of interest, segregates in a predictable fashion and helps the tagging of individual genes or small chromosome segment influencing the trait of interest. The genome is screened for genes with large effect on trait through linkage analysis. The procedure of selection for a trait by genetic marker is called the MAS.

The MAS is more efficient for traits of low heritability and secondly when the genetic variance is more explained by the marker than economic trait. The MAS can be used in early age and hence reduces the generation interval. Thus the MAS increase the rate of genetic gain by increasing accuracy of selection. The MAS has the prospects of selection for traits which can not be improved by conventional methods viz. resistance to disease etc.

## Sex determination by sexing of semen and embryos

The sex of the new born offspring can now be determined before fertilization by sexing of semen, The sperm containing X or Y chromosome are separated and the female is inseminated to produce desired sex. The separation is done using staining procedure and detecting by laser beam with the help of standard flow cytometry equipment.

Another approach of sexing is to determine the sex of the embryos. The following methods are used:

(a) Enzyme activity method – the activity of certain x-linked enzymes is measured. This is twice in case of female embryos than male because the females have two X chromosomes. This method has the limitation of embryonic mortality and not being 100% accurate.

(b) H-Y antigen detection – Male specific antigen known as H-Y antigen is immunologically detected. However, it gives an accuracy of 85%.

(c) DNA probing – One cell from an early embryonic stage is extracted and the sex is determined by localization of DNA sequences present on Y chromosome. The DNA of the biopsed cell of the embryo is hybridized to a labeled sequence of the DNA specific to Y chromosome. The presence of Y chromosome in the biopsed cell is indicated by the positive hybridization. This method has also the limitation of reduced viability of biopsed embryo.

(d) Karyotyping – some cells of an embryo are taken to examine the metaphase chromosome and karyotyped for two X chromosome or one Y chromosome.

(e) Polymerase chain reaction (PCR) method – This technique is more accurate (95%), rapid and does not affect embryo viability. It involves amplifying

Y chromosome specific DNA sequences directed by primers with a thermostable DNA polymerase from a small amount of DNA of one or more blastomers.

## DNA Fingerprinting

The characterization of one or more rare features of an individuals' genome (hereditary make up) by developing the DNA fragment band (alleles) patterns is called as DNA fingerprinting or DNA identification analysis or identity testing or DNA profiling/typing or genotyping. The bands of DNA profile are inherited in a simple mendelian fashion and behave as co dominants, both the maternal and paternal derived variants at any given locus are detectable. The band patterns also behave like independent loci. DNA fingerprinting is most important among various genome markers and like RFLP there are genetic loci for which every individual is unique and different from others. An individual inherits one or the other of the allelic status of each marker from each parent whereas another individual of the same parents inherits different marker set. However, two off spring would have some markers in common but other markers as different. However, the unrelated individuals will have no markers in common. The probability of two DNA samples matching by chance is very low (between $10^{-6}$ to $10^{-15}$).

The numbers of variable bands which appear in DNA fingerprints depend upon combination of enzyme and probe (nucleotide sequence capable of hybridizing with its complementary chain sequence). The patterns of DNA fingerprints in an individual remain same irrespective of source of DNA from any tissue of the body (WBC, semen, hair bulbs etc.) and also the band patterns do not show any difference from fresh, frozen or dried tissues provided the tissue is not contaminated. The patterns are constant from birth to death except mutation which may cause loss or appearance of one or more bands. The history of DNA fingerprinting is more recent (1985 after the work of Jeffreys et al.)

The methodology of DNA fingerprinting involves the following steps

- Isolation of DNA
- Digestion of DNA by restriction endonucleases
- Electrophoretic separation of different fragments
- Transfer of DNA on nylon membrane
- Probe labeling
- Hybridization of labeled probe DNA
- Autoradiography
- Analysis and interpretation of band patterns

The applications of DNA fingerprinting (DFP) are as under:

- Individual identification
- Pedigree analysis and parentage verification
- Zygosity testing (twins)
- Sex determination

- Conservation of genetic resources (identification of genetic relatedness).
- Demographic studies (estimation of individual and population homozygosity, effective population size, population sub division, relatedness, social organization and kin selection)
- Identification of loci controlling quantitative traits or disease resistance
- Pathogen identification
- Detection of source of tissues, particularly in meat industry to avoid adulteration
- Detection of somatic mutation or cancer
- Taxonomical tool
- Quality control of cell banks.

## (ii) Manipulation of genome

### (a) Transgenesis

The genetic composition of an individual can be altered now. The technique uses the genetic engineering technology to put single functional gene or gene clusters into the chromosomal DNA. The foreign DNA is introduced into the genome of an animal such that all the cells of an animal including germ cells are genetically changed. The animal whose genetic composition is altered by introducing foreign (exogenous) DNA is said to be transgenic. This whole process is called the transgenesis. This technique was applied first on mice (Gorden and Ruddle, 1982) and afterwords in rats, rabbits, sheep, pigs and birds.

This technology produces the animals of specific characteristics. In farm animals the purpose of this technique is to produce genuine human proteins of pharmaceutical value in large amount. The DNA gene for protein drug of interest can be transferred into another organism that will produce large quantity of protein. In dairy animals the purpose is to change the protein composition of milk. The transgenesis may allow the production of animals resistant to diseases.

The transgenesis involves the following steps:-

- Isolation gene of interest on a strand of DNA
- Cutting of DNA at specific points by restriction enzymes
- Joining the cut DNA with a Vector which may be virus or part of bacterial cell (plasmid). The gene of interest is carried by the vector into the organism that will produce the protein.

The transgenic animals are produced by three methods viz. DNA microinjection, embryonic stem cell mediated gene transfer and retrovirus mediated gene transfer.

The DNA microinjection involves a direct microinjection of gene of interest from another animal of same species or from a different species into the pronucleus of the fertilized ovum. The manipulated fertized ovum is transferred/implanted into the oviduct of a recipient female (Foster mother). However, the insertion of DNA is a random process that the inserted gene may not insert itself into a site on the host DNA that will permit its expression.

ESC mediated method involves the introduction of genetically engineered ES cells into an early stage developing embryo. The stem cells are undifferentiated which differentiate into any type of cell (somatic and germ cells) to give rise to a complete organism. These cells are then incorporated into an embryo at blastocyst stage.

The gene transfer is mediated by means of a vector (virus or plasmid). Commonly the retrovirus are used as vectors that infect the cells of an early embryo prior to implantation into a recipient female.

The transgenic livestock production research have been limited to increase growth of animals by introducing genes responsible for growth hormones regulation, disease resistance of animals (influenza resistance is caused by $M_x$ gene), and to improve the quality of animal products like wool quantity and quality of sheep, meat in pigs, and milk quantity and composition in cattle/buffaloes.

## (b) Cloning

The cloning has been successfully achieved in animals using early embryonic source material (sheep, cattle, pig), nuclear transplantation, embryonic cultured cell line and somatic cells of adult animals (Dolly sheep and cattle). Clones have been produced using embryonic, foetal and adult cells.

The cloning involves the fusion of a donor cell (embryonic or somatic) to an oocyte or zygote (of the recipient) following its enucleation. Thus the genetic material of the donor cell is transferred to the enucleated recipient cell. The recipient cell is usually a secondary oocyte which can be obtained following ovulation *in vivo* or by *in vitro* maturation of oocytes. The enucleation (removal of genetic material) is accomplished either by splitting the oocyte or by removing the chromosomes by aspiration.

The cloning technology has certain promises viz.

(i) Cloning of a proven valuable animal

(ii) Creation of thousands of precise duplicates of genetically engineered animals in a single generation

(iii) It is much simpler and effective means of conservation of breeds. Skin biopsies, hair follicles and blood samples might be suitable sources of cells to grow in the laboratory and frozen for long term storage

(iv) It may be used to increase population size

(v) It may use the embryos cloned from cells of high performing $F_1$ individuals to retain heterosis.

## QUESTIONS

**16.1.** Discuss the sequence of events along with their details which have been adopted for improvement of cattle in India. What were the shortcomings and constraints in non achieving the targeted level of milk production. (*ARS 1993*)

**16.2.** Outline the role of AI in animal improvement in India (*ARS 1982*)

**16.3.** What do you know of artificial breeding? How it has been sued as a tool in increasing rate of genetic progress through selection?

**16.4.** Refinement in A.I. and E.T.T. during the last 50 years has provided enormous incentives for livestock improvement. Discuss in detail. (*ARS 1992*)

**16.5.** Describe ONBS. How this method with the help of MOET and use of frozen semen technology can help in improving the world renowned buffalo breed (Murrah) supporting your statement with a practical example. (*ARS 1990*)

***Or***

Discuss a scheme of genetic improvement in dairy animals using ETT with MOET. How does it differ from P.T. (*ARS 1993*)

***

# 17

# BREEDING STRATEGIES FOR CATTLE AND BUFFALOES

Various animal husbandry programmes have been launched in India by different research and development organizations. As a result suitable animal breeding techniques of selection and multiplication of superior germplasm have been developed, besides expansion of infrastructure development on network of A.I., animal health care, improved management practices and milk marketing facilities which have encouraged the farmers of the country. All these combined efforts have resulted that India has come on top position in the milk production of the world, producing about 84 million tones of milk with 4.5% annual growth rate of milk production. However, based on population and production statistics there is a gap between milk requirement and per capita availability and there is also a scope for increasing the milk production ability of our cattle and buffalo population.

It is not feasible to have a uniform cattle and buffalo breeding policy in view of large number of cattle and buffalo breeds, about 80% of the population being non-descript with low milk production compared to well recognized breeds, different types of breeds (milch, dual purpose and draft), different agro-ecological regions, farmers belonging to different socio-economic level (small, marginal and landless) etc. Keeping these factors in mind, there is need to formulate various animal breeding strategies for different types of animals distributed in different agro-ecological regions. The recommended breeding policy is given here for cattle and buffaloes

## 17.1. UTILIZATION OF INDIGENOUS AnGR

The utilization implies the improvement of indigenous AnGR. The indigenous species are well adapted to local conditions. The zebu cattle, sheep and goat breeds of India have acquired by natural selection certain adaptation traits viz. high degree of heat tolerance, resistant to certain diseases and ability to survive on low feed and fodder resources. However, the production potential is poorly developed. This has been the challenge to the animal breeders to improve this potential to a desired level without sacrificing adaptational traits. The indigenous breeds of animals in India have poor production potential for the reasons of

- Poor genetic potential and improper breeding policies
- Poor environment which includes inadequate nutrition, lack of health coverage and poor managemental practices

The genetic potential depends on the genes present in an animal (genotype). The genotype gives rise to the genotypic value of a trait which is modified by the environment experienced by the animal during development and expression of the trait. Therefore, the change either in genotype or environment can lead to a change in the performance potential of the animals. The effect of environment is for a limited time and leads no improvement in next generation. The changes in genotype or genetic constitution though slow but permanent process of leading genetic improvement. Therefore, the aim is to change the genetic structure of future generation which requires the violation of any one or more conditions (assumption) of the H.W. law not to hold true. The most important are the selection and mating systems (including migration).

The **population size** for genetic improvement plays its role through selection. The selection is more effective in a large population in which there is no scope of random genetic drift and also there is ample scope for culling the undesirable/low producing animals.

The **mutation**, being a rare and random process, is not important and also beyond man's control.

Regarding importance of **mating system**, it is true that no mating system without **selection** is effective in changing the genetic structure of population. However, the selection and mating systems require the existence of genetic variability to bring genetic change. The combination of selection and mating system to change the genetic structure is called the **breeding plan**.

The **formulation of breeding plan** involves the followings:

- To decide the type of production required viz. milk, meat, egg, wool etc. This depends on the choice of owner and the market demand.
- The choice of breed as a foundation stock. This depends on the availability and adaptability of the breed.
- To take a decision whether genetic improvement within herd/flock is possible or introduction of superior genes from outside is required. Basically, the improvement can be done in two ways viz. selection, within population and introduction of superior germplasm.

The decision on introduction /migration or within herd improvement rest on the following factors:

- Performance level of the herd in comparison to other herd of the same breed or of other breed. This requires estimating the average values of economic traits.

- Genetic variability present in the population. This requires estimating the heritability and genetic correlations among traits.
- Comparative genetic value and adaptation of the introductions (G.E interactions)
- Heterotic effect

The introduction of new genes (migration) is recommended when performance of a herd/flock is lower than other herd(s) and the genetic variability within herd is very low.

## 1. Selection for improvement

The genetic improvement by selection in a generation is the function of the followings:

- Variability in the trait under selection
- Heritability (Additive genetic variance)
- Selection pressure (intensity of selection)
- Population size
- Accuracy of selection
- Generation interval

The nature and extent of genetic variability present in a herd decides the choice of selection criteria for estimating the breeding value of a trait. The individual selection for within herd improvement is advocated for traits with high heritability and for those expressed in both the sexes at an early age (growth rate). The pedigree selection can be done for traits of high heritability. The selection based on performance of other relatives viz. progeny and collateral relatives (sibs etc.) is effective when heritability of the trait is low, the character is sex limited and for the characters which are not expressed in life span of the animal. The efficient use of PT requires accurate progeny testing of bulls, intensive selection among PT bulls and extensive use of the selected bulls. This requires large population and A.I. It is better to run the associated or farmers herd PT programme in view of small population in organized farms and the nucleus herd should be raised to provide the males of high genetic merit for breeding outside the herd to transmit the benefit of genetic progress to a much larger number of animals. The genetic improvement can be sped up by use of ETT. When the genetic variation of non-additive type is important, the selection alone is not sufficient. In this case the inbreeding followed by selection or crossing the lines for their combining ability should be practiced. The breeding plans to exploit the non-additive genetic variance have been discussed in Chapter 12.

The selection for two or more characters is more useful than single trait selection. The index selection is the best method for multi trait selection compared to ICL method and tandem selection.

**Selection of female:** All the adult females at the farm are listed alongwith their phenotypic values for economic traits and graded as elite (superior in most of the traits), superior (meeting standard equal to elite but inferior in one or more traits), good and inferior. The adult females are selected according to the standard they meet for the traits under selection (selection objectives) and number of young replacement available so as the herd strength is maintained. The selection of female is made on the basis of EPA or MPPA and expected breeding value as outlined in 8.4.1. Further, the young females from inferior dams should be culled.

**Selection of males:** The males are selected as outlined under section 8.4.2.

## 2. Introduction of superior germplasm

The non descript animals can be improved by upgrading. The genetic improvement of well known breed can be done by selective breeding (within herd improvement as discussed above) or by introducing the genes of the same breed from another herd of high genetic merit (Out crossing) or of other breed (crossbreeding). The crossbreeding in the present day context is the migration/ introduction of genes of genetically superior exotic breeds in indigenous breeds. This exploits the breed differences and the heterosis for the reason that there are large genetic differences between two types of breeds. Thus genetic superiority for milk production or fleece production and quality can be combined with good qualities (adaptive traits) of indigenous breeds through crossbreeding (complementarity in crossbreeding)

Combining the inheritance of two or more breeds form a **synthetic population:** The synthetic population can be produced by *inter se* mating after achieving the desired level of exotic inheritance. When equal proportions of two breeds are optimum (desired), then the population is established by *inter se* mating of first crossbred generation ($F_1$). When higher proportion of exotic inheritance is desirable, then after making backcrossing to the exotic breed (forward cross) for one or two generations, the *inter se* mating can be started. But the *inter se* mating declines the performance in next generation because of the decrease in heterozygosity. The decline is more in a population produced by *inter se* mating of $F_1$ but the decline can be avoided by *inter se* mating of population with higher level of exotic inheritance. A synthetic population is stable in the first generation produced by inter-se mating after which the genetic structure will remain constant if no selection is done. The heterosis is exploited in individual, maternal and paternal traits in synthetic breed programme. Secondly, the population is self contained and needs no outside genetic material.

The amount of heterozygosity depends on the number of breeds forming a synthetic population and the difference in gene frequency between the breeds. The amount of heterozygosity is increased with increase in number of breeds. The proportion of maximum heterozygosity retained in *inter se* population is

$H = 1-\Sigma p_i^2$ (Dickerson, 1973)

Where $p_i$ is the proportional contribution from $i^{th}$ breed.

Or $H = 1-1/n = (n-1)/n$ for n breeds each contributing equally (1/n)

The assumption is that all breeds differ equally from one another in gene frequency. The level of heterozygosity with different proportion of genes of two breeds (exotic and native) is:

| Proportion of exotic genes | Proportion of native genes | Level of heterozygosity* ($H = 1-\Sigma p_i^2 = 2pq$) |
|---|---|---|
| 0.125 | 0.875 | 0.22 |
| 0.25 | 0.75 | 0.37 |
| 0.375 | 0.625 | 0.47 |
| 0.5 | 0.5 | 0.50 |
| 0.625 | 0.375 | 0.47 |
| 0.75 | 0.25 | 0.37 |
| 0.875 | 0.125 | 0.22 |

*H = 2pq in case of a two breed synthetic population

Where, p and q are the proportions of the two breeds.

The genetic distance among temperate breeds is less and the same is true among tropical breeds. Therefore, there is slight increase in heterozygosity by including another temperate breed in crossbreeding programme. The same is true for adding a second tropical breed. The animals to be crossed must be genetically different so as to exploit heterosis. This is the reason that little is gained by using more than one exotic breed and one native breed. Any number of breeds can be used in rotational crossbreeding wherein crossbred males are not used for breeding but the crossbred females are mated to males of various pure breeds – the breed of male alternating from one generation to the next.

### 3. Other methods of genetic improvement

The followings are some of the methods of genetic improvement

- Exploitation of non-additive genetic variation
- Marker assisted selection

Unmasking of genetic variation by environmental shock treatment (decanalization)

## 17.2. BREEDING STRATEGIES FOR CATTLE

The improvement of local non descript cattle which are very low milk producing can be made by infusion of superior germplasm from well recognized breeds of *Bos indicus* and *Bos taurus*. The non descript cattle are about 80% of Indian cattle population and hence these should be the target population for improvement. The well recognized breeds should be improved by selection breeding.

The traits of economic importance in cattle and buffaloes are:

The most important trait is the milk production which involves whole complex reproductive system, mammary tissue development during pregnancy, the age at which the production starts (AFC), for how long the milk production continues in a lactation (lactation length), and for how long the milk production is interrupted (dry period) which decide the milk yield per day of time as well as the lifetime milk production which is the function of longevity and number of lactations completed. Likewise the service period and number of services required for pregnancy are important reproductive characters. The birth weight and gain in body weight at different ages determines the growth rate and sexual maturity. In case of males, the important characters are the libido, semen production, its quality and freezebility etc.

### 17.2.1. Grading up of non-descript cattle with zebu breeds

The grading up of non descript low producing cattle with well recognized breeds is the recommended breeding policy. The bulls to be used for grading up should be the progeny of superior dams having lactation yield of more than 2000 kg for those belonging to milch breeds (Sahiwal, R.S., Tharparkar, Gir) and more than 1500 kg for dual purpose breeds (Hariana, Ongole, Kankraj etc.). The recognized zebu breeds recommended for grading up programme of non-descript cattle are different for different states and these can be summarized as:-

- Sahiwal and Tharparkar to be used on local cattle of Punjab, Hariana, MP, UP and West Bengal.
- Red Sindhi to be used on local cattle of H.P. J&K, UP, Bihar, Orissa, Assam, Arunachal Pradesh, Karnataka, Kerala, Goa and Manipur.
- Tharparkar for Kerala, Tripura, Delhi, AP, Bihar and Rajasthan local cattle.
- Gir for Gujarat, Rajasthan and MP local catle.
- Hariana for local cattle of almost all the states except South Indian states
- Ongole for M.P. and AP local catle
- Kangayam for Kerala local cattle.
- Hallikar for T.N. and A.P. local cattle.
- Kankrej for local cattle of Gujarat

The upgrading programme is expected to make an improvement in milk yield by more than 5 % annually.

### 17.2.2. Grading up or crossbreeding of non-descript cattle with exotic breeds

The choice of exotic breed to be used for crossbreeding of non-descript cows depends on the availability of the quality feed and fodder resources in adequate quantity and the market facilities. In general, Holstein Friesian should be used in the irrigated plains and Jersey cattle in hills and coastal areas. Based on the experience of crossbreeding results, the level of exotic inheritance should be 50 to 75%. The crossbreeding programme is expected to increase milk production for more than 5 times compared to non-descript cattle with low age at first calving and shorter calving interval.

The crossbred cows produced should be mated with crossbred bulls of high breeding value. However, the level of exotic inheritance should be around 50 to 75%.

This crossbreeding programme has certain requirements viz. net working of infrastructure facilities in terms of A.I. facilities, supply of quality semen from superior sires for which bull mother farms, semen banks and trained manpower are required to run the programme effectively. In addition to this, animal health care and facilities for marketing of milk preferably through cooperative milk union are also required.

- Holstein Friesian should be used in the states of Delhi, Haryana, Punjab, UP, Gujarat and Karnataka.
- Jersey is recommended for Assam, Arunachal Pradesh, Bihar, Goa, Haryana, Punjab, HP, J&K, MP, MS, Orissa, Rajasthan, Southern states, Manipur, Tripura, UP, WB.
- Brown Swiss is being used in Kerala.

### 17.2.3. Selective breeding within zebu breeds

The milch breeds and dual purpose breeds (Hariana, ongole, Kankrej) need to be improved genetically by selective breeding through progeny testing programme. The selective breeding is expected to yield around 1% genetic gain per year in organized herds whereas the genetic improvement in farmers herds is expected to be around 10%. The indigenous breeds of cattle need to be improved by selective breeding in their breeding tract. This programme can be more effectively run under associated herd progeny testing programme by associating atleast 2-3 herds of each breed of organized farms, gaushalas as well as farmer's herd under field conditions. The methodology of progeny testing has been outlined under section 11.7. The ONBS with or without MOET is a better technique.

### National Cattle Breeding Policy

On the basis of experiences, results and constrains of earlier policies/ programmes, there is need to implement the following cattle breeding policies at national level for the improvement of cattle wealth in the country.

- Selective breeding in indigenous breeds for improvement of milk, draft and both through associated herd progeny testing programme.
- Crossbreeding of non-descript low producers with exotic breeds stabilizing 50-75% exotic inheritance in areas of plenty of feed, fodder and adequate milk marketing system.
- Grading up of non-descript cattle with bulls of indigenous breeds of the area.
- Conservation of endangered indigenous breeds.
- Expansion and strengthening of Central Herd Registration Scheme.

## 17.3. BREEDING STRATEGIES FOR BUFFALOES

There is a large degree of genetic variability in the buffaloes of India. About 60% of the total buffalo population of the country is non descript and the rest 40% is descript classified into 19 breeds according to FAO but into 15 breeds according to ICAR. Two breeding strategies are recommended for improvement of buffaloes – One is for the non-descript population and second is for the recognized breeds.

### 17.3.1. Grading up for non-descript buffaloes

The non descript buffaloes of the different parts of the country should be upgraded by mating them with superior bulls of high genetic merit belonging to Murrah, Nili Ravi, Mehsana and Surti breeds. This will increase the milk production by 2-3 times from about 500 kg milk of non-descript buffaloes to about 1200 kg of first generation upgrade buffaloes. With continuous grading up of upgraded buffaloes in 4-5 generations will replace the non descript low producing buffaloes by comparatively high producing upgraded buffaloes which may be very nearer in conformation to the well defined breeds.

The grading up of non descript buffaloes with Murrah have been recommended in the states of Assam, Bihar, W.B., UP, Orissa, AP, TN, MS, Rajasthan, Haryana, Goa and Delhi. The Surti is the breed of choice for Karnataka, Kerala and some parts of Gujarat and Rajasthan. Murrah and Surti bulls can be used in Karnataka. The use of bulls of Murrah and Nili Ravi breeds has been recommended for Punjab.

### 17.3.2. Selective breeding for well defined breeds

The selective breeding under progeny testing programme for buffaloes on large scale needs to strengthen the existing organized farms of well known breeds like Murrah, Nili Ravi, Mehsana, Surti, Nagpuri, Bhadawari and Jaffarabadi and some more farms should be developed for the production of breeding bulls. Murrah breed is preferred as a breed of choice in the states of Haryana, Punjab, Delhi and some part of UP. The Surti breed is preferred in the states of Gujarat, Rajasthan and Karnataka. The Mehsana and Jaffarabadi are the breeds of Gujarat. Whereas Nagpuri and Pandharpuri are the breeds of Maharastra state. The Nili Ravi has good population in Punjab whereas Bhadawari are present in UP. As the population size of the organized herds is small, the P.T. programme should run in associating different herds as well as the farmer's herds. The methodology of P.T. is similar to that of cattle.

## QUESTIONS

**17.1.** Describe genetic basis for utilizing breed differences. How these can be utilized and what factors will determine the choice of breed(s) and breeding system? (*ARS 1984*)

**17.2.** Describe how various genetic factors/situations direct the choice of breeding plan.ARS 1984

**17.3.** Discuss how and why about the breeding plan that you would recommend for breeding crossbred cattle in India with the ultimate object of developing of tropical cattle with high milk production. (*ARS 1978*)

***Or***

It is proposed to evolve a commercially profitable herd of dairy cattle in India using exotic germ plasm. Outline in detail and explain a long term breeding programme for meeting the target in India. (*ARS 1982*)

**17.4.** What is cattle breeding policy in the country and supporting research programmes? Are these fulfilling the need of improving cattle for different functions for which these are reared in India. (*ARS 1985*)

***Or***

Give a suitable breeding programme for cattle so as to attain the target of about 60 MT of milk production annually by the year 2000. Justify your programme with scientific explanation. (*ARS 1990*)

**17.5.** Enumerate the traits of economic importance in dairy cows and buffaloes. Which of the two species would you consider more economic and important for augmenting the national milk productivity and why? In regions where feed and fodder resources are meager and insufficient, what kind of dairy animals would you recommend? (*ARS 1992*)

**17.6.** Suppose you are charged with development of a new breed of cattle that would be superior as a breed (do not think about its combining ability) for milk production in India. (*ARS 1994*)

*a.* What kind of stock would you employ? Explain.

*b.* What traits would you consider?

*c.* On what basis would you select for those traits?

*d.* Would you employ a selection Index?

*e.* Sketch a breeding programme you might follow & why?

*f.* Indicate roughly the population size that you think would be desirable, giving your reasons.

*g.* In your opinion what is the minimum number of years for which efforts in such a way should be committed in advance and why

**17.7.** Briefly review relevant research work on inheritance of economic production traits of Indian buffaloes and discuss the scope of improving buffaloes for growth, reproduction and milk production. (*ARS 1976*)

**17.8.** Give the genetic parameters of economic production traits of Indian buffaloes. Which of the 3 traits can be used for selection of breeding stock to produce meat animals for export purpose? What other traits may be necessary in selection to make this production economically remunerative. Give your breeding plan. (*ARS 1976*)

**17.9.** Suggest a suitable breeding programme in detail for improving the efficiency of milk production in Indian buffaloes. (*ARS 1891, 1982, 1984*)

**17.10.** Discuss the various steps involved in the development of breeds of domestic livestock through evolutionary crossbreeding. (*ARS 1985*)

**17.11.** (*a*) Give steps for evolving a new breed of sheep for fine wool in India. (*ARS 1995*)

(*b*) Discuss the role of inbreeding and crossbreeding in developing new breeds/strains. (*ARS 1981*)

**17.12** Discuss the perspective and prospective planning for development of dairy cattle in India (*ARS 1995*)

# 18

# BREEDING PLANS FOR SMALL RUMINANTS AND POULTRY

The sheep and goat are two different species and classed as small ruminants. These two species are kept for different purposes to some extent. The sheep are raised for fleece production (fine wool and carpet type), meat and pelt production whereas the goats are raised for milk, meat and fibre (pashmina). Thus the traits of interest are different in two species.

## 18.1. TRAITS OF ECONOMIC IMPORTANCE (SHEEP & GOATS)

In **sheep**, the wool traits are greasy fleece weight, staple length, fibre diameter, medullation percentage, ratio between secondary to primary follicles (S:P ratio). The other characters in wool breeds are birth weight, weaning weight, adult weight and fertility characters like tupping percentage, conception rate, lambs born per ewe joined or lambed etc. A fibre is produced from a follicle in the skin. The follicles are of two types viz. large primary follicles (P) that grow coarse fibres and the small secondary follicles (S) that produce finer fibres.

The characters in sheep for meat are body weight at different ages (birth, weaning, yearling, and adult); fertility in terms of number of lambs born, weaned, dressing percentage, fleece weight etc.

**Difference between wool and hair:** Wool fibres are smaller in diameter than hair. The hairs are always medulated. Wool fibres are crimped but hairs are never crimped like fine wool but sometimes have wavy like coarser wool. Most wool is free of pigment but hairs have pigment within the cortex. Fine wool sheep may have about 50000 fibres/sq inch of skin area but in coarser wool sheep these may not be more than 5000/sq inch.

**Growth and structure of wool fibre:** The wool fibres grow from follicles in the skin and the growth is at the base of the fibre but not at the tip. The wool fibres contain two layers of cells viz., **epidermal layer** which is outer one and scale like, the main part of the fibre known as **cortex** which is underneath the epidermal layer. Some wool fibres may have a third layer of cells which is in the middle of epidermal and cortex. This third layer is called as **medula** which may contain air or granular pigment material. Medulated fibres differ from kemp which are chiefly medullary cells with only a very thin layer of corticle and cutical materials. The medulated fibres are coarse, uneven in diameter, having low elasticity and pliability but with considerable tensile strength and these fibres are not desirable.

The pure wool is composed of mainly the keratin which is also the chief component of hair, feathers, hooves and horns. Keratin is closely related to some of the proteins but not digestible in gastric juices like proteins.

**Goats** produce a variety of products viz. meat, milk, fibres including pashmina fibres, mohair fibres and hairs, skins and manure. Some of the Indian breeds of goats like Jamnapari, Beetal and Barbari have been used as improver breed in India and other neighbouring countries to upgrade the regional non descript, small and dwarf breeds. They have good adult body size and milk yield. The other traits of economic importance are meat quality, fecundity, disease resistance, grazing habit and skin characteristics in development programme of goats.

An increase in meat production potential with some attention for milk production should be the thrust of goat development. Further, the meat and skin traits are of common commercial interest, the milk in plains and fibre production in hills are the traits of distinct interest.

## 18.2. BREEDING PLAN FOR SHEEP

The indigenous sheep have low level of performance for fleece weight, its quality and mutton production. The fleece weight and quality traits have medium to high $h^2$ estimates and hence respond to selection, though the rate of progress is low. The selection should be made for fleece weight at the yearling stage as this character has high estimates of heritability and repeatability. The best animals of both the sexes (rams and ewes) are selected by performance test. The fleece weight is phenotypically and genetically correlated with live weight. Thus the animals can be selected on the basis of live weight. Selective breeding had made some improvement in average fibre diameter and medullation percentage in Deccani at Pune, Bikaneri and Lohi breeds at GLF Hisar.

The non descript population should be either upgraded with recognized breeds of the locality or may be crossed with fine wool exotic breeds (Rambouillet, Merino) or mutton breeds of exotic origin (Suffolk, Dorset).

**Fine wool:** The crossbreeding of native breeds of hilly region, Nali and Chokla of Rajasthan, Patanwadi of Gujrat and Nilgiri of T.N. with Rambouillet and Merino rams has been recommended for fine wool breeding having 50-75% exotic inheritance.

**Corpet wool:** Selective breeding for improving carpet wool in breeds like Marwari, Jaisalmeri, Magra and Pugal should be considered in development programme incorporating six monthly body weight, fleece weight and medullation percentage. The upgrading of sheep breeds of Southern India may be done with some of the North Indian carpet wool breeds (Nali, Magra). The inferior carpet wool breeds (Malpura, Sonadi, Jaisalmeri, Muzaffarnagari) may be improved for better carpet wool quality by crossing them with exotic fine wool or mutton breeds stabilizing the exotic inheritance at a 50% level. Similar crossbreeding of other native breeds like Deccani, Bellary, Shahabadi and Chhotanagpuri with exotic breeds can improve the carpet wool quality.

**Mutton:** The mutton production characters have medium to high heritability estimates and hence respond to selection but with slow rate. Therefore, the upgrading of non descript population and crossbreeding of inferior native breeds with superior native breeds or with exotic breeds can bring rapid improvement. The native breeds viz. Malpura, Sonadi, Muzaffarnagri, Mandya and Nellore should be crossed with Dorset and Suffolk on the basis of earlier crossbreeding results.

**Pelt:** Regarding pelt production, the crossbreeding of coarse carpet wool Indian breeds with Karakul had good potential for pelt production. The native breed like Malpura and Sonadi can be used for crossbreeding.

## 18.3. BREEDING STRATEGIES FOR GOATS

There are nearly 20 well recognized breeds of goats in India which are nearly 20-25% of the total goat population and rest population is mixed and non descript. Secondly the goats in India are mostly raised by farmers and small size holders of different states of the country.

The breeding strategies for improvement of indigenous stock should involve the followings:-

- The non descript population should be surveyed and characterized.
- The non descript females should be mated with bucks of high genetic merit of recognized breeds for the improvement of milk as well as meat. Thus, the **upgrading** with improver breed of the area is recommended.
- The **selective breeding** within recognized breed is recommended. This programme should also revolve around at farmer's level by selecting the best males from breeding tract of each breed of milch and meat type.
- **Crossbreeding for meat** with Boer breed of South Africa has ben undertaken in Maharastra in farmer's flock with encouraging results. This can be started in Rajasthan also because the Boar breed was developed in relatively dry region. The crosses of Boer with local goats and also with Sirohi goats have shown good growth.
- **Crossbreeding** is also recommended **for pashmina fibre production** in Changthangi breed in J & K state with exotic breeds from Russia (like Orenburg which is best quality Pashmina breed). The crossbreeding is expected to increase productivity of fibre.

In addition to the above breeding plans, emphasis should be given to prevent the dilution of best indigenous breeds for milk (Jamnapari), meat (Black Bengal) and fibre (Chegu, Changthangi). Not only this, but the threatened breeds viz. Surti, Beetal, Jamunapari should also be conserved.

The implementation of the above breeding plans for genetic improvement of goats in the country require provision of superior germplasm with A.I. facilities, trained manpower, recording of performance data and marketing facilities etc. The successful implementation of the long term programme also needs the coordination between different agencies viz. state A.H. Deptt.; NBAGR, Karnal; CIRG Makhdoom (Mathura) and SAU's.

## 18.4. IMPORTANT ECONOMIC TRAITS OF POULTRY

The formulation of the breeding plans requires the knowledge of the economic traits, their performance level, the phenotypic and genetic variability and covariability of different traits etc.

A large proportion of the total cost of a bird is the cost of food. Thus the efficiency of feed conversion to meat and egg is the critical trait in profitability. The poultry are kept for two purposes viz. egg and meat.

The growth rate is of great concern for breeders of **meat birds** (Broilers). The fast growing birds converts its feed most efficiently. The profit can be more by eliminating feed wastage by spillage and fouling (dirty) and by reducing death rates through diseases. The meat birds must have a large breast with fleshy thighs and short lags. Attempts are made to reduce the fat depot inside the body cavity so that the feed consumed is converted directly to edible meat. The traits of interest in broilers are the body weight, carcass weight, proportion of breast meat to total carcass, shank length, feed consumed per unit of dressed carcass and disease resistance.

In **egg producing birds**, the traits of interest are egg size, egg number and weight, good hatchability, hen housed average, egg quality traits (yolk height, yolk colour, shell texture, shell thickness and colour, thickness of white), body weight and feed conversion. Besides these, the birds should start laying eggs at earlier age without pausing (stop laying) during production and should not grow broody. The persistency of laying eggs for a long time is also required.

## 18.5. BREEDING PLAN FOR POULTRY

The breeder is interested in egg number, size and weight which are all moderately heritable and hence respond to selection. Thus selection for these traits directly is recommended. They are all correlated both phenotypically and genetically. However, an increase in egg number results in the production of smaller eggs of light weight. The exploitation of non-additive genetic variation is also very important through crossing different lines/strains/breeds in all possible combinations alongwith reciprocals. The recurrent selection and reciprocal recurrent selection should be used. On the basis of combining ability (GCA and SCA), the commercial hybrids are produced.

Direct selection for egg quality trait is advisable. The superior parents should be identified through performance testing and then progeny testing. The best parents can be used in family selection and exploited by crossing.

The **meat production** traits have fairly high heritability estimates and hence respond to selection by performance testing. There should be selection against fat deposition inside the body cavity. The egg production in broilers is also important atleast to multiply the highly selected birds. To meet this objective a sire of meat line is crossed with a female of egg laying line to produce the market hybrid.

# QUESTIONS

**18.1.** Set up breeding goals for wool and mutton breeds of sheep and outline briefly breeding plans to improve the Indian sheep population. (*ARS 1984*)

**18.2.** Discuss the genetic aspects of skin follicle and birth coat types and their possible role in improving fleece production and quality (*ARS 1985*)

**18.3.** Discuss the importance of fibre producing animals at national level. What are different types of fibres produced by different kinds of animals? How would you plan an effective breeding programme for increasing the sheep wool production in the country? (*ARS 1997*)

**18.4.** Give a scheme for genetic improvement of sheep in Himalayan region. What are the steps involved in evolutionary process for a new breed? (*ARS 1993*)

**18.5.** Give steps for evolving a new breed of sheep for fine wool In India. (*ARS 1995*)

**18.6.** What is the scope of improving Indian goats for milk production? Give steps needed. (*ARS 1976*)

**18.7.** Review and discuss the information available on the inheritance of various economic traits in goats for developing breeding methods for increasing their productivity in India. (*ARS 1978*)

**18.8.** How the meat traits of Indian goats could be improved? Give suitable breeding plan for the same. (*ARS 1982*)

**18.9.** Enumerate the important economic traits for commercial poultry in India and outline a breeding plan for high egg production (*ARS 1982*)

**18.10.** Name the economic traits along with their breeding goals for egg type poultry and discuss the extent and type of genetic variability in and co-variability between the two important economic traits related to returns from egg type poultry. (*ARS 1984*)

**18.11.** Give the different methods of genetic progress for broiler production. How will you proceed in estimation of different components in a diallel cross data. (*ARS 1994*)

***

# References

**Basu, S.B. 1996.** *Quantitative Genetics Research Techniques.* Kalyani Publishers, Ludhiana.

**Chaudhary, S.R. and Chhikara, B.S. 1996.** *Breeding and Management of Camel.* Published by Mrs. Sawa Kaur, 152, Saket Colony, Hisar.

**Dalton, D.C. 1985.** *An Introduction to Practical Animal Breeding.* 2nd Edn. ELBS/Collins.

**Falconer, D.S. 1988.** *Introduction to Quantitative Genetics,* 3rd Edn.

**Hafez, E.S.E. 1969.** *The Behaviour of Domestic Animals.*

***Indian J. of Animal Genetics & Breeding* (1999, 2000 and 2001).** Published by the Indian Society of Animal Genetics & Breeding.

**Lasley, J.F. 1972.** *Genetics of Livestock Improvement.* 2nd Edn. Prentice Hall, Inc., Englewood Cliffs, N.J.

**Lush, J.L. 1945.** *Animal Breeding Plans.*

**NBAGR, Karnal. 2001.** Summer School on *Recent Advances in Characterization and conservation of AnGR.* Compendium of Lecutures.

**Nicholas, F.W. 1987.** *Veterinary Genetics.*

**Parekh, H.K.B. and Srivastava, P.N. 1998.** *Practical Manual of Genetic Improvement in Livestock and Poultry.* Kalyani Publishers, Ludhiana.

**Sunderasan, D. 1975.** *Livestock Breeding in India.* Vikas Publishing House Pvt. Ltd., New Delhi.

**Tomar, S.S. 1996.** *Text Book of Population Genetics.* Vol. I. Qualitative Inheritance, Universal Publication Centre, Karnal.

**Tomar, S.S. 1998.** *Text Book of Population Genetics.* Vol. II. Quantitative Inheritance, Kalyani Publishers, Ludhiana.

**Warwick, K.J. Legates, J.E. 1979.** *Breeding and Improvement of Farm Animals 7th Edn.* Tata McGraw Hill Publishing Co.Ltd.